THE MOHICANS OF STOCKBRIDGE

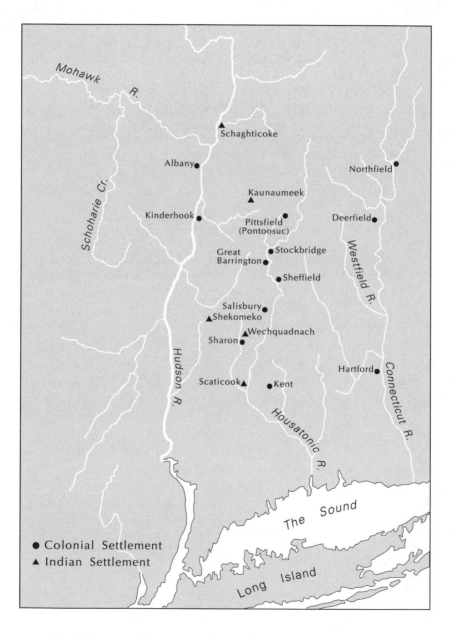

The Hudson and Connecticut River valleys.

THE MOHICANS OF STOCKBRIDGE

Patrick
Frazier

UNIVERSITY OF NEBRASKA PRESS
LINCOLN AND LONDON

Permission to reprint quoted segments of the following is gratefully acknowledged: L. Kinvin Wroth, ed. *Province in Rebellion: A Documentary History of the Founding of the Commonwealth of Massachusetts, 1774–1775.* Cambridge: Harvard University Press, 1975.

Library of Congress Cataloging-in-Publication Data
Frazier, Patrick.
    The Mohicans of Stockbridge / Patrick Frazier.
        p.   cm.
    Includes bibliographical references and index.
    ISBN 0-8032-1986-5
        1. Stockbridge Indians—History.   2. Mahican Indians—History.
I. Title
E99.S8F72   1992
974'.004973—dc20   92-6494
                                                        CIP

Publication of this book was assisted by a grant from The Andrew W. Mellon Foundation.

The paper in this book meets the minimum requirements of American National Standard for Information Sciences—Permanence of Paper for Printed Library Materials, ANSI Z39.48–1984.

To the Stockbridge Indians

CONTENTS

ILLUSTRATIONS

PREFACE

On a small reservation in Shawano County, Wisconsin, live several hundred descendants of people immortalized by James Fenimore Cooper. While Cooper was a boy growing up in New York, these people lived about fifty miles from him. Before that, their ancestors had concentrated along the Housatonic River in western Massachusetts in a small village called Stockbridge. It was this village that gave them the name by which they are officially known today, the Stockbridge Indians. That name, and the effort to subsume them into colonial culture, virtually obliterated from American consciousness the fact that they were—and their descendants today are—Mohicans. The mythic characters created by James Fenimore Cooper probably helped sustain the impression that, like the Knights of the Round Table, Mohicans were legendary figures of a misty romantic past, who may never have existed.

My hope for this book is that it will bring public awareness to the existence of these people and their contribution to a significant segment of American history. The story is not one of noble savages or strong, silent men of nature with infallible instincts, loyally guiding frontiersmen through the dangers of wild America. But it is the story of genuine nobility of spirit, quiet strength, and loyalty almost beyond belief, demonstrated by a people who were physically, emotionally, and economically close to tragedy much of their lives. This story is, then, the sometimes tragic but ultimately triumphant story of a people who were nearly the last of the Mohicans.

In 1735 the Mohicans were at a critical juncture. For 125 years they had been trade allies with the Dutch and later with the English along the Hudson River. The lucrativeness of the peltry trade changed their economy, which, along with an increasing foreign population, affected their lives significantly. No longer just hunters, subsistence farmers, traders, self-supporters, and warriors in inter-Indian wars, the Mohicans became trappers, wholesale suppliers, consumers of European goods, soldiers of fortune in colonial wars, debtors, dependents, and victims of disease and alcohol.

Yet despite prolonged contact with colonial Americans, for the first hundred years the Mohicans were relatively isolated since the Hudson River Valley remained sparsely populated. They retained their indigenous social and religious traditions in the small villages along remote portions of the river and in the valleys among the low, rocky mountains and upland bogs eastward. By the end of the first quarter of the eighteenth century this separateness, too, confronted change. While the Mohicans' own population had decreased probably tenfold, the Hudson River Valley population was increasing as rich descendants of the Dutch patroons multiplied and installed tenants on their extensive domains, many of which had been obtained from the Mohicans legally or illegally. From the east and the south the Mohicans were being pressed by expanding New England populations moving from the rich and entrepreneurial Connecticut River Valley. In 1709 the Massachusetts governor stated that for the past six years the colony (which included Maine) had received one thousand immigrants annually.[1] One year's worth of immigrants roughly equaled the entire Mohican population at this time.

The New England character offered something of a contrast for the Mohicans, however. Their experience with the Dutch had often come from dealings either with feudalistic landlords who considered Indians as vassals or, more frequently, with uncouth Albany and backcountry traders who seemed to regard the cheating of Indians as an art form. The Dutch nevertheless concentrated mainly on mundane matters and did not try hard to mold Indians socially, politically, or religiously to their own image. The New Englanders, numbers of whom on the frontier were no models of Christian civilization themselves, at least held their Bibles in nearly the same esteem as their account books. In general they were more religious than the Dutch, and the responsible ones among them attributed any material success to the blessings of God, whom they believed had ordained them to go forth to conquer the wilderness and convert the natives (or vice versa). Although New Englanders viewed Indians as occupying the low rung on the ladder of humankind, they also believed that what kept them there primarily was an ignorance of the undeniable truths of Calvinistic Christianity. The missionary spirit toward Indians, therefore, was more alive in the New Englanders than in the Dutch. On the other hand, New Englanders also had more experience of one kind with Indians than did the Dutch—bloody, devastating wars. By the end of the seventeenth century New Englanders formed roughly two attitudinal groups: those whose consciences made them believe that the Indians were instruments of God's wrath on a sinful people, whose sins included those of neglect or oppression of the Indians; and those who felt that New England air would be healthier without any Indians breathing it. Fortunately for Mohicans, the conscience-stricken colonials controlled the reins of society. But "pure" Puritanism was a thing of the past. America's abundance had made the pursuit of individual gain an acceptable manifestation of God's favor, and if that gain came at the expense of the Indians, then it must be God's will. By the 1720s, a changing New England society was encountering a changed Mohican society. And at a time when the Mohicans were probably most in need of some sort of spiritual infusion, frontier New Englanders were beginning to experience a revival of religious spirit that would become known as the Great Awakening. Charity, conscience, and fear of God's wrath were the fashion again among practitioners, as was concern for the natives' souls. But most New Englanders by now preferred the liberal progress toward salvation, characterized by material comforts and a competitive rather than a cooperative spirit. The Mohicans would encounter both attitudes and would gain from, and suffer from, both. Meanwhile, New Englanders would gain Indian allies to help them cope with a dangerous frontier. And of course the colonials would also eventually gain territory for their expanding population as the heavy price they exacted from the Indians for their conversion and education.

This book is the result of a several-year odyssey among the collections of about twenty-five institutions. The Bicentennial inspired many collection guides and publishing projects, which with the availability of microfilm produced an amount of material that dictated the reduction of an anticipated one-hundred-year history by half. But the fifty years from 1735 to 1785 are the most interesting, varied, and dynamic in terms of changes to Mohican society and its interrelationship with colonial society. Each decade introduced events and people that had notable impact on the tribe and that contributed to a rich, colorful chapter of American history.

As abundant as the material is, there are still agonizing gaps. Had they been fillable, the Mohicans' story would be clearer and more complete. Sources did not surface, for example, that gave adequate descriptions of the Indians' material culture, or of much of their day-to-day activities during the mission period. Samuel Hopkins, the Springfield minister who wrote the historical sketch that is the basis for the Stockbridge story, had access to several years of missionary John Sergeant's journal, Stephen Williams's description of events during an important Mohican gathering, and correspondence that may have shed further light on particular events, none of which has since been located. There was even a disappointing dearth of material on the activities of the colonial families who settled in Stockbridge and western Massachusetts. These gaps often made definitive analysis and interpretation of the principals' motivations difficult. What the material reveals, nonetheless, is that the Stockbridge Indians and the Mohicans in general willingly, albeit reluctantly among some groups, accepted Christianity as a spiritual replacement for their traditional religion. In the hope of accommodating themselves to the dominant culture surrounding them, the Indians tolerated a mission and town development that too quickly sought to turn their traditions around. They also received from that culture negative impressions that convinced them to retain their identity as Indian Americans, not simply Americans. Further, despite a professed desire to acculturate the Indians within Christianity and New England civilization, Massachusetts continually differentiated them as Indians in its dealings with them regarding land, trade, guardianship, and especially war, where it sought to encourage the aspects of Indian warfare that would terrorize an enemy.

I have sparingly changed paragraph structure, punctuation, and capitalization in quotations to bring the text closer to today's compositional style. From the various spellings of Mohican personal names I have chosen the most frequently used version or the version that became standard by the nineteenth century. Pre-Gregorian calendar dates are rendered in modern form; thus February 8, 1734/35, becomes February 8, 1735. I have also retained the traditional English spelling of "Mohican" rather than the Dutch and subsequent ethnological spelling "Mahican" in order to make the work more generally familiar. Neither version should be confused, however, with "Mohegan," the term used for the Indians concentrated mainly in Connecticut who at one time were part of the Pequots. After the Stockbridge Indians achieved the ability to write and communicate in English, they referred to themselves as "Muhheconnuk" or "Moheakunnuk." The pronunciation of the first syllable, therefore, is with the short "o" (as in "Monday").

ACKNOWLEDGMENTS

I wish to acknowledge and thank the following institutions, which granted permission to quote from their manuscript collections: The Baker Memorial Library, Dartmouth College; The Beinecke Rare Book and Manuscript Library, Yale University; the Burke Library, Hamilton and Kirkland Colleges; the Case Memorial Library, Hartford Seminary Foundation; the William L. Clements Library, University of Michigan; the Dwight Collection, The Norman Rockwell Museum at Stockbridge; the Longmeadow Historical Society; the Massachusetts Historical Society; the Massachusetts State Archives; Mission House, Stockbridge, Massachusetts; the National Archives, Washington, DC; The Newberry Library; The New-York Historical Society; the Public Archives of Canada; the Franklin Trask Library, Andover Newton Theological School.

Reprinted by permission are quoted segments from *Province in Rebellion* by L. Kinvin Wroth, ed., Cambridge, Mass.: Harvard University Press, Copyright © 1975 by the President and Fellows of Harvard College.

Among all the institutions whose collections are cited in this work, the individuals who helped make this book possible are too numerous to mention. Certain individuals, nevertheless, stood out not only in the amount of assistance they offered, but in the friendly graciousness with which they offered it. Among them were: Polly Pierce, Stockbridge Library Historical Room; Kay Blair, Library of Congress; Frank

Lorenz, Burke Library, Hamilton College; and Diana Yount, Franklin Trask Library, Andover Newton Theological School. I am also grateful to James Axtell for his encouraging words about the manuscript.

Throughout the course of research I also found myself wanting to express thanks to those often unknown, unheralded staff, past and present, who compiled useful indexes, checklists, and similar finding aids to make research among primary sources a little less formidable than it might otherwise be. Thanks to you all.

1

DECLINE

OF

THE

SPIRIT

A small council meeting in July of 1734 in a simple village along the Housatonic River in Massachusetts would affect the course and survival of a nation. The issue under consideration would demand four long days of discussion, reflection, hope, and apprehension. A captain in his early forties and a lieutenant in his late thirties, both weighted with the future prospects for their people, would figure prominently in the council's decision. The path they were considering would take those who followed into a world of people who thought, talked, believed, worked, and even fought differently. Their children might forget the ways of their ancestors and their heritage. But the new path just might save the nation. They must do something, or they might indeed be among the last of the Mohicans.

The captain's name was Konkapot, the lieutenant's was Umpachenee, and they belonged to the Housatonic tribe of Mohicans. Each was principal man in villages that lay eight miles apart on the Housatonic River, among the steep Berkshire Hills of southwestern Massachusetts. And the subject that they must weigh most heavily was whether to accept a Christian mission. It was a time, perhaps, to get a sense of direction, to recount the tribal history, the traditions, and the changes Mohicans had experienced.

The old tribesmen related, in what may be an early Indian confirmation of a Bering Strait crossing, how in ancient times their ancestors had "emigrated from west by north of another country; they passed over the great waters, where this and the other country is nearly connected," and where there were islands close together. They had lived beside a body of water affected by tides, this traditional history maintained, which gave rise to their name, Muh-he-con-nuk, meaning "great waters or sea, which are constantly in motion, either flowing or ebbing."[1]

The elders said that their ancestors had been more civilized than Indians now were, "until there arose a mighty famine which obliged them to disperse throughout the regions of the wilderness after sustenance, and at length lost their ways of former living. As they were coming from the west, they found many great waters, but none of them flowing and ebbing like Muhheakunnuk, until they came to Hudson's River; then they said one to another, this is like Muhheakunnuk our nativity."[2]

Related versions of this history incorporated it with that of the Delawares, who claimed to be the parent stock for most eastern Algonquin tribes, including the Mohicans, "a people who by intermarriages had become a detached body, mixing two languages together, and forming out of the two a dialect of their own, choosing to live by themselves." Though the historical time frame is unclear, the intermarriages and the new dialect may have involved the Shawnees, whom the Mohicans rescued from hostile tribes in the South. The Mohicans then interceded with the Delawares to allow the Shawnees to settle in Ohio and Pennsylvania, while according to Delaware tradition "others were conducted by the Mohicans into their own country, where they intermarried with them and became one people."[3] Whether through blood relation or political alliance, these traditions were enhanced by the kinship terms used by the tribes in addressing one another. The Mohicans called the Delawares grandfather and the Shawnees younger brother. Other linguistically related tribes east and west received similar appellations, such as the Mohicans' grandchildren, the Chippewas, Potawatomies, and Ottawas.[4]

The various Mohican tribes had occupied the Hudson River Valley north to Lake Champlain, east to the Westfield River, and west to Schoharie Creek. Some of the main villages with principal chiefs were located on the Hudson's eastern bank or on its islands. By 1609 the Mohicans were a vigorous Indian nation with a thousand warriors, who claimed respect and influence among others and held substantial territory in which hunting, fishing, gathering, subsistence agriculture, and intertribal trade provided sustenance. In the fall of that year, as their forefathers told it, a Mohican walked out from one of the main villages and saw a strange sight on the river. Thinking it was some sort of great fish, he ran back

Seventeenth-century representation of Mohican villages. Detail from the map "Belgii Novi, Angliae Novi. . . ." Courtesy of the Library of Congress.

to the village to tell the others. Two more went out to investigate more closely and found strange, pale men in a large boat. Henry Hudson was in their midst. As with most nations during early contact, a mutually attractive trade quickly developed. The Mohicans soon made a covenant with the newcomers as strong as a steel chain, and they kept this covenant chain shining with beaver's grease, a metaphoric way of describing the beaver trade that kept the two cultures linked in commercial exchange.[5]

That was 125 years before this council. Konkapot's and Umpachenee's ancestors had been many, the Europeans few. The Mohicans had sheltered them. Then more came to trade for beaver pelts, and before long the Mohicans were active in a lucrative market. Ships that came up the Hudson each year brought the Mohicans fascinating goods that eventually made them dependent on the trade. Trade became one of the primary passions that would affect all relations. For a time the Mohicans prospered, and the newcomers prospered even more.

But prosperity brought more Europeans, and it brought the Mohicans jealousy and competition from another tribe, the Mohawks of the Iroquois League. In the early seventeenth century the Mohawks had fought Algonquin and Abenaki tribes to the north and east, probably over the competition for the fur trade with the French in the Saint Lawrence Valley. The French, however, aided their Indian allies in repulsing the Mohawks. The same year that Henry Hudson first encountered the Mohicans, for example, Samuel Champlain and two French companions used their muskets to help their Indian allies drive off a Mohawk attack. Thus 1609 was a significant year for the Mohicans. The Mohawks became inveterate enemies of the French and their Abenaki and Algonquin allies, and they turned their competitive, intrusive attention to the east, where the Dutch were establishing trade with the Mohicans.

For nearly twenty years peaceful trade and coexistence prevailed among the various Indian nations and the Dutch.[6] But around 1628 the commander at recently built Fort Orange involved the Mohicans in a needless war, apparently over trade issues. The Mohawks wanted guns, and they were frustrated in trade by having implacable French and Indian enemies keeping them from commerce in the Saint Lawrence River Valley. They were also obliged to pay tribute to the Mohicans and their allies, who controlled the Hudson River Valley and access to Albany. This time the Mohawks, acknowledged by colonial observers to be the most warlike and fierce of all the tribes, were not cowed by the guns used by the Dutch and their Mohican allies. A vicious battle ensued, the principal Mohican chief fell, and the Mohawks soundly thrashed the combined forces. The Mohawks' sun began to rise, while that of the Mohicans began to set.[7] For the next forty-five years the beaver trade waxed and waned, and the Mohicans alternated between peace and war with the Mohawks. Throughout these wars the Mohicans often had allies among the Connecticut Valley Indians, as well as the northern tribes allied with the French. These conflicts were bloody; at one peace conference the Mohawks asked the Mohicans to tell them what had been done with the heads of their warriors.[8] The Mohawks, on the other hand, were said to occasionally cannibalize their captives.

Next the Dutch and the English struggled for control of New York, further disrupting the beaver trade and the Indians' peace. By the 1630s the English, represented mainly by the Pynchon family, had established a trade center at what is now Springfield, Massachusetts, and began to probe northward and westward. John Pynchon was probably the first English colonial of note to make contact with the Housatonics when he established a short-lived post among them in 1662. He represented what the Dutch saw as English infringement not only on their trading prerogative but also on their territorial prerogative. But there were fortunes to be made in the fur trade, particularly when the Mohawks would pay up to twenty beaver pelts for a gun, and another handsome amount for powder. This enriching opportunity even led what was supposed to be a Dutch agricultural plantation to turn heavily to the Indian trade.[9] In a few years, the balance of Indian power tilted to the Mohawks, who now controlled the western side of the Hudson River and received tribute from the Mohicans and from tribes as far away as the seacoast. Finally, by 1675 the Mohawks, the Mohicans, the Dutch, and the English had all buried the hatchet. As the Mohicans put it, "the English and the Dutch are now one, and the Dutch are now English." The Mohicans also declared that their scattered tribes—those along the Hudson, the Housatonic, and in the New York Highlands, such as the Wappingers—were now one. The Wappingers, who had traditionally claimed the land on the east side of the Hudson from Manhattan to northern Dutchess County, acknowledged that they and the Mohicans, whose language differed very little, constituted one nation.[10]

Among the scattered villages that remained along the Hudson and in the mountain valleys eastward the Mohicans also accommodated some Indians from the east, Connecticut River Valley tribes and possibly Wampanoags, refugees from King Philip's War. New York governor Edmund Andros purchased land from the Mohicans and in 1677 established the village of Schaghticoke at the confluence of the Hoosic and Hudson rivers for numerous such refugees from several tribes.[11] Some of the tribes on the Westfield River had relocated among the Hudson River Mohicans a year before the outbreak of the war, apparently because of hard times, or perhaps in anticipation of the forthcoming struggle, and were probably early occupants of Schaghticoke. Unfortunately for these relocated Indians and for the Mohicans, Philip and about six hundred of his men chose to winter nearby on the Hoosic River. And according to a Hatfield prisoner among them, either the relocated Indians or the Mohicans or both "kindly furnished them with provisions," a natural, usually unavoidable tradition among Indians. Further, he said, some of them were with the war party that had originally captured him.[12]

Both New York and the Mohawks denied powder and lead to Indians whose intentions were uncertain, and with a few exceptions Mohicans were apparently included in the ban.[13] The restrictions may have caused resentment among a few young men, pushing them into the warring camp, which now included most of the remaining Connecticut River tribes who had always been closely allied with the Mohicans. The Mohicans as a nation, however, remained neutral out of respect for Governor Andros and for John Pynchon, who had helped protect them during previous Mohawk wars.

Fortunately for New Englanders, three hundred Mohawks attacked Philip's men at the Hoosic encampment in the winter of 1676, killed a considerable number of them and captured others, including at least one Mohican, and drove the rest back across the Connecticut River. With the Mohawks striking in Mohican territory and the English threatening from the east, the Mohicans fled their lands for parts unknown. The Mohawks apparently then wanted to take advantage of the struggle to again attack the Mohicans, but Andros not only prevented them, he demanded that the one Mohican captive be turned over to him and then set him free. Andros further convinced the Mohicans and their friendly allies to return to the protection of his government. When unfriendly Indians began to mix with the Mohicans under this offer of shelter, they were offered similar refuge, and many concentrated at Schaghticoke.[14] In April of 1677, John Pynchon, as a New England representative, met with the Mohicans at Albany to express gratitude for their neutrality, declaring them "friends and neighbors" to the English.[15]

Despite the additions of Indians from the east, and despite the alliances, the Mohicans admitted that in the life span of one tribesman they had become small and weak compared with the new Americans. They reminded the officials at this same Albany conference that in the early days, when their status was reversed, they had allowed the newcomers to remain in their territory and live in peace. They now hoped that they would not be exiled or destroyed by the English.[16]

Some of the diseases that their new neighbors had brought with them, however, had already destroyed Mohicans. Between 1689 and 1698, during the protracted skirmishes with French Canadians and Indians called King William's War, the Mohicans and the Indians at Schaghticoke, often collectively called "River Indians" by their allies, were devastated by the loss of 160 men—64 percent of their warriors. A hundred of these were lost to smallpox.[17] Other diseases like tuberculosis took their toll more slowly, but just as assuredly.

But the real killer was alcohol, introduced to them by Henry Hudson himself. Indians who brought furs from the hinterlands to Albany might not get home with their earnings before pouring them out of a bottle. A Mohican chief from Hudson River named Aupaumut had stated their predicament to the New York governor in 1722: "When our people come from hunting to the town or plantations and acquaint the traders and people that we want powder and shot and clothing, they first give us a large cup of rum. And after we get the taste of it crave for more so that . . . all the beaver and peltry we have hunted goes for drink, and we are left destitute either of clothing or ammunition. Therefore we desire our father to order the tap . . . to be shut and to prohibit . . . selling of rum, for as long as the Christians will sell rum, our people will drink it." [18]

Dutch and English colonial officials both enacted laws forbidding the unlicensed sale of rum to Indians, but such laws were nearly impossible to enforce. The problem had been incessant ever since Europeans landed, to the perpetual dismay of responsible Indian leaders and colonial officials alike. For whatever reasons, the Indians were attracted to alcohol, and colonials of all ranks found it profitable to engage in its sale despite heavy fines and threats of imprisonment, banishment, or even death. Some of the Dutch increased their profit margin from the Indians by watering down the alcohol considerably. Indian drunkenness nonetheless often resulted in mischief, vandalism, and more serious attacks on colonial buildings, livestock, and people, including other Indians. One eighteenth-century clergyman noted, "when they are thus intoxicated they fall out among themselves, fight and sometimes kill one another, and some have drunk themselves dead on the spot." [19] Intoxicated Indians were also subject to frequent cheating or even physical abuse by crude provincials. In 1654 a Mohican known by the epithet of "whoremaster" got drunk on brandy at an Albany house. Even though he had money to pay for his drinks, two men decided to beat him anyway. Afterward, the Mohican vented his own anger and frustration by making "a good deal of trouble here and there." [20] But colonial governments did not completely outlaw the sale of alcohol to the Indians, just unlicensed distribution of it. Alcohol was an integral part of colonial American life, so the Indians had plenty of company.

If alcohol was the new enemy, at least the Mohicans had reconciled issues with their old enemy. Peace with the Mohawks had lasted since 1675 and seemed likely to continue. The two tribes now spoke of each other in kinship terms. The Mohicans called the Mohawks uncle, and they showed deference to their uncle.[21] When New England representatives in 1689 tried to encourage the Mohicans and the Schaghticokes to take up the hatchet against Canadian Indians on the Maine border, the

Mohicans acknowledged their dependence on the Mohawks for direction: "What they shal think fitt and order us to doe wee will joyn with them and doe it."[22]

New York mediators of the final peace, which was crucial to the stability of trade, may have had a part in underscoring the ranking distinction between the two Indian nations. The peace had been arranged at Albany in November of 1671 with considerable diplomatic fanfare and a pooling of large amounts of gifts and wampum by the English and the Dutch, who likely gave preferential status to the Mohawks because of their military dominance and their favorable position as middlemen in the fur trade with western tribes. But the Mohicans' Connecticut Valley allies, such as the Pocumtucks, who had also fought against the Mohawks, were reluctant to conclude terms that awarded the Mohawks a higher status.[23] This probably further explains why the Mohawks were prompted to attack these Indians while they were encamped with Philip's men near the Hoosic.

The Mohicans may not have liked the status arrangement any better, but having been the enemy closest to the Mohawks, they would receive the brunt of any attacks in a continuing war. In addition, the Mohicans were primarily dependent on and influenced by Albany merchants and patroons, who obviously wanted the advantage of trading with tribes whose connections extended west through Iroquois country, while keeping trade open east and north into Algonquin and Abenaki territory. The peace compromise undoubtedly offered some concession to the Mohicans, perhaps designating them as middlemen for trade coming from the north and east, while guaranteeing them unmolested travel to the west. They did have some additional status as intermediaries for peace and trade involving their western cousins such as the Ottawas and the Miamis.[24] And despite Mohican diplomatic deference to their uncles, the Mohawks were not exactly unafraid of the Mohicans, especially since the Mohicans still had connections among the northern and eastern Abenakis and Algonquins. During the peace conferences, and even shortly thereafter, groups of Mohawks and Mohicans alike asked colonial officials for protection from the other. Yet the desire for peace between the two tribes, both devastated by wars and disease, was strong enough that more than forty-five years later Mohican descendants referred to it as "the old agreement made by our forefathers . . . that if anything happened to the one, it happened to the other, & that we might live and dye together . . . that we are inseparable til death."[25]

In the years following the peace, the Mohicans' political and military

alliance with Canadian and northeastern tribes loosened. With both encouragement and indirect threats from the English, the Mohicans were
willing to consider them as mutual enemies in time of war.[26] At this point,
the Mohicans obviously decided that it was to their benefit economically and militarily to plan their future with their uncles and the English.
Earlier hints of their common interest with the Mohawks had surfaced
during the wars between the Dutch and the Esopus Indians, a division
of Munsee Delawares who occupied the Hudson's west bank at present-
day Kingston, New York. The Mohawks, the Mohicans, and Mohican
allies, concerned about the consequent disruption of trade and their
own safety, served as active intermediaries to effect peace.[27] And during
King William's and Queen Anne's wars the Mohicans and the Mohawks
joined hands with the English against the French. The Mohicans also
periodically accompanied the Mohawks on raids during the late seventeenth century against Indians in Maryland and Virginia, where again
the contention seemed to be about trade.[28]

The kinship frame of reference between the two tribes became deeper
than just trade accommodations and military alliances when a Mohican
chief married a Mohawk woman who produced the famous Mohawk
chief Hendrick. By 1710 Hendrick and Mohican sachem Etowaukaum
joined two other Mohawk chiefs in a visit to England to appeal to Queen
Anne to send a force into Canada against the French and Indians there.
A daughter of Etowaukaum subsequently married Umpachenee, one of
the two Housatonics now considering the mission, and this marriage
undoubtedly enhanced Umpachenee's prestige.[29]

But Mohican prestige in general seemed debatable by 1734. The Mohawk wars, the French and Indian skirmishes, the beaver trade, rum, and
disease had all debilitated the nation. Fighting and murders within tribes
and within families were more prevalent than before the Europeans came.
Drunkenness, with its consequent family and social disruption, increased
as the stress of radical change took its toll. The women, also victimized
by alcohol and cultural change, were bearing fewer children, and many
of these died in infancy.[30] Many colonials simply viewed the Indians'
natural way of living as pitiable, and the Indians themselves probably did
not perceive their condition to be deficient. But the sympathy for "the
wretched and forlorn circumstances" of the "poor natives," "half naked
and almost starved" and "in need of . . . charity," expressed by one contemporary of the Housatonics, seemed to confirm the Indians' marginal
existence, which often had a "feast or famine" aspect. "How low, how
dispirited, how miserable and brutish these few are who live within our

*Etowaukaum, also known as Nicholas, one of the "Four Indian Kings"
to visit Queen Anne in 1710. Called "King of the River Nation" by his
British hosts, he may not have been grand sachem of the Mohicans,
since he apparently was a member of the turtle clan. Mohican tradition
held that the sachem usually came from the bear clan. Courtesy of the
Library of Congress.*

borders is too manifest," this observer remarked. "And whether we, by our ill treating of them have not contributed to their misery, is worthy of a serious inquiry."[31]

Even wild game was less available than in Konkapot's father's time. The demand for hides and furs had greatly diminished the once abundant animals, as had the clearing of land and the competition from colonial hunters. A heavy European market for deer leather made that animal another trade commodity, and deer were no longer as limitless as they had once seemed. The Mohicans depended on deer for food and clothing and as a medium of exchange. Without it or some other barter item they would incur debts that often led to trouble. Some were perceptive enough to see that one of the causes of their dependent and weakened state since the Europeans' arrival was the use of animals as a commodity rather than as a staple. Konkapot and his fellow tribesmen had once lived closer to the Hudson, but moved east to the Housatonic, where among other things it was less crowded and where game was probably more plentiful.[32]

To earn part of their living many Mohicans worked fall harvests for the landed Dutch gentry in New York. In agriculture, too, the Indians had come to rely on the variety of colonially produced staples that were more abundant than those traditional Indian agriculture could provide, especially when trade, war, or social dissolution intervened. In February or March of each year the Mohicans set up camp among the sugar maples for about six weeks to tap the trees and make sugar, much of it for sale. They might also get a few trade goods for their baskets, brooms, garters, mats, wooden cups and bowls, and an occasional canoe. The lucky and prudent ones could furnish themselves comfortably.

An account of one Mohican woman's possessions was probably typical, or perhaps better than typical, of the average Indian household. She had a mare and a yearling colt, a saddle and two bridles, two lengths of wampum, one large and three small hatchets, a silk shirt, three large and three small kettles with two chains on which to hang them, two mortars for grinding meal, and a small assortment of awls, pans, bottles, mats, bags, and wooden utensils. The one lesser length of wampum was considered sufficient to pay off a debt of three pieces of eight and six guilders, but it would take the sale of the colt, the hatchets, awls, mortars, and chains to provide clothes for her daughters.[33] The majority of Indians, however, even more so than the small colonial and tenant farmers, led a marginal existence. An early frost, a severe winter, scarce game, or rapid colonial currency inflation could send them into the woods foraging.

The Indians did have one more negotiable commodity—land. And the Mohicans had been yielding it periodically for a hundred years. The Mohawk victories had cost them some towns on the west side of the Hudson. Though a few Mohican villages remained there, the Mohawks now sold land above Albany, for example, at their pleasure, giving any Mohican claimants only a token gift of acknowledgment that the land had been theirs.[34] Most of the land east of the Hudson from Albany southward had been yielded to the Dutch for their trading posts, and to the oversized plantations of wealthy men like the Van Rensselaers and the Livingstons. Some of this land's ownership, however, was in question. Aupaumut, speaking for the Hudson River Mohicans, had said, "We have no more land. The Christians when they buy a small spot of land of us, ask us if we have . . . more land. And when we say yes, they enquire the name of the land and take in a greater bounds than was intended to be sold them. And the Indians not understanding what is writ in the deed or bill of sale sign it and are so deprived of their lands."[35] It had reached the point, Aupaumut continued, where many of his people had to lease land from whites to raise their corn. They paid the lease with half their corn crop, and then might lose the other half to a rum trader.[36]

The current chief sachem, Mtohksin, had himself been involved in land sales in northwestern Connecticut, where the townships of Salisbury and Sharon were developing around Mohicans.[37] Meanwhile, Wappinger kinsmen had an unsteady hold on part of the Highlands in New York, and there were scattered villages remaining between the Hudson and the Housatonic. Konkapot still claimed land east of present-day Sheffield and south to the head of the Farmington River. Other Mohicans claimed hunting grounds northward into what is now Vermont, and several families claimed most of Massachusetts west of the Westfield River, though settlers were making incursions there. After King Philip's War and Queen Anne's War appeared to lessen the perceived Indian threat in the region, real estate activity boomed and colonial population began expanding westward from the Connecticut Valley and eastward from Albany County.

The Mohicans tried to be cautious in what they sold. In their own words, "the tribe . . . do not sell lands in a private manner but always make it an invariable rule to convene the fathers and principal heads and chiefs of the tribe on such occasions, that all sales of lands may be transacted in a publick manner as may be, we Indians having no other way of recording and keeping in remembrance what is done from one generation to an other."[38] But there were always a few Indians willing to turn a profit at the expense of their fellow tribesmen, just as there were always a few colonial Americans encouraging them to do so.[39] About 1728, for example, one provincial bought more than 3,000 acres from a Mohican for £30 and a suit of clothes.[40] In a slightly better deal, when Massachusetts wanted to create two new townships, Konkapot and Umpachenee, along with nineteen other tribesmen, sold about ninety square miles of land that surrounded their two villages for £460, three barrels of cider, and thirty quarts of rum. But ten years later, some of the money had not yet been paid, its value was depreciating, and the rum and cider were long gone. So here the Housatonics sat in July of 1734 to sort out the pieces of their Indian ways: what to keep, what to throw away, and what had already been lost.

Konkapot and the rest knew that many of the old ways had gone forever. The trade, commerce, technology, transportation, agriculture, and even politics that Europeans had introduced from Albany southward had been in the Mohicans' midst for several generations, and they could not be unaffected. Some Mohicans along the Hudson were becoming more dependent for a living on trade and crafts than on hunting. Those who worked occasionally as farm laborers certainly represented a significant change from the old ways, and so did those few who intermarried with colonials. The simple ownership of a horse, as another example, could change the way of life and economy of its Indian owner. Guns, powder, and shot were preferred to bows and arrows. The wooden war club had given way to the steel hatchet, and earthen pots yielded to brass kettles and tin pans. Everywhere metal implements replaced those of stone and bone. Wool blankets and European cloth were competing with deer hides. Even wampum, still necessary for currency, for decoration, or for the conduct of public affairs, was being provided by Albany and Springfield traders, who had many other material things that Indians now needed or wanted. More important, these new Americans had the knowledge of how to make them or had the ships to import them. And the Mohicans could not help but notice that those New Englanders who had the most material goods attributed their abundance to the blessings of a god who spoke to them through their Bibles. Perhaps, then, the Housatonics who inclined toward Calvinistic Christianity felt as some coastal Indians had nearly a century earlier, when they told the Massachusetts government, "We do desire to reverence the God of the English, because we see he doth better to the English than other gods do to others."[41]

The Mohicans observed also that the English god, as the religious colonials themselves believed, seemed to make the English victors in every war with the Indians. Even the war with the Dutch ended with an English victory, and the sporadic conflicts with France were at least standoffs, followed by more English than French populating the land. This trend alone may have played a part in the Housatonics' consideration of a mission. With the English approaching from the east and the south, the Mohawks controlling access to the west, and the French holding the north, the Mohicans' physical world was shrinking. Why not, then, try to learn the successful ingredients of the surrounding culture and cast one's lot with those who were most often the winners? After all, they and the Mohawks had already committed themselves militarily to alliances with the English.

It is not hard to understand, therefore, why the Mohicans would associate the Christians' material well-being, population increase, successive military triumphs, and less debilitating effects from rum and disease with the religion they practiced. Again, the Puritans themselves believed that these blessings were outward signs of God's favor. Further, the most influential and successful men with whom the Mohicans had had recent contact, like the Pynchons and John Stoddard of Northampton, were strongly religious. And just as important to future Indian survival in the new order of their environment was the education that usually accompanied Christian conversion. The ability to read and understand those documents that had caused trouble might well enhance their ability to survive intact as a nation. At least it might offer their children a better chance for adaptation.

Jonathan Edwards, who was acquainted with the Housatonics, once remarked in a mixture of paternalism and condescension reflective of the times that "the Indians, wild as they are, have some sense of the shamefulness of vice and of the value of virtue, good order and civilization, and they have some sense of the worth of knowledge. If any one among them is able to read and write, it is looked upon as a great attainment. And they esteem it as a thing much to be valued to be able to read and understand the Bible." [42] During their 1710 visit to Queen Anne, Hendrick, Etowaukaum, and the others asked for missionaries to be sent among them. And whether through baptism or colonial appellation, these chiefs already had Christian first names. Etowaukaum, for example, was also known as Nicholas.

Yet the impulse among the Indians to accept a new religion was not simply pragmatic. In times of upheaval, stress, or significant social changes, people often turn to religion or change religions, seeking a supernatural solution to their plight. This impulse manifested itself more than a dozen years prior to the Housatonics' conference, when a spokesman for a Mohican delegation to Albany told an official of "a great inclination to be Christians and turn from this heathenish life we are bred up in."[43] The contemporary state of Mohican society may have made it ripe for seeking some sort of metaphysical help. It is clear, from their oft-repeated description of themselves as a tribe small and weak, from the lectures to them against drunkenness even by Albany civil officials, and from the pressure of a steadily shrinking environment in which their way of living—and even living itself—was being threatened, that the Mohicans had enough psychological pressure to make them receptive to anything that looked like salvation.

The Indians were also aware of the substantial influence of the Jesuits and their religion among their Canadian Indian cousins, who had succumbed to the religious, political, and economic influence of the French. From the latter seventeenth to the early eighteenth century the Six Nations tribes, the Mohicans, and the Schaghticokes alike often requested that ministers or priests be sent to them. Not only did they hope thereby that their prodigal brethren would return to New York, but also it seems that a Christian cleric was becoming a gradual replacement for the pow-wow—their shaman or medicine man. Beginning in 1712 the English provided one minister for the Mohawks. Twenty years later Massachusetts stationed a missionary who was also to be military chaplain at Fort Dummer, a trading post on the upper Connecticut River near a relocated band of about eighty Indians, Schaghticokes mostly.[44] None, however, had yet been assigned to the steadily loyal Mohicans, so perhaps the Housatonics thought that their turn had come.

Another influence less subject to logical scrutiny may have affected their disposal toward Christianity at this point, an influence shepherded by Jonathan Edwards himself. A phenomenon had been occurring the previous year up and down the Connecticut Valley and was reaching westward, a religious revival that would come to be known as the Great Awakening. Its influence was growing, and it is conceivable that the Indians were also affected.

Many Mohicans felt, however, that there were reasons to be wary of Christians, and undoubtedly the Housatonics' council was not unanimous in its deliberations. Christians—even ministers—kept slaves. And they had made slaves of some Indians farther east. There were those who told the Housatonics that the New Englanders would do the same to them.[45] Sons and daughters of refugees from King Philip's War could tell the Mohicans stories of eastern Indians who were sent to the Caribbean as slaves, not to mention those about loyal Christian Indians who were abused, harassed, uprooted, herded onto offshore islands, and even murdered out of suspicion or pure hatred.

Certainly the New England way of dealing with the indigent, the widowed, and the orphaned—crowding them into an almshouse with little social or sexual separation from vagrants, prostitutes, and the insane—did nothing to impress Christian social caring upon Indians. The Indians furthermore feared the colonial practice of imprisonment for minor wrongs or for a simple debt. Massachusetts had passed a law in 1672 preventing anyone from being imprisoned for debt, so instead some colonials drew Indians into an agreement to repay a small obligation by binding themselves or their children as servants for a number of years. In 1700 another law made these indenture agreements more reasonable, but this whole state of affairs was hard for a proud, freedom-loving people to abide.[46] And this same love for freedom could make it difficult to follow a settled Christian life, especially for the men, who were reared to be hunters, trappers, fishermen, and warriors. The Mohicans called their warriors heroes, and numbers of them had gone to live among western tribes such as the Ottawas, where they could continue to be heroes and maintain Mohican prestige.[47] And even the majority of those who remained up and down the Hudson preferred to keep as many of their Indian ways as possible.

Nonetheless, by the spring of 1734 word had come to the ministers at Springfield that the Housatonics at least, and Konkapot in particular, might be receptive to a mission. Konkapot was considered by his colonial neighbors as just, upright, temperate, and industrious. In May he and Umpachenee were in Springfield to pick up military commissions sent by Gov. Jonathan Belcher, when they were approached by two clergymen. Both Indians listened to the ministers, Samuel Hopkins and Stephen Williams, who told them that benevolent people in London and Boston were concerned about the Indians' souls. These people wanted to send a man among them who could help them along an enlightened path to the fruits of Christian, English education.

Konkapot was in fact interested in Christian religion and education. The seeming inadequacy of the religion of his forefathers made him uneasy. The family idols were ineffective.[48] Their powwows produced few revelations or any magic that helped the Indians now. The powwows themselves admitted that they had no power over Christians. Though some tribesmen believed that the sun was god or was his home, most believed in a being who was responsible for good and one who was responsible for mischief among men. Others believed in nothing.⁴⁹ Still, a couple of things about this new proposal worried Konkapot. If he, his family, or the Housatonic bands embraced Christianity, they might be outcasts among their own people. The principal Mohicans at the main council fire on the Hudson might not like an independent decision of this magnitude. Another concern was that many of the Christians with whom he had had contact seemed poor models for ethical living.

Umpachenee was less enthusiastic about the proposal but said that he would not stand in the way of a mission. Though skeptical, less temperate, and more proud than Konkapot, he had compassion for his people and knew that the old beliefs did not serve them. Umpachenee had considerable influence among the Housatonics, so his opinions carried weight. But both chiefs told the ministers that they spoke for themselves only and would have to consult with their brethren. The four agreed to rendezvous with the rest of the tribesmen on the Housatonic in July.

On July 9, Stephen Williams and a Westfield minister, Nehemiah Bull, met at one of the Housatonic villages with about twenty tribesmen to formally put forward the proposal. Williams had firsthand experience with Indians, having been a boy captive among those at Saint Francis after his family was carried off following the raid on Deerfield in 1704. Despite his own hardship among them and the fact that his mother and several other women and children had been tomahawked to death on the way to Canada, Williams maintained an empathy for the Indians. This was due in part to the poignant situation of his younger sister, who had been captured at age five, grew up with the Indians, married one, and had no inclination to return to colonial society.

It was after this visit by the ministers that the Housatonics spent four days weighing the decision. The debate may have focused on the potential benefit or harm in abandoning traditional ways for Christian ways. But one overriding consideration prevailed. One of the men later told Reverend Williams that their great reduction in population (now probably fewer than a thousand) might have been due to their heathenism. He had told his fellow tribesmen, "since my remembrance, there were ten Indians where there is now one. But the Christians greatly increase and multiply and spread over the land; let us therefore leave our former courses and become Christians." ⁵⁰ They would accept a missionary. Stephen Williams gave them a belt of wampum to solemnify the event. The new path was begun.

2

DECLINE

OF

THE

SPIRITUAL

The people in London who wished to save Indian souls were professionals and businessmen who belonged to a philanthropic dissenter organization known as the Company for the Propagation of the Gospel in New England and Parts Adjacent in America, later called simply the New England Company. Since 1649 its members had been interested in furthering the Puritan version of Christianity and had sponsored a number of Indian missions, including those of John Eliot and Thomas Mayhew. The company operated through its American representatives, known as Commissioners of the United Colonies, who in 1734 were headed by Massachusetts governor Jonathan Belcher.

Converting the American natives to Christianity had ostensibly been the principal aim of the Massachusetts Bay settlement, according to the charter of 1628. A century later some believed that this aim had been forgotten. Solomon Stoddard, a respected clergyman, suggested in 1723 that recent epidemics, Indian wars, and Indian alliances with the French might be signs of God's anger with the English for failing to spread the gospel among the natives. Massachusetts also had critics in London, and even Governor Belcher claimed that the colony had done little to live up to the goal of its charter. In March of 1730 he had suggested to the New England Company that it ask the provincial government to lay out a tract of land for the Indians to share with a minister, a schoolmaster, and some tradesmen, who could teach civilized Christian living and provide apprenticeships for Indian children.[1] Three years later the company made money available to fund such a mission. Having learned of this, Samuel Hopkins suggested the idea of a mission for the Housatonics to Stoddard's son John, who was an influential member of the governor's council, the richest and most powerful figure in western Massachusetts, and an uncle of Jonathan Edwards. John Stoddard knew that the Mohicans were not influenced by the French and that a mission among them had some chance of success. His influence and the successful visit to the Housatonics by Stephen Williams and Nehemiah Bull convinced the New England Company's commissioners to authorize the mission. The ministers already had a young man in mind for the job of missionary, a short, dark-haired, and dark-eyed twenty-four-year-old Yale tutor from Newark, New Jersey, named John Sergeant.

Sergeant came to academic and religious life literally by accident. He apparently would have followed the course of a gentleman farmer, but when he was a boy a scythe cut the nerves and ligaments near his left wrist, causing the hand to wither. A scholar's life then became more practical, and his stepfather decided to pay for a liberal education at Yale, where Sergeant enrolled at age fifteen. By the time he finished his studies, a religious stirring had aimed him toward the ministry. Along the way, the young man developed sympathies for the Indians.

Sergeant held the traditional Puritan view of the Indians as representative of man in the state of original sin. Charitable New Englanders viewed them as he did, "a people naturally ingenious enough, but for want of instruction living so much below the dignity of human nature." But like Governor Belcher and the concerned Protestant clergy, he was disturbed that the "Romish" papists, "whose religion is so corrupted that it may scarcely be called Christianity," were much more energetic in converting Indians than were the New England Calvinists, "who at least think we profess Christianity in much greater purity."[2] Sergeant told friends that he would rather be called as a missionary to the Indians than as a pastor to an English congregation. In September, Stephen Williams and Nehemiah Bull arrived in New Haven to offer him a chance to fulfill that wish.

Sergeant felt that he couldn't call himself a man, much less a Christian, if he refused to help cultivate humanity "among a barbarous people" or to "promote the salvation of souls perishing in the dark, when the Light of Life is so near them."[3] He knew, though, that he would not be like Daniel in the lion's den among the Housatonics, since the Mohicans had already been friendly toward the English. Besides, there were already several settlers on the land that the Housatonics had sold near their villages, and the two ministers assured him that the mission had a fair prospect of success.

Still, Sergeant preferred to test the religious waters before jumping into them. He agreed to go to the Indians and remain with them until December. If his stay with the Housatonics convinced him that there really was hope for their salvation, he would devote his life to teaching them. The commissioners consented to this proposal, and Sergeant set out in October with Nehemiah Bull on a trek to the Housatonic River, through what Sergeant called "a most doleful wilderness and the worst road, perhaps, that ever was rid."[4]

They met the Indians midway between the two villages at what is now Great Barrington. There must have been quiet apprehension as the Indians encountered Sergeant. The man who had been sent to save them was small and frail and had a dead hand. His pale, solemn visage and somber clothes contrasted sharply with those of his hosts and with the brilliant hues of a New England autumn. The young man gazed on a group of natives, some tattooed darkly with totemic signs or marks of past deeds, their ears and noses pierced with baubles and their bodies draped with a mixture of Indian and European fashion.[5]

A Housatonic who spoke English acted as interpreter. Sergeant adapted his short talk on Christianity "as well as I could to their capacities and manner of thinking."[6] There were no words in Mohican to express the fine points of Christian theology. Whatever he said must have made an impression, for the interpreter later told him that one Indian who had been unreceptive to the whole idea of a mission was moved and wanted to learn more.

As for the interpreter himself, he was much interested in Christianity and had a fair understanding of its principles. He had lived with the English for a time, possibly at Springfield, where he occasionally visited Stephen Williams and was known by the Christian name of Ebenezer Poohpoonuc. He had probably also served under chief Aupaumut when the chief and Hendrick scouted for the English.[7] After Sergeant's talk Ebenezer announced that he wanted to be baptized by Reverend Bull. A few days later, at Umpachenee's hut and in front of the assembled Indians, the minister tested Ebenezer's resolution to lead a Christian life. Ebenezer replied to Bull's questions as one prepared, saying that "he would rather burn in the fire than forsake the truth."[8] Reverend Bull then baptized Poohpoonuc and set the Mohicans on a new course.

The woods between the Housatonic and the Hudson were already vibrating with the new wind that was blowing. After the ceremony, Ebenezer showed John Sergeant a young Housatonic lad who had felt the wind. The boy and his father had been some distance away in the forest when they learned that Sergeant would be coming to the village and would teach the children to read. The youngster, who was very fond of his father, insisted nevertheless on returning to the village to learn, though he would have to go alone. His father, perhaps to test his son's conviction, warned him that there would be no one to take care of him, clothe him, or feed him. Neither the warning nor the attachment between the two kept the boy from returning.

Sergeant was impressed by such sparks of interest. The Indians agreed to build a large wigwam for a winter meetinghouse and huts for themselves at the midway point between the two villages. But by spring they would have to return home for planting. Sergeant was not ready to winter in a wigwam, however, so he decided to stay at a nearby settler's house.

Since the minister and the missionary had allowed the Indians to watch a Christian ceremony, the Housatonics offered to return the favor. They invited Sergeant to attend one of their deer sacrifice rituals at Konkapot's wigwam the next day. Sergeant kept an open mind. Reverend Bull had left, and here was a chance to learn more about the thinking and customs of the people whom he hoped to convert.

When he arrived the following day, the Indians were inside sitting around a low bark platform that would serve as an altar. A large kettle sat on a fire nearby. Sergeant took his place, and after a while two men took down a freshly killed deer that hung from a ceiling pole. They skinned and quartered the animal, then placed the hide and quarters on the altar in such a fashion that the deer might again appear whole to the watching eye of Wauntheet Monnitoow (Manitou), the Great Spirit.[9] One of the old ones presided over the offering. He stood and began to pray in a loud voice that Manitou might hear: "O great God, pity us, grant us food to eat, afford us good and comfortable sleep, preserve us from being devoured by the fowls that fly in the air. This deer is given in token that we acknowledge thee the giver of all things."[10]

The man who had killed the deer and was offering it for sacrifice gave the old one a string of wampum for his services. The old man called aloud again for the Great Spirit to take notice of what they did. After this ceremony the Indians cut up the deer further to boil it for a small feast. When the meat was done, it was passed around to everyone. The skin and innards were given to a needy old widow, but the Indian who had killed and sacrificed the deer took nothing. It was his gift.

Sergeant asked where they learned this "piece of religion." The Indians told him that it was a tradition among their forefathers, who had learned it from the great hero and prophet who came down from heaven. This hero drew the Indians' awe and respect, they said, by clearing the land of monsters that had overrun it. He also introduced snowshoes to them and taught them this ceremony, which was a custom from his homeland above. The hero took a wife from among the Mohicans, and she bore him two children. He served as their powwow during the deer sacrifice, just as the old man had on this occasion. One day he began to pray during the ceremony, while his two children sat on his knees. As he continued praying intently, he began to rise gradually from the ground. Still praying and rising, he neared the top of the wigwam. The others called out to him to leave at least one of his children behind. He broke from his trance long enough to hand a son down to them and then passed through the smoke hole and disappeared from sight. The son also proved to be an extraordinary man, and the Indians had several remarkable stories to tell about him.[11]

Sergeant had learned another piece of Indian religious lore from Ebenezer, the celestial bear chase. The bear figured prominently in Mohican culture and legend. Not only was it a fine source of meat, clothing, and by-products, it was also the totemic symbol for one of the three tribal clans, the clan that claimed the hereditary station of grand sachem of the nation. And the Mohicans, according to one sachem a century earlier, traditionally believed that after death the soul went westward to a joyous meeting with others deceased, all of whom would wear black otter or bear skins, which were "signs of gladness."[12] Sergeant heard the old Mohican legend according to which the stars that made up the Great Bear constellation were men in heaven who hunted the bear. The chase began in the spring and lasted through the summer. In the fall the hunters wounded the bear, and his blood fell, turning the leaves red. By winter the sky Indians had killed the bear, and its fat was the snow that fell to the earth. The approaching summer melted the fat and turned it into the sap that rose in the trees. Sergeant viewed these beliefs as pitifully childish examples of the benighted state from which he hoped to rescue the Indians.

During November the Indians gathered their families in wigwams around the new meeting place to hear more of what the Christians believed. Sergeant thought the future held promise. They were curious and listened intently to the Christian message. The young ones especially seemed willing and able to learn. There would be trials, though, to test

Sergeant's fortitude as well as the Indians'. The first trial came just a few days before the minister left for New Haven. Some Dutch traders from the Hudson River were in the vicinity during the first week in December selling rum, and a number of the Indians indulged themselves for three days. They had not recovered by Sunday, and Sergeant's congregation was sparse: "This was the most discouraging week I had; for the Dutch traders, I was told, had been very industrious to discourage the Indians from being Christians, thinking it would lessen their trade with them, or at least they would not be under so good advantages to cheat and impose upon them. For they make vast profit by selling them rum, and making bargains with them while they are drunk. "These traders tell them that the religion we are about to teach them is not a good one; that we design in the end to serve ourselves by them, to make slaves of them and their children . . . and the like." [13] The traders also told them that the Massachusetts law forbidding private individuals from selling rum to the Indians was a prime example of how the government wished to restrict their freedom. The Indians were upset. Umpachenee's brother, a prominent tribal member, was particularly incensed. Even Umpachenee, who along with Konkapot had stayed away from the spree, was concerned that the traders might be right. John Sergeant was able to persuade them, however, that the traders were merely afraid of losing the advantage over the Indians if they became educated Christian farmers. The two Housatonics then demonstrated their trust in their new friend by allowing him to return to Yale with their sons, who could help him learn Mohican: Konkapot's nine-year-old and Umpachenee's eight-year-old, a grandson of Etowaukaum.

Stephen Williams and the other ministers in the meantime had found another young volunteer, a twenty-five-year-old named Timothy Woodbridge, the son of a minister at West Springfield and a great-grandson of John Eliot. [14] Woodbridge apparently had no designs on the ministry, but his education and religious background qualified him for teaching the children, and he may have already known the Mohican language. [15] He arrived at the meeting place a couple of weeks before Sergeant set out for New Haven, and Sergeant noticed that the children quickly became fond of him.

Sergeant was warming to the idea of a mission. He reiterated that he would prefer to teach the Indians than his own people. The Housatonics liked him, and he believed that they were capable of learning to lead a civilized Christian life. He considered Konkapot an excellent, respectable man, already filled with a Christian spirit. Sergeant was not a revivalist zealot, but his was a demanding and uncomfortable religion for the Indians, as it was for many colonials. And the ones with whom most Indians had contact on the frontier were often the least exemplary Christians. Stephen Williams looked around him at Springfield and put it more graphically in 1728:

> Facts: Vices abound, visible and manifest evils among us— decay of ye power and godliness—divine institutions neglected by many—some unbaptized—great multitudes never join themselves to the churches of Christ—low esteem of ordinances— strifes and contentions—extravagant dress beyond our estates and degree—family govt and instruction neglected—how many children ignorant of the first rudiments of religion and without civility—yea and without instruction in reading and writing— intemperance, much drunkennesse, tavern haunting and cheating one another; breaches of the 7th commandt and not to insist on the abounding of adultery, how amazing does ye sin of fornication abound, sinful company keeping, and wanton managements.[16]

These traits sounded like the ones that made the Housatonics skeptical about Christians, and Springfield court records would support Williams's contentions and more. A hundred years had effected change in New England culture, too. Despite the incipient revival, the stringent Puritanism of the preceding century was fading. The people who were gradually populating western Massachusetts were not just the transplanted English country gentlemen and entrepreneurs with separatist faith and moneyed genealogy who worked for the glory of God and the commonweal, while perpetuating their own estates. The traders, the tenants, the millers, the carpenters, the smiths, the merchants, and even the ministers who followed them to western settlements like Northampton, Westfield, and Springfield saw opportunities to create their own modest estates. In the second half of the seventeenth century, in fact, such Puritan elders as Roger Williams, Increase Mather, and William Howard were decrying the greed for land that seemed to be weakening the social and religious fabric. Sometimes the opportunities presented themselves in the form of Indians who wanted alcohol or guns or credit that had to be paid off with land. After all, no one forced the Indians to drink alcohol or to accept the trade. And if the Indians wanted guns they would certainly get them from the French if the English wouldn't sell them. Even if there was a risk that the Indians might someday aim those guns toward the settlements, the settlers themselves bore most of the responsibility for

Stephen Williams of Springfield, one of the ministers who introduced the mission proposal to the Housatonics. Courtesy Pocumtuck Valley Memorial Association, Deerfield, Massachusetts.

their own defense. And so far the victors in war usually had been the English, renewing their confidence in pushing westward. One incident dramatically highlighted the change from the Puritan ethic to mercenary temptation. Around the time that the Housatonic mission was being considered, the New England Company's Boston treasurer embezzled nearly £6,000 of charitable funds to cover his own commercial losses.[17]

The experiences of rank-and-file New Englanders had not necessarily instilled in them charitable notions about the Indians. In general, those one contemporary called "the common people" often hated the Indians and made no distinction between heathen and Christian Indians, or "such English as were judged to be charitable to them."[18] Residents of the Connecticut River Valley, for instance, had seen traditionally friendly Indians turn enemies in King Philip's War. Inhabitants of remote towns had been surprised in their homes or in their fields, set upon without warning by Indians who harbored grievances against other colonials for indignities or injustices committed or who were simply venting pent-up rage at the relentless invasion by colonials. In that rage the Indian style of warfare did not defer to European sentiments against torture and killing or against capturing women and children. And those who did not experience such terror firsthand, by the first quarter of the eighteenth century could vicariously experience captivity through at least half a dozen harrowing narratives, including Stephen Williams's father's account in *The Redeemed Captive Returning to Zion*.

Yet some of the same accounts related acts of genuine kindness and generosity by the Indians, and undoubtedly some people who had day-to-day experiences with them recognized and appreciated those traits. And it seems plausible that after more than a century of contact with the Indians, some of their character and culture was rubbing off on colonial Americans. In the rough, competitive frontier world of trading, however, the one-on-one relationships too often resulted in the Indians' being cheated, debased, or assaulted. Albany townsmen sometimes tried to keep the Indians confined to one part of town when trading with them. This same negative view was reflected in the Dutch name for one Mohican sachem, Aepjen, meaning "Little Ape."[19] Among the more civilized colonials, too, the Indians represented a standard object of contempt. A Springfield man, speaking abusively about his father-in-law, remarked that he had no more respect for him than for an old Indian.[20] And in describing a fellow civil official's decline, even Governor Belcher said that he had "shrunk into an old Indian squaw."[21] Belcher exhibited a more cosmopolitan view of Indian-colonial relations, however, when he expressed to a British official his wish that the English settlers would intermarry with the Indians as the French did, since it tended to eliminate the distinctions between the two groups and to enhance the Indians' opinions of Europeans.[22]

The consciences of responsible, God-fearing New Englanders nevertheless dictated charity to the Indians. Pragmatism dictated that given the increasing tension with the French, whose Indians occasionally terrorized the countryside, it was better to have the Indians make the Calvinistic covenant with Jehovah than to have them make the Catholic sign of the cross. Reverend Hopkins maintained that although trade with the Indians was a profitable endeavor, "Indians, simply consider'd, are not of such great consequence to us. We can subsist without them. . . . But if we consider them with relation to peace or war, as attach'd to us or to our enemies, . . . they certainly have the balance of power in their hand, and are able to turn it for or against us."[23]

Even men without strict Puritan conscience recognized the spiritual and political worth in providing the Indians with clergy. On more than one occasion in the early 1700s New York's Robert Livingston had recommended it for the Mohicans and the Schaghticokes. "For these Indians, how contemptible soever they seem to be, have done signal services for this government in the late war [King William's]." He acknowledged that they and the Mohawks "fought our battles for us, and [have] been a constant barrier of defence. But the late long war, and the great loss which they sustained in their youth hath almost dispirited them." He therefore recommended to England's Society for Propagating the Gospel in Foreign Parts that it send a minister to each of the Iroquois nations and to the Mohicans. The society agreed to send two ministers to the Iroquois, but as an indictment of the limits and motivation of its charity, a spokesman cautioned that the Mohicans were "no longer formidable to us, they having been almost consumed in former wars."[24] To the New Englanders' credit and the credit of their dissenter backers in England, they either viewed the Mohicans in a more respectful light or had more charitable instincts toward them. John Sergeant's mission would, in their view, be good for the Indians and good for the English interest in America.

3
=

APPROVAL

ON

BOTH

SIDES

Despite Sergeant's optimism and the Housatonics' enthusiasm, the mission was not yet a foregone conclusion. Konkapot and Umpachenee were concerned about what the principal Mohicans would think of them. According to rumors, or what the Indians called flying birds, the Mohicans at the main council fire on the Hudson highly resented the Housatonics' acceptance of a minister and a schoolteacher without approval by a full council of the nation. These same birds said that there was already resentment over Konkapot's and Umpachenee's military commissions. There was even talk of a plot to poison the two. It is possible that traders started such rumors to scare the Housatonics away from a mission. But it is also quite possible that Mohicans who preferred their nation to remain Indian held contempt for those who would choose Christian over Indian ways. Konkapot and Umpachenee, therefore, sent word east that they would like the support of ministers at a January council of the several tribes to be held at the Housatonic. Sergeant knew that such a conference would either encourage the mission "or almost entirely quash it." He wrote the Indians a letter of encouragement: "I know you have many temptations to draw back. They cannot be your friends that try to discourage you. They only endeavour to keep you in ignorance, that they may be under better advantage to cheat you. Knowledge is certainly good: it is to the mind what light is to the eye. You would think them your greatest enemies that should endeavour to put out your eyes, especially if you were traveling a difficult road." [1]

Stephen Williams and Capt. John Ashley of Westfield responded to the Housatonics' request and attended the council at Umpachenee's village in January, where Williams preached to nearly two hundred Mohicans. Among them was sachem Mtohksin.[2] Consultation, discussion, and debate followed. Williams later said that the visiting tribes were satisfied to the extent "that they thanked us for the pains we had taken, and desir'd Mr. Woodbridge might continue among them (at Housatunnuk) and that Mr. Sergeant would return to them; and said they would give an account to their several towns of what we had offer'd to them; and gave us encouragement that they would as a nation submit to instruction." [3] Now the mission would not only go forward, it had official Mohican endorsement.

After the ministers left the Indians held a dance and drinking fest. The ministers' departure and the rum brought about a different disposition from that reported by Williams. Some of the visiting tribesmen chided the Housatonics about the mission and taunted them for imitating the English. Clearly, not all Mohicans cared to start carrying Bibles and wearing powdered wigs. Although Mohican leadership was generally sympathetic toward Christianity, individuals and factions within communities, the men in particular, disdained Christian civilization as effeminate. This was especially true of the Indians who lived along the upper Hudson under Dutch influence or in remote villages where the colonial cultural presence was less pronounced. Further, as one eighteenth-century expert in Indian affairs observed, whenever the more remote, traditional tribesmen met with missionized Indians, those from the seacoast for example, the missionized Indians always appeared poor and deficient in the qualities that traditionalists admired: "[The mission Indians] make so many complaints about the loss of their lands, that the rest despise them, hate us as the cause of their misfortunes, and not being capable of perceiving that they have made any material acquisition to compensate for what they lost, entertain a prejudice against Religion itself." [4]

Shortly after the ministers' visit, several Indians became extremely ill, including most of Umpachenee's family. Trailing closely behind the rumors of attempts on the lives of Konkapot and Umpachenee, the incident convinced the Housatonics that somebody had poisoned them. For the next few days those who lay sick with fever began, despite the jolt to their quest for religion, to turn to Christianity. They asked that Timothy

Woodbridge come to pray for them. When he did, the Indians requested that if they died they be given Christian burial in a Christian graveyard. Two men did die, one of them Umpachenee's brother-in-law. Woodbridge arranged for the men to receive the burial they had requested. The women and the men's relatives in turn refrained from their own ceremonies and from the customary loud wailing at the funeral.[5] At least, some Mohicans clearly were ready to carry Bibles.

Whether the two deaths were intended or merely resulted from a general sickness is uncertain. John Sergeant had learned of behavior at Indian dances that may have made Mohicans prone to illness. Inside a wigwam they danced and danced around a fire until they were wet with sweat and nearly exhausted. Then they would go outside, strip naked, and stand in the cold night air or roll around in the snow to cool off, only to return to the wigwam for more dancing. They would repeat this sequence four or five times in a night. If they accompanied the ceremony with liberal amounts of rum, they might fall dead drunk overnight, buried in snow.[6]

Konkapot and Umpachenee nevertheless believed that the two who died had been poisoned, indicating that other Mohicans "hate us for what we have done" in accepting the mission.[7] A few weeks after the fest, Konkapot told Timothy Woodbridge that he was going to Umpachenee's wigwam to join the men there in discovering who was responsible for the poisoning. Woodbridge thought they were simply going to council on the matter, until Ebenezer told him that powwows were going to try to conjure up the murderers. The schoolteacher immediately saddled a horse and rode through the dark to the village.

He arrived at Umpachenee's wigwam just before the ceremony was to begin. Inside, nearly forty Indians sat around several fires for almost the entire length of the wigwam. Each had two sticks about eighteen inches long, one of them split on the end. At a far end of the lodge sat four powwows. Woodbridge asked if they minded his watching their "devotion." The eldest powwow lifted his eyes toward heaven to ask the Great Spirit for an answer, then told the teacher he could stay. A night of scenes followed that the preacher's son found almost "impossible to describe." The Indians began rapping their sticks together and singing, while the old man sat uttering incantations. After an hour of this sound montage, Woodbridge saw a powwow get up and strip down to his breechclout, clamp his eyes shut, contort his face, then dance and gyrate from one end of the wigwam to the other.

When he had exhausted himself, the second one picked up where the first had left off, and the third and the fourth followed him. All through the night the powwows entreated the Great Spirit to give them a vision of the murderer. They interrupted this ceremony only briefly so that all might dance or smoke their pipes. After it was over, the schoolteacher gave them a lecture: "I took an opportunity to inform them how improper such a method of worship was; how sinful and displeasing to the great God. Upon which they told me they knew no harm in it—they made their application to the Great God, and to no other. "I informed them that God was not to be worship'd in such a manner; and when I had instructed them as well as I could, they resolv'd never to do so any more, and those of them who had been best taught were much troubled that they had taken so wrong a step."[8] An essential element for a Calvinistic Christian conversion had been planted—guilt. Those like Konkapot, who wanted to obey the new religion, were sensitive to any missteps on their part.

Even when the Indians had to leave their villages to set up camp among the sugar maples, they sought to reassure the ministers at Springfield that this move did not indicate a disenchantment with religion: "We do humbly thank you for your care and kindness towards us in instructing us in the Christian religion, which we acknowledge to be the best religion in the world, and the religion which we intend to stand by and follow as long as we live. Altho' there are a great many difficulties in the way, yet we have no thought of giving out."[9]

In early May of 1735 Konkapot, Ebenezer, Umpachenee, and his brother went to New Haven to bring back the two boys. Sergeant entertained them for a couple of days, showing them the sights at Yale, and he was impressed by the Indians' civil behavior. Umpachenee's brother, he claimed, had formerly been mean "and a very bitter enemy to the Gospel." But recently he had had a turnabout and had even begun learning to read.

During a two-week return visit to the Housatonic, Sergeant found the Indians emotional and tearful. Some of the Indians, at least, were experiencing a genuine spiritual stirring. The young Yale graduate was now convinced that his call was to their ministry. He did not overlook temporal concerns, however, and hinted to the mission officials that his annual £100 salary was barely sufficient. He also hoped that Timothy Woodbridge would be supported as a teacher.[10]

Governor Belcher was planning to meet in late August at Deerfield with a contingent of Caughnawaga Mohawks. The Massachusetts government thought that the conference would also afford a judicious opportunity to announce the dedication of an English missionary's life to

the service of Indians. The Caughnawagas were a tribe of Catholic Mohawks situated about nine miles above Montreal on the south side of the
Saint Lawrence River. Some Hudson River Valley tribesmen, including
Mohicans, had lived among or near them at various times.[11] They and
their Catholic Abenaki neighbors, the Saint Francis tribe, also harbored
King Philip's War refugees from the western Connecticut Valley who,
unlike the Schaghticokes, preferred French company to English and were
still seething over the loss of their land. These Indians and some of the
Schaghticokes in the 1720s had joined with Indians along the Maine
frontier—Norridgewocks, Penobscots, and Micmacs—to fight against
any settlements bordering on Indian territory. A peace was concluded
in 1725, but peace seemed always tenuous along the frontier. The upcoming conference with the Caughnawagas was to be a renewal of that
peace. Launching the mission to the Housatonic Mohicans at the same
time would be a strategic demonstration of Massachusetts's concern for
Indian welfare and would, it was hoped, help neutralize French influence.

The Caughnawagas also had a strategic role in the sometimes vexing,
sometimes deadly, trade between Albany and Canada. They occasionally
conveyed intelligence concerning the French, but undoubtedly performed
a like service for the French regarding the English. Their blood relation to the New York Mohawks and their connection with anti-English
Algonquin and Abenaki tribes made them a pivotal tribe with which
to maintain friendly communications. The Massachusetts House of Representatives emphasized the importance of the upcoming conference by
appropriating £600 for presents for the Indians and £1,200 for Belcher's
trip. It also allocated £100 for wine and rum.

In August the Housatonics—forty-three men, women, and children—
gathered at Deerfield. Sergeant contracted a fever and did not join them
until later, but in time for the conference. Both he and Woodbridge had
contracted a malady that Samuel Hopkins said affected every newcomer
to the Housatonic. They did not know it, but the upland bogs hosted a
mosquito that carried a mild form of malaria. Chief Aupaumut of Hudson River was supposed to attend the conference, but he too was sick
and sent a son in his place. By the last week in August Deerfield would
host more Indians than it had since the raid of 1704.

It was an appropriately symbolic place to stimulate friendship with
the Indians. Jonathan Belcher sat at a long table inside a large tent topped
by a British flag. Most of his council was there, as well as a committee from the house of representatives and assorted men of influence.
A distance away 170 Indians encamped—Caughnawagas, Saint Francis,

Housatonics, and Schaghticokes. The governor spent the first day with the Caughnawagas, exchanging friendly greetings and wampum. The next morning Belcher welcomed the Housatonics, saying that he rejoiced in their desire to receive the gospel and hoped they were satisfied with John Sergeant and Timothy Woodbridge. "Religion is a serious thing," he lectured, "and it ought always to be borne on your minds." After Belcher and Konkapot drank a toast to King George's health, the chief replied, "We are very glad the Governor takes so much care of us. It takes all sorrow from our hearts, and we hope (as God shall enable us) to perform what your Excellency has recommended to us."

The following morning Stephen Williams read Konkapot's speech to the governor:

> We thank your Excellency as our father, that we have received your kindness and love, and we would express our duty and subjection to our rightful sovereign King George whom we pray God long to preserve.
>
> We are desirous to receive the gospel of our Lord Jesus Christ, and hope that our hearts are in what we say, and that we don't speak only out of our lips. And we are thankful that Mr. Williams and other ministers are come to us, and especially that Mr. Sergeant and Mr. Woodbridge have been sent to us, and pray to the great God to keep them and cause they may have health, and live long with us.
>
> And sir, our father, we did not come to you of ourselves and tell you that we wanted any thing, and yet you have taken care of us as your children, and given us learning, &c. No child says to his father, "I would have so and so," but a father when he sees his children in want, is ready to help them. And so we think your Excellency as our father is willing to do to us upon every account.

Konkapot then asked that John Stoddard be the Indians' representative, in effect, in the legislature:

> Sir, our father, our children are afraid of strict laws and of being brought into trouble and put in prison for debt, &c, and we pray that care may be taken by your Excellency as our father and by the General Assembly, that we be not hurt by the severity of the laws, seeing we don't understand how to manage in such affairs, so as that there may not be any danger at any time that our children be taken away from us for debt, &c.
>
> We don't pretend to desire any thing but that if any of our

people should commit murder or any other crying wickedness, they should be liable to the law.[12]

From the Indians' perspective, Konkapot was making a noteworthy acknowledgment of, and concession to, provincial control over Indian lives. But from the government's point of view he was merely echoing what had become an unquestioned rule in Massachusetts's relations with the Indians. Konkapot nevertheless sought assurance, for the sake of their children's future, that the law also worked in the Indians' favor. He concluded: "Sir, our father, we are concerned for our own children as we think you, as a father, are for us, and therefore we pray that it may be given us in writing (or established by a law) that our children after us be not wronged or injured."[13] Afterward Konkapot presented a bundle of deer hides to the governor, and the two again drank a salute to the king's health.

The next morning the governor responded to Konkapot's speech, thanking the Indians for their loyalty to the king, though he said he was even more gratified to hear of their devotion to the King of Kings. He encouraged them to keep the faith. As for their fear of debtor's prison, he was reassuring. "There are good laws provided by this government to save you and your children from being hurt, or from their being taken away from you for debt; and if you should meet with any difficulty on this or any other account (as you have desired) you may with the greatest freedom apply yourselves to Col. Stoddard of Northampton, whom I have directed to take particular care of you, and you may depend on his favor and friendship."[14]

Further, Belcher promised to recommend to the legislature that the whole Mohican nation be cared for by Massachusetts. Konkapot thanked the governor for his concern for their souls and for his hospitality during their stay.[15] This exchange between Konkapot and the governor reveals a conflict in the perceptions of the relationship between the two cultures that usually worked to the detriment of the Indians. When they acknowledged a colonial authority as "father," when they asked to be protected from the severity of the laws, and when they requested, as Aupaumut had more than a decade earlier, that "the tap be shut" so that their people could not get rum, the Indians represented themselves in English eyes literally as children for whom officials must assume paternal guardianship. And of course parents dictate the rules of guardianship.

But the Indians were not children. They were simply adults unfamiliar with the intricacies of the dominant culture around them, who attempted to put the relationship in the diplomatic, kinship frame of reference they themselves used. Yet the agony for individual Indians, the men especially, was that within *their* frame of reference they were as good as, or better than, colonials. That frame of reference was being disassembled, and their efforts to maintain their traditional roles did not fit the more complex English cultural pattern around them. Konkapot and the others who embraced the mission may have recognized that the Indians must at least begin to change that framework, but they also wished to maintain their dignity as a people. They did not wish to sell their souls to New Englanders.

On Sunday, August 31, the Housatonics sat in a gallery reserved for them at the Deerfield meetinghouse, while many Indians from the other tribes joined the rest of the congregation to watch the ceremonies. One of the attending ministers publicly asked whether Governor Belcher, as representative of the New England Company, was willing that John Sergeant be made missionary to the Housatonics. The governor said he was. John Sergeant was asked if he was willing to be the Indians' minister, and the young man said yes. The other ministers laid hands on Sergeant, ordained him, and asked God's blessing.

Stephen Williams then turned to the Housatonics, who sat with quiet dignity in the gallery. Through an interpreter he asked if they were willing to have John Sergeant as their minister, and if so, to give a sign of their approval. The Housatonics said nothing. Some of their faces reflected the solemnity of the occasion. Some beamed with joy. But in an instant, all of them rose to their feet. A flock had claimed its shepherd.[16]

The ordination and the four-day conference had been conducted in a fashion not far removed from the Indian style in formal councils, and the Indians were impressed. The government even supplied them with enough provisions for the trip home. The head Caughnawaga went so far as to compare his treatment with what he might expect in heaven, and he doubted that he would be able to control his tears when he left the governor. If cost were an indication of the importance attached to the treaty, the Indians had reason to be impressed. The bill for the whole affair totaled more than £3,000—£1,200 over what had been appropriated.[17]

The Housatonics were equally impressed with the governor. Umpachenee, however, did not attend the conference or the ordination, suggesting his less than enthusiastic acceptance of the mission. It is highly doubtful, for example, that he would have endorsed Konkapot's apparently wholesale submission to the laws of Massachusetts. Instead of attending the conference, in fact, Umpachenee went to Westfield and was reportedly "unfit and ashamed to see the Govr." Belcher later remarked on the incident, "I hope he has since that [time] effectually seen the sin and folly upon putting himself upon a level with an ox or a bear—nay worse." [18] Umpachenee's absence nonetheless put him in the position of seeming to at least passively accept the mission, but his ambivalence presaged the stresses of future adjustment for the Indians.

For the next several months Sergeant spent long Sundays at the central meeting hut, explaining Christianity in greater depth, answering the Indians' endless questions, and baptizing them. The fledgling minister and the fledgling Christians were infatuated with their new lives. November and December of 1735 were intense months. Sergeant baptized Konkapot and his family, Umpachenee and his family, and another principal Mohican, Naunauneekanuk, who had served in the militia. New names sounded in the Berkshires: John Konkapot, his wife Mary, their daughter Katherine and son Robert; Aaron Umpachenee and his wife Hannah and son Jonas; David Naunauneekanuk. At their request, Sergeant also remarried the Poohpoonucs and Konkapots in a Christian ceremony and baptized Ebenezer's wife. By the end of 1735 he had baptized nearly forty Indians, young and old.

"Their whole hearts seem'd to be engaged in the matter," Sergeant declared as a way of explaining his baptismal exuberance, "and I have reason to think that the imperfection of their knowledge is made up by their zeal and integrity. Those who have been baptiz'd have behav'd very well, tho' they have several times been tempted to exceed the rules of temperance. They seem surpriz'd with the change they find in themselves; expressing the difference between their former state and the present by infancy and manhood, dreaming and being awake, darkness and light, and the like metaphors." [19]

It had been a year since the two Indians died mysteriously after the conference with Stephen Williams, and it was time to end the mourning period at Umpachenee's village with a Mohican ceremony called a Keutikaw. Invited guests brought appropriate presents for the relatives of the deceased. After an appointed speaker gave a commemorative address, he distributed the presents to the bereaved, offering them consolation and urging them to forget their sorrow. Then followed a feast and dance to help heal the wounds. Rum was often used to help the healing process.

The converted Indians decided to ask Sergeant's opinion about the upcoming ceremony and were prepared to drop it if he objected. After determining that it was not a practice of Indian religion, the minister saw no harm. But he was concerned that it might end in a drunken spree that would disgrace them. The Indians promised that there would be no drinking, and most of them kept that promise. Sergeant was impressed at how little drinking there was. Not only did Umpachenee hold himself in bounds, but he and a visiting Susquehannock monitored the others.

Umpachenee was clearly the Indian who made the most vivid impression—good or bad—on his contemporaries. Sergeant almost glowed in his description of him: "a clear-headed, smart man, of a deep reach and pleasant humour, and is one of the best speakers we hear; is free in conversation and talks excellently well. He has entirely left off drinking to excess, and declaims against it; shews great compassion towards the rest of the Indians and seems heartily to lament their miserable condition; wishes they were come to the Gospel; is thoro-ly convinced of the truth; and his knowledge does not puff him up. And tho' he is reckoned somewhat haughty, yet always shews himself modest and teachable enough." [20] Sergeant also once observed, reflecting his own naïveté as much as Umpachenee's sophistication, that he had been stunned when the chief matter-of-factly asked his opinion on the Catholic Church's rule of celibacy for priests. The young minister presumed that the chief wouldn't have been aware of such issues. But Umpachenee was one who would give much thought to comparative religion.

During these months, and even for years to come, Indians from near and far would appear at the mission to witness the new Indian life. Some came to watch and listen for a while, some came to stay. One Sunday at Umpachenee's wigwam Sergeant preached to about eighty or ninety, half of whom were strangers. The Susquehannock, for instance, was a reformed alcoholic who in late November 1735 came with two sons more than two hundred miles from the west, near the Susquehanna River in Pennsylvania. The Mohicans maintained contact with Indians there, and several Housatonics had visited the area in the early summer, likely telling them about the mission. The Housatonics also claimed that on this journey they encountered many Indians who expressed dissatisfaction with their native religion. [21]

The Susquehannock stayed a month listening to Sergeant preach and talking with him at length about his past. He was impressed enough to leave his sons behind to attend the school. The minister also noticed that the visiting Indians had been impressed by the Housatonics' conduct at the Keutikaw. A divine hand seemed to be guiding the mission, Sergeant thought. He hadn't mastered their language yet, but he understood enough to know that the Indians frequently discussed religion, which the Dutch interpreter confirmed. This initial success was achieved in part because Sergeant was not a hardline Calvinist, as evidenced by his numerous baptisms without rigorous instruction or examination of the converts and his tolerance of Indian social customs. Samuel Hopkins described the young minister as having "a most generous and catholick temper . . . and he was far from the rigid and narrow spirit those are of who confine salvation to themselves with those who think just as they do."[22] In this respect Sergeant's methods paralleled those of the Jesuits with the Mohicans' northern cousins, who received baptism easily and without cultural submersion. Success was also possible because the Indians were enthusiastic and hopeful for a new life after decades of decline, and because some Indians were experiencing precisely that renaissance of spirit that people have found for millennia in religious conversion. They were as capable of revivalism as were their colonial neighbors. Perhaps the Housatonics also felt a new sense of pride for having been the first Mohican tribe to acquire a resident clergyman.

When the spring maple syrup season arrived in 1736, Sergeant and Woodbridge chose to relocate to the temporary camps rather than interrupt the progress of religion. The two bookish young men would spend six weeks in and out of fragile wigwams, walking on snowshoes over a foot and a half of snow, sleeping on a blanket-covered deer hide spread over spruce boughs, with three more blankets on top of them. Sergeant told a friend that they would stay with the Indians at the camp as long as they could hold out. He also hinted that something other than religion was on their minds:

> Perhaps we shall be so taken with them and their way of living, that we shall take each of us a wife from amongst [them] and sadly disappoint all other fair ones that may have any expectation from us. And indeed I am almost of opinion this will be our wisest course, lest if we don't disappoint them [the fair ones], they will us.[23]

For the next several weeks the two young men shared the Indians' meals, saying grace and reciting in Mohican the prayers that the interpreter had helped write, gathered eager children around them during the day, and at night taught them to sing while sitting around a fire. Sergeant reported that he ate well, slept well, and felt well, perhaps better than he had in some time. Maybe the Indian way of life could offer the missionary something as well. The Indian camaraderie did not eliminate his desire for company of his own kind, though, and before long he would have it.

4

CENTRALIZE,

CHRISTIANIZE,

CIVILIZE,

PROSELYTIZE,

CAPITALIZE

When Stephen Williams and John Ashley spoke to the Mohicans in January of 1735, they not only talked of religion, they mentioned a government plan along the lines of what Governor Belcher had suggested in 1730. If the Indians agreed and the General Court approved, Massachusetts would lay out a tract of land large enough to accommodate both Housatonic bands and any other scattered Mohican tribes. The tract under consideration was one adjoining the north side of the upper Housatonic township that the Indians had sold in 1724, which included Konkapot's settlement and sufficient meadowlands to support crops. The Housatonic River winds east to west at this point and turns south around the base of a small mountain. A large pond nestles in the upland, and the small, steep Berkshires are clustered throughout the area.

The site contemplated would actually take more than 9,000 acres out of the new township and require relocation of several claims, as well as removal of some settlers. At the Deerfield conference Governor Belcher had mentioned the subject to the Housatonics, and he later recommended the plan to the legislature, although he indicated to them that the Housatonics had broached the idea. The legislature agreed to the plan and appointed a committee to meet with the Indians and settlers who would be involved. John Sergeant suggested that certain exemplary English families be settled among the Indians to help in the anglicizing process. Belcher agreed, "for to *civilize* will be the readiest way to *Christianize* them." [1]

When Sergeant informed the Indians that a government committee would be coming to discuss resettlement, the Indians reacted with less enthusiasm than he had expected. He attributed it to "enemies of the Gospel," but it is likely that the proposal had never been fully explained to the tribe. The Indians decided to council among themselves to determine what to say to the committee.

From the government perspective the Housatonics should have been eager to settle together on a tract of land large enough to accommodate them, especially since many Mohicans did not have any land to call their own. There was also a chance that the legislature would approve expenditures for a permanent meetinghouse. As John Stoddard put it, "These things are great tokens of kindness towards the Indians, and they should be very careful how they put a slight upon them." [2]

But these things also had tokens of kindness for others. The plan was to get Umpachenee's people to give up their east-west strip of land, which separated part of the two 1724 townships, thereby making the colonial settlements contiguous. If the scattered tribes did concentrate in one spot, these frontier settlements would have less reason to fear Indian attack from different directions in the event that Mohican allegiance switched to the French. Settling the Indians on one tract also had advantages for the minister and the schoolteacher, since some of the township's acreage would be allotted to them. And Sergeant's idea of incorporating English neighbors would give him the civilized company he wanted.

A government committee met with the Indians twice in February of 1736 and again in April. Gathering the bands together on the Housatonic meadowland appealed to the Indians, and they were willing to grant some of the land to their minister and their schoolteacher. But they were reluctant to accept the two or three English families that were suggested, though their inclusion sounded reasonable in theory. Before agreeing, the Indians would have to know how much land they themselves would have, because to become Christians meant gradually changing from hunting to farming for a living. [3]

When the committee returned to Boston the government acted swiftly, granting a township of six miles square along the north border of present Great Barrington. Much of the tract was already claimed by Mohicans, however, so the province was exhibiting no grand largess. The grant allowed John Sergeant and Timothy Woodbridge each a one-sixtieth part of the township, or 384 acres.[4] The other English families would get "a sufficient quantity of land" to accommodate them. John Stoddard would select these additional families to live among the Indians, despite their reluctance. There would be four families, not two or three, and the committee would decide how much land they would receive.

Quite simply, Massachusetts was gradually assuming, or perhaps presuming from the Indian point of view, a trustee or guardianship role over the Housatonics. Attempts to turn Indians into independent Massachusetts colonials in the previous century merely by providing a minister and a teacher to explain civics had not worked to the government's satisfaction. Indians still preferred some of their traditional ways of dealing with problems. And the so-called praying towns established on the coast had made Christians and settled tribesmen of the Indians, but had not really enabled them to manage their own affairs within the Massachusetts legal system. After 1694, therefore, the province began appointing commissioners who were authorized as justices of the peace and guardians of Indian welfare. These guardians sometimes had the assistance of other officers, and they themselves had broad civil powers as well as mediating power in nonlegal problems involving Indians. John Stoddard, with the Housatonics' apparent blessing, was assuming part of this role, but he lived in Northampton. The head of one of the new resident colonial families would take over those duties.

Circumstances on the western Massachusetts frontier, however, were not like those in the settled English-dominated areas of the east. This tribe had lived in relative isolation from colonially populated areas, had an alliance with the Mohawks and intercourse with troublesome tribes of the northern and northeastern frontiers, and had been exposed to other European influences in the sparsely developed Hudson River Valley. Perhaps this is why nothing survives to indicate a thorough plan of execution for the mission township. This ambiguity allowed more latitude for a frontier mission, but the Indians were apprehensive about the width of the latitude.

John Stoddard and the committee met again with the Housatonics in April to relay the government's efforts on their behalf. Umpachenee responded for the Indians. He said that he was very aware of his nation's miserable circumstances, ignorance, and vice, and of his own formerly unhappy life. Though he was not sure he yet understood all of the Christian principles, he was convinced of their truth and hoped that the rest of his nation and the children especially would embrace them. But he wondered why, if Christianity was as true and good as he believed it to be, so many Christians lived vicious lives that were contrary to their religion.

A few more things nagged at him. He wondered why the Indians' spiritual and temporal welfare had been neglected until now. If this sudden show of charity was motivated purely by kindness and goodwill, he for one was extremely grateful. But perhaps there was some hidden motivation; if so, such gratitude might not be warranted. Further, one committee member's questions seemed to cast doubt on the Indian claim to land. Granted, they had no written documents, and to prove ownership they would have to call in friends and witnesses. Yet their title to the land, according to Indian laws and customs, was as valid as anyone's. In light of this, Umpachenee expressed concern that the Indians' descendants might not be able to prove title to the township land to the satisfaction of future generations of other Americans. In any case, other residents of the township might feel superior to the Indians, since the land was being given to them as charity. How could the Indians be sure that their children would be free from servitude?

John Stoddard assured them that the Christians were motivated solely by their concern for the Indians' best interests. He mentioned the commitment to their conversion as stated in the Massachusetts Bay charter, and he cited John Eliot's early work and other missions. As for the behavior of some alleged Christians, which he agreed was shameful, it sprang from man's corruption rather than from a defect in Christianity. The committee member whose questions had bothered Umpachenee then claimed that he had asked about their land only to learn their laws and customs.

Stoddard concluded by assuring the Indians that they would have titles to their land and enjoy the protection of the law just as Massachusetts citizens did. Moreover, specific laws had been passed to protect Indians. No one could predict the future, but they and their children would always be free to stay or leave as they chose. Stoddard obviously had in mind the formal, titled allotment of land to individual Indians. Just as any colonial freeman could, any Indian holding a deed for land could then keep it, pass it on to his heirs, or sell it. The Indians, however, perceived Stoddard's explanation to be an assurance of their freedoms and of the protection of their land by the government so that they could continue to keep it or dispose of it in their tribal ways. Stoddard's answers therefore satisfied Umpachenee for the present.[5] But this was another example of how differently a concept could be perceived, leading to later misunderstanding and resentment.

When the committee dealt with the English and the Dutch whose claims and homesteads were to be displaced, they found them less co-operative than the Indians in doing their Christian duty. Most of them soon acquiesced, however, either under pressure or because of attractive land swap offers that would have been hard to refuse.

By May the Housatonic bands had settled on the river where it flowed from east to west in their new township. They had planted three times as many crops along the river as they had in previous years, in anticipation of new Indian families moving into the settlement. By mid-June ninety Indians were there, and the number of baptisms increased by twelve over the previous year. The two Christian chiefs soon had an opportunity to act as apostles. A Hudson River Mohican had committed a murder, and when Konkapot and Umpachenee were called there to council with the other tribes, they used the occasion to proselytize. Many of the head men agreed with the two Housatonics. They were on the wrong path, serving the evil spirit rather than the Great Spirit. Several said they would come to the Housatonics' new town and listen to the word of the Christians' god.

Further charity flowed to the Housatonic from London, especially from Isaac Hollis, a wealthy minister whose money was paying Sergeant's salary. The Indians were touched by the generosity of strangers thousands of miles away. Guided by their minister, they sent a letter thanking all those in England who had helped to bring the gospel to them and their children. "And from the small measure of knowledge we have (being now as it were just wak'd out of sleep) we are so sensible of the benefit of the Gospel that we wish and pray that our whole nation may be brought into the same way."[6]

At the end of July, John Sergeant and about thirty Mohicans, half from the Hudson River and half from the Housatonic, arrived in Boston with further thanks and another gift of deer hides for Belcher. Among them was chief sachem Mtohksin, whose presence again signified a serious commitment to the Christian path. On Sunday they attended church in Boston, where a local paper reported that they "behav'd themselves with exemplary decency and gravity."[7] Belcher conferred with them on three consecutive days. Umpachenee, whom Sergeant described as eloquent, again spoke for his people. He expressed their sincere thanks for all the government had done, for the demonstration of Christian love and concern, and for setting up their township. He also asked for help to build a meetinghouse. "We are nothing and can do nothing of ourselves. As you were first led into the way of wisdom, you have shown your love to us in sending it amongst us." He reiterated his hope that the children would become wise and attentive to Christ's teaching. But knowing how hard it would be for his people to adjust, he asked that the government have patience with them.[8]

Belcher promised to put their request for a meetinghouse before the General Court. He later sold his gift of deer hides to provide books for the Indians. Mohican generosity, however, was not to be outdone. Besides the deer hides, they bestowed upon the government a strip of land twenty-six miles long and two miles wide that flanked "the path used by our fathers from Westfield to Housatunnock." Even Samuel Hopkins remarked that "the land . . . these Indians gave up . . . should be esteemed no inconsiderable return for the favour bestow'd."[9]

At the fall legislative session, Belcher not only brought up the meetinghouse proposal, he asked that a large excise tax be laid on liquor, because "gaming and excessive drinking . . . seem to threaten the ruin of this people now more than ever."[10] He may have learned that some of the Housatonics had drunk too much at a Keutikaw in another village, only three weeks after leaving Boston. It was easy to see why Umpachenee asked for patience.

On paper, at least, the province was trying to bring order and fairness to its Indian relations. Because of abuses by private traders, particularly on the Maine frontier, Massachusetts placed the Indian trade under the control of government owned and financed trading houses. In an effort to woo Indians from the French interest and to stop the violation of Protestant sensibilities through "the taking of unreasonable or excessive prices for the goods sold unto them," the province sold trade goods to the Indians at wholesale prices, yet paid Boston market prices for hides brought to the interior posts. Fort Dummer on the upper Connecticut River was one of the posts, conveniently located for Mohicans and more northern tribes. Operators of the posts generally could not extend credit to the Indians (thereby getting them into troublesome debt), and they initially were forbidden to sell alcohol under severe penalties, even of death. By the 1720s proscriptions had been lifted against the sale of moderate amounts of rum. Private sale was still prohibited, however, and in 1735 the province passed a law that allowed conviction of illegal traders simply on the basis of face-to-face accusations by Indians to whom such illegal liquor had been sold.[11] The policy of providing goods at wholesale prices was successful in diminishing French influence, but enforcement of the alcohol ban was difficult and sporadic, as was guaranteeing that only honest men traded with the Indians. Nevertheless, in contrast to the greed and chicanery of the previous hundred years, the trade policy may have deepened Mohican affection for Massachusetts. But it also allowed Boston to presume a more paternalistic role toward Indians, and this role not only assumed protection, it dictated policy.

Both John Sergeant and Timothy Woodbridge, meanwhile, began settling down to a commitment of patience. The schoolteacher finished a house in the new Indian town in January of 1737 and moved into it with his bride. The minister lodged with the Woodbridges until March, but then he was on his way to look for a wife. "I pray God to smile upon him," wrote Stephen Williams after the missionary stopped by his house during the search.[12] Where Sergeant went to look and whether God smiled on him are uncertain, but by late April he was preparing to build his own house, which he finished eight months later.

On May 7, 1737, Governor Belcher issued a patent or charter for the township to the Housatonic Indians and their descendants, "to their use and behoof, forever."[13] By August work on a meetinghouse and a schoolhouse for the Indians was under way, thanks to a grant from the General Court.[14] Now comfortably situated, the minister could concentrate on his duties, and he had learned enough Mohican to preach directly to his people without an interpreter.

Interest in the mission accelerated. Sergeant baptized another principal Mohican family named Yokun, Chief Aupaumut's son, and a Shawnee lad who had been with the Housatonic congregation for about a year. Next the missionary visited a small Mohican village of about ten families, called Kaunaumeek, about eighteen miles northwest of the Housatonics near present-day New Lebanon, New York. About thirty Indians were there when the minister arrived with several Housatonic chiefs. He delivered a prepared sermon in Mohican, which apparently made a favorable impression. His religious message was enhanced this time by the enthusiasm of his Housatonic converts, especially Umpachenee, whom Sergeant said "talk'd a great deal, and very well, upon the subject."[15]

The Kaunaumeek chief had already adopted some colonial secular ways and lived comfortably by farming. Though he had reservations about Christianity, the words of the minister and of the Housatonics haunted him in the coming months. Before long he eagerly sought the

Christian path and came to the Housatonics' village to be baptized with his daughter, whom he left to attend Timothy Woodbridge's school. Two other Kaunaumeek families came to be baptized and to stay.

By June of 1738 there were even more new faces in town and more on the way. Timothy Woodbridge's wife delivered the town's first non-Indian baby, a girl, on April 2, 1737, and another was on the way.[16] The schoolteacher had had a head start on producing his family. He and his bride, who as exemplary Calvinists were to teach the Indians rigid Christian morals, had confessed themselves "guilty of the crime of fornication before marriage." Each had to pay the Hampshire County Court a fifty-shilling fine.[17]

Two other English families arrived shortly thereafter to help fulfill the ideal set forth in the Massachusetts Bay charter: to be "soe religiously, peacablie and civilly governed as their good life and oerderly conversation may win and incite the natives of country to the knowledge and obedience of the only true God and Savior of mankind, and the Christian faith."[18] They built along a narrow plain on a high hill north of the river. One family was headed by Ephraim Williams, a forty-seven-year-old cousin of the wealthy and influential Israel Williams of Hadley. Ephraim was from Newton, where over a period of twenty-two years he had held most of the town's civil offices. He appears also to have been a middle-class farmer, an entrepreneur, and a part-time real estate broker. In 1737 he and a partner had purchased from Konkapot and ten other Indians about 11,000 acres for £300.[19]

The second family was that of thirty-seven-year-old Josiah Jones of Weston, a brother-in-law of Ephraim Williams. Jones had been a selectman and town moderator in 1721. His father was a merchant, so perhaps Josiah was likewise. When he moved to the Indians' town he brought with him his wife, mother, and six children.[20] For men of this maturity to uproot their families from the comfort and safety of eastern communities and relocate to a remote, raw, and insecure region, they must have had strong incentive, religious or otherwise.

In 1739 the pace of Christian development in Mohican territory quickened. The baptized Indians were receiving communion now, and the Boston commissioners provided a silver set for this purpose. Though Sergeant feared that Umpachenee's lack of sobriety and questionable state of grace might prevent him from receiving the sacrament, the lieutenant reinstated himself to the minister's satisfaction. Mohicans from outlying areas continued to visit the Housatonic, groups from the Hudson Highlands and from the small village at Sharon, Connecticut, called Wechquadnach.[21] John Sergeant also made proselytizing trips to the Indians at Hudson River. The Kaunaumeek chief and several tribesmen accompanied him to help testify to the religious progress in the Housatonics' town. At Aupaumut's island Sergeant again explained Calvinist doctrine to about thirty Indians. "Some approv'd of what I said, but three or four shew'd themselves very averse to Christianity. A great many Dutch people were present at the service, to whom I preach'd in English; but their behavior was much more disorderly than the Indians; . . . they seem'd to consider the Lord's Day rather as a season for frolicing than for religious duties."[22]

By late spring, Ephraim Williams decided to ask the government to incorporate the Indians' settlement in order to "hold and enjoy town privileges &c."[23] Williams had recently been appointed a justice of the peace in Hampshire County, and as such he would be the principal manager of Indian affairs in the town. John Sergeant presumably would have endorsed the idea, especially since it came from his prospective father-in-law. The minister and Williams's daughter were to be married in August.

On June 22 the legislature incorporated the Indian town under the name of Stockbridge. The next day Konkapot, Umpachenee, and Williams were authorized to assemble the town's freeholders to choose a town clerk and other officers. Who exactly constituted the freeholders at this point is uncertain. The plan for incorporation, with all its inherent duties, apparently had not been fully explained to the tribe. Sergeant remarked in a probable understatement that "this affair made some talk and difficulty, as every new thing does among the Indians."[24] Some of the talk may have involved the question of why the Indians' town was to be called Stockbridge instead of Muh-he-con-nuk. And some of the difficulty may have been caused by the feeling that their new neighbors were trying to undo generations of cultural tradition and tribal government in four years.

This latest proposal, following so rapidly on the heels of their relocation and the thrusting of new colonial families among them, understandably caused consternation among the Housatonics. Up to now, the methods used by Sergeant and Woodbridge to convert and catechize the Indians had interfered little with the Housatonics' hunting, maple syrup harvesting, or tribal government. The proposal for a formal, political township threatened these traditions. In agreeing to become Christians, the Housatonics and other Mohicans probably did not understand fully that they would be getting the whole New England social and political package, nor were they seeking it. Yet the township became fact,

Ephraim Williams became town moderator, and the Indians in general acquiesced and struggled to adapt.

Another complicated event in 1739 seemed at first to work to the Mohicans' benefit. They always chose river bottoms and meadowlands for their planting grounds, of course, and the Stockbridge Indians would need as much as possible now that they were concentrating in the township and hoping to have others join them. Konkapot had already given the Dutch interpreter quite a few acres along the river, however. But the interpreter had fallen into debt, and in March he borrowed £100 from John Sergeant, giving him a mortgage for the land as security.

The ink was hardly dry on the mortgage when the Dutchman sold the land for £450 to an interesting group. In the name of charity, the new landowners offered to trade with the Indians 280 acres of this prime bottomland for "equivalent" land outside the township. They persuaded the Indians that the equivalent was 4,000 acres adjoining the northeast edge of Stockbridge, land that today constitutes much of the town of Lenox. The group included the very ministers involved in establishing the mission—Stephen Williams, Samuel Hopkins, and Nehemiah Bull. John Sergeant, Timothy Woodbridge, Ephraim Williams, and John Stoddard's nephew Jonathan Edwards formed the rest of the partnership. Stephen Williams, Hopkins, Sergeant, Woodbridge, and Edwards each received 480 acres. Bull's share was 700, and Ephraim Williams acquired 900 acres plus a 130-acre pond.[25]

The timber alone on the ministers' new property would be worth the several pounds each man had spent. They themselves had no plans to live on the land to help spread the gospel among the Indians. The land was an investment in their future, not in the Mohicans'. With land-hungry New England farmers and entrepreneurs moving westward, the property would ensure that the ministers, as they grew older, would not have to depend solely on their congregations. Nehemiah Bull especially welcomed such insurance because a year earlier he had had to file a court suit to force his Westfield parishioners to pay his salary.[26]

When Stockbridge was originally being planned, the "equivalent lands" arrangement had been the means to turn some of the relocated English settlers' protests into cooperation. The Indians apparently were not aware of those transactions, however. In any event, now at least it seemed that virtually the whole town of Stockbridge proper belonged to them—except what the minister, the schoolteacher, and the other four English families would have. Yet the allotments of the four families were never specifically defined. All that is known is that they entered into a vague agreement with the tribe to settle in the eastern part of town, while sharing a traditional New England common with the Indians.

John Sergeant's impending marriage to Williams's daughter, Abigail, seemed to have been arranged in heaven. He considered that God had made her "as if on purpose for me, and giv'n her to me as if he tho't it not good for me to be here alone."[27] The two were married on August 16, 1739, by her father. Ninety Indians attended the wedding with appropriately serious deportment, according to an observer, "and seem'd exceedingly well pleased that their minister was married."[28] The couple's new life was helped along by charitable contributions from the mission's well-wishers in New England and abroad. Sergeant blushed at "how unworthy I am of the divine bounty and repeated benefactions of men of charity. . . . I covet not wealth, but I would gladly live as free as possible from the perplexing cares of life, that I may attend the proper business of my calling without distraction, which truly requires the most prudent and diligent application."[29]

Returning to Stockbridge after a month-long absence, Sergeant was saddened to learn that one of the baptized Indians, in a drunken rage, had murdered a fellow non-Christian tribesman.[30] This was a discouraging blow to the newlywed minister and an embarrassment, and perhaps doubly so for the Indians. Not only had one of them violated a commandment of their newfound God, he had also violated the tribal law and morality. Drink had made him forget the homily that, according to tribal history, Mohican mothers recited each morning to their children: "you must never commit murder, the Great Good Spirit will be angry with you, and your life will be in great danger; also the lives of your dear relations."[31]

The tribal history conveyed more than moral persuasion.

It was . . . the custome of our ancestors, when any murder was committed in the nation, to have the murderers executed by a relation of the murdered person. If the murderer repented of his crime, had been useful to his friends and relations, and was beloved by them, in such a case they collected a quantity of wampum and gave it as a ransom for his life. Or, if this was not done, the murderer, to save his life, might go a great way till he should find some enemy of his tribe from whom, if he could bring a prisoner to die for him or a scalp with wampum, either was received as Nanptanteon, or a ransom instead of his own death. But such murders were seldom committed before white people brought many evil spirits across the great waters to this island.[32]

What atonement was offered by this murderer is not known, nor what action, if any, was taken by civil authorities.

In addition to this setback, Umpachenee was again slipping into the grip of the "evil spirits." Sergeant reported that his proclivities were abetted by a few "evil minded" Indian women who made money by bringing alcohol into the settlement. Neighboring settlers and a certain tavernkeeper in Great Barrington supplied the women. Ephraim Williams admonished the tavernkeeper and reported him to the authorities, who reprimanded him and threatened to revoke his license. The tavernkeeper, who had known the Indians longer than the newcomers had, persuaded Umpachenee and his friends that trying to restrict their access to rum was Williams's first step toward gradually enslaving the Indians. This made them suspicious of Williams, so they bought and drank rum defiantly. Sergeant claimed that the Indians interpreted their freedom as "unbounded licence to do whatever their inclinations lead them to without any restraint at all." When Umpachenee was drinking, he would malign the English in general, and in particular Williams and even Sergeant.[33]

Adding to Umpachenee's irritation at about this time was John Stoddard's arrival with an assignment from the General Court to divide the meadowlands among the Indians. The government assumed that the Indians, as colonial landowners and inhabitants of an incorporated provincial town, should have individually allotted lands, which would be deeded and entered into a proprietary ledger. But the Indians resisted. Although the Mohicans counted themselves as loyal subjects of the king, not all chose to consider themselves subjects of Massachusetts. They feared that as duly recorded landowners they would be governed from Boston.[34] As the full implications of New England township living were gradually revealed to them, not all the Indians were willing to become English colonials.

Nevertheless, Stoddard and Williams persuaded twenty-four of them to at least divide among themselves meadow plots along the river for planting their crops. Stoddard and Williams sent a plan of the division to Boston, with the accompanying paternalistic statement: "The above platt contains all the intervale land in Stockbridge that we thought would be of any present advantage to the Indians."[35]

Umpachenee continued to blame Ephraim Williams and John Sergeant for his fall from grace and argued with them over religious principles. His truculence continued into the winter, and he was intoxicated for the entire first week of February. Sergeant reported that he "gave the utmost disturbance to his own family and neighbors, as he is the most turbulent creature in the world when in liquor; for his natural haughtiness then breaks forth without any restraint." Sergeant felt that he might be compelled to excommunicate Umpachenee, but whether he did is unknown.[36]

One bright spot was the new meetinghouse, which was near enough to completion that the Thanksgiving service could be held in it. Another was the arrival of four plows, through the charity of the New England Company.[37] There was also the one-room schoolhouse, where the children would continue to learn their letters and their catechism. The minister and the principal tribesmen saw hope for a better future in the children. Maybe God would give them strength to resist the alcohol that had become a way of life for some of their grandparents. Sergeant had long ago despaired of the old ones' salvation, claiming that "nothing but the extraordinary power that attended Christianity in its first propagation will be sufficient to reform them."[38]

Temperance was the main concern in the mission for the rest of the year. With the help of his English brethren, Sergeant persuaded some of the principal men to impose a fine of £40 on any Indians who brought rum into town. The Dutch traders and tavernkeepers were again urged not to sell rum to the Indians, especially to those who tended to drink to excess. But the Dutch simply redoubled their propaganda, and the temperance battle was seesaw at best. Sergeant reported that traders evaded the Massachusetts law against maverick rum sales by leaving the alcohol just outside the provincial border for the Indians.[39]

As the new year approached, Sergeant worried that the Indians would follow the Dutch example of celebrating with an all day drinking fest, since there was still plenty of rum in town. To forestall this, the minister announced that he would hold a church service on New Year's Day. To his surprise, the strategy worked. "The Indians were universally at meeting, and there was no drinking at all, . . . which was a rare instance of moderation at that season."[40]

The ups and downs of some Mohicans reflected the stress that the proximity of Indian society to colonial society produced. Though principal men like Konkapot embraced the mission life as a spiritual and possibly temporal salvation, the pace of change made adjustment difficult, and some Indians preferred not to adjust at all. They were caught between the colonials' conflicting attitudes of charity and disdain, fear and condescension, fraternalism and paternalism. Meanwhile the Dutch were telling them that the English would enslave them, and the English were telling them that the Dutch already had enslaved them with rum. Yet the English also sold rum and the Dutch were also Christians.

Despite their suspicions and their struggles, the Mohicans found beneficial elements in English colonial society. And some of them could see harmful elements in the Indian ways, especially given the inroads of the past hundred years against traditional Indian living. But they hoped to preserve the good things from both worlds. In the coming years they would try to emulate their colonial neighbors while attempting to maintain the respect of other Indians. These goals were sometimes mutually exclusive and occasionally invited disrespect from both groups.

Several Indians began to build and furnish New England colonial houses and to fence their gardens, paying for the expenses with money they had earned, borrowed, or made on land transactions. Twenty Indian houses would go up in the next nine years.[41] Konkapot and others signed a ninety-nine-year lease for land around Taconic Mountain to help defray their expenses.[42] (By this means some of their clever new neighbors were able to get control of Indian land without violating Massachusetts law against purchase of it.) Umpachenee and another Indian went to Hartford to sell a strip of land near the Massachusetts-Connecticut border.[43] A few of the Stockbridge Indians apparently tried land speculation themselves. One deed records that for £12 Jehoiakim Yokun and another Indian bought all the unsold land between Stockbridge and Pittsfield from two fellow tribesmen. Yokun added this to the considerable territory that he and other principal families claimed throughout western and northwestern Massachusetts.[44]

Mohicans continued to resettle at Stockbridge, whether attracted by the word of God or by the promise of better things. In 1740 there were 120 Indians in the town. Measuring births against deaths, though, the Mohican population had decreased. This was the hardest strain on Mohican culture. For several years the infant mortality rate was about 50 percent.[45] Death seemed determined to prowl the Berkshires. Hannah Umpachenee died on July 14, 1740, after a long, hard bout with tuberculosis. A few days beforehand she asked John Sergeant to pray with her. She told him that "she was content to die, hoping by that means to be free from sin, which was now her burden; and if her life was lengthen'd out, it was likely thro' temptation she should be prevailed upon to commit more sin." Sergeant said she died "with a comfortable hope . . . of eternal life; spending her last moments in exhorting her husband and children to godliness."[46] Hannah Umpachenee had been enthusiastic about the mission from the start. It was said that she was so eager to learn to read that Timothy Woodbridge regretted having to turn her away to give time to others. She, her sister, and Mary Konkapot were all anxious to learn and to adopt the new ways.[47] Less than a year later Mary Konkapot also died of tuberculosis, "having enjoyed," her minister said, "all along in her sickness, a good hope thro' grace, of a happy eternity."[48]

The Mohican women were usually more constant in the faith than were the men. Whether the women had any say in the original deliberations concerning acceptance of the mission is not known, though one contemporary observed that they were not admitted to tribal councils.[49] Mohican women did have the right to hold and convey land and chattels, and descent among Mohicans was through the female lineage. Perhaps the new way seemed to offer an improvement over the current amorphous state of Mohican society.[50] Ideally, the Christian emphasis on the sacredness of marriage would bind their husbands closer to them and the children, ensuring their support. If the men became farmers, they would not be absent for such long periods hunting or trapping for the peltry trade and could share the women's agricultural burden. The traditional female role included clearing land, planting, and reaping the crops.

When Mohican marriages ended in separation the woman always kept the children, the domestic possessions, and the domestic responsibility. The man kept his gun and his freedom.[51] Orphaned children, if not adopted by two Indian parents, usually became the charge of a woman.[52]

Those who were old and in ill health, like Hannah and Mary, may have thought that new skills such as spinning, weaving, and soap making would make their tasks easier. For the young women, the new religion would abolish the rite of first menstruation, when they had to cut off their hair and go alone into the woods for several weeks.[53]

Young Mohican women were also frequently under pressure when it came to marriage arrangements. If one was the object of a young man's nuptial intentions, his parents would consult with his friends and their families. Those in favor of the match would contribute presents, which were given to the bride to be. If she accepted the presents, the match was considered made, and she turned the gifts over to her friends to help provide for a wedding feast that might last several days. The intended bride could refuse the gifts and forestall the proposed wedding, but with friends and relations looking forward to a festive occasion, she often felt bound to comply, whether the match was agreeable or not.[54]

With the deaths of the two chiefs' wives, providence seemed to be turning against the Stockbridge Indians. An early frost in the summer of 1740 destroyed their corn crop, and by the following spring they were out of food. John Sergeant described their need as so acute that without assistance they would have to disperse to forage. He appealed to the company's commissioners at Boston, and they voted £60 for the Indians' relief.[55]

Fate and more charity may have sobered some of the wayward Indians. Less than a year after these events John Sergeant wrote that "many notorious drunkards seem entirely to have broke off from their beloved strong drink, and of their own accord, and some the most unlikely to human appearance have resolved to taste no more strong drink, among whom the Lieun. [Umpachenee] is one and is again reconciled to our conversion, and we begin to conceive good hopes of him, tho' we are not altogether without fears."[56] A holy spirit still seemed evident more than a year later, when a dying young Indian urged his father to receive baptism.

During this period the other two English families who had originally been authorized to join the mission did so. The three-year gap between their arrival and that of the first two families may have been planned to gradually accustom the Indians to an increased colonial presence. Timothy Woodbridge's older brother, Joseph, arrived with his wife and eight children.[57] The other family was that of Samuel Brown, a deacon in the church at Watertown and a tailor by trade. His connection was likely with the Williams clan, since Brown's father had been Ephraim Williams's guardian after his father died.[58] Perhaps Brown was selected to instruct the Indians in making clothes. But presumption is all that is possible, because there is no known record of the actual day-to-day activities of these families in direct relation to the Indians. Obviously these men's experience in civil offices demonstrated to the Indians the functions and responsibilities of New England town government. And it is safe to say that nearly every colonial of their stamp had some farming experience to impart.

Several new Mohican families appeared in town who would figure prominently in the coming years of Stockbridge Indian affairs. Among these were the Yokuns and the Mtohksin family, undoubtedly related to the head sachem. Some had land claims near present-day Canaan, New York, ten miles northwest of Stockbridge. Others came from along the Hudson River and its islands. Dutch first names—Hendrick, Jehoiakim, and Johannes—may indicate that some Indians had been baptized by

Dutch ministers at Albany and already inclined toward Christianity. The man who would become head sachem arrived in the 1740s and began to hold office in Stockbridge.[59] Benjamin Kokhkewenaunaunt, popularly called King Ben, was in his late sixties and had produced many children, among them David Naunauneekanuk.[60]

Now that prominent Mohican families and the sachem were here, had been baptized, and were becoming practicing Congregationalists, the commitment to the Christian path seemed assured. Stockbridge during this decade became the main council fire of the Mohican nation.[61] It also would become a hub of diplomatic activity for the Mohicans and other tribes and nations. Mohican traditional history suggests this in its description of the role of the sachem and those associated with him. At the same time, their history provides an intimate view of the long-standing Mohican culture and government now reluctantly yielding to the colonial influence surrounding them:

> The Sachem always have Woh-weet-quau-pe-chee, or counsellors, and one Mo-quau-pauw, or Hero, and one Mkhook-que-thoth, or Owl, and one Un-nuh-kau-kun, or Messenger or Runner, and the rest of the men are called young men.
>
> The Sachem is looked upon as a great tree under whose shade the whole nation is sit. His business is to contemplate the welfare of his people day and night—how to promote their peace and happiness. He also ever take pains to brighten the belt of friendship with all their allies. When he find any business of public nature, he is to call his counsellors together to consult with them; and then they will determine what is good for the Nation. The Sachem must be a peaceable man—has nothing to do with wars—but he is at times go from house to house to exhort his people to live in unity and peace.
>
> The Sachem has no stated salary for his services; for it was a disgrace or reproach any man to ask reward for any of his public services; but whatever he does for his nation must be done out of friendship and good will. But it was the custom to help their Sachem voluntarily in building a long We-ko-wohm, or wigwam, all complete; and the hunters, when they returned from hunting, each man give him a skin. The women also at times, some give him Mkith-non or Muk-sens [Moccasins], some belts for the body, others garters, and some other ornaments—as wampum to be for his own use. They are also to bring victuals to Sachem's

to enable him to feed strangers; for whenever strangers arrived at their fireplace they are directed to go to sachem's house. There they stay until their business is completed.

The Sachem is allowed to keep Mno-ti, or peaceable bag, or bag of peace, containing about one bushel, some less.—In this bag they keep various Squau-tho-won, or belts of wampum; also strings; which belts and strings they used to establish peace and friendship with different nations, and to use them on many occasions, and passed as coin. In this bag they keep all belts and strings which they received of their allies of different nations. This bag is, as it were, unmoveable; but it is always remain at Sachem's house, as hereditary with the office of a Sachem; and he is to keep the Pipe of Peace, made of red hard stone—a long stem to it.   .   .   .   .   .   .

The office of counselors was not gotten by hereditary, but it was elective; therefore, the wise men were only entitled the office of Counselors. They are called Chiefs. Their business is to consult with their Sachems in promoting peace and happiness for their people. They will also at all times exhort young people to every good work.[62]

Two runners left Stockbridge in late January 1744 to announce to Mohican villages in New York and Connecticut that a new chief had been chosen in Stockbridge. According to protocol, the runners were then to determine how the news affected the villagers' friendship toward the Stockbridge Indians.[63] Whether this announcement referred to the choice of a sachem or to that of a counselor is unclear. It seems likely that the chief was either Benjamin Kokhkewenaunaunt or Umpachenee, who had assumed increasing importance in Stockbridge Mohican affairs. If Stockbridge was to become the center for traditional Indian political and cultural activity while trying to replace Indian ways with New England political and cultural activity, clearly the seeds of discord were being planted.

5

CHRIST'S

DIFFERENT

DRUMMERS

Christianity, either the prospect or the revival of it, seemed to be blossoming everywhere as the ecumenical fervor of the Great Awakening spread. At least in this aspect of cultural adaptation, the Mohicans were right in step with their colonial brethren. Several Indians from Stockbridge accompanied Sergeant on a proselytizing journey in the spring of 1741 to a Shawnee village on the Susquehanna River in Pennsylvania. The Mohicans preached to their younger brothers like true Calvinist converts: "This is the way to life." "If you pity your body and soul you will receive the Christian religion." "The only true light which enlightens the eyes is the Christian religion." [1]

The Shawnees, however, responded coolly to the Mohicans' message, and when it was Sergeant's turn to address them, many of the local Indians left, including the chief. The rest started arguing with the missionary. These Shawnees had received their present site from the Senecas, who were pro-French and had warned the other Indians never to receive Christianity from the Protestants. In addition, the Shawnees had formed a low opinion of Protestants, Sergeant said, "by their own observation of the behaviour of that vile sort of men the traders, that go among them; for they said (which I believe is an unhappy and reproachful truth) that they would lie, cheat, and debauch their women and even their wives, if their husbands were not at home. They were further prejudic'd against

Christianity from the inhospitable treatment they had sometimes met with from those who call themselves Christians."[2]

Closer to home, prospects looked a little brighter. In 1739 the Kaunaumeek chiefs had told Sergeant that ten families there wanted to know "the way to eternal life, which they look'd upon as a thing of the greatest importance."[3] The Indians finally got their wish on April 1, 1743, when David Brainerd, a twenty-four-year-old Yale missionary, arrived on horseback in the Kaunaumeek village. Financed by a philanthropic missionary organization based in Edinburgh, the Society in Scotland for Propagating Christian Knowledge, Brainerd was living testimony to the mental havoc that Calvinism could wreak on those prone to emotional instability. He was an anxiety-ridden, melancholic manic-depressive, filled with guilt and self-loathing. His preoccupation with death and fear of divine judgment were occasionally relieved by what he described as "sweet" feelings and the tranquillity of God's presence.

Brainerd kept a diary of his metaphysical misery, and this introductory passage was typical of its tone: "One night I remember in particular, when I was walking solitarily abroad, I had opened to me such a view of my sin, that I feared the ground would cleave asunder under my feet, and become my grave; and would send my soul quick into hell, before I could get home."[4] Brainerd's troubled spirit was accompanied by a troubled body, gnawed by tuberculosis. His life had been further complicated by his expulsion from college in his junior year after commenting on the lack of grace among administration officials. Though he never graduated, he was considered sufficiently learned to be granted a license to preach.

Unlike John Sergeant, Brainerd gave up most of his worldly estate in devoting his life to the Indians. This decision stemmed in part from his lack of concern with mundane matters and in part from his mistaken belief that he would not need material goods among the Indians. Brainerd initially stayed in a Scottish immigrant couple's primitive log cabin two miles from Kaunaumeek. Almost every day he walked to the village to preach, sometimes only to find the Indians away on business. When he returned to the cabin, his night was spent on a thin layer of straw over boards barely raised off the ground. During the summer Brainerd stayed in a Kaunaumeek family's wigwam while he built a cottage nearby, which he furnished with a bed, a few blankets, an iron kettle, a teapot, and a Bible.

In general Brainerd found the Kaunaumeeks receptive to his preaching, though occasionally resistant to reform, as Sergeant had experienced with the Stockbridge Indians. And like Sergeant, Brainerd considered the

Dutch traders to be a hindrance: "They have no regard to the souls of the poor Indians; and by what I can learn, they hate me because I come to preach to them."[5] The Kaunaumeeks had little land of their own, and because of the village's close proximity to Albany the Indians were probably more subject to temptation and more dependent on the Dutch than those at Stockbridge had been.

The following winter Brainerd began learning Mohican from John Sergeant. He also had the services of a twenty-year-old Kaunaumeek Mohican named John Wauwaumpequunaunt, whom Sergeant described as having "superior abilities, an innocent behaviour," and an apparent disposition toward religion. When he was twelve or thirteen, John would steal away without his parents' consent to attend Timothy Woodbridge's school and even cried to be allowed to stay. After a while his parents relented, and he came to Stockbridge to live and to learn more.[6]

After less than a year, Brainerd thought "that God designed good to them." The Indians had abandoned idol worship and had almost given up "their Heathenish custom of dancing, hallooing, &c." They kept the Sabbath and disciplined their children. And he at least hoped "that they were reformed in some measure from the sin of drunkenness." Ever haunted by doubt, however, he saw some discouraging signs and feared that the improvement might be "like a morning cloud, that passeth away."[7]

To the Kaunaumeek Indians, their new missionary may have seemed like a morning cloud. Before his first year with them was over, Brainerd was reassigned to Indians on the Delaware River in Pennsylvania. Disappointed, the Kaunaumeeks tried hard to persuade him to stay. Having heard so much about the need to save their souls, they said, they could no longer live without a minister. Brainerd was able to convince his little flock to join the Stockbridge congregation, where they would get not only religion, but also some land from the Housatonics. Most of the Kaunaumeeks heeded Brainerd's advice and moved to Stockbridge in April of 1744. After a farewell sermon to his people, the young missionary gave up his few modest possessions and mounted his horse, which would carry his wracked body, tortured soul, and worn Bible further into the wilderness.

Mohicans and the other Indians east of the Hudson who had not been gathered into the Stockbridge fold were not being neglected. About thirty miles southwest of Stockbridge on the west side of the Taconic Mountains in New York lay the small Mohican village of Shekomeko, which had less than a hundred inhabitants, including a smattering of eastern Indians and Highlands tribesmen.[8] East of the Taconics in Connecticut were the forty-five Mohican souls at Wechquadnach.[9] And several miles south near Kent was a village of more than a hundred eastern Indians who came to be known as Scaticooks, whose chief was Umpachenee's cousin.[10] Attempting to gain these souls for Jesus were young Moravian missionaries. Their base was Herrnhutt in Saxony, and their message was rather different from that of New England Calvinism. They had no well-defined creed, and they eschewed academic theology. Moravian missionaries and preachers in America often had little or no preparatory religious schooling, as did graduates of Harvard and Yale, and did not receive regular salaries from their churches or congregations.[11] They were uncomplicated men, many of whom practiced trades, and their wives worked equally hard in the missions.

Their sermons were simple, often impromptu messages based on the Bible, but centering on Christ as a personal savior. In the early exuberant years of evangelism they so stressed Christ's crucifixion and the wounds he suffered for man's redemption that these sensuous, emotional symbols became an integral part of religious conversion. Christ assumed such a personal presence that some communities elected him as their elder and believed that he actually made important decisions through lots cast by churchmen. Moravians practiced foot washing in emulation of Jesus, and they held communal religious suppers called love feasts.

A religion of heart more than of head, it lavishly used music and hymns to stimulate religious experience. The Moravians took no part in wars and swore no oaths. Their everyday life was communal, with most of the work and material gain devoted to the community. All members of the community—though they were not necessarily missionaries—saw themselves as members of the evangelical mission. They dressed simply and uniformly, emphasizing discipline and adherence to communal rules, and they followed a written code of ethics for missionary conduct among the Indians. The communal center in America was Bethlehem, Pennsylvania, which served as a base of support for several missionary satellites.

The first Moravian missionary to encounter Mohicans was Christian Rauch, who practiced medicine as well as religion. In New York City in the summer of 1740, only a few days off the ship from Germany, he sought out an Indian delegation that had come to talk with the governor. But he had to wait for a day when the Indians were sober. Two tribesmen from Shekomeko, one lame and the other with a snake tattooed on each cheek, spoke in rough Dutch with the young man. Like Konkapot and Umpachenee before them—at about the same age—the two Indians expressed a desire to improve themselves and to learn the Christian version of salvation.

The tattooed Mohican had visited Stockbridge a year earlier to learn something about religion after experiencing what he called a vision during an alcohol-induced stupor. In the vision he saw a great number of Indians lying distressed, cold, and naked in the woods, unable to escape from "nasty water" being pumped over them. A voice warned him to take note of their wretchedness and to avoid imitating their wickedness. Then a violent blast of wind dispersed the Indians into the air, like so many autumn leaves. He told John Sergeant and Timothy Woodbridge that with one exception since that vision he had given up drinking.[12] This trip to New York was apparently the second exception. At his next meeting with the two Indians, Rauch found them too drunk to speak or stand. But on the third encounter the three agreed that the missionary should come to Shekomeko to preach.

Rauch's reception by the Shekomeko Indians in mid-August alternated between warm and cool, however, and at times they openly scorned and laughed at his preaching and ignored, avoided, or actually threatened him. As Sergeant and Brainerd had, the Moravian found that colonials in the general vicinity, whose interests might be threatened by sober, Christianized Indians, helped turn the Mohicans against him. Some, playing on a prime Indian fear, told them that Rauch intended to take their children away and sell them as slaves overseas. Other colonials harassed Rauch themselves. Just when Rauch thought he was having some effect on the Indians, they became agitated to the point of threatening to shoot him if he didn't leave. One intoxicated Indian came after Rauch with a hatchet but during the chase fell into a pond and nearly drowned.

Even the lame Indian, who had invited Rauch to Shekomeko, threatened to shoot him. This man was being persecuted by his relatives for allowing the Moravian to preach to them, especially by his mother-in-law, who was keeper of a leather idol decorated with wampum. It had been handed down from her grandmother, and being the oldest member of the household she had the privilege of insisting that the family worship the idol. She told her son-in-law that he would be worse than a dog if he failed to believe in it. Some of these Mohicans were undoubtedly the same ones who disdained their Stockbridge brethren's acceptance of Christian living.

The missionary lodged with a nearby friendly settler during the difficult periods, but continued his visits to Indian huts in Shekomeko,

Wechquadnach, and the Scaticook village. He preached God's love for them and taught some Indians to read. He ate with them and slept in their huts, and he tried to heal their physical as well as spiritual ills. His ingenuous persistence, his self-denial, and his genuine concern for souls began to impress the Indians. He did not come to them asking for land. He was as poor as or poorer than some of them. And he had not sought out Indians with good reputations, who would be easy converts, but patiently worked with a tribe that stepped on every commandment. The lame one, observing his guest sleeping in his hut, remarked to himself, "This man cannot be a bad man, he fears no evil, not even from us, who are so savage, but sleeps comfortably, and places his life in our hands." [13]

Witnessing the missionary's exemplary behavior and hearing his message of hope to a people who were losing hope, this rough Mohican, who had crippled his leg during a drunken fit, became a devoted follower of Christ. His new fervor was as intense as his debauchery had been, and he began to influence other tribesmen. Gradually the Indians from the three villages drew to the Moravian's preaching and schooling, and Rauch witnessed the same tearful, heartfelt concern for their souls, and the same ups and downs in religious constancy, that Sergeant and Brainerd had observed.[14] The Great Awakening was marching deeper into Indian territory.

By 1742 the Moravian missionary effort was gaining strength as more missionaries and their wives circulated through Mohican villages. The hierarchy preferred them to rotate among the missions to discourage the Indians from forming strong attachments to them.[15] Settlers and Indians alike commented on the change in the Shekomeko Mohicans. Some Connecticut Indians visiting the village told one of the Moravians that the Shekomeko tribesmen prior to their conversion "were like wolves and the worst in all this part of the country." [16] A visiting Moravian patriarch, Count von Zinzendorf, described these Mohicans as "a confessedly worthless tribe of Indians . . . naturally fierce and vindictive, and given to excessive drinking." Yet he also characterized them as "tender hearted, and susceptible of good impressions." When the Shekomeko converts attended a conference on the affairs of the mission, the count noted that "they deliberated in a manner which astonished us." And although, like the Calvinists, he considered the Mohican language inadequate compared with his own language to describe the Christian experience, he acknowledged "how unsatisfactorily . . . we give utterance to the emotions and aspirations of our hearts!" [17] Zinzendorf's initially negative view of the Indians applied to the Mohawks. The traits that he observed

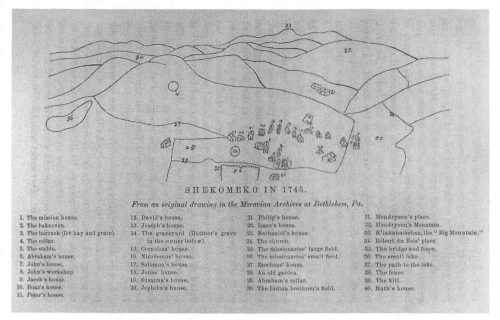

SHEKOMEKO IN 1745.

From an original drawing in the Moravian Archives at Bethlehem, Pa.

1. The mission house.	12. David's house.	21. Philip's house.	31. Hendrysen's place.
2. The bakeoven.	13. Joseph's house.	22. Isaac's house.	32. Hendrysen's Mountain.
3. The barrack (for hay and grain).	14. The graveyard (Büttner's grave	23. Nathaniel's house.	33. K'takanatschan, the "Big Mountain."
4. The cellar.	in the corner below).	24. The church.	34. Robert du Bois' place.
5. The stable.	15. Cornelius' house.	25. The missionaries' large field.	35. The bridge and fence.
6. Abraham's house.	16. Nicodemus' house.	26. The missionaries' small field.	36. The small lake.
7. John's house.	17. Solomon's house.	27. Zaccheus' house.	37. The path to the lake.
8. John's workshop.	18. Jonas' house.	28. An old garden.	38. The fence.
9. Jacob's house.	19. Susanna's house.	29. Abraham's cellar.	39. The kill.
10. Boaz's house.	20. Jephtha's house.	30. The Indian brethren's field.	40. Ruth's house.
11. Peter's house.			

A Moravian sketch of Shekomeko in 1745. Source: A Memorial of the Dedication of Monuments Erected by the Moravian Historical Society *(New York and Philadelphia, 1860).*

may have been symptoms of the toll that colonial contact had taken on both Indian nations.

Amid sixteen Indian wigwams the Moravians built a simple mission house at Shekomeko, with a leaky, bark-covered church attached and a bake oven nearby.[18] They also built a hut among the sugar maples so that they could be with the Indians in the early spring. The missionaries set aside God's acre, planted corn and wheat, introduced turnips to the Indians' gardens and sauerkraut to their diets. They taught the Mohicans to sing hymns, called the faithful to church by blowing a horn, and kept the Indians from passing snuff during the services. They washed feet, held love feasts, and on at least one occasion baptized outdoors by moonlight. One missionary even married a Wampanoag woman who had been catechized by David Brainerd.[19] The crippled Mohican was baptized Johannes, his tattooed compatriot became Abraham,[20] and Abraham's son became Jonathan. By the fall of 1743 Shekomeko was home to forty-seven baptized Indians and served as a base for the missionary excursion into western Connecticut and other parts of New York. The Moravians usually traveled between villages on foot. When they did get a horse at Shekomeko, it was stolen.

This new and different religious activity, the changed behavior of some New York and Connecticut Indians, and the travel by missionaries and Indians alike soon attracted attention, just as Stockbridge had. The first week in October 1742, about twenty Stockbridge Indians visited Shekomeko, accompanied by John Sergeant and the minister from Sharon. Sergeant received Rauch's permission to preach to the Indians, who assembled in Abraham's house that evening and again the following morning to hear the Stockbridge minister speak to them in their tongue. After agreeing to allow one of the Moravians to preach in Stockbridge, Sergeant and the Sharon minister left. The Stockbridge Indians stayed, however, and asked that one of the Moravian missionaries preach to them. They apparently were interested in comparing religious messages.[21]

The following January Rauch went to Stockbridge and several other Indian villages, including Kaunaumeek, where he shared their spartan life. David Brainerd, in turn, visited Shekomeko in June, saying that he had heard a lot about the Moravians, both good and bad, and wished to judge for himself. He received an indifferent reception from the Indians, so he climbed on his horse and headed for Wechquadnach.[22]

A chess game for souls was developing, and the Indians seemed to be both pawns and players. The Mohicans at Wechquadnach were struggling to hold on to what land they had left after the towns of Sharon and Salisbury were established. Umpachenee was involved, since he had an interest in the area, and he and others petitioned Connecticut in mid-May of 1742. They complained that more land had been taken into the boundaries than had actually been sold, leaving the Wechquadnach Indians nowhere to live. These Indians apparently had intended to reserve a tract for themselves, as Umpachenee and Konkapot had, and thus emulate the Stockbridge example. In the petition they also requested religious and civil instruction for themselves and their children.[23]

A typical government committee came to Sharon to investigate. While agreeing that a portion of Salisbury, which was being encroached on by settlers, had not been sold by the Indians, the committee failed to accept the Indians' assertion that they had not sold the Wechquadnach village, planting ground, and improvements. The committee suggested a gratuitous grant of 50 acres in compensation and recommended that a minister be assigned to teach and preach to the Indians. They refused to consider less than 200 acres, especially since they maintained that some of the deeds were fraudulent. Connecticut ultimately paid the Indians who claimed the Salisbury tract—and who now lived in Stockbridge—but dragged its feet on the Wechquadnach situation. The Sharon minister was to instruct the Indians.[24]

In the meantime the Moravian missionaries had been working with the Wechquadnach Mohicans, and the Indians were undecided between them and the government-subsidized minister. The Sharon preacher was friendly and near at hand, but some Wechquadnachs had been baptized by the Moravians and inclined toward them. The principal man finally decided on the Moravians, after two of the missionaries threatened to exclude him from the brotherhood and the services at Shekomeko if he accepted the Sharon minister. This turned out to be the right choice, because the Sharon clergyman had a drinking problem that eventually caused the town to dissolve its association with him.[25]

The Scaticooks at Kent were faced with a similar choice, between the Moravians and a Presbyterian minister, and they also opted for the Moravians. Freedom of religion in those days, however, was not guaranteed. Connecticut passed a law in 1742 prohibiting any unorthodox or unlicensed schools and seminaries. The Moravians were certainly unorthodox for eighteenth-century New England. In many eyes their practices too closely resembled those of Catholicism, and a religion of that ilk mixed with Indians smacked of the French and Indian menace. Paranoia and intolerance led some New Englanders and New Yorkers in the vicinity in 1743 to seek the arrest of the Moravians. In March residents of a small settlement a dozen miles from Shekomeko began keeping a night watch, fearing an attack from the Mohicans. A sheriff came to the Scaticook village near Kent in June and arrested three missionaries and one of their wives. In the course of six days they were brought before the local minister, the justices in New Milford, and finally the governor, who released them but refused to issue them a license to preach to the Indians in Connecticut. The Moravians retreated to Shekomeko. Several of the baptized Scaticook Indians followed them, and the rest maintained contact with the missionaries despite local pressure against it.[26]

For the Stockbridge Indians, the Moravian missions among their fellow Mohicans added another dimension to their own quest for adaptation to a new order, sometimes reinforcing, sometimes complicating that quest. Their frequent visits among their own villages and among colonial communities offered the Indians opportunities to compare and contrast approaches to God and to life. When Christian Rauch was visiting John Sergeant at his house in Stockbridge, an Indian came to the Moravian and said that the Brethren in Shekomeko spoke much of a "new heart."

The First Fruits, *by John Valentine Haidt, date unknown (possibly the mid-1750s). Haidt, a Moravian artist of the eighteenth century, here depicts the church's missionary philosophy that in every country a few individuals were eagerly waiting for the gospel and would accept it readily, although mass conversions were not to be expected. Each of the individuals Haidt painted was the first convert, or first fruit, from his or her nation. The two Mohicans depicted are the figure immediately at the left hand of Christ and the figure at the viewer's far right. Courtesy of the Archives of the Moravian Church, Bethlehem, Pennsylvania.*

The Stockbridge Indians had been listening to Sergeant for eight years, and he had never told them how to get one. The Indian wanted Rauch to tell him now, and the missionary did his best.[27]

During a visit to Shekomeko, one of Sergeant's converts asked to be allowed to stay and plant. The missionaries denied him permission, explaining that he must not abandon his wife in Stockbridge.[28] Sergeant once asked another convert (a half-Dutch, half-Mohican Sheffield farmer named John Van Guilder, who was married to a colonial woman) whether he had heard the Moravians preach, and if so, what he thought of them.[29] Van Guilder had heard them preach and told Sergeant that the

Moravians went straight to the truth with words that touched the heart, whereas Sergeant seemed to talk around the truth. Further, Van Guilder said, after baptizing the Indians the Stockbridge minister seemed to care little for the cultivation of their souls, like a man who planted maize but never watched to see how it grew.[30] Some Stockbridge Indians thought that Sergeant was losing interest in them and that consequently they were losing affection for him.[31]

Sergeant may have become somewhat discouraged by the erratic moral progress of his mission, or he may have become distracted by his own secular progress. Samuel Hopkins noted that for the first five or six years Sergeant's journal was "indeed something large and particular . . . but after that time it consisted only of a few brief hints, two or three pages . . . containing the space of a year; and for two or three years it was wholly wanting." Sergeant's living arrangements may have had some symbolic impact on the Indians. His first modest house was on the plain above the Housatonic, along with the meetinghouse and many of the Indians' dwellings. Later, he built more elaborately on the hill above the plain, where most of the colonial families lived. Hopkins, a staunch defender of Sergeant, nevertheless declared that Sergeant's flock "from first to last had a great veneration and hearty affection for him as their father and best friend."[32]

The Moravians reported several instances of individual Indians experiencing doubt, suspicion, and even emotional stress in coping with the different religious arguments, as well as with the conflict between traditional ways and Christian ways.[33] The Moravians and their converts also learned that their brand of Christianity did not spare them from tragedy. As had happened in the earlier Stockbridge incident, a drunken fight at Shekomeko ended with one Mohican murdering another. But the Moravians gained an important friend when one of the Stockbridge chiefs, probably Umpachenee, came to Shekomeko with ten other Stockbridges for the victim's burial and to arrange compensation for his relatives and friends. The missionaries' hospitality and Christian persuasion won the chief's affection and endeared the Moravians to him. One missionary noted what must have been an ironic circumstance for the Stockbridge converts and proselytizers: "Our [Moravian] Indian brethren have preached to them day and night."[34]

So the battle went for hearts, minds, and souls. The Moravians, while admitting that Sergeant's flock was fairly civilized and somewhat educated, considered them to be spiritually dead.[35] The Moravians also believed that Sergeant's tolerance of moderate drinking and dancing was morally suspect. Sergeant apparently was criticized for his unorthodox leanings by conservatives within his own church as well. "He tho't himself very ill-treated and much abus'd," Samuel Hopkins reported, "by those who represented him as being unsound in his principles." Sergeant, while admitting that he was not familiar enough with Moravianism to pass judgment on the sect, thought that its converts were overly emotional and bigoted. He felt congenial enough toward the Moravians, however, to send greetings to Shekomeko on behalf of himself and his flock and to ask that they be remembered in the Moravians' prayers.[36]

As for the Mohicans, their views and beliefs varied according to individual needs and perceptions, and many probably chose the religious community that could best serve their material well-being. Yet at a time when most Indians were being ignored or abused by colonials, a genuine show of concern for their well-being was usually rewarded with loyalty. And the presence of another religious sect of men and women with different practical skills to impart, who expressed concern for Indian welfare, gave Mohicans alternative options to follow for salvation, social and spiritual.

Both Christian communities, however, required discipline that the Indians found difficult to accept, and both sects reserved the right to exclude from their communities those who failed to follow the rules. The Stockbridge Indian who was denied permission to join the Shekomeko community because he would be abandoning his wife continued to visit the Moravians. One day he claimed that Sergeant had excommunicated him for preferring the Moravians and their beliefs. The Moravian community appears to have accepted him in spirit, though years later he was still living in Stockbridge. The Moravians, on the other hand, had been confident they could fill the vacuum left by Brainerd among Kaunaumeek souls, but lost that flock to Stockbridge.[37]

6

BEHAVE LIKE CHRISTIANS, FIGHT LIKE INDIANS

The Kaunaumeek Indians who settled in Stockbridge in 1744 found it quite changed from the days when Konkapot's people and a couple of Dutchmen lived along the Housatonic in primitive isolation. About twenty Indian families were now established in the growing village, trying English-style self-government, or at least blending it with their traditional methods. The Indians as well as the English were holding office, and one of the Kaunaumeeks' own band, Solomon Waunaupaugus, had just completed three terms as a selectman. Waunaupaugus, whom Sergeant described as a "grave and sober man of good behaviour," had been baptized a Catholic. Nevertheless, according to Sergeant, "as he had lived altogether in heathenism, he was willing to be baptized by me." [1]

Stockbridge had a gristmill, a sawmill, and the beginnings of new roads. Fruit trees were blooming, corn, beans, oats, and other grains were growing, cattle, sheep, hogs, and horses were grazing, and rail fences were being built, along with framed houses and more wigwams. Indians were becoming tithingmen, surveyors, constables, and hog reeves. The Stockbridge Indians seemed to be adapting to the New England way. Konkapot had a barn, its roof shingled in colonial fashion. Umpachenee was on a committee to build a bridge across the Housatonic River and to repair the meetinghouse. One upstanding Mohican was a deacon in the church, and David Naunauneekanuk was a town surveyor. Several young women were learning to sew and were making cloth shirts and other garments. Some Indians were able to read their Bibles and catechisms, and a few had learned to write legibly.[2]

Besides the appeal of land and a minister to call their own, the Kaunaumeek band and the other Mohicans had another good reason for locating at Stockbridge. As early as 1740 birds were flying among the Indians that warned of the possibility of war. On January 20 a large gathering of outlying tribes came to Stockbridge to promote a neutrality pact in case the colonials began fighting one another. The Mohawks sent word that they had decided to stand neutral and wanted the Mohicans and their brethren to do likewise. The Mohicans, Wappingers, and Schaghticokes, in turn, sent runners from Stockbridge with three wampum belts to related northeastern tribes—the Norridgewocks and probably the Penobscots—some of whom were hunting north of Albany: "Brother at Wtanshe-kauntukko . . . Let us have a tender regard to our families. The white people . . . with whom we respectively live in alliance, are about to enter into a war. We only destroy ourselves by meddling with their wars. They are great and strong and so tall as to reach to the clouds. Let us only sit and look on when they engage in war. Don't let any of your people assist your allies in their wars, but while they fight let us sit and smoke together."

To the Norridgewocks went a sterner message: "Brother at Naunauchoowuk: Though you had begun a war with the English, you would regard us if we should desire you to desist. You will without doubt not intermeddle if we insist on advice to this purpose. Perhaps the English think the Indians prevent their conquering their enemies, the French; therefore let us sit and smoke together and see who will be the conquerors."[3]

In March of 1741 the English families in Stockbridge and six of the principal tribesmen petitioned the governor for help in building a fort to defend against possible raids. The petitioners felt that a fort also might draw in the scattered neighboring tribes whose neutrality was suspect.[4] But the war clouds were thin yet, and the governor did not grant the request. By the fall of 1743, however, war was imminent. The Kaunaumeeks received word of this from Stockbridge in October, which may have been a major incentive for their relocation, especially after the Massachusetts government allotted Stockbridge £100 for its defense. On June 2, 1744, the new governor, William Shirley, received King George's declaration of war against the French. Governor Shirley instructed John Stoddard to alert the frontier towns and to outfit men to scout for possible enemy movement from Crown Point on Lake Champlain. Later that month

Stoddard, along with other representatives from Massachusetts and Connecticut, met at Albany with forty-seven Mohicans and Schaghticokes, who reaffirmed their alliance with the Mohawks and the English.[5]

John Sergeant may have recognized for the first time his vulnerability as a frontier missionary. Johannes, the lame Shekomeko convert, reported that Sergeant trembled in fear of the French and their Indians. Having learned of this, the new chief in Stockbridge goaded the minister and tweaked Calvinism by asking Sergeant why he was so fearful: "You must certainly not have the true faith nor ye right God, for if you had, He is strong and can help you. What can anyone do unto you, nothing can happen to you but what he wills. But I think you don't believe on him in your heart, and therefore you are so afraid." Though Sergeant apparently tried to drop the subject, the chief kept up his harangue. As a consequence, the two were now feuding.[6] Some Mohicans remained cynical about the Christianity practiced by the New Englanders.

To frontier colonials, war included the chilling prospect of Indian involvement, and no one could be sure how tribal allegiances would affect the conflict. Settlers anxiously watched for signs of Indian intent, regardless of their past behavior. Just before the formal notice of war, the Mohawks and the Mohicans had met in a cordial council.[7] The Mohicans wanted again to verify what they had heard about an agreement between French Mohawks and English Mohawks to stand neutral in the conflict, and to ask the Mohawks' advice on what their own position should be: "If you say we must sit still, we will sit still. If we see those Indians help their friends, we must help ours."[8] The Mohawks confirmed the pledge of neutrality, and so it rested for a time.

But many colonials in the frontier settlements between the Housatonic and Hudson rivers believed that another potential enemy was in their midst—the Moravians. The missionaries at Shekomeko, already under suspicion for their religious beliefs, refused militia conscription in the spring of 1744, citing their ministry to the Indians and their religious conscience. In mid-June hundreds of Indians were rumored to be in the area set to strike, awaiting a signal from the Shekomeko Indians and their missionaries, who had been secretly supplied with powder and ammunition. Stories circulated of outlying families having been killed. People in the new townships of Sharon and Salisbury armed themselves in fear of the Wechquadnach and Shekomeko Indians.

The rumors were unfounded, but in response to growing panic in Poughkeepsie, a sheriff's posse arrived in Shekomeko on June 19 to search for arms and ammunition. They found no ammunition "and as few arms as could be expected for 44 men."[9] The posse informed the missionaries that they were suspected of being "disaffected to the Crown." Denying this, the Moravians claimed that they, too, were afraid of the French and their Indian allies. The posse then demanded that the Moravians take two oaths, one to King George and one disavowing certain tenets of Catholicism. The principal missionary, an ordained clergyman named Gottlob Buettner, replied that those oaths reflected their own sentiments but that for conscience' sake they declined to swear them. The sheriff's group left, but within a month militia arrived at Shekomeko with the governor's orders again to search for arms. This group also failed to find anything unusual.

Meanwhile, Buettner tried to assure the minister at Sharon and his armed congregation that the Mohicans intended no evil against any settlers.[10] A militia captain nevertheless took thirty men to Wechquadnach to check for themselves. They approached the Mohicans, who were working in their cornfields, and bluntly asked if they were friends or foes. Friends, the Indians replied. One Moravian convert wryly told the captain that their preachers did not teach Indians to kill colonials just as the captain's preacher did not teach him to kill Indians.[11]

Several times that summer the Moravians were obliged to prove their pacifism before various officials of New York. In August the Moravians appeared before the governor in New York City, where threatening mobs and general sentiment railed against them. They still refused to take the oaths, but after examining them, the governor gave them a written acquittal, with a warning to conduct themselves to avoid suspicion. Despite the acquittal and the sentiments of those who sympathized with the Moravians and their work, the legislature passed an act declaring that "no vagrant preacher, Moravian or disguised Papists, shall preach or teach either in public or private" without taking the prescribed oaths and obtaining a license from the governor, under pain of fines, imprisonment, or banishment.[12]

The missionaries were unwilling to abandon the Indians, so a month later they were ordered to leave the province.[13] They did not leave immediately, however, and two of them were imprisoned in New York during February and March of 1745. Others came to Shekomeko despite the ban. One missionary had told the governor that if the Moravians were ordered to leave, the Indians might follow, and the "Mohawks might take it ill."[14]

Gottlob Buettner was not to leave at all. Throughout two years of severe missionary life Buettner had been in the advanced stages of tuber-culosis. After three months of intense suffering, he died on February 23, 1745, at twenty-eight years of age, while his Indian brethren sang hymns at his bedside. He left behind a pregnant, sickly wife and a grief-stricken band of Mohicans, who wrapped him in white and buried him in their own graveyard.[15]

The remaining Moravians planned to remove to Bethlehem tempo-rarily while a community for the Shekomeko Indians was established in the Wyoming Valley in Pennsylvania. The Mohicans, led by Abraham, opposed the idea. Almost all of Shekomeko belonged to Abraham and his family. The mile square tract had been reserved out of a much larger area that was sold in 1724 to New York, which turned development over to several partners in land speculation. There was a serious difference of opinion between Abraham and the speculators as to whether the land had been paid for. In 1738 he believed he had the governor's assurance that he would receive payment. But the matter remained unresolved in 1745 as far as Abraham was concerned, and he still hoped to get justice. To leave Shekomeko would give the impression that the Indians were forfeiting their rights.

Further, Abraham maintained, the Wyoming Valley was a bad place. It was close to the warrior's path, with too much temptation to drink and dance for the young people, and the courtship and marriage customs among the Indians in that vicinity differed greatly from theirs. Abra-ham claimed that his people would not go to the Wyoming Valley even if they were driven from Shekomeko. Neither did they care to move to Bethlehem, because in the current atmosphere of suspicion, colonials there might launch a preemptive strike against the Moravian commu-nity. Many colonials did in fact believe that Bethlehem might become a launching point for Indian attacks on surrounding settlements.[16]

As if civil and spiritual matters were not complicated and upsetting enough for the Mohicans, they had the pending war itself with which to contend. The new Stockbridge chief and Umpachenee, along with the principal men from Wechquadnach and Scaticook, came to Shekomeko in late April of 1745 to hold council. They also wanted Abraham and Johannes to accompany them to New York to confer with the Wap-pingers and the governor. The Stockbridges had received word from the Mohawks that they were now considering war against the English. The Mohawks wanted the Mohicans to help and awaited their answer. If the Mohicans did not join them, the Mohawks would kill the Mohicans and the English both. The Stockbridge chief had built a fort for the Indians at Stockbridge, and he was inviting Indians from other villages to take refuge there and defend against the Mohawks should they attack.

The Mohicans consulted for three days. Abraham declared, in true Moravian pacifist fashion, that he did not want to help kill anyone. The Stockbridge chief agreed as far as the English were concerned; using the kinship frame of reference, he asked whether the child should kill the father. He would be foolish to kill the one who had taught him everything good, the Moravians reported the chief as saying.

The issue of whether the Shekomeko Indians should even retreat to Stockbridge evoked anxious, mixed reactions. Some of the converts thought they should trust in the Lord to protect them, but others thought they should trust in the solid wood of the fort. Abraham and Johannes wanted to stay in Shekomeko, as they believed the Savior wanted them to. But if they had to heed the call of the Stockbridges, they would. For now, they would wait to see if war developed. Abraham would go to New York with the others, but his main interest was in settling his land claim. As the Stockbridge chief saw it, he had to try to please the Mohawks, the governor, and the New York Mohicans. He wanted the Moravian Mohicans with him, since their seemingly direct communication with God might give them the words to accomplish this feat.[17]

The Mohicans achieved little in New York, partly because the Wappingers drank heavily nearly the entire week they were there and were unfit to conduct much business. The Stockbridge chiefs relied on Abraham for moral protection against temptation in the big city. They boarded with some Moravian Brethren and were surprised to be treated so well by New Yorkers. The new chief subsequently made Abraham one of his right-hand men in diplomatic affairs.[18] Mohican regard for Moravians thus was strengthened.

The New York governor did meet with Johannes and Abraham, and he told them how glad he was that the Moravians had left Shekomeko. They had been driven out of Germany and were looking for land, the governor said, and now he feared that they might ally themselves with the French. None of this was true, as he undoubtedly knew. He reportedly gave Abraham and the principal Scaticook some coins minted with his image, to present to anyone trying to take their land. If these were not respected, they were to report to him for help. This show of interest reinforced Abraham in his stance against removal from Shekomeko, a position that was now becoming divisive.[19] The governor's propaganda against the Moravians probably was an additional wedge.

In mid-June of 1745 several Stockbridge chiefs visited Boston to pay their respects to William Shirley. The Massachusetts governor learned that they were firm friends of the English, and the General Court secured the friendship with several presents, besides paying their traveling expenses and tavern bill.[20] The Mohicans also received an invitation to attend an upcoming conference at Albany along with the Six Nations and representatives from New York and New England. Colonial officials had learned of the Mohawk discontent, conceivably from the Mohicans' visits to the two governors. The conference was to provide the Mohawks with a forum for complaints and at the same time to determine the intentions of the other Six Nations tribes in the current conflict. Forty to fifty Mohicans convened in Albany, on October 13, including representatives from Shekomeko, Stockbridge, Wechquadnach, and Scaticook. All were told to sit down by the governor's door, which they did, holding a good deal of venison as a present for the governor. His secretary, however, wanted neither to admit the Mohicans to the governor nor to accept the venison. He sent for Conrad Weiser, an experienced Pennsylvania hand in Indian affairs.

The secretary damned the Mohicans, saying that they brought the meat only to get ten times as much back in provisions from the governor. Weiser reminded the secretary that the Mohicans had been summoned by the governor, and it was therefore reasonable that they should have provisions during their stay. He further advised the secretary that it would be better to accept the venison, even if he threw it out the back door, than to offend the Indians. The refusal to accept an offer of food was, among Indians, a high form of insult. The secretary grudgingly ordered servants to take away the venison. The Mohicans sat by the governor's door for another hour and a half, but were finally sent away without seeing him.[21]

The governor and the other colonial officials were concerned more about meeting with the Iroquois, whose allegiance was suspect, than with the friendly Mohicans. And it was probably just as well that the Mohicans were not there when Mohawk chief Hendrick spoke. Venting his frustration and expressing his people's fear of losing their land and becoming subservient to colonials, he said, "We the Mohawks are apprehensive we shall be served at last as our brethren the River Indians, they [the English] get all their lands and we shall soon become as poor as they. You in the Broad way (addressing himself to Coll. Stoddard) have got our lands and driven us away from Westfield, [where] my father lived formerly." [22]

As 1745 drew to a close, alarms and rumors of enemy attacks grew more frequent among the frontier towns, and militia rushed to Stockbridge from other parts of western Massachusetts and Connecticut. The tracks of enemy Indians were reported several times around Stockbridge, and Indians were accused of burning a barn within the town's boundaries in the middle of December.[23] This was a direct threat to the Mohicans' heartland, and the Stockbridges had to act, especially if their colonial brethren were not to suspect their allegiance. A week later the Stockbridge Mohicans sent a war belt to the other villages, declaring war with the French.[24]

Frontier attacks by Indians allied with the French increased in 1746, and full-scale Indian commitment seemed inevitable. Some officials, among them William Shirley, were reluctant to use Indians in colonial warfare because of their tactics, but the governor was considering fighting fire with fire. On May 30, 1746, he received a letter that helped persuade him. John Sergeant and Ephraim Williams urged Shirley to start using Indians who were already aligned with the English interest.

The governor and the General Court quickly approved the idea by voting to raise more men for the frontier, sixteen Stockbridge Indians and four colonials.[25] This measure would also benefit the Stockbridges, who would be able to fight and defend themselves with government support. The Indians wanted Timothy Woodbridge to be their commander, but the teacher pleaded "bodily disability." The governor was disturbed at any complications in engaging the tribe. He instructed John Stoddard to find someone else acceptable to the Indians and to enlist Woodbridge in a subordinate function. He also wanted John Sergeant to accompany the men as chaplain. Sergeant obviously did not have the constitution for war, however, so a fresh young minister from Great Barrington took his place. Already a soldier in the Great Awakening, this nephew of Samuel Hopkins was also his namesake.[26]

Meanwhile, the Stockbridges noticed that no men from Shekomeko had responded to the war call. They sent another wampum message two weeks after the first, with the sharp implication that the Shekomeko Indians should send some men against the French. The day after this message arrived, two nearby settlers who were well disposed toward the mission came to Shekomeko to report that the people at Rhinebeck, New York, had armed themselves before attending church; they feared an attack from Shekomeko, since a number of Indians had arrived there recently. The visiting Indians and a Moravian missionary were actually in Shekomeko for a church service and supper. The Rhinebeck folk, nevertheless, had gone so far as to ask a local justice for permission to kill the Indians at Shekomeko. The justice told them to ask someone else.

Following this news, Abraham called the Indians together for a conference. They soon decided that, since they were friends with the English and the English were in trouble, they would send several men to help. Four Indians offered to go immediately. This action might also assuage the dangerous fears of those at Rhinebeck. But four days later all the volunteers had returned, and the missionary claimed that Christ had willed them not to go soldiering. Abraham and others continued to express uneasiness about getting involved in military affairs.[27] Moravian pacifism was clearly having an impact on this tribe. The Stockbridges renewed the call for fighting men, however, and several unbaptized Shekomeko Mohicans volunteered.

Those at Shekomeko who did not share Abraham's interest in staying had had enough. The suspicion and threats against them and their missionaries, the land problem, and the general harassment of the war induced ten families—about half the population—to move. The same problems also forced the Moravian elders at Bethlehem to end the mission at Shekomeko by the summer of 1746. A new community about thirty miles from Bethlehem, called Gnadenhutten, was established that year at the junction of Mahoning Creek and the Lehigh River. Some Indians moved there right away, and others dispersed temporarily to Wechquadnach and other places, including Stockbridge.[28] Those who remained in Shekomeko began to lose touch with the Christian ethic after the missionaries left, and Abraham began to regret the decision to stay. Before the decade was out he and his family had joined the pilgrims at Gnadenhutten, leaving his village to the land speculators, who soon destroyed everything but the cemetery.[29] To John Sergeant's dismay, the Moravians drew off some of his flock from Stockbridge.[30]

The tempo of attracting Indian allegiance in the war effort increased as the New York governor and Massachusetts officials held another conference in Albany beginning August 19, 1746. This time the Mohicans' presence was acknowledged. The governor addressed them, delivered wampum belts, and smoothed over his former effrontery, telling them how glad he was that they had attended so they could renew and brighten the ancient covenant chain. He reminded them of recurring French and Indian attacks against their colonial brethren in Massachusetts and announced an intended joint Iroquois-English retaliation against Canada, which he urged them to join: "You will not only gain honor and renown but also safety and prosperity, to your selves, your wives and children for ever afterwards, and for which ends I will furnish your fighting men with arms, ammunition, clothing, provisions, and every thing necessary for the war." [31]

For three days the Mohicans held council among themselves. After the Six Nations' representatives agreed to take up the hatchet, the Mohicans, who had committed themselves to the fighting anyway, responded: "Father. You have told us what mischief the French have done and what murders they have committed upon the Christians, therefore we declare from our hearts and not from our lips that as you have ordered us to shed the enemies' blood in return for what they have done we are resolved to do it, and we will live and dye with you in the common cause." The Mohicans were aware, however, that Canadian tribes would not be restrained from retaliating by a peace treaty signed in Europe: "when you Christians are at war you make peace with one another, but it is not so with us; therefore we depend upon you to take care of us, in confidence of which we now take up the hatchet and will make use of it against the French and their Indians." [32] A Mohican hand reached out and offered a wampum belt and a hatchet to confirm their commitment. A war dance underscored the agreement.

The timeliness of this agreement was boldly punctuated by the French capture and burning of Fort Massachusetts, about forty miles northeast of Stockbridge, on the same day that the Albany conference had begun. Five hundred French with two or three hundred Indians came down from Canada and besieged the fort, which held just over twenty men and a few women and children, all of whom surrendered and were carried off to Montreal.

Massachusetts in the meantime had fully committed itself on paper to employing Indian-style warfare against the enemy. The province offered a £5 incentive simply for going after prisoners or scalps. The scalp of each male over twelve would bring £38, and if there were a breathing Frenchman or Indian under the scalp, it would fetch only £2 more. The rate for females and boys under twelve was £20 for prisoners and £19 for scalps. [33] So much for the Christian ethic. In April of 1747 about a dozen Stockbridges were outfitted for duty at Northampton and sent to Fort Massachusetts, where some of the forces destined for the Canadian expedition were stationed. [34] For much of the year the town of Stockbridge accommodated seven hundred soldiers, who must have put a considerable strain on local resources.

One of Ephraim Williams's sons was commissioned a major at Fort Massachusetts. On May 19 Major Williams left for Albany with a com-

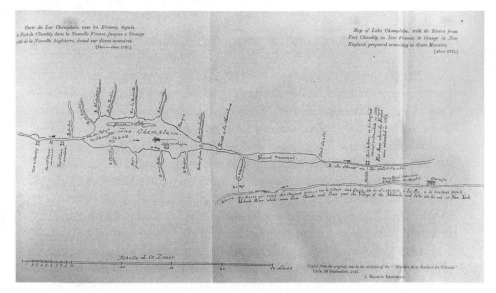

A composite French map of the area from Lake Champlain to Albany about 1731. Source: Documents Relative to the Colonial History of the State of New York, *ed. E. B. O'Callaghan (Albany, 1853–87), vol. 9.*

pany of men, including some Stockbridge Indians, to procure supplies for the fort. Among the Stockbridges was Ensign Konkapot, probably the chief's son Robert, who was about twenty-two. Returning from Albany with a convoy of wagons, Williams kept Indian scouts and a road crew out in front. When this advance party got close to the fort, they stumbled onto a nest of about twenty enemy Indians, who opened fire on them and the fort at the same time. The skirmish was hot but brief. Major Williams's convoy approached while those inside the fort discharged cannons toward the swamp where the enemy Indians lay. They fled, leaving most of their outfits behind, but not before venturing out to retrieve a strip of scalp from the only man killed in the action—a Stockbridge Indian.[35]

The Mohicans informed the Mohawks of this casualty, identifying him as one of their principal young men. The Mohawks were short on sympathy since they put their own losses so far at fourteen, four of them chiefs.[36] The Mohicans commiserated with the Mohawks' losses in a meeting at the home of William Johnson, the rising colonial figure in Indian affairs. With wampum and sympathy the Mohicans metaphorically gathered together the scattered bones of the Mohawks' men, women, and children, to be buried in one place. But they also sought to reinforce Mohawk adherence to the English, which may have been wavering and which in turn might strain the friendship between the two tribes.

"There is many clouds arise about us," the Mohicans told their uncles, "and if we are not carefull we shall get into difficulties, let us keep those dark clouds from comeing between us least we should not be able to see one another. "Unkle, do you keep steady at your place and I will at mine then we shall always know where to find one another. . . . The friendship we made long ago with the English we must maintain firm and un- shaken." Referring to Johnson as a representative of their father the king, the Mohicans observed, "We behold him as a strong tree with spreading roots standing fast having goodly limbs and leaves. Let us gether about him and stand around him and if he falls let us fall with him." [37]

For the Stockbridges, the loss of even one man was a blow, since at the time their strength was only about fifty men. This was proving to be a year of deep grief for the small tribe. Konkapot had earlier lost his daughter Katherine, and David Naunauneekanuk's daughter had died the following month. [38]

Wampum messages, flavored with metaphorical, cryptic diplomacy, were exchanged between the Stockbridges and other tribes to report con- ditions, to offer advice, and to encourage perseverance. From a village near Detroit came a message in February of 1748, probably from the Mohicans among the Ottawas: "My Father at Mahekun, I have already compassed the Frenchman round and laid close siege to him. Where ever he peeps out I kill him. He is so strongly fortified, that I cannot take him. I can only starve him out."

The Mohicans answered: "My Child, your Father hears your cries, being himself in poor miserable circumstances by reason of the distresses of the war. When I lie down at night, I am afraid I shall not live till morning, and when I rise up in the morning I am afraid I shall not live till night, I am so harrass'd with the war. What you told me of the wind blowing is now come to pass, which is the occasion of my calamities." [39]

By late summer the war was all but over. The Indians allied with the English were disturbed at having been drawn into it on the strength of the supposed expedition to Canada, which never took place. Many among the Six Nations were particularly upset, since a number of their kins- men were held prisoner in Canada, and they had hoped that a Canadian invasion might free them. Even John Sergeant had cause for disappoint- ment. Having apparently conquered some of his trepidation about war, he acquired two guns and served as "chaplain in the designed expedition against Canada," but failed to receive the £5 sterling due him.[40] In July of 1748 Shirley and the New York governor again met with the Indians. To appease their discontent and offset the loss of their fighting men, the Indians received wampum belts, gifts, and the king's gratitude for being Indian, not just Christian, soldiers.

7

THE
SHEPHERD
GONE,
DANGER
FROM
OTHER
SHEEP

The hardships of frontier life began to take their toll on John Sergeant's frailty. In the last week of June 1749 he contracted an illness attended with fever and an inflamed throat. The minister sensed somehow that this sickness was ominous. He began to put his affairs in order with a calm, businesslike manner. On July 1 he delivered a portentous sermon to his Mohican followers. He told them that recently he had been afraid that a heavy judgment might be hanging over them because of their wickedness, and that some of them grew worse despite all that God and their minister had done for them. He warned the Indians that the Lord had his ways of dealing with sinful people: "It may be God will take me from you, and then my mouth will be shut and I shall speak to you no more."[1]

The sickness and pain grew, and Sergeant was confined to bed. The Mohican congregation became concerned. They climbed the hill to visit him often. He continued to urge them to piety and learning. The Indians gathered in the little church to pray for their shepherd's recovery. But on July 27, 1749, the minister fulfilled his own prophecy. He died at age thirty-nine, and a light went out for the Stockbridge Mohicans.

Abigail Sergeant said that her world was like a dark and gloomy place without her husband, and the minister's "poor bereaved flock . . . are incessantly lamenting this judgment upon them."[2] The judgment upon the Indians indeed may have seemed supernatural. Only three weeks earlier a Moravian missionary, who had visited Stockbridge several times at the sachem's request, died in Wechquadnach three days after one of these visits.[3]

A month after Sergeant's death Ebenezer Poohpoonuc and one of King Ben's sons visited Stephen Williams, who noted that "they seem greatly affected with ye death of Mr. Sergeant." Williams prayed that God's judgment would have a "suitable" effect on them and that the Lord would "repair this great breach" in their lives. Williams himself filled the gap for a month during the following winter and found the Indians trying to keep steady in the faith.[4] For the next few years, keeping the faith would be a major chore.

Tension had developed about a year before Sergeant died. The minister, the schoolteacher, and the heads of the four other English families had petitioned the General Court, complaining of irregularities at a March 1748 town meeting and asking that the proceedings be declared null and void. The colonials had tried unsuccessfully to persuade the Indians that the meeting itself was illegal, because it was announced by a selectman rather than by a constable. This petty legal point could have been resolved easily in Stockbridge, and there was no need for Sergeant and the rest to make such an issue over it, considering that the Indians were still learning the nuances of town government.

The real purpose of the petition was to force the Indians to confront the issue of land proprietorship. At the town meeting in question, the colonials had attempted to assign unnamed tracts ranging in size from 20 to 70 acres to several Indians.[5] Other Indians, under Umpachenee's influence, apparently protested the formal English way of recording these tracts. The colonials, preferring neat property lines to traditional tribal boundaries, became upset. They wanted to hold another town meeting, but the Indians refused to cooperate.[6]

The upper half of Stockbridge, which Massachusetts had presumed to grant to the Indians, was already claimed by Mohicans who did not want to submit their claims to the township for free. Most of the English families, therefore, had pooled resources with several principal Stockbridge Indians and bought out these claims. The Indians allowed the English to establish their settlements in the northeast quarter of town, and the Indians took the northwest quarter. Some of the Indians then sold about a square mile of their part to Timothy Woodbridge for £200, and another 800 acres to Samuel Brown. These purchases, without General Court approval, were illegal. To complicate matters, Umpachenee claimed a large share of the proceeds from the sale, and felt he had still more coming to him. These haunting, unsatisfied Indian claims undoubtedly made the settlers nervous. It would be reassuring if they could pin the Indians down to defined limits once and for all.[7] The settlers already seemed to be taking more of an interest in the Indians' land than in their souls.

In June of 1749 Massachusetts directed the town officials to reconvene, but the Indians apparently refused, since no meeting was held. A government-appointed committee then met with the Indians and the English families at Stockbridge in November to investigate. They soon learned that the Indians had grievances against everyone, including their late missionary.

The first complaint was about the schoolteacher, who they claimed had bought the mile-square tract without the full consent of the tribe and then included it in a deed for other acreage that the tribe had earlier consented to sell. Woodbridge replied that some of the Indians had "importuned him" to buy the tract so that they could have money to build English-style houses. Because that land was so rocky and swampy, he had agreed only when they offered him an additional 150 acres south of the tract. His version of the transaction differed considerably from the Indians' version. The committee nevertheless recommended to the General Court that Woodbridge be allowed to keep all the land, despite the fact that "the sale of the Indians land without liberty of the General Court is not legal and it is uncertain whether the Indians understood the deed to include the whole 150 acres." After all, "Mr. Woodbridge has spent the prime of his life and most of his estate in the service of the . . . Indians."[8] The report neglected to mention that Woodbridge had obtained most of his estate *because* of the Indians.

Several Indians next told the committee what happened when they were looking for land for crops and pasture. John Sergeant had instructed Jehoiakim Yokun to select a suitable spot for plowing. Yokun found 50 acres adjoining a Williams plot, and after getting the minister's and the schoolteacher's blessing, eighteen of the Indians spent about two weeks cutting and splitting enough logs to fence the land. When Ephraim Williams returned from an excursion and learned of the project he objected, and John Sergeant told the Indians to quit. The Indians claimed that this incident "discouraged all Indians making any further attempt to clear land." It must also have discouraged them with regard to their minister's priorities.

Williams's only rebuttal was that this particular land had been promised to the English by other Indians, that it lay between two English lots, and that it was therefore "very inconvenient that the Indians should have it." The committee recommended that the English be allowed to take possession of the cleared property and pay the eighteen tribesmen £10 for their labor.[9]

Next the Indians pointed out that Samuel Brown, despite having procured a vast acreage for himself, had measured off 19 acres of their land and built a house on it. True, Brown replied, but it was a surveying mistake, and he now agreed to pay the Indians £28. Since his house was already on the property, the Indians conceded to the cash settlement, and the Boston committee recommended that the government confirm Brown's claim. Following a similar complaint by Konkapot, that Joseph Woodbridge had fenced 10 acres of his land, the committee recommended a new survey. If part of the New England town experience was to learn surveying from these families, the Indians must certainly have questioned the value of their education so far.

The Indians also claimed that Ephraim Williams had previously promised to give them 8 acres of meadowland in exchange for some upland. Williams replied that he had never promised absolutely, but would consider doing so as soon as he found something that suited him. He had also somehow acquired a 30-acre lot and built a sawmill that the Indians said was of little use to anyone. They were becoming seriously disenchanted with the Williams clan.

Next the Indians complained that the English residents in general laid out land for themselves in a manner and in amounts unfamiliar to the Indians. None of the acreage the colonials took included swamps or ponds. That ambiguous government statement about "sufficient quantity of lands" to accommodate the English families was subject to interpretation. The settlers admitted that perhaps their own survey had included a little too much land and agreed to submit to a new survey by the General Court. The survey, if it was ever recorded, does not appear in the records.

Finally, the Indians reminded the committee, when they agreed to settle together there were to be only four English families besides the minister and the schoolteacher. Now there were about ten non-Indian families in Stockbridge. The committee explained that as the colonials multiplied, they would naturally let their children settle on their land. This concept by itself was reasonable, the Indians replied, but no one had told them beforehand that more than four would live in their town. The committee ignored this rebuttal altogether.

According to the committee, some of the Indians seemed to favor a plan for assigning land among themselves in order to keep stricter account of their claims. Since some of the colonials were accidentally spreading onto Indian land, the Indians probably thought it advantageous to record on paper exactly what was theirs. The committee therefore suggested that the Indians form a proprietorship and enter their names, landholdings, and future transactions into a book. The Indians appeared to agree, and when they met again with the committee shortly afterward, told the members that there were fifty-six proprietors, but they did not provide a written list.

"It appeared plainly to us," the committee reported to the General Court, "they had a jealousy, that thusly they would be brought to submit to the laws of the government. Upon which we endeavoured to shew them what benefits they would receive by conforming to the laws, many of them appeared willing to be governed as English men; but their chief leader Umpachena was very averse to be governed by the laws, though at the same time he allowed they were good, so far as he knew them. But as to their being formed into a propriety, they told us they were willing to submit to what the Court should order in that affair." [10]

Umpachenee was confronted with the same dilemma he had faced in 1736, when John Stoddard and the government representatives proposed the relocation of the Housatonic bands to Stockbridge. He wanted to maintain Indian independence by handling land in Indian fashion, yet he wanted the government to assure that future generations of Americans would recognize Indian claims. Dividing the land among individual tribesmen made obsolete the traditional methods of dealing with land issues in a full tribal council. But if Umpachenee wanted future generations to recognize his descendants' rights, it was better to submit to the English system. And some individuals within Stockbridge, Indian and colonial alike, apparently were already undercutting the tribe's traditional methods of land disposal.

On the committee's recommendation the General Court issued an edict ordering the Stockbridge Indians to form themselves into a formal record-keeping proprietary. It declared that, Umpachenee's objections notwithstanding, "the Indian inhabitants of the Town of Stockbridge are and shall be subjected to and receive the benefit of the laws of this government—as other his Majesty's subjects of this province—provided always that nothing in this order shall be understood to enable any of his Majesty's English subjects to become purchasers of any part of the Indians land, contrary to the provision made by law for preventing the same." [11]

So to complicate matters even further, the government was maintaining that Indians were the same as everyone else, but they were different.

They were free English subjects except when it came to selling their own land. Here was another dilemma to upset Umpachenee. This law, ostensibly beneficent, would later cause problems for the Indians, and it was ignored or circumvented by provincials who chose to do so. And despite the government's moral tone, there is nothing in the order to indicate that it resulted in rescinding the illegal purchases made by Brown and Woodbridge. Further, at the committee's recommendation, the survey that followed restricted the Indians to a maximum of 100 acres per man, without imposing any restrictions on the English. These continuing disparities in perceptions between the colonials and the Indians, and even among the Indians themselves, about how Indian affairs should be handled in Stockbridge, undoubtedly retarded the tribe's total acceptance of Christian culture. Samuel Hopkins acknowledged that the Stockbridge Mohicans "were for a considerable time considerably jealous that we had some ill design upon them, even in the favours they received at our hands." [12]

The government committee, obviously more disposed toward the colonial interest than toward the Indians, nonetheless may have seemed like an objective third party to the Indians, and its official nature may have induced them to comply with the government's orders. Sergeant's death probably continued to affect many of them as they wondered what lay ahead for the mission. Yet some Mohicans brooded over their treatment. Umpachenee and Solomon Waunaupaugus were supposed to be selectmen on the town council when it reconvened in March of 1750, but only three colonial selectmen were present at the meeting.[13] When the government surveyor arrived in June to start marking off territory, however, the head tribesmen did provide a written list of Indian proprietors, each of whom received his individual land allotment.

But neither their colonial neighbors nor the government could completely control how the Stockbridge Indians conducted their affairs. Although the Indians accepted individual allotments for house and garden plots, the tribe maintained common land for its general benefit, and within part of this common land individuals and families retained certain additional rights. An Indian committee, serving a similar or supplementary function to the traditional Indian council, held jurisdiction over any common land sold for general tribal benefit. Whereas individuals were free to sell their own house and garden lots, the sale of a right in the common lands required the committee's approval. Deeds were seldom issued in sales or assignments of land among Indians, but each grant was surveyed and recorded. And primogeniture had not yet gained acceptance, though this would gradually change, at least to the extent that sons began using their fathers' last names. Massachusetts did assert itself by restricting new residents from other tribes from selling land granted them by the Stockbridges, and town rules stipulated that the newcomers be "orderly inhabitants here and do common duties with others." But even here the Stockbridges made sure that the selling restrictions applied not only to Indians, when they also prohibited the resale of an 80-acre grant to the son of their old Dutch interpreter.[14]

In September the Indians felt stung again when they learned that Ephraim Williams had had the surveyor mark out another 155 acres for him in the western part of the township; one of Williams's sons also acquired a piece of Indian property, which he believed might contain iron ore. So upset were some of the Stockbridges that they "had concluded to leave the place," but they decided first to appeal to the kindness and mercy of the government.[15] Another Boston committee journeyed to Stockbridge, and after observing that 60 of the contested acres lay between two of Williams's established claims, pronounced that for Williams not to have the land would be "inconvenient".[16] A compromise of sorts was worked out whereby Williams paid the Indians £100, gave up the meadow and mill lots, and kept the 155 acres.[17] Ephraim Williams was a practiced bargain hunter. He also convinced the New England Company to reimburse him for the £9 he had paid for John Sergeant's tombstone.[18]

Whatever Sergeant's relationship with the Indians in the later part of his life, his presence seems at least to have been a moral restraint on rising secularism in Stockbridge. His death, however, apparently unbridled the town's pecuniary impulses. One month after the missionary died, the county court granted Josiah Jones a license to establish an inn and tavern in Stockbridge, with permission to sell liquor. Three years later Elijah Williams, another of old Ephraim's sons, procured a license to sell alcohol "out of doors."[19] Temptation was now in the Indians' back yard.

For two years following Sergeant's death, the Stockbridges were virtually unguided. Ministers in the general vicinity, such as Stephen Williams and Samuel Hopkins of Great Barrington, paid spiritual visits, but some of the faithful preferred the visits from Moravian missionaries. The Moravians could now operate more freely, thanks to a protective decree from England. Umpachenee, who had grown very fond of them, was undoubtedly the prime force in getting the missionaries to come to Stockbridge. Less than two weeks after Sergeant's death Umpachenee, his new wife, his son, and a number of Stockbridge and Wechquadnach Indians had visited Bethlehem and Gnadenhutten. They may have been probing the possibility of Moravian involvement with the Indians at Stockbridge, or perhaps a segment of the tribe was considering relocation among the Moravians. While in Bethlehem, one of the Stockbridge Indians was baptized by the Brethren. And there Umpachenee saw for the first time a painting of the crucifixion. It moved him deeply, especially since he had heard so much of the Moravian emphasis on Christ's wounds, blood, and death. He told Abraham and his son that he would never forget that painting, and that every time he thought of it, his heart wept.[20]

Moravian missionaries did visit Stockbridge on request, preaching, singing hymns with the Indians, and encouraging them to trust in Jesus. During one visit, two Moravians met a former acquaintance, Ebenezer Poohpoonuc. He apparently had fallen from grace and was out of favor with the other Indians, no longer serving as their interpreter. As the two Brethren told Ebenezer of Christ's love and death for him, tears ran down his cheeks. He confessed his need for a savior. He also asserted that Stockbridge could not continue in its present state and wished that the Indians could be delivered from there.[21]

The following spring the Nimham brothers, members of the Wappinger tribe, told one of the Moravians that the Stockbridges were living like Indians in the wild, drinking and indulging in all kinds of vices. The perfervid Moravians faulted the Calvinist ministers, who rotated at Stockbridge and would baptize any Indian who requested it.[22]

Things were obviously not well with the Indians at Stockbridge in this postwar period, though possibly not as bleak as the Moravian accounts suggested. The Indians had lost men in the conflict, and the economy and morals of Stockbridge undoubtedly had suffered from the presence of military contingents. Then in August 1751 two awesome events occurred. The renowned theologian Jonathan Edwards officially became the Indians' minister. A few days later, Aaron Umpachenee died.[23]

Umpachenee had fallen ill in May. Sensing death, he asked a visiting Moravian missionary from Scaticook to convey his greetings to his brethren in the Moravian communities, because he might not see them again. The Moravian urged the chief to commend himself to the will of Jesus, and Umpachenee agreed that he would.[24] Perhaps Umpachenee's spirit kept him alive throughout the summer, a summer of sickness for many in Stockbridge, but he gradually deteriorated. By the first week in August it looked like the end was near. The Scaticook chief, four of his tribesmen, and their Moravian missionary visited Stockbridge on

August 11 and went straight to Umpachenee's bedside. Aaron was unable to recognize his visitors until the Scaticook chief told him who they were. Umpachenee summoned strength enough to thank them for coming to see him and, anticipating their message, told them that he had been thinking of Jesus' own suffering and death for him. Umpachenee again asked his visitors to convey greetings—his last—to his Mohican brothers in the other villages. When the missionary and the Scaticook chief visited Aaron the next day, he was too weak to talk. Ten days later the Stockbridge Mohicans lost an intelligent, perceptive champion. Runners arrived at Gnadenhutten four weeks later to announce the death, and they told the Moravians that the chief had spoken about the brethren until his last hour and died more contentedly than anyone they had ever seen.[24] Samuel Hopkins probably would have concurred. He reported that after straying from the Christian path, Umpachenee had "recover'd from his apostasy; confessed his wickedness, was resol'vd to charity, and walk'd orderly to the day of his death."[25]

It may have eased Umpachenee's mind before he died to know that at last a minister had been selected for his people, someone who he hoped could help them continue to bridge the difficult gap between the old ways and the new and keep on the path down which he and Konkapot had led them. It would take history to establish Jonathan Edwards as a theological giant. To the Indian flock he was simply a new shepherd. But to some of his Massachusetts contemporaries he was an eccentric, outdated clergyman.

Edwards's sermons and writing expounded the old, stern Puritanism, and recently his theories had become a little too stern for some of his more worldly and influential parishioners in Northampton. The principal agitators against him were related to the Williamses of Stockbridge, who did not favor Edwards as the new missionary. They were joined by Josiah Jones and a few others who, according to Abigail Sergeant, were "very bitterly against it" because Edwards did not know the Indian language and because "they don't like the man."[26] The Woodbridge clan and Samuel Hopkins of Great Barrington favored him, however. The teacher's sway over the Indians worried the Williams faction, who felt that Woodbridge had his own interests to serve. Woodbridge, on the other hand, apparently felt that the Williamses were seeking to further their own influence by feverishly attempting to enlist another young Yale tutor, Ezra Stiles. Stiles did not know the language either, but he had preached twice to the Indians and was on friendly terms with Abigail

*Jonathan Edwards, missionary to the Stockbridge Indians, 1751–57.
Courtesy of the Library of Congress.*

Sergeant. Woodbridge objected to Stiles ostensibly on religious grounds, but was said to have warned the Indians that such a young man might marry into the Williams family and thus come under their influence. Woodbridge's remarks and the controversial state of Stockbridge affairs effectively killed Stiles's candidacy.[27] By February of 1751 no other viable candidate appeared to be interested, and after Jonathan Edwards auditioned for the Stockbridge congregation, it voted to receive him. The English members of the church would offer him a little more than £6 a year and twenty loads of firewood, and the Indians would provide eighty loads of wood. The New England Company paid the bulk of Edwards's annual salary, £70 sterling.[28]

The firewood supply was no small consideration, since timber was becoming scarce in the heart of Stockbridge. Edwards thought that even the congregation's supply, however, would not be enough for him and his family, and he petitioned the General Court for permission to purchase from the Stockbridge Indians 100 acres of timberland, as well as 50 acres for a home site. The Indians had about five times more timberland than they would ever use, according to Edwards, and those colonials who had suitable land near the town center wanted too much money for it.

Edwards's petition was rejected by the government, but a Massachusetts official sent an informal note to the inhabitants of Stockbridge, saying that he was directed by the General Court to strongly recommend that they grant Edwards's request. Edwards, therefore, over the next few years, set about buying parcels of land in town from the Indians, circumventing the provincial law by having the purchases approved by county justices just as his fellow colonials did.[29]

Ephraim Williams, Jr., was Edwards's most outspoken opponent and apparently did all he could to prevent Edwards's appointment. But Williams sardonically claimed otherwise: "I am sorry that a head so full of divinity should be so empty of politics. I would not have him fail of going for 500 pounds, since they are so set for him, not that I think he will ever do so much more good than an other, but on account of raising the price of my land."[30]

Edwards was a popular attraction outside of Northampton and as far away as Virginia. The Williams pecuniary instinct overrode religious objections. It was quite possible that Edwards's settlement at Stockbridge would raise land values, and the congregation might get a good return on an investment of £6 and one hundred loads of firewood. Of course, Edwards's own 480 acres just outside Stockbridge would also benefit from the appreciation.

Despite the Williamses prejudice, Ephraim's initial objections to Jonathan Edwards as a missionary are worth noting:

1. That he was not sociable, the consequences of which was he was not apt to teach.

2. He was a very great bigot, for he would not admit any person into heaven but those that agreed fully to his sentiments, a doctrine deeply tinged with that of the Romish church.

3. That he was an old man, and that it was not possible for

him to learn the Indian tongues, therefore it was not likely he could be serviceable to the Indians as a young man that would learn the tongue. Why no more pains should be taken with the old Indians to save them, that as it were they must be under the necessity of being d . . . d I knew not.[31]

On this last point Williams was either unaware of or chose to ignore his late brother-in-law's sentiments regarding the redemption of the old Indians, which paralleled Edwards's.

But from the standpoint of a mission to Indians barely in touch with Christianity, Williams's other points were legitimate. Edwards's approach to religious conversion was stricter than Sergeant's and might be harder to digest. In some scratchy notes he prepared for lecturing the Indian children at Stockbridge, Edwards dwelt on the options of going to heaven or to hell, depending on their goodness or wickedness. To young souls who had just awakened to life he would preach the need for an awakening to religion. Those who failed would "go down into a Great Fire."[32]

As for the language issue, the Indians certainly preferred to be preached to in their own tongue. But Edwards indirectly defended his deficiency in Mohican by contending that the real problem was that the children were not learning English well enough. His first order of business was to correct this shortcoming. He maintained that they were merely mimicking the sounds made by the teacher and learning to associate those sounds with related words on a printed page, but that they were not learning the sense of the language or of a given lesson. As a consequence, the youngsters had learned little of substance in the last fourteen years, "their own barbarous languages being exceedingly barren, and very unfit to express moral and divine things."[33] Edwards also had a curious notion that if the Indian children learned to sing sacred hymns they would "renounce the coarseness and filth and degradation of savage life, for cleanliness, refinement and good morals."[34] He apparently was unaware that the Stockbridges had sung hymns with the Moravians. Yet despite Edwards's moral pomposity and his tendency to have his head in ethereal clouds, his avid young follower Samuel Hopkins reported that "to Indians he was a very plain and practical preacher; upon no occasion did he display any metaphysical knowledge in the pulpit. His sentences were concise and full of meaning; and his delivery, grave and natural."[35] Hopkins's assertion is borne out by at least one sermon against drinking, wherein Edwards warned the Indians that God would be angrier with them than with those Indians who had not had Christian instruction, and that they would "have a hotter place in Hell than the heathen that never heard of [Jesus Christ]."[36]

Edwards further discounted his need to speak Mohican by availing himself of John Wauwaumpequunaunt's assistance. Although John drank too hard on occasion, Edwards warmly praised him, describing him as "on some accounts an extraordinary man, understands English well, is a good reader and writer, and an excellent interpreter." Edwards boasted that perhaps no other educated American Indian better understood divinity and the scriptures.[37] John had put aside hunting and planting for clerical work, became a town constable in 1753, and married a woman with an English name.[38] One of the Moravian missionaries, however, described Wauwaumpequunaunt as "an arrogant creature."[39]

In any case, as William Johnson once explained, translating Christian theology into Indian languages was precarious. In Johnson's presence, a preacher from one of Boston's religious societies once delivered a sermon to Indians on the text "God is no respecter of persons." The preacher's interpreter, though the best in the area, rendered the translation as "God had no love for people such as them." Johnson had to interrupt to rescue the passage and the rest of sermon.[40]

The question of Edwards's qualifications was moot, since he assumed the Stockbridge missionary duties in the summer of 1751. His wife and six children joined him the following winter, and the Indians soon appeared pleased with both him and his family.[41] Even Abigail Sergeant reluctantly admitted that Edwards had so far conducted himself "with wisdom and prudence, & I must confess I am not a little disappointed in him. He is learned, polite & free in conversation & more catholick than I apprehended. He has treated me with much respect & complasance."[42]

Edwards's daughter Esther was immediately charmed by Stockbridge. She enjoyed watching Indians and settlers arrive at church on horseback or on foot with babes in arms and gliding in silent canoes along the Housatonic. She described Stockbridge in January as "delightfully suited for winter sports." The frozen river hosted skating parties, and the steep, snow-covered hills afforded ideal sledding. With her cheeks flushed and pulse pounding she gushed to her diary one winter day: "My sister and I had two Indian boys to pull our sleds for us, and to guide them over the crust . . . we speed from one descent to another until we finally reach the level of our quiet street." Woodmen's sleighs with their "merry sleigh-bells" and sledding parties, sometimes followed by dancing, enhanced the romantic setting.[43]

Warm, human vignettes like this undoubtedly were commonplace throughout the years of the mission. Not all was difficulty and contention between Indians and colonials, and the Stockbridges enjoyed good times as well as or better than their neighbors. Certainly children found things to enjoy as they grew up together. Six-year-old Jonathan Edwards, Jr., heard Mohican more than English outside his own home, to the extent that over the years his thoughts frequently ran in Mohican and he knew the Indian names for things he did not know in English. The Indians flattered him (as they had John Sergeant) on his superior linguistic knowledge.[44] Similarly, John Sergeant, Jr., grew up sharing the language and the frontier experience with the Stockbridges, forming lasting bonds. A Mohican teenager whose father had died chose Samuel Brown, Jr., instead of another Indian as his legal guardian.[45] Ephraim Williams, Jr., the nemesis of Jonathan Edwards, at one time included in his will a provision for an annual contribution to the Indians' education.[46] Even among the adults, where differences were likely greater, there were surely light moments of laughter, empathy, storytelling and shared wisdom, enthusiasm, and joy.

Adding to the town's bucolic quaintness, one of the Indians blew a conch shell every Sabbath and lecture day to call the faithful to worship. The people considered its use important enough, perhaps with defense in mind, to provide payment to the Indian who sounded it. "At first it seemed wanting in solemnity," Esther Edwards said of the clarion, "but now we are used to it, the shell begins to have a sacred sound, and the summons is speedily heeded."[47] Stockbridge was becoming the quaint New England town that Norman Rockwell would portray two hundred years later—with no Indians in the picture.

8

PROFITING

FROM

EDUCATION

Pastoral tranquillity would not be the rule in Stockbridge in the coming years. The Edwards family had barely settled when they found themselves involved in yet another controversy. This time the storm center was a new building in town, a boarding school, which had been John Sergeant's pet project before he died. It was a different attempt to civilize his flock, but it was also evidence that the mission had not been succeeding to his satisfaction. Within eight years after the mission started, Sergeant recognized that something more than divine light was needed to keep the Indians steady in the Calvinist ethic. He observed that the tradition of Indian women alone doing the agricultural work, for instance, was hard to overcome. Although the Stockbridges had been given plows, they still preferred to have plowing done for them. So when the men were not following their traditional pursuits of hunting, fishing, and trapping, they were, in the English view, idle or "indolent," a condition worse than intemperance to the religious mind. The women, in turn, never had time to learn the arts of "housewifery."

Seasonal projects like the maple sugar excursions involved whole families and took children back into an uncivilized environment. At times families also accompanied men to distant hunting camps for extended periods. Fathers, of course, wanted to teach their sons hunting, fishing, and trapping, and most boys would naturally listen more to the call of the outdoors than to the lectures of teacher or preacher. Even during war, some fighting men took their families with them to English forts, where they might be safer than in their own villages and where the women could help provide for their husbands. These military forts probably exerted the worst influence on Christian morals.

Further, Indians generally did not discipline their children as Europeans did. Spanking or hitting was forbidden, for example, and Sergeant remarked that while the Indian children were cute, agreeable, modest, and even bashful, they showed no deference to their parents, which was unacceptable in Christian society. The Moravians experienced similar frustrations in dealing with Indian children. All the rough edges that wilderness living offered, combined with the lack of New England-style discipline, the lure of the trading post, and the temptation of rum, together produced a formula for frustrating the Christian living and child rearing practices with which the missionaries sought to replace Indian culture. And from the 1740s onward, the proportion of ingredients for this formula increased for the Stockbridges. In Great Barrington there were two refreshment taverns, and a third was being contemplated, while the town's population amounted only to about thirty families. Young minister Hopkins, having observed some of his parishioners drunk in one of the taverns, helped prevent construction of the proposed third one, incurring the wrath of several townsmen.[1]

The war and the material appeal of Stockbridge had attracted scattered Mohicans who had little or no interest in Christianity. This complicated matters further for Sergeant, since drawing these Indians to Stockbridge was one of the mission's stated purposes. By January of 1747 he lamented: "nothing affects me with more grief than to observe the little fruit of my labors. Some of those who have appear'd the most promising converts have to my great grief and sometimes even to my astonishment, strangely fallen away—which has almost wholly discouraged my further attempts." "The truth is," he added, "the Indians are perhaps as fickle and irresolute in their determinations as any people in the world; and when they seem to be wholly recovered from their vice easily relapse into their foolish and wicked national habits."[2]

Anxious to keep his congregation in the Calvinist camp, John Sergeant thought that a self-sustaining boarding school would offset many distracting influences. Indian children between the ages of ten and twenty would be trained in farming, trades, and domestic industry, besides their letters and catechism. This, he said, would "change their whole habit of thinking and acting; and raise them as far as possible into the condition of a civil, industrious and polish'd people; . . . and withal . . . introduce the English language among them instead of their own imperfect and barbarous dialect."[3] Sergeant hoped to turn the young ones into English Americans.

In April of 1743 Sergeant had claimed that the Indians were "mightily taken" with the idea of a boarding school. He convinced them to donate 200 acres about a mile from the meetinghouse to accommodate it. When David Brainerd coaxed the Kaunaumeek Mohicans into moving to Stockbridge, the proposed boarding school may have been part of the inducement. The Shekomeko Indians, and most recently the Wechquadnachs, had been looking for a place of refuge from their shrinking land base. When the Stockbridges invited them to their town, Sergeant likely took the opportunity to advertise his plan. The Moravian converts, however, influenced by their missionaries, tended to view the liberal atmosphere at Stockbridge as dangerous for their souls.[4] Nevertheless, before the decade was out there were more than two hundred Indians in Stockbridge, though only a little over half of them had been baptized and just a third of these received communion. The majority of Mohicans remained scattered up and down the Hudson, holding on to their ways as much as possible.

Sergeant wanted to attract these and other Indians from near and far. He eventually asked William Johnson's help in encouraging Mohawks to send children to the school. The Society in Scotland for Propagating Christian Knowledge was apparently willing to supply funds, and the New England Company voted £100 sterling for the venture. Sergeant's proposal reached Isaac Hollis in London, who liked the idea and opened his purse even wider.[5] Eight of the English Stockbridge residents and two visitors pledged more than £115 toward the project, to be paid over a ten-year period. David Brainerd had sold his teapot and an iron kettle to the Woodbridge brothers before he left, and he offered the proceeds from these meager possessions to Sergeant for the proposed school.[6] But New England charity virtually ended with these pledges. John Sergeant's proposal was published and distributed to religious figures, government officials, and educators in Massachusetts, New York, and Connecticut, with little response. The war interrupted the effort, and Stockbridge was preoccupied with defense and hungry soldiers.

Things were different on the other side of the Atlantic. The prince of Wales started off one fund drive that included other royalty. His chaplain sent a more personal gift, a two-volume illustrated Bible for the Indians and £20 sterling for the minister. But it was clear that this level of charity during King George's War had a mundane motive—to keep the Indians in the British camp. John Sergeant did not fail to exploit this angle in his subsequent appeals for the school.

The project would entail significant expense for the building, livestock, and equipment, as well as salaries for several instructors. After the war less than £200 of New England money trickled into Stockbridge. Yet by the summer of 1749 the shell of the boarding house was complete. Then Sergeant died, with debts approaching £600. From his list of debts it appears that he had borrowed some money intended for the boarding school.[7] Ephraim Williams claimed that his son-in-law's salary had been inadequate, and that "had it not been for his very good friends he might have been oblig'd to have deserted his mission or beg his bread."[8] Nonetheless, Sergeant had managed to start construction of the school only by going further into debt. This was just the edge of the cloud hanging over the school.

By 1751 the English residents and the Stockbridges alike had begun a concerted effort to persuade Chief Hendrick and his Mohawks to send their children to the proposed school. Though initially wary of English intentions, the Mohawks agreed and thus encouraged other Six Nations tribes to send their children. Before the end of the year, families of Oneidas from the headwaters of the Susquehanna and several Tuscaroras and Mohawks arrived in Stockbridge and enrolled ninety-five boys in the boarding school. Many of their parents stayed in wigwams nearby.[9] Considerable financial support for the project then emerged from official and private sources both in New England and in London, since Iroquois presence considerably strengthened the western area against French and Indian attack.[10] Once again, Christian charity seemed to blend perfectly with colonial security.

The boarding school project, with its need for logistics, supplies, and salaries, created enviable jobs and contracts for those involved. And those most involved in its direction were the Williams clan. Ephraim Williams contacted his connections in Boston and London to elicit additional government support and to promote his daughter Abigail as mistress of a contemplated girls' boarding school. The New England Company subsequently authorized her as mistress and provided her with a £30 salary, plus enough to clothe and feed ten girls for a year. They advanced her money to begin the experiment in her home. Williams in the meantime sent to London a deed made out to Princess Augusta for one-quarter of his Stockbridge land. This was ostensibly a charitable contribution to accommodate the Mohawks, though he evidently hoped to arrange another "equivalent" land exchange. He asked a relative, however, to be sure that the deed was not registered on the proper records in London, since it was not recorded in his own county.[11] In other words, the deed was illegal. The grand finale of the Williams clan's nepotic orchestration was Abigail's marriage to Joseph Dwight. A prominent merchant and a brigadier general in the militia, Dwight was now an appointee of the General Court to oversee the new boarding school program.

Jonathan Edwards began to observe that little of the mission money was being used as it was intended, and that affairs in general were being mishandled. Considering Isaac Hollis's noble charity and how his money was being used, Edwards said, "it is enough to make one sick." [12] He was joined in this sentiment by Timothy Woodbridge and most of the population of Stockbridge.

Edwards objected to Abigail as boarding school mistress, claiming that her health and her responsibilities for Sergeant's and Dwight's families would preclude her from effective administration. Yet at the same time he described her as a woman of considerable abilities with a love for public affairs and a domineering personality, which she had used on John Sergeant and would likely use on Joseph Dwight. The Stockbridge Indians were more blunt in describing her, he said, as proud, jealous, and untrustworthy. And though great pains were taken to get students for her, only three Stockbridges and one Mohawk attended the nascent girls' school, and there were complaints of her rough, impatient treatment of them. She managed—or mismanaged, according to Edwards—Hollis's money by dispersing it as she saw fit. Her new husband, as resident trustee, would be the only one to oversee her accounts.[13]

Joseph Dwight meanwhile had apparently found a way to further the family interest in the name of charity to the Indians. Edwards charged that Dwight was proposing himself as steward of both boarding schools, with Abigail directing one and his son directing the other. Two other sons and two daughters would receive a free education, another family member would serve as a tutor, and personal servants would be paid as school personnel. At the same time, Edwards said, because the boarding school was built on Williams land, produce from the students' farming lessons would grace the Dwight dinner table. Dwight would also be supervising the schoolhouse construction and supplying the Indian children's needs from his own business in Brookfield, where he sold everything from pocket knives to an occasional slave. In addition, Ephraim Williams and one of the new men in town, David Pixley, were profiting from the sale of beef, wheat, and mutton for provisions for the Mohawks. Jonathan Edwards also questioned the size and expense of the girls' boarding school, but felt that his question was answered when the Dwight family moved into the new building.[14]

Edwards also was unhappy with the instructor who had been employed with boarding school money since 1748. He was a sixty-two-year-old militia captain, licensed trader, and former Mohawk captive from Newington, Connecticut, named Martin Kellogg. Edwards described him as old, lame, temperamental, illiterate, and unsuited for anything productive. Some of the boys under his tutelage reported that he had clothed and fed them poorly, while using them mainly to work his Newington farm. Edwards claimed that John Sergeant himself had been concerned about Kellogg's conduct and expense accounts.[15] The New England Company's commissioners in Boston, meanwhile, had appointed a young Yale graduate named Gideon Hawley as official instructor for the Indian boys. He arrived in Stockbridge in early February of 1752, moved into the boarding school, and began teaching Mohawks and Oneidas. But with the backing of the Williams clan, Martin Kellogg refused to give up his position. The Indian boys became the object of a tug-of-war between the two.

With the support of Edwards and Timothy Woodbridge, Gideon Hawley informed the Indian parents that their children were not being properly instructed by Kellogg and advised them to remove their children from his tutelage. Seven boys were shortly withdrawn from the school. The Iroquois in Stockbridge were unhappy with the contentious state of affairs. Most of the town residents as well were disturbed with the Dwight-Williams-Kellogg clique and formally protested to the provincial government. The town also elected Timothy Woodbridge as its representative to the legislature for the coming session, and several tribesmen joined him on a trip to Boston to present their grievance.[16]

During this time the Williams faction was far from silent. Dwight and Ephraim Williams, Jr., both waged war on Edwards and Woodbridge. They harped on Edwards's inability to speak Mohican, charged Woodbridge with irregularities, and suggested that Edwards wanted to turn the girls' school over to his daughter. Dwight refused to attend church, and most of the English residents felt that he was putting public worship in contempt and demoralizing the Indians, especially the Mohawks. Joseph Woodbridge swore that he had heard Williams describe Edwards as a plague in the town, declaring that he would have no such plagues. Edwards claimed that some of the Williamses and their allies had asked two Indian boys to sign a petition to get rid of him, and when they refused, plied the boys with wine to get them to cooperate.[17]

Complicating the Williamses' strategy during this period was the declining physical and mental health of Ephraim Williams, Sr. One fall morning in 1752 he arose before daybreak and with cash in hand awakened several English residents, and then hotly pressed them to sell him their farms, offering high prices but insisting that the deals be completed immediately. Unsuccessful in this endeavor, he then roamed for a month throughout Massachusetts and Connecticut, at one point imagining that he had been appointed to negotiate Indian affairs in New Haven. His daughter Abigail, sensing potential damage to the Williamses' contest with Edwards, pleaded with her brother at Boston to stop their father before he ended up in front of the General Court. His appearance, she said, would undermine "our publick affairs & . . . intirely ruin us, for he is . . . by no means . . . in one quarter of his notions." By February of 1753 the whole argument was becoming moot. Disgusted Mohawks were beginning to drift away, Isaac Hollis decided to put his charity in Jonathan Edwards's hands, and that month the boys' schoolhouse burned to the ground. Gideon Hawley lost most of his possessions in the fire; years later he intimated that the Williams faction had been suspected of arson. And Ephraim Williams, Jr., soon dropped the provision in his will for the Indians' education.[18]

The raging controversy stifled any meaningful attempt to educate the Indians. The unsettled atmosphere apparently discouraged the Wechquadnach Mohicans from moving to Stockbridge despite several invitations. Nearly all the Wechquadnachs chose to join the Moravian community at Gnadenhutten, and others went to Oneida country on the upper Susquehanna.[19] The Stockbridge Indians had taken their children out of the boarding school earlier because of Kellogg's inadequate attention. Only Timothy Woodbridge's school remained for basic education.[20]

The Iroquois decision to leave Stockbridge was hastened by an incident involving a member of the Dwight-Williams clique. While visiting the boarding school, he struck an Iroquois lad on the head with his cane. The resulting furor had to be settled by the perpetrator's making restitution to the offended tribesmen—an important concession to Indian customs, which indicated that their traditions did not go unheeded in a frontier town like Stockbridge. The incident also widened the breach between the Edwards and Williams factions.[21] Some Mohawks stayed in Stockbridge through 1753, but Chief Hendrick directed all of them to return home by the spring of 1754. Even so, the parents of three Mohawk boys begged to be allowed to stay so that their boys could be taught. Edwards reported that the Stockbridge Mohicans, on the other hand, were so disgusted with the Williamses by the summer of 1752 that they, too, had talked again of completely disbanding and leaving town. This threat struck a nerve among the Stockbridge colonials, since abandonment by the Indians would make Stockbridge especially vulnerable to Indian attack. The colonials' un-Christianlike feuds, greed, and pride had self-destructive implications. To placate the Indians, the lieutenant governor followed Edwards's advice and made Timothy Woodbridge a justice of the peace in Stockbridge.[22]

Woodbridge, known to the Indians as Solohkuwauneh, by now had an established reputation. Jonathan Edwards claimed that "Mr. Woodbridge, from his childhood, has had the character among all that have been acquainted with him, of being a man of uprightness, and of a generous disposition, and one who greatly abhors any mean, clandestine and injurious management from private views, and of a very easy, placable natural temper. By his long proved justice and integrity he has gained a vast esteem with the Indians, who are a people in that respect peculiar. If once they find that a man is a mean, deceitful man, they never will trust him again; but their friendship is mightily gained by upright dealing." In this regard, Edwards said, the schoolteacher had greater influence among the Stockbridge Indians "than perhaps all other Englishmen put together."[23] Abigail Sergeant put it less flatteringly: "he thinks he can gett ye Indians to say just what he bids 'em."[24]

Gideon Hawley described Woodbridge as a "gentleman of abilities . . . always poor, and had a powerful party against him; but he rose to be the first man in the county of Berkshire, was always esteemed for his sense; but had few who wished to promote him."[25] Hawley and Edwards were allies of Woodbridge in the contest with the Williamses, so their comments were not likely to be unfavorable. Others, however, saw Woodbridge's rapport with the Indians as a means to further his own interests. Besides his Stockbridge arrangements, the schoolteacher was involved in the controversial Susquehanna Land Company. He tried to use his influence with the Indians to gain a foothold for Connecticut emigrants in the Wyoming Valley of Pennsylvania, a settlement effort that resulted in bitterness and violence for more than forty years. When the Indians in that area appeared to be pulling back from a transaction in which money had already changed hands, Woodbridge sent them an obnoxious, whiny letter. He warned that God would punish the Indians for cheating him out of his money, and that they must not hurt him if he chose to settle a hundred families in a township there. The Indians were upset enough to bring the letter to William Johnson's attention, and Thomas

Penn of Pennsylvania went so far as to speculate whether a reward of £50 could be offered for Woodbridge if he ever came to the contested area. Mohawk chief Hendrick sent his dark regards to Woodbridge through Gideon Hawley, asking the young minister to "inform [Woodbridge] that he would before long meet with some misfortune." [26]

Woodbridge obviously did not become "first man in the county" on his salary, which in 1749 was only a little more than £87 for six months of teaching. He had a wife, nine children, and a slave-servant couple with their own child, all of whom had to be supported.[27] It is hard to reconcile Gideon Hawley's description of Woodbridge as "always poor," since connections with the Indians frequently reaped rewards from them as well as from the provincial government. As an educator, therefore, he had something of value to teach the Indians—that both students and teachers could profit from education.

9

ADDING INJURY TO INSULT

Besides the boarding school fiasco, several other developments impeded the progress of religion and New England civilization among the Stockbridge Mohicans. First, a new market enticed the Indians into the woods to hunt for a cash crop. Ginseng was in heavy demand in Europe for the China trade, and New England forests yielded a prime grade. Young and old Indians gathered the root and headed for the Albany trading posts, trying to recapture the heyday of the beaver trade and leaving church and school behind. According to Springfield's Samuel Hopkins, too much of the Indian trade was controlled by unscrupulous colonials. Hopkins maintained that although "their lust after drink exposes them to be cheated out of what little they have, yet this gives us no right to deal unjustly by them. They have a natural right to justice, and may with great propriety challenge it at our hand, seeing we profess to be subject to the law of Christ."[1]

An ominous incident occurred next, in April of 1753. While collecting maple sap in the woods southeast of Stockbridge, Solomon Waunaupaugus's son and grandson heard a commotion nearby. They started chasing two men who appeared to be stealing horses. One of the men shot and killed Solomon's son. The Stockbridge Indians were outraged. They held an elaborate ritualistic funeral in the Indian tradition, defying Christian standards.[2] Mohicans from other villages came to learn what was being done about the killing. The threat of Indian justice seemed real, and everyone in Stockbridge was on edge. Joseph Dwight saw several Indians with blackened faces, a sign of preparation for war.[3]

Samuel Brown, Jr., acting as sheriff, apprehended both men and eventually took them to Springfield for trial. One was acquitted and the other found guilty of manslaughter. This action gave no consolation to the family, and the Indians felt that the Waunaupaugus family deserved greater satisfaction. Timothy Woodbridge wrote to Governor William Shirley, asking him to send money to wipe away Solomon's tears, as the Indians put it. Woodbridge feared the consequences if the gesture was not made. Coming from a man of Woodbridge's reputation among the Indians, this judgment reflected the severity of the situation. A year after the killing, even though the governor and his council had authorized a £6 payment, the Indians had not yet received it. In any case they did not consider the amount to be any consolation.

The incident sparked smoldering Indian resentment, and the English families became concerned for their safety. The common fear quickly buried the differences between the town's factions, and the residents asked both Woodbridge and Dwight to do something. Ugly rumors spread. A couple of black servants told the Colonials that some of the Indians were plotting a general revenge. Alarming signs appeared: formerly friendly tribesmen became surly; several of the looser sort were congregating and drinking in the woods outside of town; a few English guns were missing. Jonathan Edwards noted that the killing of Waunaupaugus's son seemed to affect the remaining Mohawks as much as the Mohicans. An Indian close to Edwards told him that several young Stockbridges had recently visited the Shawnees and were told that they were fools for putting up with the English, who were bent on exterminating them and were merely awaiting the right moment. These young Stockbridges returned home and formed what Edwards thought was the nucleus of a conspiracy. When a number of the Indians were called together and asked directly about a plot, most of them seemed completely ignorant of it. Timothy Woodbridge and Joseph Dwight believed otherwise. Together they coaxed Boston into increasing Waunaupaugus's restitution to £20. Edwards pointed out in his appeal to Governor Shirley that if outlying tribes heard of the killing, they would be more susceptible to French influence. He pleaded with the governor to send the approved money speedily, and he recommended compliance with Indian custom by delivering it via an official from Boston. The government approved the new amount, which was to be forwarded to Joseph Dwight as soon as possible.

The settlers' responses to this incident and the official compliance with Indian custom demonstrated that Stockbridge and its Indian citizens had a different status than other provincial towns or even eastern Indian towns, Boston's indignation over the land allotment issue notwithstanding. The local tension was exacerbated by the larger events that transpired as a confrontation developed between Britain and France. War appeared imminent, and French colonials and their Indian allies were making menacing moves. Frontier settlements like Stockbridge had the most to fear. In the late summer of 1754 a Stockbridge Indian hunting party led by Jonas Etowaukaum, Umpachenee's son, was in Albany when they learned of an impending attack on a tiny Dutch settlement on the Hoosic River, about twenty-five miles northwest of Stockbridge. Etowaukaum warned some men at a gristmill in that area, and the next day, while the Stockbridges were hunting on Mount Greylock north of Stockbridge, the party heard shots coming from the settlement. They slipped down to investigate and saw a large group of Indians killing cattle and burning buildings. The Stockbridges hurried back to town to alert their fellow residents.[4] Frontier nerves grew more taut. Three days later, on Sunday, September 1, those nerves snapped.

A latecomer rushed into Jonathan Edwards's church service with the news of a nearby massacre. Passing the cabin of Samuel Brown's son-in-law, he had seen an Indian dragging a child outside and gave chase. When the abductor saw the man pursuing him, he tomahawked the child and fled. Returning to the cabin, the churchgoer found a servant and an infant dead and the father and two other children cowering under a bed.[5]

Word spread like wildfire and so did panic. Outlying settlers north of Stockbridge flocked into town and many Stockbridge families fled south. Young Samuel Hopkins was reading a psalm to his congregation in Great Barrington when villagers burst into the church with the news of the killings. People began screaming, shouting, running back and forth, and some fled even farther south. "Women, children and squaws presently flocked in upon us from Stockbridge," Hopkins said, "half naked and frightened almost to death; and fresh news came that the enemy were on the plains this side of Stockbridge, shooting and killing and scalping people as they fled."[6] Rumors grew wilder and panic spread as Stockbridge refugees arrived covered with blood, and others claimed to have witnessed killing and scalping.

The militia was hastily summoned to Stockbridge, and a fortification was quickly built around Jonathan Edwards's house, since it was in the center of town. Suspicion focused on the Stockbridge Indians. According to Edwards, "Multitudes came from various parts for our defense that night and the next day; and many of these conducted very foolishly toward our Indians—suspecting them to be guilty—charging them with it, and threatening to kill and the like."[7] The man who had discovered the cabin murder scene thought that one of the Indians he had seen there was a Stockbridge, but he changed his mind several times and wouldn't swear to it. Moreover, Edwards learned that this Indian and another suspect had been seen in the heart of Stockbridge that day by several reliable persons. Etowaukaum's hunting party was suspected next, until one of the men who had been at the Hoosic gristmill stepped forward to acknowledge Etowaukaum's timely warning, which undoubtedly saved several lives. Besides, the hunting party had returned to Stockbridge three days before the murders. The man was grateful enough to invite Etowaukaum to Jones's tavern for a treat.[8]

But suspicion continued to hang over the Stockbridges. Rumors grew more distorted as they traveled outside Massachusetts. Esther Edwards, married and living in New Jersey, heard that all but two or three Indian families had left Stockbridge disgusted with the English, and that they were thinking of enlisting a neighboring tribe to help them kill all the settlers.[9] Such a scheme would have been inconsistent with the Stockbridges' tested behavior and proven loyalty to the colonials around them, but they certainly had grounds for anger: the boarding school embarrassment; the killing of Waunaupaugus's son; being suspected of a conspiratorial plot. Now they were suspected of murder and their own lives threatened. Some of the militia currently in Stockbridge were compounding the grief by insulting and abusing the Indians.[10]

Then two soldiers added abomination to insult and injury. After it was finally decided that the attackers were Canadian Indians, a reward was offered to anyone who would bring in a Canadian Indian scalp. One night two soldiers dug up a fresh Stockbridge Mohican corpse, scalped it, and presented the scalp as that of a Canadian Indian whom they had killed in the woods. When their sacrilege was discovered, the settlers produced speedy justice to quell further Indian discontent. The offenders were tried in Great Barrington and found guilty. Given the choice of heavy fines or whippings, the two chose the post. One received thirty lashes and the other twenty.[11]

Timothy Woodbridge ultimately learned at Albany the full story behind the Canadian Indian attacks. Some Caughnawaga sachems told Woodbridge that the Schaghticoke Indians had invited Abenaki tribes at Bécancour to revenge themselves on the English for the deaths of several tribesmen. The Abenakis could then escort the Schaghticokes to permanent residence in Canada. The Canadian Abenakis represented tribes who had been driven from the Connecticut Valley during King Philip's War, and who continued to complain to the French governor about that loss. They therefore needed little encouragement for the deeds, but Woodbridge believed that they probably received such encouragement from the governor anyway.[12] After the attacks the Abenakis escorted the Schaghticokes—more than fifty men, women, and children—to Crown Point, and from there a French ship carried them to Canada over Lake Champlain.[13]

The Mohicans may have been aware of the Schaghticoke intrigue, which could account for the furtiveness that Woodbridge and Edwards sensed among the Stockbridges after Waunaupaugus's son's death. By July of 1754 tension had developed between the Mohicans and the Schaghticokes on some issue to such a degree that at the Albany Congress the Mohicans were neither speaking to the Schaghticokes nor having anything to do with them. The traditional presents that the colonial representatives had planned to deliver as one package to both tribes had to be given separately. The Mohicans also insisted on replying independently to the New York governor's speech.[14] Perhaps the Mohicans realized that the Schaghticokes' propensities could spell misery for them through English suspicion or retaliation.

Alarm over the Stockbridge cabin murders flowed quickly down the Housatonic to Sharon and Kent. The new inhabitants of these two towns believed the Stockbridges to be the guilty Indians, and they warned the Scaticooks against going to Stockbridge or even leaving the area without official permission. Anxiety was heightened by an incident in Sharon that led to gunfire when a town prankster pretended to be an Indian. Yelling and whistling, he pounded on the cabin walls of a settler whose right to the property had been warmly contested by an Indian now living at Stockbridge. One result of the incident was that the Indian soon got paid for his claim to 200 acres.[15]

Young Samuel Hopkins drolly commented on the current alarmist state: "Two Indians may put New England to a hundred thousand pounds charge, and never much expose themselves. . . . The troops that came to our assistance are now drawing off; and what have they done? They have seen Stockbridge and eaten up all their provisions, and fatigued themselves, and that's all; and now we are left as much exposed as ever."[16]

Jonathan Edwards and his family bore the burden of feeding and housing those who helped build the fort, since the minister's residence became the garrison site.[17] To add to Stockbridge miseries at this juncture, some colonials continued to sell rum to the Indians without restraint.[18] And despite the shabby treatment the Stockbridges were receiving, the local settlers had the gall to question the Indians' devotion to the English interest in the growing conflict with the French. The Stockbridges pointed out that the soldiers' conduct toward them did not inspire enthusiasm. More to the point, the climate of suspicion and the ill treatment made them afraid to go into the woods not only for war, but even to hunt. If the French or enemy Indians did not kill them, the English might.[19]

Serious doubts about Mohican allegiance were expressed by Ephraim Williams's rich and arrogant cousin, Israel Williams, who headed the Hampshire County militia. He recommended to the government that more men be assigned to Stockbridge as protection from Indians outside and possibly inside the town. Governor Shirley authorized forty more men to be sent to Stockbridge for six weeks, since "there appears great danger of the total defection of the Stockbridge Indians."[20] To Joseph Dwight's credit, however, he told Williams that "we are, and too often have been, witnesses of the many insults and abuses which [the Indians] have suffered from the English soldiery—their lives and scalps threatened to be taken, and they called everything but good, charged with the late murders, and actually put into such terror as to not know which way to turn themselves."[21]

Though there was some doubt about the allegiance of the Stockbridge Mohicans, Jonathan Edwards felt that they could be induced to go on the "scalping design" for the English, but that they would probably follow the lead of the Iroquois. Timothy Woodbridge believed that if the Stockbridges did commit themselves, they could persuade other tribes along the Hudson to join them. Male Indian disposition was such that it would be impossible to keep them from going to war, Woodbridge asserted, and to try to stop them once they had the urge for war would be unwise, since blood would be shed one way or another.[22] The elder Samuel Hopkins felt confident, however, that the Stockbridges were "our hearty and fast friends, . . . willing to live or die with us, whether in peace or war."[23]

In fact, the Stockbridges had been talking of joining in the skirmishes for some time. At the Albany Congress they reminded colonial delegates of the ancient covenant chain between them and the English. They reiterated the change in the nature of the relationship between the two nations—how once the Mohicans had been powerful and protective of the newcomers, but now were few and weak and looked to the English for protection: "We view ye now as a very large tree, which has taken deep root in the ground, whose branches are spread very wide, we stand by the body of this tree, and we look round to see if there be any who endeavour to hurt it, and if it should so happen that any are powerful enough to destroy it, we are ready to fall with it."[24]

The Stockbridges may not have known it, but they were nearly insulted again. When Benjamin Franklin told New York's lieutenant governor James Delancey that the Stockbridges had arrived to attend the congress along with the Iroquois, Delancey was petulant. He replied that the Stockbridges had not been sent for, that New York had not usually supported the tribe at any treaty in Albany, and that Massachusetts should bear the expense. When New York's records of Indian affairs were examined, however, the governor's memory was refreshed. He was reminded that Mohicans did usually attend treaties with the Six Nations and that a speech was always made to them. Delancey agreed to speak to the Stockbridges but wanted the other colonies to contribute to their support in Albany.[25]

Late in 1754 a Massachusetts government committee recommended that the Stockbridges be "received as soldiers in the province service" with appropriate pay and subsistence for six months, to be under the care "of some good officer that will use them well." As an incentive, the committee further recommended that the Indians be advised to bring their complaints to the General Court, or that yet another committee could be sent to redress any grievances.[26] Obviously the government sensed that the Stockbridges needed wooing. Joseph Dwight called together the Indians who were in town and conveyed the government's message. They in turn sent runners to summon those out hunting or trading. After a full council debate and many questions put to Dwight, most of the Stockbridge Indian men were glad to join the service. Others were away, and a few refused to join because it would interfere with their "private affairs." Perhaps New England culture or Moravian pacifism was distilling some of the warrior spirit. Those families most committed to trodding the Christian path probably decided not to interrupt the process of learning its crooks and turns, especially in the case of the young men who were potential leaders.

But for the majority of young men the call to war reaffirmed their warrior status and gave them the identity with which they felt most comfortable during this period of uncertainty. On the practical side, it was also an opportunity to temporarily escape their creditors or earn money to relieve their debts. Joseph Dwight, as a brigadier colonel in the militia, had already taken a little frontier initiative and sent three willing Stockbridge Indians to reconnoiter some rumored enemy movement at the Carrying Place, the usual area of portage between Lake Champlain and Lake George. He commissioned Jacob Cheeksaunkun as a lieutenant and paid the trio more than the usual wages because of the danger.[27] In early December Cheeksaunkun, John Wauwaumpequunaunt, and Jehoiakim Yokun were sent to the fort at Pittsfield to obtain powder, shot, knives, pipes, and a few rounds of rum.[28]

At this stage of Stockbridge Mohican history some new names became prominent. Old warriors like John Konkapot and David Naunaunee-kanuk, now both in their mid-sixties, sat this war out. Naunauneekanuk apparently limited himself to performing odd jobs around Stockbridge.[29] Konkapot, along with King Ben and twenty-seven-year-old Johannis Mtohksin, helped monitor domestic affairs. Mtohksin was an educated church member who served as the tribe's interpreter. He had held various town offices since 1748 and was currently a selectman. Mtohksin's value to the tribe was such that he apparently did not serve in the war. And his services must have been sufficiently rewarded since he was not poor. He seems to have been disposed toward real estate schemes, particularly with enterprising men in Connecticut, and could hold his own in their wheelings and dealings. One colonial suspected Mtohksin "of being a cheat." [30]

The two principal heroes now were Jacob Naunauphtaunk and Jacob Cheeksaunkun, who had been in Stockbridge for about ten years. Naunauphtaunk had four sons, who were also rising in tribal prominence. He had a farm in the township and had served at various times as hog reeve, constable, surveyor, and was currently a selectman.[31] Cheeksaunkun was well established among his Indian peers, since he was Benjamin Kokhke-wenaunaunt's grandson. Next in the ranking came Solomon Uhhaunau-waunmut, who may have been related to the two Jacobs.

As the war grew more heated, a few outlying tribes moved to Stockbridge for the security it might afford. The Nimham clan and nearly two hundred of their fellow Wappingers arrived around 1756 for the protection of the women, children, and old men. Thirty-year-old Daniel Nimham and Aaron, probably a younger brother, were the principal tribesmen. Before their move to Stockbridge they were more closely identified with the government of New York than with Massachusetts. But from this point forward, the Nimhams at least would be Stockbridge Indians.

Prewar anxiety and political tension had in the meantime reached the Moravian Mohicans at Gnadenhutten. These Indians found themselves not only surrounded by potentially hostile Indian factions, but caught among competing interests attempting to use them as pawns. The Six Nations were pressuring the Moravian Mohicans to remove to the Wyoming Valley as part of an increased Indian presence there. Such a move might provide an Indian buffer against further English encroachment and would consolidate Indian strength in case of French attack. William Johnson favored the move, and for different reasons so did the Stockbridge Indians. The Stockbridges conferred a chieftainship on Abraham with a belt of wampum, and Abraham subsequently agreed in the spring of 1753 to relocate. The Stockbridge sachem encouraged the Gnadenhutten Indians and all western Mohicans to live together with a missionary on the Susquehanna. The Stockbridges may have been hoping for an eventual welcome to that territory themselves, though the Iroquois would not currently allow it.

When Abraham broke the news of the agreement to the Gnadenhutten congregation, however, not all the Mohican and Delaware converts received it with joy. It seemed that the relocation compact excluded missionaries. The Indians who were devoted to the community felt that Abraham had exceeded his authority. The ensuing debate created divisiveness. Abraham nevertheless felt bound by the agreement, and in late April of 1754 he and Delaware chief Teedyuscung led sixty-five Brethren on a tearful journey up the Susquehanna. For a year after this removal the remaining Gnadenhutten Indians, more than thirty-five of them Mohicans, received periodic demands, pleas, and threats to relocate, but they steadfastly refused.[32]

Meanwhile, the young Stockbridge heroes were willingly being drawn into the political and military arena. Frontier attacks by French Indians increased as 1755 approached, so Massachusetts decided to keep a company of Stockbridges in pay and supplies from late January to early July. For at least one nine-week period Jacob Cheeksaunkun served as a lieutenant under Joseph Dwight.[33] Then the Stockbridges were ordered to meet William Johnson at Albany for his planned assault against the French fort Saint Frédéric at Crown Point. William Shirley also arrived in Albany to enlist Indians for his planned expedition against Niagara, and the Stockbridges found themselves the confused objects of yet another power play, this time between Johnson and Shirley. Shirley felt that as commander-in-chief it was his duty to dictate the military use of Indians. Johnson believed that as head of the Six Nations for the expedition and as an expert in Indian affairs he should be primarily responsible. Although Johnson had authorized the raising of the Stockbridges, he seemed disinclined to use them after they got to Albany. But according to Shirley, Johnson forbade him to employ the Indians in the Niagara expedition. "And what makes this more extraordinary," Shirley pointed out, "is that these Indians are no part of the Six Nations, but chiefly inhabit within my own government, and are dependent upon it."[34]

Johnson thought Shirley's method of raising Indian companies was wrong. Johnson preferred to have a militia captain for Indian parties, thereby relieving the head warriors of unfamiliar administrative duties and freeing them to be interpreters for and guardians of their men. Shirley, on the other hand, put Indian officers in charge of a company, down to the ensign rank, a rank Johnson thought superfluous. Johnson also believed that Shirley was offering Indians more pay than was usual, abetting what he described as their mercenary temper. Johnson was further piqued by Shirley's employment of a shady Albany trader as an Indian agent.[35]

Several Stockbridge chiefs and about thirty warriors nevertheless decided to go with Shirley. According to Abigail Sergeant Dwight, whose disdain for her late husband's flock was beginning to show, each Indian who would go with the governor was offered $15 a month—"a fine pay for 'em"—plus a gun, a shirt, and other supplies. Cheeksaunkun was to be made an officer in the king's army for life, she said (though this was not true). As a consequence, she claimed, "the ordinary encouragement together with Drink had brought 'em into absolute determination to go." Abigail did not think that the Indians were worth the price, and yet she felt that Stockbridge would be safer if the Indians stayed in the township. She said further that the Stockbridges had recently proved in several situations that they would not fight other Indians if they could help it.[36] Subsequent events would fail to support such an observation, yet there may have been something in her assertion. Indians probably did prefer to fight non-Indians in the colonial wars declared by European monarchs they had never seen.

While William Shirley proceeded on his long march to Niagara, enlisting a hundred Oneidas on the way, the Stockbridges returned home to seek the enlistment of other Mohicans along the Housatonic and the Hudson. The call presented problems for the Scaticooks. Some of them now held pacifist convictions, and Kent authorities had prohibited the Scaticooks from going to Stockbridge. When the head man got his people together he found that none of them wanted to go to the Stockbridge conference, so he and one other Indian went after notifying the nearest justice of the peace of their intentions. After several days of conferring, the Scaticook chief declined to commit his men to enlistment with the Stockbridges.[37] His decision may have been based on religious conscience and on the fear of leaving his own town vulnerable. But at least two Scaticooks—and baptized Moravians at that—joined the military before the year was out.[38]

The Stockbridges assembled a company and left in time to join Shirley's army on August 12 at its encampment between the Mohawk River and Wood Creek. Progress toward Niagara bogged down, however, so the campaign had to be abandoned in late September, partly because the Indians realized that it was too late in the season and requested leave to return home.

The Stockbridges were lucky that they had not chosen to go with William Johnson. After beginning construction of Fort William Henry at the southern tip of Lake George, Johnson sent a force of one thousand men to meet a French and Indian detachment coming to impede his progress. Leading the English contingent was Ephraim Williams, Jr., and old Mohawk chief Hendrick. Failing to send out any advance or flanking scouts, Williams marched his men headlong into an ambush, and he and Hendrick fell dead from the first enemy volley. The panicked militia fled back to Fort William Henry, where Johnson rallied the men to drive back the pursuers and capture their leader. Then two hundred relief militiamen stumbled onto the retreating enemy and gave them a thrashing. But the day's events cost the lives of about two hundred English and forty Mohawks.

The Stockbridges were also lucky to be living in Massachusetts and not with their kindred in Pennsylvania. On the evening of November 24 more than a dozen Moravian missionaries were either shot or consumed by fire in a raid by hostile Delawares on the Gnadenhutten communal house. A few missionaries, along with their Indian converts, escaped or hid in the woods while the hostile Indians burned the entire mission to the ground. Most of the refugee Indians, thirty-five Mohicans and thirty-eight Delawares, relocated with their brethren at Bethlehem. The rest decided that it was now prudent to join their comrades in the Wyoming Valley. But there they were in turn threatened by pro-French Indians who accused them of being English. Along with other scattered tribes the refugees applied to William Johnson for guns, bullets, and a small fort to defend themselves. Johnson instead arranged for the Mohicans to resettle with the Nanticokes and friendly Shawnees in their village at Otsiningo, near present-day Binghamton, New York. The Mohicans, including those who had left Gnadenhutten with Abraham and seventy-five who were scattered along the Hudson River from Fishkill to Albany, agreed and settled at Otsiningo in the early spring of 1756.[39]

That summer at his own fortified estate William Johnson entertained 196 Mohican men, women, and children. He promised to aid the Pennsylvania Mohicans until they could provide for themselves, and he urged them to actively join the English and the Six Nations in the common cause against the French. In front of some Delaware, Shawnee, and Iroquois chiefs, Johnson clothed and armed the men from head to foot and provided them with wampum, ammunition, war paint, and accessories for war. Three days later he decorated the Delaware and Shawnee chiefs and the Mohican sachem with medals. The gratified and impressed Indians responded that night with a war dance. Within a year, however, the New York Indians found that they were no longer suited to sustain themselves by hunting, and they asked the Stockbridges to take them in so they could better support themselves by making brooms and baskets.[40]

The Stockbridge Indians, meanwhile, continued firm in their commitment to the English interest and eagerly reenlisted for William Shirley. They decided that a blacksmith was needed in town to keep their arms in order during the war. An all-Indian committee found a blacksmith, granted him 50 acres as an inducement to settle in Stockbridge, and had Massachusetts confirm the arrangement.[41]

In late May, Jacob Cheeksaunkun, then a town selectman, was commissioned captain, Jacob Naunauphtaunk lieutenant, and Solomon Uhhaunauwaunmut ensign of a company of about fifty Stockbridges. This time excitement and money lured eight Indians from Scaticook, six of them Moravians.[42] Their instructions were to "proceed wherever convenient for annoying the enemy, taking prisoners and scalps, intercepting enemy convoys, destroying their cattle, burning their barns and magazines, £5 sterling to be given for any Indian or French prisoner or scalp."[43] Here again was a strong inducement for the Stockbridges to retain an Indian practice, but it was an encouragement diametrically opposed to the province's professed concern for "civilizing" natives. Pounds sterling were much more valuable and negotiable than the unstable colonial currency that had been offered during the previous war.

The Stockbridges met Shirley at Albany on June 10. They were immediately sent out with a party to track down enemy Indians who two days earlier had abducted a local farmer and his son.[44] Failing in this attempt, the Stockbridge company then headed up the Hudson to a fort at Saratoga, from which they reconnoitered enemy movements along the Lake George and Lake Champlain waterways. In mid-July two Stockbridge scouts reported the sobering news that great numbers of French were now at Crown Point, and the woods thick with their Indian scouts. Some of them had spotted and chased the Stockbridges. On the way back they crossed the tracks of two or three hundred of the enemy and followed them south along the western shore of Lake George until the tracks divided. The French were inching closer to English territory.[45]

William Shirley in the meantime had been recalled to England, and the Stockbridges temporarily returned to the direction of William Johnson. The succeeding commander-in-chief, James Abercromby, didn't know what to do with the Indian company. He followed Johnson's advice to divide it into smaller units under militia officers, specifically those of Robert Rogers's rangers, which would scout and scour the woods. Rogers took a fancy to the Stockbridge Indians, and the partnership evolved into a popular guerrilla force, creating the characters that would later be romanticized by James Fenimore Cooper.

But Rogers Rangers, including the Stockbridges, were far more earthy than Cooper's noble woodsmen and savages. Rogers himself had become a soldier as an alternative to going to jail in New Hampshire for passing counterfeit money. Through the intercession of the New Hampshire governor, Rogers was allowed to work off his punishment by raising men for the war. Rogers and the men he picked had a knack for woods fighting, and they subsequently had a way with Indians that starchier military types lacked. They dressed lightly in buckskins, and their weapons were firelocks, tomahawks, and scalping knives. When William Shirley commissioned Rogers to recruit men for an independent ranger company, they were offered the same £5 sterling that the Indians received for every enemy prisoner or scalp obtained.

Rogers assigned thirty Stockbridges under Naunauphtaunk to one of his lieutenants, who added some of his own men to Jacob's company and sent them to Fort William Henry. The rest of the Indians under Cheeksaunkun accompanied Rogers and his brother to Fort Edward. The Scaticook Indians were among them, and in between a few uneventful reconnoitering missions they found time to write home. At least one of them was involved in a skirmish but escaped unharmed. Five other Stockbridges joined a New York regiment under Col. Thomas Fitch.[46]

One evening during the second week in August, sixteen of Naunauphtaunk's men and five provincials set out to scout the new French fort at Ticonderoga. They guided their boats northward on Lake George all

Robert Rogers, commander in chief of the Indians in the Back Settlements of America (October 1776). Courtesy of the Library of Congress.

night and by the next evening were camped near a mountain not far from Ticonderoga. The following morning Jacob marched his men up a hill overlooking the fort. Leaving their provisions with three of his party, Jacob and the others moved down for a closer inspection. They found two paths leading south from the fort's advance guard, and Jacob sent two of his men to determine where the smaller path led. A little later an enemy group approached along the larger path, and Jacob retreated with his men a short distance into the woods. They let the group pass while they lay hidden. Presently three stragglers came into view. The opportunity to earn some scalp money was too good to pass up. Jacob ordered his people to fire. Two of the three fell, and Jacob led the dash to their bodies. Coming upon them, he discovered that one was not dead, so he buried his tomahawk in the side of the man's head and left it there. The French would know that the Mohicans had carried the war to their territory.

After Jacob and another soldier removed their victims' scalps, the party divided, taking separate routes to an agreed upon rendezvous. When they regrouped they found that one Indian and one New York militia sergeant were missing, possibly lost or captured, the enemy presumably having been alerted by Jacob's ambush. Returning to the hill where they had left the provisions, Jacob's company discovered that one of the Indians who had stayed behind, an old man, had wandered off.

Jacob's men scouted Ticonderoga and found that the numbers there were greater than the combined English forces at Fort William Henry and Fort Edward. The next morning the party returned to the boats, where they remained until an hour before sunset, waiting for the cover of darkness and hoping that the missing men would reappear. The certainty of discovery demanded that they wait no longer, so after leaving provisions behind for the others they pushed off.[47]

Three days after their return to Fort William Henry, Naunauphtaunk and his men joined Robert Rogers's corps for a raid into Canada to destroy enemy harvests and livestock. They did not return until September 22, but apparently were able only to reconnoiter and to bring back one family as prisoners.[48] During the rangers' absence Captain Cheeksaunkun had arrived at Fort Edward with twenty-two Indians to scout the Lake George–Lake Champlain area. They returned within a week and reported to the new commander-in-chief, John Campbell, earl of Loudoun, that the French fort had only half the men reported earlier by Naunauphtaunk. While in the area, Cheeksaunkun more than matched Naunauphtaunk's trophies by bringing back two French scalps, one of them an officer's.[49]

After Rogers Rangers returned from their Canadian jaunt, the two Jacobs and about thirty Stockbridges remained at Fort Edward for scouting duty during October, encamped in huts on an island in the Hudson River outside the fort.[50] On November 1 Loudoun left Fort Edward for Albany in the company of the Mohicans and some of the Six Nations, marking for the Indians, at least, the end of the 1756 campaign. For one Indian, the son of a Moravian Scaticook, it was the end of the war. He died outside of Albany, from either a wound or disease.[51]

When it came time to settle accounts a few days later, there was some confusion over how much was due the Indians. Shirley's generosity may not have been matched by those who succeeded him. On paper the company had nearly £1,000 coming to it. Jacob Cheeksaunkun had reportedly received most of it, but the movement of Indians in and out of the service made strict accountability difficult. One of the Scaticooks, for example, had deserted and was lying low in Stockbridge.[52] Company clerk John Wauwaumpequunaunt couldn't be located to compile the list of names and length of service for the muster roll, so Loudoun angrily ordered the clerk's own name struck from the roll.[53]

Cheeksaunkun spent three months trying to straighten out the arrears, complaining to William Johnson at one point, "if this be the way . . . that we are served by our brethren we have no reason to join them any more."[54] Wauwaumpequunaunt, apparently declared unqualified as clerk, received only a fraction of what was said to be his due. Jacob claimed further that three or four of his party had not been paid, and that the Indians who had enlisted in the New York regiment for five months—but actually served seven—had not received a penny.

As the captain, Cheeksaunkun was accountable to his men. Besides putting him to a great deal of trouble, he said, "my soldiers find fault as if they suspected me of dishonesty, which name I never had before. But because I have not received it [the money] therefore I could not pay the soldiers as they expected by agreement. There were also eight guns lost of the Indians property, which they expect I answer, but if I must pay that and the arrears that remain unpaid of the wages it will leave me worse [than] when I begun. If I cant be help'd in this matter I shall go very heavily into the war if called for, but if set right shall go with all cheerfullness and delight."[55] Johnson finally promised that Jacob's complaints would be addressed, and Cheeksaunkun accepted his word.

Every time Jacob and his companions visited Johnson, they received a keg of rum, to the detriment of Christian temperance.[56]

When the young Stockbridge men returned home in the fall of 1756 they found a visitor, one whom some of the Indians may have had for a playmate years earlier, the charming daughter of Reverend Edwards. On a Monday Esther recorded in her diary a "visit among the poor Indians, which excites in me a great concern for the poor creatures' best interest." At her father's fortified home she confessed on one of her several sleepless September nights, "Almost overcome with fear, last night and Thursday night we had a watch at this fort and most of the Indians came to lodge here. Some thought they heard the enemy last night. . . . O how distressing to live in fear every moment."

The town's vulnerability once again discomforted the genteel. "This place is in a very defenceless condicion," Esther noted, "not a soldier in it, the fighting Indians all except a very few gone into the Army, many of the white people also, and this is a place that the enemy can easily get at, and if they do we cant defend our selves. 10 Indians might with all ease distroy us intirely. There has been a number seen at about 30 miles distance from this place." Predestination offered no comfort as a philosophy, and she stated flatly, "I am not willing to be butchered by a barbarous enemy nor cant make myself willing." She wanted to shorten her visit, but her father insisted that she stay for another month. So, Esther concluded, "I must tarry the proposed time and if the Indians get me, they get me, that is all I can say."[57] Esther eventually returned home safely. Within a year her father and the rest of the Edwards family would also be considering a move, but under different circumstances.

In the autumn of 1757 Princeton University notified Jonathan Edwards that he had been nominated as its president. Edwards, however, did not wish to leave Stockbridge. Despite frontier living, wartime anxiety, and the duel with the Williams clan, he had found relative inner peace there and plenty of time for cosmic contemplation. According to Esther, her father spent thirteen hours a day in his study. So far, he had written several books, including *Freedom of the Will*. In a long letter to Princeton's trustees Edwards cataloged the handicaps that he thought should disqualify him from undertaking the school's presidency. There would be the disruption to his family as well, not to mention possible financial loss if he were unable to sell his Stockbridge property. (He had just received free, albeit extralegally, an additional three acres of river meadowland from an Indian widow in gratitude for kindness shown during her late husband's sickness.) [58] More worrying to Edwards was the possibility that the Princeton post would interfere with his theological expositions, which he described with enthusiasm. Not once did he mention his obligation to the Stockbridge Indians; indeed, he did not mention the Indians at all. [59]

But decisions of this religious magnitude were not always left to the individual, not even the likes of Jonathan Edwards. He agreed with the suggestion of the Stockbridge church members to submit the matter for consideration to a council of ministers, who would meet at Stockbridge. But, he confided in Esther, "I know I cant live at Princeton as a President must on the salary they offer." He then revealed part of the motivating force within the Stockbridge mission, which was not always divine: "Deac. Woodbridge is a cunning man and an eloquent speaker; he will shine to his utmost to influence the council by his representation, and perhaps by influencing the Indians to make such representations, before the council as will tend to persuade them that its best for me to stay. . . . Not only has Mr. Woodbridge and others a friendship for me and calling to my ministry, but it is greatly against their temporal interest for me to leave them." [60]

When the council met in Stockbridge, however, it quickly overruled Edwards's objections and voted to have him assume the Princeton post. Young Samuel Hopkins reported that when the council announced its decision Edwards "appeared uncommonly moved and affected with it, and fell into tears on the occasion, which was very unusual for him in the presence of others." But these were not tears of joy and gratitude. Edwards expressed to the council his amazement that the ministers "could so easily, as they appeared to do, get over the objections he had made against his removal." [61]

Edwards nonetheless yielded to providential will and accepted the job. A little more than two months later he again yielded to providential will when he reacted adversely to a smallpox vaccination and died at Princeton, before his family had a chance to join him. Shortly after Edwards's departure, Samuel Hopkins had taken the opportunity to scold the Stockbridge Indians for what he characterized as their current lack of religious enthusiasm. He told the parable of the sower, comparing them with the bad ground upon which the seed fell. Hopkins said that all the good people in America were asking whether the word sown among the Indians was fruitful. He told them that angels descended from heaven to observe them and to report on their progress. Christ was also watching them. But what could be said about the Indians? Didn't they forget what they heard at meeting and never think about it afterward? Though they once seemed to flower from God's word, hadn't they yielded to temptation, and didn't their lusts and wickedness cause that flower to wither? Weren't their hearts as hard as rock and turned away from Christ?

One might legitimately have asked Hopkins in turn how well the seed had been nurtured if the sower spent many thirteen-hour days in a study, writing abstruse books. Of all the minister's rhetorical questions, perhaps two seemed most cogent to the Indians in light of recent events: "Have not some of you grown worse and worse while the word has been sown among you, rather than better? Are you not worse than you would have been, if you had never heard the word?"[62]

The Stockbridge congregation was eager to obtain David Brainerd's brother John as a replacement for Jonathan Edwards. Brainerd was a Presbyterian and an aspiring missionary who had learned the Delaware tongue. This knowledge and his relation to David would certainly have made him attractive to the Indians. The English families—and there were eighteen of them now—also wanted Brainerd, most likely because the bulk of his support as missionary would come from the Society in Scotland for Propagating Christian Knowledge, not from themselves. Timothy Woodbridge, Joseph Woodbridge, and Samuel Brown formed a committee to woo Brainerd, but despite their efforts he chose to devote his attention elsewhere.[63] The Stockbridge Indians' religious fields would lie fallow for a year and a half.

10

LOVED
AND
LOATHED
IN
THE
ARMY

Regardless of whether angels would have found the Stockbridges worthy
of enrollment in heaven, Massachusetts deemed their men quite acceptable for military enlistment. Though they saw little action during 1757,
the earl of Loudoun had found them of great use during the 1756 campaign, and he sought to expand enlistments by including Connecticut
Mohegans. Loudoun had been supplanted by Gen. James Abercromby,
but the effort to raise both tribes for the 1758 campaign continued. In
January the Stockbridges got a signed agreement for raising fifty privates,
a sergeant, an ensign, a lieutenant, and a captain. This time, though, the
Indians had to supply themselves with arms, blankets, and incidentals,
but they were advanced $500 toward that end.[1]

On April 12 William Johnson held a conference with the Stockbridges
and the Mohawks, during which he urged the Mohicans to alert kindred
tribes to be in readiness to join him. The Stockbridges complied and
sent word to other villages, including that of the Connecticut Mohegans,
several of whom had been serving with Connecticut troops and Rogers
Rangers.[2] By late spring there were enough Mohicans and Mohegans at
Fort Edward to form three companies of Indians for Rogers Rangers.
The British planned a major move against Canada, with Ticonderoga as
the first target, and wanted as many Indians and rangers as possible to
reconnoiter and to harass, scalp, or capture the enemy. Jacob Naunauphtaunk was soon promoted to captain of Cheeksaunkun's old company,

while Cheeksaunkun headed another company of fifty-two privates and a new set of junior officers.[3]

Rogers Rangers served as advance scouts and skirmishers for an army of sixteen thousand which would march that summer from Fort Edward to Lake George to begin its assault on Ticonderoga. Rogers designed informal uniforms for his men—buckskin knee britches, green coats with silver buttons, and green berets. Lord Loudoun and his successors, however, wanted the Indian rangers to dress Indian style, both to terrorize the enemy and to save money.[4]

Jacob Naunauphtaunk and his men had been in military pay since early February, and they accompanied Rogers's men on raiding ventures around Ticonderoga and Crown Point throughout the early spring. In May, the woods, hills, and swamps between the Hudson and Lake Champlain were humming with guerrilla movement on both sides. On the fourth of that month Naunauphtaunk with eighteen other Stockbridges and one ranger lay in wait opposite Ticonderoga, watching three approaching boats that carried an enemy woodcutting party of about fifty. Seventeen were in the first boat, and as soon as it landed Jacob's men surrounded it and took ten prisoners, while the other boats fled. Seven of the captives resisted, and as a result lost their lives and their scalps. After threading their way through enemy territory, Jacob and his men returned with their trophies four days later to Fort Edward.[5]

Late that month Jonas Etowaukaum, now an ensign in Naunauphtaunk's company, was returning south from another scout of Ticonderoga with twenty or so Indians, including Aaron Nimham, and four rangers. A party of about forty Canadian Indians meanwhile was returning north to the fort after scouting English positions. They came upon the Stockbridges' tracks about six miles below Ticonderoga and stopped to await their return. Before long Etowaukaum and his men walked into the ambush. Jonas and twelve Indians managed to escape and get back to Fort Edward, but two Indians and two rangers were killed. The other two rangers and seven Indians were taken prisoner, among them one Mohegan and Aaron Nimham.[6]

Nimham and at least one of the rangers were carried to an Indian village twenty-five miles above Montreal. Another Stockbridge and a Mohegan were taken to Quebec, sold as slaves, and put aboard a French man-of-war bound for Cap François, Haiti. Arriving there in late summer, they were again sold and assigned to hard labor. Within a few months a friendly Spaniard advised them to try to escape to Monte Cristi in the neighboring Dominican Republic, where they could probably find an English vessel. The two managed to steal a gun, some ammunition, and two large knives and slipped into the woods around late January of 1759. It took them thirteen days to negotiate the thirty-eight miles to Monte Cristi, where an English ship afforded them passage to New London, Connecticut. On February 23 they breathed free, crisp New England air again.[7]

While these Indians were in captivity, the English and colonial army prepared for the assault on Ticonderoga. By the second week in June 1758, Rogers Rangers had been sent on a final scouting and mapping expedition. Rogers, one of the Jacobs, and fifty men, mostly Mohegans and several Stockbridges, rowed down Lake George in whaleboats and landed on the east side of the Ticonderoga River. Rogers sent a lieutenant with about a dozen Indians and rangers to scout the French fort while he and three others climbed a nearby mountain to make maps. Jacob, with the rest of the Indians and several rangers, waited in the woods not far from the boats. While there, Jacob's party was surprised by a volley of shots from a contingent of more than thirty Indians under a French officer. Believing the attacking force to be larger than it was, Jacob ordered his fellow Indians to make haste for the boats, and he called to the rangers to follow their example. The rangers did retreat, but much more slowly as they fanned out and fired back at the enemy. Their resistance enabled Rogers and his companions, who were about three hundred yards behind the Canadian Indians, to skirt them and join the others. But the slow retreat also allowed the enemy to encircle them all, and the rangers had to break through the noose to their boats. At the shore the firing was intense as the French Indians closed in on the rangers, who piled into the boats and rowed off. Five of Rogers's men were killed, three were captured, and Rogers was slightly wounded. The lieutenant and the men who had been scouting the French fort were returning to join Jacob's men when they heard the melee; they, too, decided to avoid the contest. Commanding general James Abercromby was furious with Rogers for beaching his whaleboats farther down the lake than ordered, thereby allowing their discovery and the capture of three men, who might give away detrimental intelligence. At the same time Abercromby reportedly implied that Rogers had led a cowardly retreat, though the decision to retreat was more properly Jacob's.[8] In his defense, had everyone retreated quickly as he suggested, five men might have been saved and none captured.

Ultimately, however, Abercromby destroyed his own campaign by wasting his superior numbers and firepower. For six and a half hours on July 8 he sent waves of men against formidable French defenses, and after suffering 464 killed, more than 1,100 wounded, and nearly 30 missing, he turned his army around to leave Ticonderoga still in French hands.

On the evening of August 1, while the disappointed and battered army was camped on Lake George, Aaron Nimham walked into camp with a fellow ranger and a colonial, having all escaped their Indian captors nearly two weeks before. They reported that English prisoners were ill-treated in Canada. They also reported—as the Stockbridge and the Mohegan refugee from the Caribbean would confirm—that Canadians and Indians alike were suffering a shortage of food. Nimham and his companions consequently believed that Louisbourg was vulnerable. They were right. Louisbourg had fallen to a successful British amphibious attack six days earlier. Nimham and his fellow tribesmen stayed with the limping army until September 12, then headed home to their families.[9]

British authorities decided to change commanders again. To command a planned invasion of Canada, Abercromby was replaced by one of the successful generals who had taken Louisbourg, Jeffery Amherst. The Indian men were hardly back in Stockbridge before Amherst camped near Sheffield on September 30. It was an occasion that called for a visit by some of the Stockbridges. King Ben, one of the Jacobs and his son, two other Indians, and an interpreter traveled the seven miles to see Amherst, probably to discuss the coming year's campaign. They dined with Amherst and returned for another visit the next day, accompanied by Ben's wife and daughters.

In Jeffery Amherst they met a stocky forty-one-year-old man with light wavy hair and a long English nose on a full face. The expression of inner amusement that gave a twinkle to his eyes in his portraits belied a hard, starchy, and rather pompous guardian of His Majesty's kingdom. Amherst was cut from British broadcloth, a disciplinarian who expected all of His Majesty's subjects to operate by the book, and Indians were His Majesty's subjects. Amherst's answer to the desertion and lawbreaking he would encounter among the provincial troops was a quick hanging or a liberal application of the lash. He attempted to outlaw alcohol for the army except in special instances and introduced in its place a decoction of molasses and spruce, known as spruce beer.

Given this approach to his fellow Englishmen, one can imagine Amherst's attitude toward the Indians. He loathed them. He perceived their temperament to be contrary to everything he held sacred: they responded to orders on their own schedule and chose to ignore others; they got

Jeffery Amherst. Courtesy of the Library of Congress.

drunk at posts or on their way to them; they brawled among themselves; they were rough and careless with their guns and would easily lose them to thieves or gambling adversaries and then ask for replacements; and just as they shunned women's work at home, they shunned it equally at military encampments. They resisted digging trenches or throwing up earthworks, cutting wood, and maintaining the fort. None of this lack of soldierliness was extraordinary, of course, since Indians were specialists. They could not be expected to wear themselves down with camp duty and then at a moment's notice go into the woods with light rations for extended periods. They were signed into the army to do what Indians were known to do, not for engineering or housekeeping. Judging by the Stockbridges' refusal to perform camp duty, the New England town experience so far had not converted them from native warriors to provincial militiamen.

Another of His Majesty's stuffy officers, Thomas Gage, viewed Indians—and the Stockbridges in particular—much as Amherst did. Gage became acquainted with the Stockbridges when he commanded the light infantry in Abercromby's army. In late 1758 or early 1759 Gage arbitrarily delayed four letters from Robert Rogers to the two Jacobs, asking them to meet him at Fort Edward to discuss enlistment for his corps.

Rogers did not share the British officers' opinion of the Stockbridges, and he wrote to Amherst about their desire to reenlist. But Jacob Naunauphtaunk traveled to New York in February to find out for himself whether the new commander wanted their services. Amherst did not answer Jacob directly, but wrote a letter for Jacob to deliver to Rogers, asking Rogers's opinion of the Stockbridges' service, under what terms they would serve, and whether they were worth these terms.

Gage in the meantime offered his opinion of the Mohican heroes: "These Indians were last campaign so great a nuisance to the army and did no manner of service. Some people say they were not properly managed. I own myself ignorant of the management that is proper for those gentry; can only say that neither orders nor entreatys could prevail on them to do service, always lying drunk in their hutts, or firing round the camp."[10] Amherst replied, "I know what a vile crew they are, and I have as vile opinion of those lazy rum-drinking scoundrels as any one can have; I shall however take them into His Majesty's service for the next campaign, to keep them from doing mischief elsewhere, and as I am in hopes we shall be able to act offensively and successfully, they may be of more service than they have hitherto been. The French are afraid of them, and tho' they have but very little reason for it, it will be right not only to keep up their terror, but to increase it as much as we can, . . . and I shall for that reason engage as many of them as I can for the ensuing campaign." In a postscript Amherst added "that the great warriour Capn. Jacobs marched off to Fort Edward without taking the letter to Major Rogers, as he was directed to do." Amherst had the letter forwarded to Rogers, and two days later the general expressed his unflattering estimate of the Stockbridges to the British secretary of state, William Pitt.[11]

Their previous lack of compensation had apparently left an impression on the Stockbridges. When Naunauphtaunk met with Gage at Albany, Jacob refused to go farther north until Robert Rogers came from Fort

Edward to satisfy him with an agreement on the terms of service. Rogers also wrote again to Cheeksaunkun and to Uncas of the Mohegans, asking them to raise their companies. Gage later told Amherst that "Mr. Jacob has given me some hints that money must be advanced him to raise his people, which I am by no means inclined to grant him." This news did not endear the Stockbridges to Amherst: "Capt. Jacobs has behaved just like himself and all the drunken good for nothing tribe. I hate them all, but as things are, they may do some good by doing mischief, of which we have a great deal to do, to be at par with the French." [12] Robert Rogers, however, told Amherst that both Jacobs' companies would be very useful and would amply repay the government's expense.

Amherst went to Albany to gather his forces and equipment, and he expected the Stockbridges there by April 28. Naunauphtaunk arrived a few days late with his company of twenty-five Indians, two of his sons among them. Six Scaticooks had joined Jacob's company, to the chagrin of the Moravian missionaries, who in vain advised them against it. According to the Moravians, some of the Indians were leaving because they were greatly in debt to colonials and others were simply confused, lost sheep straying from the Moravian ethic. Five of Jacob's company were boys. Amherst discharged one Indian, probably for being too old or too young in the general's estimation. Nine of the Indians had no guns, and two others had guns that didn't work. The general ordered that they be outfitted and their equipment accounted for, so that "we may be able to keep some check over those kind of gentry." He added four non-Indians to their company and finally got them off to Fort Edward on May 9, when he wrote to a colonel there: "Capt. Jacob's drunken crew did not quit this place as soon as I ordered, but they are at present all out of town, and I hope will arrive sober to you; the Captain promises great things." [13]

Late in May, Cheeksaunkun arrived in Albany with thirty followers, four of whom were boys. They were short five guns and three of those they had were not working. Ten of Jacob's men had decided to follow William Johnson, who was on his way to attack Fort Niagara with hundreds of Iroquois. Three of Jacob's company had decided to stay home. Amherst wanted the company to leave for Fort Edward on May 26, but, he complained, "Rum put it out of their power to walk." And though Jacob promised to leave with his men the next day, they instead spent the day recovering from a drunken brawl that had nearly killed one of them. About halfway to the fort Jacob and "his mirmidons," as Amherst called them, left two more men behind, who were then chased by some lurking French Indians.[14]

Amherst quickly learned that the Stockbridges were not his sole headache. The rangers were not ideal soldiers either, and the general claimed not to give the least credence to their intelligence reports. He described them as "the most careless, negligent, ignorant corps I ever saw. . . . M. Rogers is a good man, but I must rub his corps up, or they are worse than nothing."[15] The same day that Cheeksaunkun's men were nursing hangovers, Amherst noted with regret in his journal, "The provincial troops deserted most shamefully."[16] Amherst had reason to be out of sorts, since he was a month and a half behind William Pitt's schedule for moving against Canada. By the middle of June he had gathered seven thousand men at Fort Edward, only to march fifteen miles to Lake George, where he spent another month building a fort close to the ruins of Fort William Henry.

On the night of July 4, Jacob Naunauphtaunk set out in three whaleboats with thirty men, including his two sons and a few rangers, to scout Ticonderoga and to avenge the blood of some New Jersey men who had been killed in an Indian ambush. Three days later, Jacob's party was discovered in broad daylight in enemy waters in a narrows below Ticonderoga. Several canoes of enemy Indians appeared in pursuit, and as Jacob directed his men toward shore the two forces opened fire. Two English soldiers and a Stockbridge were killed. The whaleboats were slower than the canoes, which closed swiftly on Jacob and his men as they reached shore at the base of a steep mountain. Jacob was among those providing cover fire while the rest scrambled up the mountain. Just as he and one of his sons were being hotly chased and fired upon, they became separated. Two days later ten half-starved members of the party, one of them a wounded Indian, made it to the British encampment, and about five more straggled in the following day, but Jacob was still missing. Amherst's comment on their misfortune was that "they all deserved to be taken for setting out in their boats in the daytime instead of the night." He ordered some of the colonial troops to instruct the remnants of Jacob's company in British military discipline, "how to form, and to enforce silence among the men and obedience to their officers, &c."[17]

For two days in a row Amherst sent a detail of Rogers' Rangers with several Stockbridges, some light infantry, and a few decoy fishing boats down each side of Lake George, hoping to draw the enemy into a skirmish and pick up any additional survivors from Jacob's company. The first day they encountered one survivor on his way back to Fort George. On the second day Rogers and his men routed twenty canoes filled mostly with enemy Indians, but not before a sergeant was killed and an Indian wounded.[18] By mid-July there was still no sign of Jacob Naunauphtaunk. His son was grief stricken and wanted vengeance on the enemy. Then on July 17, under a flag of truce, a French party arrived at the English camp and announced that Jacob and four other Indians had been captured and carried to Montreal. The rest presumably either had been killed or were unaccounted for, and the Stockbridge Indians believed that Jacob was as good as dead.[19]

Preparation for a grand flotilla assault against Ticonderoga intensified as the rainy summer lengthened in 1759. On a cool and cloudy July 21 the rangers and the Indians finally led the way onto the lake, ahead of seven thousand men and heavy artillery. At Ticonderoga the English forces paused and girded themselves for four days as the French welcomed them with their own heavy artillery. Unbeknownst to Amherst, the fort was manned by only four hundred men, who abandoned it on July 26 after trying to destroy it. The French plan was to yield Lake Champlain by giving up Ticonderoga and Crown Point, and then to fall back to more defensible Canadian posts. By July 31 Amherst had inherited two damaged but reparable forts without much of a struggle, and he decided to spend two months rebuilding them.[20]

While Amherst's men were refurbishing the Crown Point fort, Brig. Gen. James Wolfe on the Saint Lawrence River was engaging the French as he closed in on Quebec. To ensure that Wolfe received his messages, Amherst sent one via a solitary ranger following a roundabout route. But the general also sent two British officers accompanied by Jacob Cheeksaunkun, his sergeant, and four other Stockbridges, one of whom was probably Naunauphtaunk's eighteen-year-old son, John, on a riskier, more direct journey.[21] Naunauphtaunk's son naturally wanted to go on this trip, which was to include stops at several Indian villages under French influence, in case he could learn something about his father. Amherst reportedly offered a handsome reward to those who volunteered to take the more hazardous way to Wolfe. In addition to a truce flag they were to carry a large wampum belt from Amherst urging Indian neutrality. The tribes who accepted his proposals were to take their answer to Wolfe. Amherst's attempt to get his message through to Wolfe under a truce flag and possibly under escort of French Indian allies failed. When the emissaries approached Canadian territory, a hunting party of Saint

Francis Indians captured them and took them to the French commander-in-chief, General Montcalm.

When Jacob and his men set out to scout Ticonderoga in early July, Solomon Uhhaunauwaunmut and two ranger officers were with another scouting party of twenty-seven about sixty miles below Crown Point. They spotted a birch canoe containing a keg of powder and some bread tucked away in a creek that fed the lake. After hiding in an encirclement, they settled down for a long wait in the soggy woods. Around eight o'clock on the morning of August 23 three Canadians and six Indians with two English captives came in sight. Spotting tracks, two of the enemy Indians stayed with the prisoners while the others moved warily toward the canoe. When they were within range, Solomon's company opened fire. The Canadian party returned the fire and began to run. In the excitement two rangers were wounded by their own men. One English captive broke loose from the Canadian Indians and ran toward the rangers, but the other was unable to escape. The rangers pursued the Canadians a short distance but had to give up the chase, fearing that the three French sailing vessels on the lake just below them would hear the firing. Solomon's men had killed one Indian and believed they had wounded two others. They took the dead one's scalp, a significant trophy since it belonged to the Indian who had captured the now-free soldier.

Solomon and his men took the canoe, and when they returned to their own vessel the French ships were sailing toward them with the wind at their backs. The rangers rowed furiously and outpaced the French, arriving back at Crown Point that same afternoon.[22] The Indians, proud of their mission, fired their guns and raised the scalp yell for the fort to hear; Amherst sourly retorted, "and a very great noise for a very little they have done." Most likely he was upset with the Indians for having opened fire too soon, thus allowing the enemy Indians to escape. Nor was he happy with the rangers' performance, especially wounding their own men.[23]

Amherst's pique escalated on September 10, when a letter informed him that his emissaries to General Wolfe had been captured.[24] The general apparently cared little about Cheeksaunkun and the Stockbridges, but he was incensed that two British regular officers had been taken by Indians while carrying a truce flag. His anger and frustration with the Indians led him to authorize an expedition that Robert Rogers had long advocated for his rangers—an attack on the Saint Francis Indian village about halfway between Montreal and Quebec.

This would be a treacherous adventure. French boats reigned over much of Lake Champlain, and three forts guarded the Richelieu River as it flowed from the lake's outlet. The raid would take place more than fifty miles beyond the northernmost fort, deep into enemy territory. Thirty days' rations and extra equipment were issued to nearly two hundred handpicked men, among them about twenty-five or thirty Indians, about half of whom were from the Stockbridge companies. Their destination was supposed to be known only to Rogers, but word soon spread that a Canadian Indian village was the target.[25]

Seventeen whaleboats set out on the night of September 13. Ten days later the raiders had gotten only as far as Missisquoi Bay, the northernmost portion of Lake Champlain. Their delay was caused by sickness, which had struck the group shortly after they left Crown Point. First to become ill and head back was a Stockbridge Indian. The contagion spread quickly; within a short time forty men had to return. Less than two weeks after leaving Crown Point, Rogers had lost about a fourth of his little army to sickness or accidents, many of them Indians. At most fifteen Stockbridges and Mohegans out of the two Indian companies were able to continue the journey.

Nearly a week of hard rain and continual wetness made the rest of the journey miserable. At Missisquoi Bay the company went ashore and attempted to hide the boats and provisions. Rogers left two Indians there to watch the supplies from a distance, while the rest of the army marched toward the village with what sustenance they could carry. If enemy scouts came upon the cache, the Indian lookouts were to overtake Rogers and alert him. After trekking two days northward through soaking swamps, the party turned to see their two Indian allies following them. The boats had been discovered. There was no returning the way they had come, and there would be no supplies for the return. Nine more days of tedious marching lay ahead if they pressed on to Saint Francis. They would have to elude the French parties that would be scouring the country for them in both directions. And if they made it to Saint Francis, they would have to march overland 150 miles through rough terrain to return to Crown Point.

As a contingency plan Rogers sent seven men back to Crown Point to ask Amherst to send supplies to the ruins of an old fort on the upper Connecticut River. After they hit Saint Francis, the rest of the rangers would return in a southeastern arc to this rendezvous where supplies would be bearably closer.

After nine rugged days, the rest of the men reached the Saint Francis

River and drier terrain, fifteen miles from the Indian town. Rogers and two officers moved forward at night to scout the village and found that the Indians were preoccupied with a dancing feast in a council house. He and his cohorts returned to the main force, where they lay still until the next morning. In the early hours of October 6 they moved close to the village and encircled the perimeter. According to Rogers, about six hundred scalps were draped on poles around the town. A half hour before dawn they struck. Half-dazed Indians woke too late to stop the thrust of bayonets or the thud of tomahawks. Some never woke at all. In the screaming, yelling confusion that followed, some of the Saint Francis villagers were clearheaded enough to reach their canoes at the river, only to be cut down by a shower of ranger musket balls. Others rallied in a building and held off the attack briefly, until ranger torches made the house a flaming sepulcher. By 7 A.M. it was over.

Rogers claimed that at least two hundred enemy Indians had been killed. French accounts, however, listed only thirty dead. According to a Saint Francis tradition, one of the Indians from the Stockbridge company warned a Saint Francis child during the night, and though some of the tribe did not heed the warning, most hid in nearby woods.[26] Rogers's men put torches to the village, including the church, and may have believed that the other Indians died in the fire. If the Saint Francis tradition is correct, however, the question remains why the hidden Indians did not counterattack, since their number probably equaled that of the rangers. Perhaps the survivors were mainly women and children.

The major reported only one ranger killed—a Stockbridge Indian. Saint Francis tradition also holds that when the tribesmen returned to the village to look for friends, they found an unbaptized enemy Indian named Samadagwis still alive on the side of a road and killed him with one stroke of a hatchet to his head.[27] This may have been the Stockbridge Indian mentioned by Rogers.

The rangers captured twenty women and children and liberated five English captives. Three of the village's structures held corn, and the wise rangers stuffed their packs with it. Others loaded themselves with booty. After eight days on the return march the corn gave out and the weather turned cold and stormy. Rogers's men divided into several parties, hoping to increase their chances for forage or game on the way to the rendezvous. For many, the return became nightmarish. One detachment was discovered by the enemy and twelve of them killed. Several starved to death. Some had to sustain themselves on bark, leaves, and their own leather accouterments. Two groups who found the mutilated remains of dead comrades satisfied their hunger on the bodies. When Rogers and some of the men finally reached the appointed spot, where they expected to find provisions, they found nothing but a smoldering camp fire. One of Rogers's own lieutenants, who had been waiting with the supplies, after only a few days assumed that the raiders were not returning at all. He had left with the supplies only hours before Rogers arrived.

The men's despair was inexpressible. Rogers and three others hastily built a raft and pressed on another fifty miles to a post farther south on the Connecticut River, leaving nearly sixty starved and weakened men in the woods. Five days later, on November 4, Rogers and the trio dragged themselves into the fort, and Rogers began directing relief back to the others. A party of seventeen, most of them Indians, had come back toward Crown Point on a more direct but more dangerous route down Lake Champlain, and by November 7 they had arrived at Otter Creek. Among them were three captives from Saint Francis and a freed colonial woman. One Indian ranger went ahead of the others and arrived at the Connecticut River fort that afternoon, as the season's first snow fell. Apparently confident that the rest of the party would soon follow, he did not tell Amherst about those left behind for several hours. Nettled again by Indian vagaries, Amherst quickly sent out a relief party. Most of the party was brought back the next day, but a few were now missing.[28]

The mission was finally over. New England rejoiced more in its success than in the fall of Quebec to General Wolfe, which had occurred five days after Rogers's expedition set out. But forty-nine lives had been lost since the day of the Saint Francis raid, and more than thirty of these were the result of starvation. The lieutenant who had failed to wait at the rendezvous was court-martialed and removed from the service.[29]

While Rogers was on his epic raid, the bulk of the Stockbridge Indians had remained behind at Crown Point. Amherst was trying to organize his army for an assault on a French fort at Ile-aux-Noix, but the season was getting late, and the Stockbridges were undoubtedly restless to return home for the hunting season. On September 24 Amherst grumbled, "I had the Indians mustered . . . a most idle worthless sett and if their Capts. were not taken prisoners I should send them all to their homes. If I send them on a scout they all come back in twelve hours sick, and here they will do nothing but eat and drink except forced to it."[30]

Indeed, the Indians' susceptibility to disease was another good reason for them to leave the crowded fort. Sickness was reported at several posts by this time of year. The unsanitary conditions of military life made communicable illness a greater killer and debilitator than battle. On October 11, when Amherst finally got his army afloat, twelve Stockbridge Indians who were sick stayed behind. Amherst, becoming increasingly irked, left orders that any sick Indians who recovered while he was gone were to busy themselves working on the fortifications. Twelve subsequently were sent home after refusing to work around the fort.[31] Among these were six of the Scaticook men. The seventh died after a bout with what was termed the bloody flux, most likely dysentery. After contracting measles at Fort Edward at the outset of the campaign, he had been constantly sick. His wife was told that he saw the end coming, prayed often, and stayed cheerful until he died.[32]

Nine days after these Indians headed home, several Massachusetts soldiers and more Stockbridges reported sick. The Stockbridges requested leave to go home, since Amherst had abandoned his intended assault due to stormy weather and the campaign was over for the year. The general grudgingly let them take minimal supplies and one boat to carry their sick across the lakes.[33] Not admitting to himself that he had given in to their request to go home, Amherst recorded in his journal that "to save unnecessary expenses to the government and our provisions I got rid of the Indians. Sent them to Albany to return to their own homes, 43 in number and as idle good for nothing crew as ever was."[34]

The general's ire may have abated somewhat when the remnant of the Stockbridge company straggled in ten days later from the rangers' successful raid on Saint Francis. Following their recuperation at the fort, the Stockbridges left for home on a cold and snowy day late in November, nearly a month after their fellow tribesmen had gone. Joining them were Cheeksaunkun's sergeant and Naunauphtaunk's son, who had been released as part of a prisoner exchange with the French.[35] The Stockbridges could return home with lighter hearts now that two of their important young men were back. They knew that Cheeksaunkun was alive, and the Indian grapevine undoubtedly had relayed to John Naunauphtaunk that his father was alive.

11

FINISHED
COLONIAL
BUSINESS,
UNFINISHED
INDIAN
BUSINESS

When the Stockbridge heroes returned home they found a new minister. Stephen West was another Yale man and an old-guard Calvinist, long on Christian exactitude and discipline, short on Christian compassion. He seems to have had only one special credential to head the Indian mission. He, too, had married one of the Williams girls. On June 13, 1759, West became pastor, according to him, "with the delightful agreement and unanimity of the inhabitants." As was expected of them, the Stockbridges granted him 50 acres.[1]

The returning men had little time to acquaint themselves with the pastor. It was late into the hunting season, and consequently they extended their stay in the woods. Many of the men were still pursuing game in mid-April, which delayed somewhat their entry into the 1760 campaign. One of the Jacobs' sons was in Scaticook on May 1 to recruit, but the Indians there had already signed with militia companies.[2] Jeffery Amherst, despite his disdain for them, wanted the Stockbridge Indian companies back, and he wanted them at Albany by May 1 ready to march at a moment's notice, with their guns in good working order. Any Indians who in his view were too old or too young, too weak or too lazy should stay home.

Since the two Stockbridge captains were still prisoners, Amherst offered Solomon Uhhaunauwaunmut command of their two companies. If the men conformed to his stipulations and proved useful, he promised to reward them better than ever before—an interesting gesture from someone who considered the Indians worthless. With some advance cash as incentive, Solomon, who spoke fluent English, agreed to the terms.[3]

Solomon and forty-one of his men arrived a week later than promised, and it was the end of May before Amherst could prepare them to leave Albany. They were to join Rogers at Crown Point for some disruptive sorties against three French forts in the north. Rogers was eager to move, and at his suggestion the commanding officer at Crown Point warned every post between there and Albany to keep rum away from the Stockbridges. By May 30 they had started on their way when the Indian officers realized that they had not received their commissions in writing from Amherst. Their experience with pay problems probably convinced them to go no farther without their commissions.

When Amherst learned of this recalcitrance he was furious. He considered it mutinous and ranted in letters to Rogers and the Crown Point commander that the Stockbridges were scoundrels, that he didn't have the least use for them, and that if not for Rogers's high regard for them he would send them packing. He also admonished Solomon for allowing his men to mutiny: "I myself told you that as soon as time would permit, I should send them [the commissions] after you, and how after that you could permit such behavior is astonishing." Amherst was probably stung more by the Indians' reluctance to accept an English officer's word than he was by the insubordination. He wrote Solomon that if he and his men were not at Crown Point by the time they received the letter, he "hoped" they would march there immediately. If not, he would consider it a breach of orders and would "punish the delinquents as they deserve."

Amherst nevertheless sent the commissions by a lieutenant, who found the Stockbridges still waiting. The general knew that Indians were necessary, but he disliked having to admit it. When soldiers from Crown Point once failed to locate an enemy Indian canoe reported to be nearby, Amherst commented that the Indians were the best people for such searches: "if those from Stockbridge would make themselves any ways useful, it would be upon such services, for I have no opinion of them for anything else." Despite his stern warnings to Uhhaunauwaunmut, Amherst maintained a diplomatic facade with the Indians. He signed his message, "Your friend."[4]

When the Stockbridges had not arrived the first of June, Rogers felt that he had to begin his mission anyway. A group of soldiers wandered into camp, claiming that the Indians had either deserted or gone off to join William Johnson, who was organizing several hundred Iroquois for part of the thrust against Canada from the west. Amherst discounted their report, because he doubted that the Indians had spirit enough either to desert or to travel that far west: "Depend upon it they are loitering on the road and will sometime or other come into Crown Point."

The general assumed that Rogers would not want the Stockbridges anymore, and not wanting them to lie idle at Crown Point, he told the commander there to have the Indians camp on the other side of the lake, away from the rum. Amherst thought they might guard against enemy scalping parties: "I do not mean that they would act offensively against them, on the contrary I dare venture to say, they would run away even at the sight of a fresh track." But he thought that the Stockbridges could at least report sightings of the enemy so that the English could organize a chase: "If you send a ranging officer and some few white folks with them they may be of some sort of service. Keep them employed and do with them as you think best."

Amherst was wrong. Rogers did want the Stockbridges to follow him. When the general learned this he grudgingly yielded to Rogers's judgment: "I wish they may overtake the party, as Major Rogers is very fond of them, otherwise I think he would be as well without them." [5]

Solomon and his men did not arrive at Crown Point until 10 P.M. on June 3, two days after Rogers and his men had set out on the lake. There were only thirty Indians now. The other twelve probably did follow William Johnson, since there were twelve Mohicans among the more than thirteen hundred Indians Johnson assembled on Lake Ontario later that summer.[6] Of the thirty at Crown Point three were sick and two stayed behind to care for them. Smallpox had again plagued the posts over the winter months, and several rangers at Crown Point had died. The commander tried to keep the deaths a secret, lest the provincials fail to reenlist. Naturally, the Indians were the last to know.[7]

The Stockbridges learned something else at the fort. A ranger sergeant who had recently escaped from Montreal reported that Jacob Cheeksaunkun was in irons on board a French ship and that Jacob Naunauphtaunk was in difficult straits. Naunauphtaunk had attempted to escape the previous fall, but after suffering frostbite had to return to his captors at Montreal. He eventually lost three of his toes.[8] Now the Stockbridges had a genuine motive for helping to subdue Canada and its Indian allies.

The Stockbridges finally caught up with Rogers a couple of days after a battle in which several rangers had been killed or wounded. After waiting for more provisions from Crown Point, the combined force of 220 moved their boats down the lake and then marched at night toward the strategic French fort Saint John. Finding that fort too stoutly defended, the men headed for the next one, Saint Thérèse, nine miles north. They reconnoitered Thérèse at eight o'clock in the morning and found it lightly manned. Most of the occupants were busy carting hay into the fort from nearby fields. Rogers and some of his men crept close to the fort while other detachments silently approached the surrounding farmhouses. As a hay wagon entered the fort, Rogers and his men rushed forward before anyone could close the gate. The French were caught completely off guard, and the rangers took the fort without firing a shot. Nor was a single shot fired as the others rounded up bewildered civilians in their homes. Seventy-eight were caught in the net, but fifty-one were women and children.

Rogers freed the women and children, who were to make their own way to Montreal, but the men were to be taken to Crown Point as prisoners. Before leaving, the raiders put the torch to the fort, the houses, the hay, the supplies, the wagons, and the boats, except what was needed to cross the Richelieu River.[9] Because of the need to avoid French pursuers and to transport prisoners, the return trip took a week. By June 23 the rangers were in Crown Point, and the next day the Indians were in their own camp across the lake.[10] The Stockbridges had cause to celebrate. Four days earlier more than 120 captives had arrived at Crown Point from Montreal, among them Jacob Naunauphtaunk.[11] On June 27 these former captives continued south toward Albany, and Jacob was probably among them, since he was in no shape to rejoin the rangers. His condition must have been very poor in fact, and his fellow warriors had only temporary reason for joy. Within six months Jacob was dead.[12]

Sometime in July or early August, forty more Indians joined the English at Crown Point. On August 16 the army fanned out on the lake with six hundred rangers and seventy Indians in whaleboats a half-mile in the lead. This army was the centerpiece of a three-jawed vise closing on Montreal. Amherst's army was moving east with William Johnson and his Indians from Lake Ontario down the Saint Lawrence; a second army was sailing up the river from Quebec; and the Crown Point army was approaching from the south via Lake Champlain and the Richelieu River. By 10 A.M. on a rainy August 20, the rangers and light infantry touched ground on the east bank of the river within sight of a fort on Ile-aux-Noix. Not one soldier had fallen from enemy fire yet, but a gale two days earlier had churned up violent waves that split some of the boats and sent several rangers to the bottom of Lake Champlain.

For the next four days the army laid siege to the fort, and by August 25 a contingent decided to try to capture the French ships anchored in the river north of the island. The rangers, the Indians, and some light infantry stole unnoticed through the woods along the east bank, pulling three artillery pieces with them, and planted themselves opposite the vessels. The first shot from a small cannon was a lucky one, cutting the main ship's anchor cable. A westerly wind blew the ship toward land and into the attackers' hands. The other ships headed down the river toward Fort Saint John, but after two miles they all ran aground. The rangers raced to the ships. While some rangers provided cover fire from land, others swam out to one of the ships and climbed on board, brandishing tomahawks. The crew surrendered quickly, and those on the other ships soon followed suit.

The besieged island's main means of communication and supply was now cut off. Two days after the ships were captured, the French abandoned Ile-aux-Noix, slipping away at midnight. They began a hurried march to Fort Saint John, leaving behind a few sick comrades. The next day the English forces took possession of the island, and the following day Rogers and six hundred rangers and Indians were in hot pursuit of the fleeing enemy. Rogers's men traveled twenty miles in boats by night, and when they arrived at Saint John at daylight they found the fort in flames. Rogers had orders to proceed no farther, but the enemy's smell was in his nostrils. The rangers moved ahead and captured a couple of stragglers, who told Rogers that about fifteen hundred French and a hundred Indians had left the fort only ten hours earlier and planned to encamp halfway to Montreal. Many of them were ill, however, and they probably would not reach the encampment before afternoon.

The enemy's scent was even stronger now. Two hundred rangers remained at the fort to guard the boats and supplies. Rogers and the rest, including the Indians, overtook about two hundred of the French rear guard and charged to the attack immediately. The intense onslaught broke through the guard, which flew to join the main body. The rangers nipped at their heels, hoping to take on the entire enemy army. But the French forces retreated over a portable bridge across a river to their fortified camp, and then pulled up the bridge behind them. A body of water and common sense halted the rangers. In the pursuit only two rangers had been killed and two wounded, and according to Rogers, they had lessened the enemy considerably more. They turned back and rejoined their own army, which was arriving at Saint John.[13]

By early September the three English jaws were closing on Montreal. While the rangers and the Indians had been chasing the French, Amherst's army and William Johnson's Indians had subdued their target forts along the Saint Lawrence. During the evacuation of Fort Lévis near Montreal, most of Johnson's Indians wanted to invade the fort for the plunder and a few scalps. Amherst refused to allow it, despite Johnson's warning that without this concession the Indians might leave the army. The general still refused, and nearly 700 Indians marched home. About 170 remained for the assault on Montreal, among them the twelve Mohicans. Amherst later rewarded these Indians with silver medals for their faithfulness to the English standard.[14]

On the night of August 29, three days after Amherst had taken over Fort Lévis, a few Indians from the French side arrived seeking peace. As evidence of their sincerity their peaceful intentions were put in writing by Jesuit missionary Jean Robaud and sent via their prized captive, Jacob Cheeksaunkun, now free to join his Stockbridge brethren. Little more than a week later, after the English army descended on Montreal, the governor-general of New France saw that war in North America was futile. On September 8 he surrendered the country to Great Britain. Two weeks after this, Amherst sent the Stockbridges home.[15]

Yet for some of the Indians in the Stockbridge company the war was not quite over. The Cherokees were still resisting peace in the Carolinas, and to help subdue them Amherst sent troops to South Carolina, including a few Mohawks and Stockbridges. The Indians started on this mission later than Amherst wanted, as usual, but they finally sailed from New York to Charleston in March of 1761. There they joined some Catawbas and Chickasaws to provide about seventy Indian scouts for the army in the heart of Cherokee country. The combined forces caught up with the Cherokees for a few skirmishes, but they were primarily effective in destroying several Cherokee towns and burning their crops and provisions. It was enough, however, to make the Cherokees sue for peace by midsummer.[16]

More direct to the Stockbridge interest was a score they had to settle with the Saint Francis Abenakis, who had captured Jacob Cheeksaunkun's party two summers before. One of Jacob's men was a former Saint Francis Indian, probably named Peter. He had joined the Stockbridges in about 1752 and had a Stockbridge wife and child.[17] When he was captured, the Saint Francis clan to which he had formerly belonged gave him the choice of returning to the fold or being punished as a wartime deserter. He remained defiant to his former tribesmen, so they killed him.[18] Jacob considered this a serious offense, and he demanded retribution. With William Johnson's endorsement and a victorious English army to back it up, the Saint Francis Indians were obliged to comply. After almost a year and a half of negotiations, the Stockbridges finally agreed to accept as a replacement an Indian slave in his twenties whom the Abenakis had purchased from another tribe. William Johnson and Father Robaud orchestrated the arrangements, and two belts and several strings of wampum sealed the agreement. Obviously, Christian influence had not yet affected this traditional method of restitution.

In the presence of Mohawks and other Iroquois, an Abenaki chief confessed: "We see the head of our Brothers the River Indians is bleeding, occasioned by the wound we have given them by the death of one of their Nation whom we killed, and therefore with this belt of wampum we take the axe out of their heads, and sink it in a rapid stream which shall drive it to the bottomless sea, that it can never again be found, and that all the past may be forever forgotten." Further, the Abenakis wanted Johnson to make their restitution known to all the Indian nations, "that they may forget what hath passed, and that an everlasting friendship may subsist between us and our posterity." Johnson agreed to comply with their wishes, admonished them for their past transgressions against the English, and helped restore peace between the two tribes.[19]

The Stockbridges shortly had occasion to repay Johnson through military service in the western Indian uprising called Pontiac's Conspiracy. At a conference in July of 1763 several Stockbridges offered to raise sixty men to help fight the western tribes. Johnson thought that under good officers the Stockbridges might be useful, especially because of "their implacable hatred . . . particularly to some of the Nations." He further believed that the Mohicans might attract some of the eastern Canadian Indians as allies. But since Jeffery Amherst was still commander-in-chief, Johnson had to seek his approval. Amherst initially dismissed the seriousness of the western troubles. In any case, he growled, "I would on no account whatever think of engaging the Stockbridge Indians, I know them to be a worthless tribe." Johnson reluctantly sent the Stockbridges home, thanking them for their offer.[20]

As reports of overthrown forts and killed settlers multiplied, Amherst became as inhumane as he believed the Indians to be. He asked a junior officer, "Could it not be contrived to send the small pox among the disaffected tribes of Indians?" When the officer replied that he would try to spread an epidemic with infected blankets, Amherst said: "You will do well to try to inoculate the Indians by means of blankets, as well as to try every other method that can serve to extirpate this execrable race."

Sending a relief detachment westward, Amherst ordered them to take no prisoners, but to attack the Indians "as the vilest race of beings that ever infested the earth, and whose riddance from it must be esteemed a meritorious act, for the good of mankind."[21]

Little of Amherst's tirade resulted in action, since autumn was rapidly approaching and the hostile Indians were drawing off to go hunting. Those under Pontiac were wearying of the siege at Detroit, and some were asking for peace. In November Amherst learned that he could return to England. He met with William Johnson at Albany for a final conference on the Indian situation. Stockbridges came and addressed Johnson, possibly renewing their offer to help. Johnson did not respond to their speech then, but in mid-February of 1764, after Amherst had left, Johnson asked the Stockbridges to join with other Indians he had raised to punish the western tribes. The Stockbridges offered their men for service, and Johnson immediately sent for them.

On March 12 twenty Stockbridge warriors arrived at Johnson's place with a letter from King Ben, the elders, and the councillors, asking Johnson "to take into your bosom our young men who go to war by your call. We pray our father to keep them from all bad practices and hear our father." The Stockbridge elders recognized the debilitating effect that continued war was having on the young men and on the tribe as a whole. Twenty was only a third of the number they had originally offered. At this time there were probably only twenty healthy men of fighting age among the Stockbridge Indians, since only thirty-seven of them were over twenty-one.[22] The earlier offer of sixty men likely was based on the assumption that they could enlist other Mohicans or allied tribes. But it is also possible that many Mohicans were reluctant to fight their grandfathers and younger brothers, the Delawares and Shawnees, who constituted the remaining hostiles.

By the time Johnson, his Indians, and the British troops arrived in the west the war was all but over, as one village after another submitted peacefully. The twenty Stockbridge Indians doubtless served more as diplomatic emissaries than as warriors when Johnson met with friendly and unfriendly tribes at Fort Niagara in July to arrange the peace.[23] Ten years of war, death, turmoil, and anxiety had passed since the first attack on the cabin at Stockbridge. Now that colonial business was settled, perhaps the Indians could pursue their own business.

12

THE

DOMESTIC

WAR

Another war had started about the same time as the one with the French. It was a class war and a border war of sorts, and the Stockbridge Indians were in the thick of this one, too. At the Albany Congress in 1754 they discussed not only military conflicts, but land conflicts as well:

> When the white people purchased from time to time of us, they said they only wanted to purchase the low lands, they told us the hilly land was good for nothing, and that it was full of wood and stones. But now we see people living all about the hills and woods, although they have not purchased the lands.
>
> When we enquire of the people who live on the lands what right they have to them, they reply to us that we are not to be regarded, and that these lands belong to the king; but we were the first possessors of them, and when the King has paid us for them, then they may say they are his. Hunting now is grown very scarce, and we are not like to get our livings that way; therefore we hope our Fathers will take care that we are paid for our lands, that we may live.

The New York governor, displeased that he had to entertain the Stockbridges in the first place, halfheartedly promised to look into the affair, but warned that "most of these lands . . . were patented when you were children, some before any of you were born."[1]

The events of the past had indeed woven themselves into knotty problems. The patents of which the governor spoke were grants to several individuals for land between the Hudson and Housatonic rivers, made in the second half of the seventeenth century by various New York governors. Through creative wording in the deeds and patent applications, tracts of a few thousand acres were enlarged to claims of several square miles. Aupaumut had complained about this practice a generation earlier. A handful of men claimed most of what are today Columbia, Dutchess, and Putnam counties. As the patent holders installed tenant farmers on the land, the Mohicans gradually learned of these manipulations. By 1755 about a thousand tenant families were scattered throughout the manorial claims.

The Stockbridge Indians also became aware that Massachusetts had made more than generous land grants northeast of Stockbridge to people who yielded their acreage for the Stockbridge mission. On May 31, 1759, while the Stockbridge fighting men were at Fort Edward, King Ben and one of his sons, Nimham, and a few others came upon Israel Williams surveying land in the woods along the Housatonic south of Pittsfield. When the Indians told him that he was surveying their land, Williams related a history of the grants. The Indians laughed, replying, "very pretty, the government pretend to give the Indians a township if they will come and settle together, and pay the claimers with the Indians' own land." They then prohibited any further surveying.[2] As a complicating backdrop to this whole scene, both New York and Massachusetts assumed jurisdiction over these lands, since the two colonies disputed their boundaries. Massachusetts and Connecticut were in an expansionist mood, and farmers and land speculators were eager to find soil more productive and less expensive than ground in the east.

A shadowy Sheffield character named David Ingersoll learned of the faulty title to land held by wealthy New Yorker Robert Livingston, Jr. Seeing an opportunity for profit, Ingersoll and some other schemers, including Abigail Sergeant's new husband, Joseph Dwight, by 1751 began urging the Massachusetts government to grant new townships on the western frontier. They also tempted the tenant farmers with visions of owning their own farms and encouraged friends and relatives to move west, assuring them that they would be Massachusetts landowners. Speculators and settlers soon showed interest, and some of the tenants rebelled against their landlords, Robert Livingston and John Van Rensselaer. The aspiring landowners were encouraged by Massachusetts's increased willingness to grant townships in the area. Several legislators were especially willing because they themselves were among the speculators.

Once again the Mohicans were being squeezed in the middle. While Joseph Dwight was in Sheffield in 1755 to arrange a survey of one of these new township grants, the Stockbridges protested. Dwight assured them that the government would pay them, but the Stockbridges had no reason to trust Dwight. The boarding school fiasco was fresh in their minds. Their mistrust was sound, because there was no guarantee that Massachusetts would win the boundary dispute with New York and be in a position to pay them. To protect themselves, the Indians began to sell land independently to settlers and manorial tenants. Speculators like Ingersoll encouraged such sales, since they helped undermine the New York landlords' claims to the territory.[3] The Stockbridges said later that they had offered John Van Rensselaer a chance to buy, since he was the inheritor of one of those extravagant patent claims. But he refused, fearing it might set a precedent for other claims against his domain.[4] The Indians subsequently sold all the land bounded roughly by the present-day Massachusetts western line and New York's Taconic State Parkway.

When these sales—illegal under provincial law—came to the attention of the Massachusetts legislature, the government decided to eliminate all the Stockbridge claims west of the Connecticut River with an offer of £1,200. By including the land between the Westfield and Connecticut rivers, Massachusetts would remove any lingering guilt and ward off any potential claims by descendants of refugees from King Philip's War. The legislature appointed Timothy Woodbridge chief negotiator, and he persuaded the Indians to agree to £1,000. Half this amount was to be forwarded as a down payment, but the sum instead was diverted to the war effort.[5] Throughout the war, therefore, the Stockbridges—not really satisfied by the £1,000 offer anyway—continued to sell the land. These sales gradually allied their interests with those of the settlers and rebelling tenants, who often had the Stockbridges agree in writing that they and their descendants would defend any potential claims against these lands.

The violence between the restless New England farmers and the possessive New York landlords escalated. The landlord's forces, which often included his faithful tenants, would evict a squatter or a troublesome tenant, tear down his hut, or burn his crops. The rebels retaliated with raids on the faithful tenants or on the landlord's outlying property. The landlord would turn to the Albany authorities to arrest the troublemakers, and the rebels turned to the Hampshire County authorities in Massachusetts—Joseph Dwight and his associates—to arrest the landlord's allies. Ephraim Williams, Jr., obtained blank militia commissions for some of the new settlers and rebels, using the growing war threat as an excuse to organize an armed body. When the Albany sheriff arrived with a posse to arrest the rebel ringleaders, the rebels arrested him instead.

Tempers grew heated in the spring of 1755. One of the rebel tenants who had been involved in the sheriff's arrest was shot and killed as he tried to escape through the roof of his house. This shooting heightened the conflict by giving the rebels another cause. Sometimes disguised as Indians and sometimes accompanied by Indians, the rebels conducted vigilante raids on loyal tenants' farms and mills, looking for anyone suspected of being involved in the killing.

Not even the onset of the French and Indian War stopped the local hostilities. On November 25, 1756, the Albany sheriff and another posse, said to be unarmed, again attempted to evict several tenants and destroy their houses. One of the tenants was apparently a good friend of Mohican John Van Guilder, who with two of his sons and another settler soon arrived on horseback at the tenant's place. The Van Guilder party was armed with guns, bayonets, and tomahawks, and Van Guilder threatened to kill some of the posse if they touched the house. The sheriff ordered his men to arrest them, and as the posse approached, the Indians gave a war cry. Van Guilder leveled his gun, shot and killed one of the posse, then fled with his sons and his friend. The sheriff's men quickly captured Van Guilder, one of his sons, and the settler, took them to the Albany jail, and put them in irons. It was rumored that Van Guilder's other son vowed to involve the Stockbridge Indians, to capture one of the posse dead or alive, and to burn down Livingston's house.

With the war and the uncertain Indian allegiances in the balance, the Van Guilder incident had larger implications. Fearing a vengeful raid by the Stockbridges, the New York governor wrote to the lieutenant governor of Massachusetts, describing the New Yorkers' version of the incident. He also asked Sir William Johnson to intercede in the affair. Timothy Woodbridge in the meantime petitioned the lieutenant governor to obtain the prisoners' return to Massachusetts for a trial. The prisoners remained at Albany, but a Massachusetts investigation concluded that the Indians had not been the aggressors and that their action seemed to have been in self-defense. However, the Stockbridges were urged to abandon any plans for retaliation.

William Johnson sent an urgent wampum message to the Stockbridges expressing great concern over the killing and the rumored threat against Livingston Manor. He hoped that the rumor was false and warned that the Indians' good behavior would do more for the jailed Van Guilders than interference. Part of his message may have struck the Indians as ironic: "It is very wrong of your people to interfere or take any part in any matters or disputes between the white people, for they have good and wholesome laws for settling all disputes and differences . . . among themselves."

King Ben's reply was polite: "We are very sorry for the unhappy affair of one of our tribe's killing one of the Kings subjects. . . . We neither think it our concern nor do we have a disposition to intermeddle with the controversies of white people." They were unaware, King Ben said, of any threats by Van Guilder's son. He assured Johnson that no Indian at Stockbridge had made any threats or "made the least motion of entering into a quarrel." "However," King Ben added, "as we hear the matter, we dont understand that the old man or his son made any attempt against any man, till those people that were turning the poor families out of doors undertook to make them prisoners, and if the old man made not any resistance we cant see what right there was of attacking him or any others that was in the highway in the peace of the King. . . . We cannot think well of Mr. Livingstons severe conduct to those poor people and we think it would be better for him to desist." As for Van Guilder, the Indians wished him to be tried in Massachusetts, "since he belongs to us and we shall be willing that justice may take place."

The tribe was concerned about the Van Guilders. Jacob Cheeksaunkun visited Johnson in January of 1757 to inquire about their fate, fearing that the men might be hanged. Johnson coolly replied: "The law must take its course. If they were not guilty of the murder they would be acquitted."[6] But the Van Guilders' fate became a cause célèbre among the Mohicans, and the tribe at Otsiningo also addressed the issue in a meeting with Johnson. By coincidence, a soldier was in jail, accused of having killed a Mohican somewhere between Albany and Schenectady. Johnson relayed this information to the Otsiningo Mohicans and assured them that if the soldier were guilty, he would suffer. He gave them condolences, blankets, and clothing, according to custom, to convey to the dead man's friends and relatives, and hoped they would let the matter rest. "I am very sorry for this misfortune," he blithely told them, "but there is no recalling the dead."

The Mohicans, having long memories, used the occasion to draw an analogy. Jonathan, the son of the Moravian Mohican Abraham, spoke for the rest:

> 'Tis now 9 years ago that a misfortune happened near Reinbeck in this province; a white man there shot a young man an Indian. There was a meeting held thereon, and Martinus Hoffman [a resident near Shekomeko] said "Brothers there are two methods of settling this accident, one according to the white people's customs, the other according to the Indians: which of them will you chuse? If you will go according to the Indian manner, the man who shot the Indian may yet live. If this man's life is spared, and at any time hereafter an Indian should kill a white man, and you desire it, his life shall be also spared." Brother, you told us . . . that when a man is dead, there is no bringing him to life again. Brother, we understand there are two Indians in jail at Albany, accused of killing a man; they are alive and may live to be of service, and we beg you in the name of the great king our father that they may be released. All we that [are] here present, among whom are some of their nations, are all much dejected and uneasy upon this affair, and do entreat that these people may be let free, which will give us all the highest satisfaction.[7]

The Mohicans gave Johnson a large amount of wampum to indicate the strength of their sentiment. That night Johnson, no longer cool or blithe, wrote to the earl of Loudoun and the New York governor about the Indians' concern for the Van Guilders. The next day Johnson told the Mohicans that he was certain those two men would do everything possible to secure the Van Guilders' release. The precarious position of the British military situation in 1757 and the delicate state of Indian allegiances convinced Johnson, Loudoun, and the New York authorities that "every thing should be avoided that might give umbrage to the Indians, and that in the present posture of affairs it was absolutely necessary that this request should be complied with." By summer the Van Guilders had been released without trial.[8]

The Van Guilder family, and possibly more of the Stockbridges, were involved in yet another fray the following May. The Indians recently had sold a huge segment of Livingston's claim to tenants and squatters in the disputed area. This brought Livingston out of hiding, but in company with the Albany deputy sheriff and a small army. Arriving at a rebel farmhouse, they found about thirty armed insurgents waiting. The deputy sheriff ordered them to break up, and a few timid souls did retreat. The rest retreated too, into the farmhouse, and they answered the deputy's orders with a volley of musket balls. In the following shootout several men were hurt, and two from each side later died from their wounds. The posse finally flushed the rebels but caught only five.[9] William Johnson was especially irked by the report of Indian involvement, having just procured the Van Guilders' freedom. He sent a strained diplomatic message to the Stockbridges, warning them to stay out of the feud, "least it breed ill blood and produce ill consequences which I should be sorry for."[10]

By the end of 1757 the Board of Trade in London announced its decision on the boundary line between New York and Massachusetts, which is reflected in the present boundary. But the actual survey would not take place for another ten years. Many residents of the two provinces, therefore, considered the matter open until the line was actually drawn. Others accepted the proposed line as inevitable, and for several years the area remained relatively quiet. Livingston had the best reason for being content, since the line would leave his claims intact within New York. But for some of the settlers, and for most of the Stockbridges, trouble had just begun.

In the spring of 1762 an announcement appeared in the Boston newspapers that Massachusetts was creating nine townships in the western territory. The townships were to be put up for auction, and the proceeds would go into the public treasury. This news came as a shock to the Stockbridge Indians. They had not yet been paid for two of the townships that the Dwight committee surveyed in 1755. The Stockbridges quite rightly felt that Boston was ignoring them. They therefore again appealed for justice to William Johnson. Two principal men visited him on April 10 with a message from King Ben: "Father, we think it hard to be so treated when we have helped to subdue the French and their Indians. Now the English think they shall need us no more. They are not willing to do us justice." Since the Stockbridges' complaints at Boston had been to no avail, Ben asked Johnson to advise the Indians and to write Gov. Francis Bernard on their behalf: "If the court at Boston are determined to use us in this manner, we are determined to carry our complaints to the king, not doubting but he will do us justice."

Johnson was noncommittal, but he suggested that the tribe send two or three of its most intelligent men to Boston to represent their case to Bernard. He further assured them that the king had recently instructed the New York governor to protect the Indians against land fraud. Before leaving, the two Stockbridges again entreated Johnson to consider their situation himself, lest they have to seek the king's justice in person.[11]

For the time being, the Stockbridges took Johnson's advice and appointed Jacob Cheeksaunkun and Johannis Mtohksin to carry their petition to the General Court. This time they had legal help, since the petition was not just a plea, but an injunction to stay the pending land auction until they could be heard. Two days after Cheeksaunkun and Mtohksin arrived in Boston, a joint session of the legislature heard their complaint. The Indians reminded the lawmakers that they had been promised payment for their lands before the war started, and they pointed out once again that many of their young men had fought and died for the English in that war as well as in previous ones. From their point of view, the settlers and speculators who purchased land from them at least acknowledged the Indians' rightful claim to it, whether the General Court recognized the transactions as legal or not. The current General Court did not seem to believe that the Indians had a rightful claim.

After hearing the Stockbridges' petition the court appointed a committee to investigate their claim. What investigation, if any, this committee conducted was spurious at best, for it reported the very next day that "there has not been sufficient evidence offered to support the Indian title to the lands."[12] The committee offered no evidence, however, to suggest that anyone else had title to the land in question. It also ignored all previous cases in which the province had satisfied Indian claims, as well as the General Court's recent law reasserting the validity of the premise on which such restitution was made. Instead, the committee labeled these earlier payments "gratuities," given to the Indians only "to prevent discontent and keep them quiet."

The committee nevertheless did suggest, since "it may be of importance to the publick to keep the Indians quiet and in good temper," that the Stockbridges receive a sum not to exceed £1,000, "although in strict justice nothing is due from the government to the Indians." The governor's council would agree to this proposal only if the Indians released "all claims to any of the lands of the Province to which they pretend a title."[13]

Despite all the rhetoric, the government was considering payment to the Indians, and that was what the Stockbridges wanted to hear. Now that the concept of payment had been established, they could debate the price. A thousand pounds for all their Massachusetts claims had not been satisfactory even in 1755. Since then, inflation, debts, legal expenses, and the possibility of having to reimburse settlers who had already paid the Indians for land had increased the asking price.[14] Jacob and Johannis, the latter being no stranger to real estate matters, apparently lobbied for more money. From 1750 to 1758 Johannis himself had paid more than £1,600 for almost all of northwestern Massachusetts west of the Westfield River, which he had purchased from other Indians, mainly Benjamin Kokhkewenaunaunt and Jehoiakim Yokun. Either Johannis was rich, or he was making such purchases on someone else's behalf, as Johannis could legally do under Massachusetts law. This silent partner presumably hoped to obtain title to the land when the legal climate became more favorable for non-Indian buyers. Mtohksin apparently did sell land to speculators, who resold the land to unsuspecting settlers, who would be holding useless deeds once Massachusetts bought the land from the Indians.[15]

A week after making the original offer, the government agreed to pay £1,500. Eight months later, after the deal had finally been closed and the deed signed by all the head men of the tribe, King Ben wrote to the governor, explaining extenuating circumstances. The General Court increased the final amount to £1,700. Now the Stockbridges were satisfied.[16] Massachusetts could well be satisfied, too, because for £1,700 it had obtained enough land to lay out nine townships of six square miles each, to be auctioned at the starting bid of £800 apiece.[17] In the final analysis, the political bluster about the government not owing anything to the Indians may simply have been a ploy to intimidate the Indians into keeping their price low.

By contrast, the Stockbridges maintained their integrity throughout this ordeal, repeatedly requesting that the settlers who had bought land from them be allowed to remain on it. Late in 1764, for example, King Ben and Johannis Mtohksin discovered that they had forgotten to exclude from the government transaction 2,500 acres they had sold to a farmer, who now stood to lose everything. The Indians not only refunded his money, they petitioned the General Court to allow him to keep the land anyway. The government stuck by its assertion that the purchase had been illegal in the first place, but it did compensate the farmer with 300 acres elsewhere.[18] If all prior sales produced such complications, then the Stockbridges may not have cleared much from the sale to the government.

The Stockbridges also had to negotiate with New York. The unsettled boundary and the questionable, extravagant, and conflicting patent claims resulted in the disputed land's remaining unoccupied for years. This situation created opportunities for squatters, who asserted their own right to some of the land. Normally the Indians would have been as upset with squatters as they were with the manor holders. But the squatters, mostly emigrants from Massachusetts and Connecticut, were aware of the conflicting claims and faulty patents. They knew that technically the Indians had a legitimate claim, so if the Indians demanded satisfaction, they paid them. The Indians, in turn, were probably grateful that the settlers at least acknowledged their claims, since the colonial governments and the land barons ignored them. Further, the Indians empathized more with the poorer, aspiring farmers than with the landlords. The farmers were using the Indian purchases as a means to their own ends, of course, and how much genuine sympathy they had for the Indians is questionable.

In late December of 1762, John Konkapot, David Naunauneekanuk, and other Stockbridge elders, then in their seventies and eighties, traveled a hundred miles to tell William Johnson how his "children of the Moheekunnuck tribe have many troubles and difficulties—by means of the conduct of the King's white subjects." They related the recent history of their land sales to the English, who wanted to create three townships just west and northwest of Stockbridge. But after more than a hundred families had settled there, John Van Rensselaer not only began displacing them by installing his own occupants, he also drove off at least one Mohican family who had lived on an unsold tract for many years. The Indian elders wanted Johnson to intervene on their behalf, since according to them neither Rensselaer nor his new settlers had ever purchased the remaining tracts.[19]

Down in the Highlands, meanwhile, several Connecticut emigrants who had been tending farms in disputed territory for decades combined forces with speculators to challenge some of the old patents. One patent dating from 1697 encompassed about 200,000 acres of territory claimed by the Wappinger tribe, whose more than two hundred members were scattered in wigwams throughout the southern portion of Dutchess County. Daniel Nimham's father and his grandfather had complained frequently to the patentee and his heirs about that patent. Tenants who settled under the landlords' claim often had to pay the Wappingers some restitution, which temporarily satisfied the Indians. According to the squatting challengers, however, the original patentee maintained to his dying day that he had never fully compensated the Indians for territory included in that patent.[20] During the war, after Nimham had moved his scattered people to Stockbridge, the New York heirs to this estate— Roger Morris, Phillip Philipse, and Beverley Robinson—asserted their claim and even extended it by nearly 5,000 acres. They installed their own tenants and evicted the Connecticut settlers. When the Wappingers returned they found new faces all over their land.

Seeking redress in New York was rather a different story than it was in Massachusetts. Even more than in New England, nearly every political office in New York was occupied either by a large landholder, by his relatives, or by his close connections, from the governor's office down to the surveyor's. Judges, attorneys general, lawyers, and assemblymen saw no conflict of interest in working on cases that directly affected them. For several generations these landed families had a financial interest in every aspect of New York colonial life. They controlled the fur trade, the slave trade, the agricultural trade, the mercantile trade, and the ships that made all of it possible. They owned mills, ironworks, stores, and farms. Their influence was awesome and pervasive.

But the land barons were not without challengers, and their methods of operation invited emulation, competition, and resentment. Others besides Indians had complained about their expandable land patents. William Johnson, explaining the postwar Indian unrest, told Jeffery Amherst that "it is notorious that they have been frequently overreached and defrauded greatly by persons taking up small tracts from a few Indians, whom they have often made drunk to bring them to their purpose, and have afterwards by false surveys &c, included in the pattents much more lands than were sold by the Indians, which they have not been able to discover until of late years, by seeing us settleing thereon, of all which I could give many examples."[21]

The small farmers and tenants who simply wanted modest farms for themselves also resented the manor holders' inordinate wealth. Aspiring merchants and speculators likewise wanted to carve out their own domains. The Nimham family, for example, occasionally became entangled with patentees and squatters alike in land competition.[22] The New England emigrant farmers made up in imagination and dogged determination what they lacked in wealth and power. Samuel Monrow, a long-term Connecticut squatter who had been thrown off the New York land during Nimham's absence, had improved his farm to a worth of £500. Naturally, Monrow was a principal challenger to the old patent claims. In 1764 he and his fellow squatters decided to join their interest with that of the Wappingers. What inspired them was the royal proclamation of 1763, which not only separated Indian territory from colonial territory, but also established the concept of inherent Indian right to the soil.

Daniel Nimham, whose family had moved permanently to Stock-bridge, joined with three other tribesmen to award Monrow power of attorney over their land affairs. Together they asserted the Indians' native right to the disputed ground and posted notice that anyone holding a lease or a title not granted by the Indians would be prosecuted. At least fifteen tenants signed leases with the Indians before the landlords started eviction proceedings. Daniel Nimham, as sachem of the Wappingers, represented the tribe, and indirectly those evicted. If their case failed in New York, the antilandlord forces then would have an excuse to take the whole matter to London, on the strength of the royal proclamation. The Indians, in turn, would benefit from legal help in presenting their case to the king, a strategy they had been contemplating for some time, since several of their appeals to William Johnson had met with polite but evasive answers.

At a hearing on March 6, 1765, before New York lieutenant governor Cadwallader Colden and his council the atmosphere was charged. Much was at stake, for a decision here could set a precedent. A victory for the Indians would bolster the Stockbridges' case against the Livingston and Van Rensselaer claims. It would legitimate the Mohicans' grievances concerning the many unfair land deals of the previous century. It would also sanction the integrity of their tribal tradition as an honest record of past transactions. Moreover, it would reassert the Indians' native rights as original owners of the soil. For the squatters, the tenants, and the speculators, a victory would mean the opportunity to negotiate with the Indians for farms carved from the land barons' claims. Such a victory for the Indians thus would threaten every owner of large estates founded on old patents. And that included everyone of consequence in the government and the private sector of New York.

Daniel Nimham, speaking in English, presented the Wappinger claim to the territory based on the ancient tribal heritage. Then he interpreted the proceedings for the other Indians, while Monrow and the representative for the patent heirs debated the issues. The Indians, somewhat intimidated by the imperious air of the council, were taken aback when Beverley Robinson produced a curious Indian deed for the area in question, dated 1702 and signed by several Indians. Although one of the old tribesmen recognized the names, he recollected no transaction that the deed described. Samuel Monrow was allowed to examine the deed only briefly, but he could see flaws and possible fraud in it even so. For one thing, the deed did not specify any amount paid to the Indians. For another, it was not officially recorded at Albany. Finally, if any transaction with the Indians actually had occurred, it would have been five years after the patent was issued. The law required that a license to purchase Indian land be obtained before a patent could be issued. From the Indians' and settlers' point of view, they were facing either a fraudulent deed or one wangled from Indians who had negotiated without the whole tribe's knowledge. And all of the persons listed on the deed—Indians, purchaser, and witnesses—were long since dead.

The Indians were urged to go home and tell their fellow tribesmen to forget their alleged claim, since Mr. Robinson obviously had a deed for their land. Nimham replied that he wanted to hear from the lieutenant governor first. After conferring with his council, Colden declared that the deed was good. He told the Indians to trouble the government no more.[23]

Not only did the Indians lose their case, two days later they lost their guardian. Monrow was arrested and jailed without trial under £2,000 bail for about a year. The landlords and officials considered Monrow to be an agitator, and they asserted that only William Johnson had a right to represent the Indian interest. Keeping Monrow in jail was an attempt to silence the Indians and to prevent that first legal domino from falling against all the other flimsy land patents. Monrow appealed to Johnson, claiming that he had been imprisoned "to stop me from going to England as I intended with the Indians, in order that they might be reinstated in their rights."

Worried landlord Roger Morris wrote to Johnson when he learned that the Nimham associates were applying to Johnson for aid. Sir William walked a tightrope. Without impugning the claims of Morris and the other landlords, he replied that "an Indian claim may be verry just tho' otherwise pronounced by law, the opinion of which is founded on a pattent, which may have been obtained in a most iniquitous manner and cannot be supported, whilst any virtue or sound policy remains amongst us." Nevertheless, Johnson said, he had not given any assistance or encouragement to the Indians or the settlers in this affair, and he hoped it might be concluded to Morris's satisfaction. Johnson's "invariable rule" was that whenever a claim was presented by Indians who were of "little consequence or importance to his majesty's interest, and who may be considered as long domesticated, . . . such claim unless apparently clear, had better remain unsupported than that several old titles of his majesty's subjects should thereby become disturbed."[24]

This was the respect that Mohicans had earned by accepting Anglo-American civilization and Christianity, and by fighting and dying for the

English. Johnson would defend an Indian claim to his utmost, but only if the offended tribe were threatening. Eight years earlier he had used his influence to free the Van Guilders because he valued the Stockbridge Indians as English allies. His current views echoed the words of King Ben: "Now the English think they shall need us no more. They are not willing to do us justice." A last-ditch appeal to the new royal governor of New York, Henry Moore, in which the Stockbridges offered to remove the illegal squatters, failed to produce any substantive support.[25] The Indians, however, with encouragement from their colonial allies, were preparing to carry this domestic conflict farther—several thousand miles farther.

13

LEARNING
THE KING'S
LIMITATIONS

Plans had been under way since the summer of 1765 to finance a trip to England to represent the Wappinger case. After Samuel Monrow went to jail, Daniel Nimham hired a Connecticut lawyer named Asa Spalding, who proposed a sort of lottery. Nimham would issue tickets at £5 apiece to the emigrants and rebellious tenants in Dutchess County, or anyone else with an interest. When his territory was recovered, Nimham would give each ticketholder free and clear title to 250 acres of it, for an additional payment of £20. Spalding hoped to sell five hundred tickets. If Nimham won his case, the Wappingers would retain half their claim.[1]

The outcome of this proposal is not known, but in May of 1766 the Stockbridges arranged a deal with William Gregg, Jr., a well-to-do New Englander. Nimham, Jacob Cheeksaunkun, Solomon Uhhaunauwaunmut, and John Naunauphtaunk would serve as tribal delegates to the king for all the New York claims. Gregg would lay their case before George III and other officials. Since they expected to spend a long time in England, Gregg further agreed to support them there for three years, providing £30 New York currency a year and "meat, drink, apparel, lodging and washing fitting gentlemen," and to pay for their trip home. Gregg, in turn, would receive a deed or, for ten shillings a year, a 999-year lease to a twelve-mile-square tract of land of his choosing. Solomon, John, and Jacob (but not Daniel) also would act as Gregg's servants while they were in England. The four Indians signed the contract with Gregg on

May 29, binding themselves to a penalty of £10,000 for default.[2] That same day they petitioned William Johnson for letters of recommendation to the king, and Johnson apparently accommodated them.[3] Inherent in both of the schemes for financing the trip was the assumption that the appeals would be successful. Nowhere was there any mention of what the Indians' obligations would be if the plans failed, but no doubt the colonial backers covered themselves.

Within a month the chiefs, accompanied by their wives, set sail from Boston.[4] Gregg and the Indians brought along two interpreters. One, Bartlet Brundige, was a rebel tenant farmer from Dutchess County, who had jumped bail after being arrested for participating in a tenant riot.[5] Their need to leave New York may have been greater than the Indians' need for interpreters, since both Daniel Nimham and Solomon Uhhau-nauwaunmut spoke English.

Five weeks later the delegation landed at Weymouth in southern England. The Stockbridges would see things in England that later filled many an hour of talk at home around the hearths and the council fires, in the sweat lodges and at the meetinghouse. British officialdom was gracious. At Weymouth they were taken to visit William Pitt's family, and one of the Indians made a speech to Pitt's eldest son. That evening the guests were taken by coach to a new assembly hall, where they attended a ball. The Indians were delighted with the dancing, and entertained with a dance of their own, complete with war whoops. One of them then surprised the crowd by performing the English hornpipe.[6]

From Weymouth the visitors traveled to Salisbury, where they stayed for two days, walking its medieval streets and viewing England's tallest cathedral spire. The local inhabitants were impressed by the Indians, as reported in the *London Chronicle*:

> The sachems are remarkably tall and stout, and one of them six feet and a half without shoes, of a brown shining complexion, and bold manly countenance, dressed in the Indian manner. The women, who are ladies of fashion, are of the same complexion with the men. They appeared very modest and decent in their behaviour, and seemed remarkably delighted with a few trinkets, such as earrings, necklaces, &c, that were presented them by some ladies who went to pay their respects to them. They all came here without scrip or purse, having spent everything in their voyage; but were nevertheless very hospitably received, of which they seemed truly sensible, and desired their interpreters to return their most grateful thanks, and to signify that

they should ever remember the goodness and generosity of the English nation, with whom they had long been in friendship, and held in the greatest esteem.[7]

The statement about the Indians' lack of funds implies that their business agreement with Gregg was not common knowledge. He may have fostered this notion, in hopes that the British government would pay for their diplomatic venture. Similarly, the colonials may have advised the Indians not to speak English, as is suggested by the mention of the interpreters in the *Chronicle*'s account.

From Salisbury it was off to London. On August 2 the delegation arrived on the northwest periphery of London, where they put up in a large house in Marylebone. There was a pleasant park nearby with trellised walks, hanging lanterns, and two-story open-air kiosks, where one could dine and listen to a band and, on occasion, singers. For the next few weeks, while Gregg presumably laid the groundwork for presenting the Indians' case, the Stockbridge natives would be both entertained and entertainment. The papers published their social calendar: The Indians "will be at the Marybone Gardens to hear the music and view the new fireworks"; "Marybone Gardens; by order of the Indian chiefs and their ladies the musical entertainments will be continued every evening."[8] On August 18, a grand entertainment was held at the White Hart in Watford, farther northwest of London. It was a celebration of the Watford church's new organ, donated by the earl of Sussex, who attended with several nobility: "A fine concerto was prepared, and a grand ball was given to the ladies. The Indian Chiefs were present, and sung several of their warlike songs."[9] The next day the *Daily Advertiser* noted: "This evening the Indian Chiefs are expected to be at Vauxhall Gardens."[10]

For this treat the Stockbridges crossed the Thames by ferry to Lambeth Parish, where steps from the riverside led to the garden entrance. In the eighteenth century Vauxhall Gardens was *the* place for several levels of London society to mix, often in masquerade, to see and to be seen. It was a privately owned park with landscaping, goldfish ponds, statues, promenades, gazebos, music pavilions, and boxes for listening and dining in posh fashion.[11] Boston and Albany were nothing like this, and even Marylebone was a second-class imitation. The Indians gave Vauxhall one more interesting attraction. But for those who missed them at Vauxhall, Marylebone Gardens assured its patrons "that the Indian Chiefs will not leave Marybone till their affairs are settled by the government."[12] In the meantime, music and fireworks would continue at the gardens; admittance was one shilling.

The government soon perceived that the Indians were becoming carnival attractions. The *London Chronicle* notified its readers that "the very scandalous proceeding of making a shew of the Indian Chiefs and their ladies is put an end to by authorities." [13] Meanwhile, the real purpose of their trip came to the attention of George III, who apparently did grant them an audience. [14] He was concerned, though, that they had come to England without his consent or a recommending letter from any colonial governor. With England's postwar debts, the government was loathe to support additional expenses from the colonies. [15] Again it seems that Gregg was not publicizing his contract with the Stockbridges.

At the end of August the Lords of Trade reported their findings to the king, focusing on the Wappinger claim. In their opinion there were grounds for further investigation into the facts, especially since "frauds and abuses in respect to Indian lands . . . have so notoriously prevailed and been complained of in the American colonies in general, and in this colony in particular." Moreover, the lords stated, "the conduct of the lieutenant governor and council in directing prosecution against the guardian, agents and protectors of these Indians . . . does carry with it the colour of great prejudice and partiality, and of an intention to intimidate these Indians from prosecuting their claims." [16] During the first week of September, the four Indians consulted with the Lords of Trade in person. While in the area, they were given a tour of Saint James's, including the armory. The officer of the guard served them wine and food in the officers' guard room. A couple of weeks later three of the Indians and one of their wives attended church services in Kensington and enjoyed a tour of Kensington Palace gardens. [17]

By the second week in September the Indians had finished their business with the government. The earl of Shelburne had taken their affairs under his wing. After consulting with the king, the earl informed the Indians that he would instruct Governor Moore to give their case serious consideration and to find a just and speedy solution. Shelburne would later send the same message to William Johnson, urging him to afford "these distressed people" his "countenance and protection." [18]

Another two weeks passed before the Stockbridges and their escorts could arrange for passage back to America. On Sunday, September 28, they were awaiting passage on a merchant vessel at Gravesend, down the Thames from London. That morning they joined a large crowd at the church where Pocahontas is buried. The *London Chronicle* described the bizarre scene that occurred. After staring at the Indians for a while, a woman in the congregation began to imagine that she had been brought to the church to be sacrificed. Screaming "You have scalped my husband! You have scalped my husband!" she jumped at one of the chiefs and struck at him three or four times. She then turned on one of the wives and scratched her face badly, before falling into a fit. Hearing the commotion, the rest of the crowd panicked and stormed out of the church, thinking it was on fire or collapsing. Only the minister remained calm, later scolding his parishioners for their irreverent behavior. Four days after this incident the travelers boarded ship and left frenetic England behind. After a tedious passage of more than six weeks, they arrived in New York in mid-November.[19]

The Indians learned that in their absence land feuds had again been ignited and that the landlords had fanned the fire. A match had been struck well before, however, by the Sons of Liberty. Their protest against the British Stamp Act sparked volatile antiestablishment feelings, which spread to the rural areas and rekindled the farmers' confrontations with the land barons. Samuel Monrow's son organized Dutchess County tenants and squatters in late November to demand concessions from the landlords and to harass or throw out their recently installed loyal tenants. A terrified Beverley Robinson fled from his country mansion to New York City. It was after a similar sortie in April of 1766 that Bartlet Brundige had been thrown in jail to keep Samuel Monrow company. Monrow had soon escaped during a general jail break, and Brundige had jumped bail by traveling to England. As soon as the ship landed in New York Brundige went into hiding.[20]

As the Stockbridge chiefs sailed toward the king in late June, the king's troops had been trying to tame a few hundred of Nimham's rebel neighbors. The farmers, also calling themselves Sons of Liberty, defied even the redcoats. One leader ordered his men to "kill every son of a bitch."[21] At a skirmish near the Connecticut line they did manage to seriously wound three soldiers before the insurrection was crushed. The British, under Thomas Gage, retaliated by destroying their farms and forcing their families to seek refuge in Connecticut.

While the Dutchess County rebels were dodging the redcoats, their northern counterparts were harassing the Livingstons, the Van Rensselaers, and their tenants. The landlords reportedly were upset by the Stockbridges' envoy to the king. Knowing that they had never equitably purchased the Indians' rights, the landlords were trying to intimidate the settlers into signing leases, thereby strengthening their own claims. At the behest of the Van Rensselaers, the Albany sheriff formed a posse of about three hundred men to arrest rebel tenants and troublesome squatters who had purchased land from the Stockbridges in the Austerlitz area. Word reached the rebels that the force was coming and that it would destroy the settlement.[22]

About sixty farmers gathered at the house of one of their leaders, Robert Noble. Some crossed the border from Massachusetts, including at least one Stockbridge Indian, Johannis Mtohksin, who said that he went out of curiosity. The posse, which included some of Livingston's and Van Rensselaer's sons, approached Noble's house on horseback. About fifty yards from the house a hastily built rail fence blocked their path. The farmers stood on the other side, holding clubs and barrel staves. The sheriff ordered Noble to take down the fence or surrender. He refused, and when the sheriff tried to arrest him, his friends stepped in. Mtohksin heard a member of the posse shout "Rush on! Down with the fence! Fire!" The first shot went over the farmers' heads, and they urged the posse to hold their fire and talk. But a second shot went into the crowd, killing two of the rebels. The farmers then ran back to Noble's house for guns.[23] Noble was wounded by a shot in the back. An hourlong shootout followed, until all but twenty-five of the posse deserted. In the end another man died and several were wounded on the rebels' side, and the landlords suffered one dead and seven wounded, including one of the Van Rensselaers. Another Van Rensselaer had his horse killed under him. The sheriff's men captured only one insurgent.

When Mtohksin returned to Stockbridge he, King Ben, David Naunauneekanuk, and another elder formed a tribal committee to deal with the crisis. On June 30 they sent a testy complaint against Van Rensselaer to the mayor of Albany. Once again they claimed that they had never sold the contested land to Van Rensselaer or his predecessors, "and if he is able to shew any deed of those lands, it was either taken of Indians that had no right to make sale or is in itself a fraud." They had offered to sell their rights to Van Rensselaer before they sold the land to the emigrants, but he refused: "But now [that] it is settled at the expence and toil of others he is ready to make his purchase at the muzzle of the gun: a new way to us of maintaining claims." If this method and "horrid murder" were the approved ways of establishing claims, the Indians, too, were willing to employ them: "We have indeed applyed to the government of New York from time to time for a redress of those grievances but have been so neglected that we have sent several of our tribe to the court of Great Britain to see if we cant be heard and redressed there. We was in hopes that all contentions would have subsided about those lands till some order came from home. But it seems Mr. Ransler cannot wait the event."

The committee next appealed to Massachusetts governor Francis Bernard to intercede on behalf of the emigrants. They also felt justified to ask for orders from the governor, "whether we may engage in the quarrel or not."[24] The governor's response is not known, but the New York authorities used the violent confrontation as an excuse to involve the military. Governor Moore asked General Gage to assist the Albany lawmen and ordered every peace officer in the colony to pursue the rebels. Gage complied, but he restricted his troops to the New York border. As the redcoats approached, the rebels slipped across the Massachusetts line to sympathetic communities or melted into the woods.

The British officers abandoned conventional military tactics in favor of surprise raids, roadblocks, and maneuvers, as if they were in Indian country. To some extent they were. The insurgents had been known to wear Indian dress, but some of the Mohicans were probably allied with them. Governor Moore, in fact, wrote to England that the Stockbridge Indians "seem to be the contrivers of these riots, and from the information I have received have joined with some of the lower people in the irregularities which have been committed lately." He accused the Indians of "aiding and assisting in turning the tenants . . . and their families out of doors by force and putting in others who have promised to acknowledge them for their landlords, to the great prejudice and ruin of several families. Many well disposed persons who have refused to join in committing these disorders have been threatened by them, and are at present afraid of returning to their habitations, so that they will be reduced to great distress." Moore, who was not experienced in dealing with the Indians, made a final indictment: "The Indians in general (as I am credibly informed) make no ceremony of selling the same tract of land as often as anyone can be found who will purchase it, which has been constantly practiced by them, . . . and since a practice of this kind prevails even amongst the best sort of them, it is no wonder that it should be adopted among the Stockbridge Indians, who are looked upon by the Six Nations to be a very despicable tribe."[25]

Moore never mentioned the four chiefs, though he surely knew full well that they were in England as he wrote. In sympathy with the landlords, he portrayed the Stockbridges as a band of rogues who could not be trusted. It was propaganda obviously designed to influence the powers at home. As for reducing the farmers "to great distress," the landlords' forces were doing a much more efficient job than the Indians or the rebels could do. By late July the British troops were conducting search-and-destroy missions, while posting guards around the settlers' crops so they could not harvest. In a three-day purge of one settlement the soldiers destroyed at least seven houses, plundered the contents, burned outbuildings, and killed livestock. About twenty families fled to Massachusetts border towns like Stockbridge and Sheffield. Several families lost everything in the assault, and Massachusetts provided for them as refugees. Governor Bernard appealed to Governor Moore to at least allow the emigrants to gather their crops, but Moore refused. Instead, he demanded their extradition as fugitive rioters.

By the first two weeks in August the army had captured thirty-two of the insurgent farmers and were entering Massachusetts to pursue others, despite Gage's orders. Thinking he was still within New York, one captain established headquarters just west of Great Barrington at a tavern licensed by Massachusetts. Now the western Massachusetts settlers and the Stockbridge Indians became alarmed and angry. Nearly four hundred of them, forty of whom were Stockbridges, descended on the tavern to confront the force. They asked the officer to move his men back over the mountain. Elijah Williams, a son of Ephraim Williams and a county sheriff, was a spokesman for the group. A negotiating session lasted well into the night, interrupted on occasion by shouting from the settlers and the Indians. As the crowd grew more boisterous, the nervous soldiers fixed their bayonets and the tension increased. The antagonists finally reached a compromise. The troops would withdraw and the farmers would stop sniping at the redcoats. Both sides saved face, and within a week General Gage called off the entire operation.

Those who had not been completely ruined or imprisoned gradually drifted back to reestablish their settlements, so the situation remained a standoff. In the late fall, the positive news from England brought by Nimham and the others gave the settlers and the Indians renewed hope. The chiefs visited Governor Moore shortly after their return to inform him that the earl of Shelburne would soon send instructions to reconsider their claims. Moore told them that he would hear their case right away if they wished, but the Indians were not to be rushed. Moore then told them to return in a month, at which time he would set a hearing date.

When the Indians returned home, confident that things were going their way for a change, they started dispossessing prolandlord tenants who had not leased from them. The chiefs' treatment in England and the grandeur they had witnessed probably made them a little heady. The morale of the Indians and the settlers was further boosted by word that the earl of Shelburne had chastised both Gage and Moore for inordinate use of military force in a civil affair. But even more heartening word came from the king, who ordered the governor to prosecute John Van Rensselaer for intruding on the king's soil with his excessive patent. The Stockbridges may have noted, however, that the king did not say "the Indians' soil." [26]

Optimism was premature. First of all, the same vested interests that had scuttled the Wappinger claim in 1765 would be hearing the case. Nimham and his new lawyer, Spalding, wanted Governor Moore alone to hear the case without influence from the biased council. Moore refused, claiming that this would reflect on the council's honor. Even William Johnson admitted that the officials who would hear the Indians' claims were not disinterested. Second, Johnson's support—so instrumental in important Indian matters—was now negligible. He exposed his predisposition on the issue when he told Shelburne that the Stockbridge and Wappinger tribes were "upon a very different footing from the rest, being . . . domesticated." Claims to the lands in question, he said, were so old that "the circumstances of their case is extremely difficult to prove." Johnson also declined to attend the hearing allegedly because of trouble with an old war wound, but he did send his nephew, Guy Johnson, in his place. [27]

Governor Moore, despite his initially impetuous desire to hear the Indians' claims, delayed and inconvenienced Nimham and his allies until finally setting the hearing date for March 5, 1767. Samuel Monrow risked appearing in New York as a witness but landed back in jail instead, where he would be kept for a few more months while his family grew destitute. [28] On the day of the hearing Asa Spalding and another lawyer, along with a parade of twenty-five witnesses on Nimham's side, filed into the hearing room at Fort George. Among them was the Poughkeepsie judge who had approved Monrow's guardianship over the Wappingers, and against whom the council also wanted to take action. The judge and others testified that the original patent holder had never bought the Wappingers' rights to the land, and that the Indians had always claimed it.

Between the testimony and cross-examination of witnesses on both sides and the long, detailed closing arguments, the hearing lasted three days. The New York attorney general, who attended the hearing as an observer, believed that Nimham failed to prove his case. He felt that the tenants and squatters who had paid the Wappingers from time to time had satisfied the Indian claim. Finally, he thought that the contested 1702

Indian deed had been shown to be so fair and genuine that even Nimham's lawyers "seemed satisfied it was so," though "they made several exceptions to it."[29]

At the end, Governor Moore asked Nimham's counsel if they thought they had had a fair trial. The lawyers avoided answering directly. The "several exceptions" they had taken to the deed were, in their minds, rather fundamental legal points. Moore closed the proceedings without rendering a final decision. A few days later the decision suddenly appeared in the public press. The governor and the council declared that the patent was good and the purchase valid, that the Wappingers had no right to the land, and that they had been induced to complain by squatters who wanted support for their own illegal claims. The Wappingers' complaint was "vexatious and unjust, and . . . accordingly dismissed."[30]

The Indians could not believe that this was the final decision, given the consideration they had received from the king. Three weeks later Nimham and several others naively approached William Johnson for further help.[31] In vain the rest of the Stockbridges petitioned Governor Moore and the council to take up their own claims on New York, west of Stockbridge. Timothy Woodbridge also wrote to Johnson on their behalf. But Johnson repeated his observations about the legal documentation necessary to prove the Indian title, and about the difficulty of substantiating such old claims. Unless and until the Indians could produce such proof, there was nothing he could do.[32] Woodbridge then told Johnson, "The Indians conclude nothing will be done after all their trouble and expence and have desired me to prepare once more to the ministry at home the difficulty they meet with from the government."[33] Whether he did write and, if so, whether the appeal was acknowledged are not known.

In the summer of 1768 the Stockbridges once again sought Johnson's intercession, and he did write to Governor Moore, but to no end.[34] When the king proclaimed that officers and soldiers who had served in the French and Indian War would be rewarded with grants of land in North America, the irony was not lost on the Stockbridge Mohicans. With the help of the Woodbridge brothers they sought to recoup their New York lands. After spending more than £71 for legal services, they came away still empty-handed. The double irony was that the Indians had to use 150 acres of their Stockbridge land to pay the fees.[35]

Years later Timothy Woodbridge tried to prick the conscience of New York governor William Tryon concerning soldiers' land grants: "The kings munificence which moved him to make provision for his faithful officers and soldiers as a recompense for their toils and dangers no doubt extended to all equally who were within his majestys proclamation. These poor Indians who were near ruined in the war have by an unhappy fatality never received what they are really intitled to by his majestys gracious designes. They not being able to conduct their own affairs and having trusted it to others as ignorant or more unfaithful and designing, have faild of receiving their just rights altho' they have been at great expense to obtain it." Woodbridge obviously considered that the Stockbridges had been ill-advised if not ill-used by the New England land schemers. The Reverend Stephen West was more blunt, describing the speculators as designing, base men.

The schoolteacher also criticized the government's indifference toward the Indians' native rights to the land: "The Indians too have been illy used respecting their original claims as natives of the country. Why the Indians should not have a consideration from those who have settled on the lands descended to them [the Indians] from their progenitors, who were the first occupants of the country, I believe none can assign a reason, especially such Indians as have approv'd themselves loyal to the crown."[36]

Woodbridge's epistolary eloquence was wasted. The governor was looking for New York land to reward his own public service. When a map of all New York land grants was produced six years later, no Stockbridge Indian names appeared among the grantees.[37] There was only one concession to Mohican prestige during these dark days. The Stockbridges' position throughout these land debates had been complicated by previous sales of Mohican land east of the Hudson River above Fort Edward by the Mohawks. On September 30, 1768, the two tribes concluded an unusual, because written, treaty, in which the Mohawks said that they "now declare and make known to all people that we do freely and unanimously yield up and quit any claim we may have had to lands on the east side of Hudson's River." In turn, the Stockbridges agreed never to dispute any land sales the Mohawks had made east of the Hudson. Ironically, this agreement took place at Fort Stanwix at the same time that colonial officials and other tribes were negotiating a treaty to establish a boundary between colonial territory and Indian territory. William Johnson witnessed the Mohawk-Mohican treaty, despite his pique that the Stockbridges had come to Fort Stanwix. His only concern with the Stockbridges was to be rid of them. Two days later they left, Johnson having given them credit toward £60 sterling worth of provisions for the trip home.[38]

The other nations continued with the business of the dividing line, which was to separate once and for all the western Indian territory from the relentless spread of colonial occupation. Of course, the proclamation of 1763 was supposed to have done the same thing. The new dividing line would be heeded as little as the old one was, especially now that the combined French and Indian menace was gone. An enterprising surveyor and militia officer expressed most Americans' sentiments: "I can never look upon that proclamation in any other light . . . than as a temporary expedient to quiet the minds of the Indians, and must fall, of course, in a few years, especially when those Indians are consenting to our occupying the lands." [39] If George Washington felt this way, one can imagine the thoughts of the average colonial farmer or land speculator.

The meager Stockbridge claims, meanwhile, would be drowned as a rushing tide of emigrants swirled and settled around them and others swiftly moved westward, worrying only about the hostile tribes, not the friendly ones. Timothy Woodbridge and others were undoubtedly correct that the land rebels had a vested interest in the Indians' claims, but the Mohicans were not simply dupes. Nearly a hundred years later the Stockbridge Indians, on their own, were still seeking restitution for the lands denied Daniel, Jacob, John, and Solomon. [40] And with all the troubles of the 1760s, the Stockbridges at least gained some broad experience in the complex maze of legal, economic, and political intrigues that would help future generations cope with a new society.

14

POSTWAR

DEPRESSION

In the turbulent decade following the close of the French and Indian War, the condition of the Mohicans at Stockbridge worsened. The war had cost the lives of several men in their prime. Then in the winter of 1761–62 smallpox was rampant among the Indians, killing some of their leaders.[1] The following spring Abraham Unkamug, who had been captured with Jacob Cheeksaunkun by the Canadian Indians in 1759, murdered a fellow tribesman at Kinderhook, New York. Indian reaction to this incident reflected their further assimilation into Anglo-American culture. The victim's family sought neither blood vengeance nor material restitution, but asked that justice be done in the English court system. Another possible explanation for the family's reaction is that the victim and the murderer may have been related; sadly, one or both may have been sons of Umpachenee. The murderer was taken to Albany for trial in June, though no record of a trial survives, and he was free and back in Stockbridge by August. Pleading with Elijah Williams to accept a deed for 50 acres in exchange for £8, he claimed he was "almost ded for want of provetion"[2] Three years later his brother, known as Jacob Unkamug or Jacob Umpachenee, was jailed for wounding a colonial, and family and friends were forced to relinquish 100 acres in Stockbridge to obtain his release. Jacob, who could write only his initials, had been one of Martin Kellogg's underfed, underclothed, and undereducated students at the ill-fated boarding school.[3]

Colonial justice, despite the many problems it caused the Indians, was becoming acceptable to the Stockbridges. At the same time, they experienced a deadly ironic twist of Indian-style justice. The Indian whom the Stockbridges had obtained from the Saint Francis tribe in exchange for the executed captive was employed as a runner. On his return from one diplomatic errand he refreshed himself with one or two bottles of rum while awaiting the return of the tribal leaders, who were away. That evening he tried to coax one absent Indian's wife into sharing the rum with him at her mother's house in the woods. After she refused, escaping from him with difficulty, he went on alone, half-drunk and angry. When he arrived at the hut, the wife's mother, her lame brother, and two children were asleep.

Awakening the mother and brother, the intruder argued with them and started beating the woman and then her lame son, who tried to come to her aid. The woman escaped from the house, but as her son made for the doorway, the attacker threw a piece of burning wood from the fireplace after him. Cinders scattered on the straw inside the hut started smoldering. The two frightened Indians outside did not know that one of the children had also escaped. Thinking both children were in the cabin, the old woman returned to retrieve them. It was speculated afterward that when the woman went back to the house, the troublemaker murdered her. The only certainty was that flames eventually consumed the house, with the old woman, one child, and the ex-slave Indian in it.[4]

Incidents like these were the visible sores on an unhealthy Mohican social body. War, disease, rum, the intrigues and greed of those who pushed and pulled the Indians this way and that, the changing environment, and the inability of many to cope with the rapid changes were all enervating. Random comments by different individuals sketch the condition of the Mohicans at Stockbridge and elsewhere throughout this period.

Stephen West, February 2, 1763: "Whether this poor, wretched people will ever be reclaimed or not, God only knows."[5]

Timothy Woodbridge, November 15, 1764: "As matters stand they are in miserable circumstances and must of necessity in a very short time be intirely broken up unless something be speedily done to prevent it. . . . I am really affected with their miserable circumstances."[6]

Samuel Hopkins, March 30, 1767: "The Indians are truly in a deplorable state. . . . They are most of them drunkards; and are often got drunk, it is believed, by those who tamper with them and have ends of their own to answer by them. They are consequently idle, and of course poor, and many almost starved; which leads them to press and live on those who have something, and even to steal from them. By this means they are all reduced to straits; and most of them have nothing to eat great part of the year, but what they can pick up where they find it, as the hungry wolves in the wilderness! And how much this tends to hurt the morale of the whole, and prevent all benefit by instruction, need not be said. The sights that are to be seen among them every day are enough to make the compassionate heart of a true Christian bleed." [7]

An old Hudson River Mohican chief to Guy Johnson, April 26, 1767: "We are now in tears, we have lost everything. The Patroon has got all our lands, and we have nothing for them." [8]

Another old chief who arrived at Johnson's two weeks later with twenty-one followers: "We now come poor & naked before you but we cannot help it. . . . There are still beasts and birds left, but we have not guns to shoot them. We often take up a stick and present it, wishing it would kill game for our subsistance. We are ashamed, Father, to appear before you so bare." These Mohicans asked not only for guns and clothing, but also to "chear [their] hearts with Liquor." [9]

Two Stockbridge Indian women to a Moravian missionary, June 23, 1771: The Stockbridges are "leading a difficult and evil life and . . . they are orderly on Sunday only as long as the sermon lasts." [10]

A Moravian missionary, reporting his conversation with a Stockbridge Indian in October of 1771: "He indicated that he liked to hear about the Savior of whom he didn't hear anything in the place where he lived, for the Indians there were leading a dissolute life, drinking and dancing and being poor in body and in soul." "Life in Westenhuc [the old Dutch name for Stockbridge] is difficult and wretched." [11]

John Sergeant, Jr., January 11, 1774, after talking with some of the old Stockbridges: "They tell me that they are more wicked now than they were in my father's time." [12]

John Konkapot's son, Robert, exemplified the problems of a generation caught between conflicting cultures. By his mid-thirties he had held the offices of constable for one year and highway surveyor for another. But Robert also had a large family and expensive tastes, and by the fall of 1763 had put not only himself but his father in severe financial straits. John Konkapot was already reduced by age and infirmity. [13]

Robert was in debt to two Albany merchants, who obtained judgment against him in a Massachusetts court. Threatened with jail, Robert unwisely signed over a deed to them for 20 acres of Stockbridge meadow-land, including a house and a barn.[14] John and Robert petitioned the legislature to be allowed to sell 160 acres of woodland in order to buy back the meadow and the buildings. Joseph Woodbridge, to be helpful, he said, had in the meantime purchased extralegally 40 acres of Konkapot land. Elijah Williams took a five-hundred-year lease on another 140 from Robert. Though a self-righteous Massachusetts legislature declared that Williams's lease could not "be justified by the laws of this government," it did not pursue the matter.[15] The legislature also denied the Konkapots' request to sell their 160 acres, but proposed to provide them with a lawyer to fight for the meadow and the buildings, since that transfer was also deemed illegal.[16] By mid-October of 1766 both John and Robert were dead, leaving their problems to their heirs.

Conditions were as bad or worse for the Scaticook Indians during this period. A Moravian historian's portrait of them in the 1760s would have been familiar to those in Stockbridge: "One piece of land after the other was taken from them, by which they lost the means of their support. Thus they were obliged to run into debt, and to live dispersed among the white people, to earn a livelihood. If they could not pay, they were treated with the greatest severity, and even their poor furniture taken from them. This behavior exasperated the unbaptized Indians to such a degree, that they abused the baptized on account of their sobriety and better management of their outward concerns, attacking them on the highway, and in other places, and cruelly beating them. This occasioned some of the baptized to waver, and to become low and dispirited. Some young people were even seduced to sin, and brought into misery. A certain melancholy pervaded the congregation, and the missionary himself began to lose courage."[17]

The Moravians found that the men who had joined the war were especially troublesome. About fifteen had served at various times between 1755 and 1760. They frequently caroused, sometimes in company with the Stockbridge heroes, providing poor models for the young. The war experience undoubtedly contributed greatly to keeping the men of fighting age in an amorphous state between cultures. Though members of Christian communities dominated by New England society, their status and self-perception as warriors had been magnified by the demands of war. They scouted, scalped, killed, and terrorized the enemy as their colonial allies had hired them to do and as their own tradition demanded of them. They were then expected to drop the tomahawk and the scalping knife to pick up a plow and do what Indian tradition designated as women's work. That type of transition was easier for colonials, whose culture was so structured. It was neither easy nor necessarily desirable for Indians, even those who were neophyte New Englanders. Furthermore, they had spent several years with frontier colonials like Rogers' Rangers, whose way of life resembled their own more than did that of colonial religious and social leaders. And the disruption of traditions was certainly as unsettling for some of the women as it was for the men.

Periodic droughts, severe winters, and scarcity of game added to the Scaticooks' miseries. Famine became an occasional visitor. The Stockbridge Indians offered their town as a refuge, and by this time the Scaticooks thought the move would be advantageous. The head man who in the past had resisted Stockbridge advances died in 1760. His successor petitioned the Connecticut legislature in 1767, asking permission to sell about 200 acres the Scaticooks had occupied in Kent for twenty years to help pay for the move. Connecticut denied the petition, claiming that the land did not belong to the Indians. This seems to have frustrated the move to Stockbridge, but the Indians had begun to disperse anyway.[18]

The Scaticooks would not have escaped an enveloping population even had they moved to Stockbridge. When Stephen West joined the congregation in 1759, his was the nineteenth non-Indian family in town. There were then forty-two Indian families.[19] Only four years later Stockbridge had thirty-two colonial families. By 1770 it hosted fifty, and in another six years the total number of colonials in Stockbridge was about a thousand, whereas the Indians numbered hardly more than two hundred souls.[20] Western Massachusetts, which had been wilderness in 1735, had three to four thousand settlers in 1765, and in the next decade the colonial population increased to six times that number. There were enough people by 1761 for Massachusetts to create a new county called Berkshire, and by the end of that year the county claimed six incorporated towns.[21] By aiding the English in subduing the French and by selling their lands, the Stockbridge Indians had helped bring New England civilization to the frontier faster than they wanted.

The Stockbridge Indians began to look elsewhere. The industrious Moravians with their Delaware and Mohican converts, meanwhile, were establishing a comfortable mission town called Friedenshutten at an abandoned Delaware Indian village on the upper Susquehanna in present-day Bradford County, Pennsylvania. The Stockbridges and Scaticooks sent a message to the Six Nations in the spring of 1765, asking to join their brethren on the Susquehanna "because they were so hemmed in among the white people that they could hardly move any more." The Six

Nations objected, however, because the Mohicans wanted to bring along a few colonial neighbors whom they considered good friends.[22]

The Six Nations were still attempting to keep settlers out of the Wyoming Valley, especially those under the auspices of the persistent Susquehanna Company. The Iroquois knew full well that the Stockbridge Indians were under the influence of Timothy Woodbridge and might be used as a shield to protect advancing settlers. The Stockbridge Indians, therefore, apparently suffered guilt by association with Timothy Woodbridge. Although Woodbridge and his associates may have encouraged the Stockbridges to move to the Susquehanna, several within the tribe were already attracted to the Moravian communities.[23]

In early April of 1768 William Johnson sent a wampum message to the Mohicans, urging all of them to concentrate at Oquaga on the east branch of the Susquehanna with the Oneidas and the Tuscaroras, who had their own English missionary. Later that month, while touring New England, Johnson met with the Stockbridges west of Pittsfield, but little seems to have come from either the suggestion or the meeting.[24] Occasional probes west and a trickle of emigrants were all that Stockbridge yielded in this decade, while gaining a few Indians from remnants of nearby tribes.[25] The Indians at Friedenshutten moved west in 1772 to a branch of the Ohio River in western Pennsylvania, and west again a year later to two villages on the Tuscarawas River in Ohio, one of which revived the name Gnadenhutten. As the decade of the 1770s began, there were more than a hundred Mohicans west of the Alleghenies, vainly hoping, along with other nations, that the line established by the king between them and the colonials would hold.[26]

The Stockbridges in the meantime tried to hold the line in their own town. How did they get into such straits after the war? Probably one major reason was the expense of pursuing their New York land claims. It hardly seems coincidental that in the same year the chiefs visited the king, the Indians issued thirty deeds for land within Stockbridge. From 1765 to 1769 the total was seventy-four. Much of the Stockbridges' trouble can also be attributed to their becoming surrounded by colonial culture without being absorbed into it, making them increasingly dependent on their Anglo-American neighbors for support. According to Timothy Woodbridge, for example, the Indians kept no oxen and most relied on the English for plowing and spring planting. Otherwise they were likely to starve, he said, being "an improvident people." When the men were absent, their families needed relief.[27] Other observers noted that the Indians had cultivated the same fields for so long that they were producing "very thin crops." They did not use fertilizers and seemed unwilling to clear new land.[28] Much of their unwillingness may have been due to their general discouragement. The gristmills, the sawmills, the farm equipment, the taverns, and the shops and the goods they contained were all owned by provincials. Most of what the Indians received was through struggle or charity. A further complication for those Indians who held the various town offices was that the execution of their duties often impinged on earning a living.

Another problem that contributed to the Indians' deprivation throughout the mission period, ironically, was their own tradition of hospitality. Both the Moravians and the English described the Indians as "improvident"—in the sense that many were accustomed to live more for today than for tomorrow—but improvidence was sometimes imposed on them by the steady stream of visitors to and from the mission sites. Indian custom demanded that guests be generously provided for, and colonial observers had early noted that an Indian visitor could unceremoniously walk into a compatriot's wigwam, sit down, and not utter a word about the purpose of his visit until he had been fed. Eastern Massachusetts settlers had enacted a law in the seventeenth century to prevent Indians from practicing the same habit in colonial homes. Between the numbers of curious visitors that the missions attracted and the Indians' own frequent peregrinations, those who were hosts could easily become financially strapped. After this problem was called to his attention in 1744, Gottlob Buettner had recommended to mission authorities that they reconsider the frequency of visits by the Brethren.

The Stockbridges also were being victimized by a colonial Catch-22. A Massachusetts law that barred suits against Indians for debt unless their credit arrangement had prior approval by a legal guardian expired in late 1762. Normally the courts would have applied an older law with similar requirements, which had no expiration date.[29] After the French and Indian War, however, courts in newly created Berkshire County took the convenient position that this older law did not apply to the Stockbridges because they had not been known as a tribe when it was passed.

"People here exult at the determination," Woodbridge told a provincial official in 1764, "and are getting as many obligations as they can of the Indians where they run in debt. He that can get them bound at any rate right or wrong, drunk or sober, has his action against them. Nothing is easier than to overreach and ruin the Indians in this way. I have paid hundreds of pounds in getting up their notes of hand, and it is most likely one half of them were for trifles, some I know to be so." If his conscience allowed it, he added, "I could procure obligations on the Indians for a thousand pounds for that which should not cost me one hundred."[30]

In one case two shopkeepers in Northampton had allowed a Stockbridge Indian's debts for "sundry goods" to lie dormant for five years. When he died in 1757, the two successfully petitioned the province to have his land sold to pay the bill.[31] By itself the request sounds reasonable, but in such situations the land usually was sold for a fraction of its worth. The distressed Stockbridge Indians complained in later years that traders tried to get everything the Indians owned. They took advantage of the Indians' ignorance by encouraging them to become debtors in the first place, in part by promising to wait until the Indians could repay the debt. Then the traders would immediately bring a suit or take a promissory note for more than the actual amount owed, threatening the Indians with jail if they failed to part with their lands for less than the real worth. And the Indians would part with anything rather than go to jail. Even if an Indian could afford a lawyer, he would probably lose the case and have to pay the lawyer's fees and the court fees on top of the debt.[32]

The Stockbridge Indians were at the bottom of a heap of lawsuits throughout the 1760s and early 1770s, as Berkshire County folk engaged in a litigious free-for-all. Relatives sued one another for debts unpaid, merchants sued farmers, farmers sued Indians, and even Indians sued Indians. No one, high or low, escaped suit, including several judges. But no one was trapped by the law in the way that the Stockbridge Indians were. The Indians were fettered by that provincial edict of 1749, which declared them English subjects and Massachusetts citizens, except when it came to selling their own land. In that case they were Indians and therefore could not legally sell their land without official approval. Creditors in turn held this law over the Indians' heads as a means to get their lands for about half their value, since the creditor could not be assured of a legal title. And if the Indians waited for official blessing from Boston before selling their lands to repay old debts or to buy new credit, the poor, sick, or hungry might die in the interim. And yet the Indians could not avoid prosecution or jail by taking the debtor's oath, because they owned real estate.[33] The old Hampshire County court sometimes did the Stockbridges a favor by skirting provincial proscriptions against land sales and long leases. According to the law, then, the Indians were adults when they acquired debts, but children when they tried to get out of them. "For Gods sake," Woodbridge pleaded, "don't let us under the pretence of being guardians and saviours to them insnare them and deprive them of the common and natural rights of mankind. . . . This is guarding of them in an uncommon manner. Indeed it opens several doors to the Indians. It opens the prison door, it opens the tavern door, for now there is no law to restrain the taverners from letting the Indians have as much spiritous liquors as they can pay for and as much as they have a mind for, and one door more is opened and that is to go out of the government and go for shelter where they will not be thus used." [34]

The prison doors were continually threatening to open for some of the Stockbridges and had already closed behind others. Nearly every Indian of every rank was sued for debt during these years—Cheeksaunkun, Uhhaunauwaunmut, the Naunauphtaunks, and others. Jonas Etowaukaum was jailed for debt in Albany in 1763, and a black Stockbridge man put up £40 toward Jonas's release. The black in turn received a deed from Jonas for 8 acres of meadowland and 50 acres of woodland, a fair bargain considering what others were getting. Etowaukaum's bad luck didn't end here, because two years later his house burned down. The town did at least vote him £12 to rebuild. [35]

The schemers, the cheaters, and the devious were not the only claimants against the Indians. Their friends and neighbors also held their I.O.U.s. Those in and about Stockbridge who knew the Indians were neither hesitant about taking deeds, leases, or promissory notes illegally, nor reluctant to benefit from the Indians' predicament. Joseph Woodbridge and Josiah Jones told the General Court that they and several other persons had advanced the Indians "considerable sums in provisions, clothing and the necessaries of life." [36]

For building a fence between the Indians' land and his own, one townsman received more than 44 acres from the Indians. When John Sergeant's older son, Erastus, a doctor, treated some of the Indians, they sold more land to pay his bill. And Timothy Woodbridge always received a few acres for his services. Even Woodbridge's grandson was given 50 acres by the grateful Indians, "to be laid out in the town where said childs friends shall chuse." But after the little boy died, his grandfather inherited the land. [37] Woodbridge's son-in-law sustained a loss "in having his ox killed," and the Indian proprietors had to forfeit 50 acres, the implication being that they were responsible for the mishap. [38]

Most Stockbridges were indebted to Elijah Williams at one time or another. [39] Williams practiced some form of trade and owned an ironworks in the western part of town, probably on the ore-bearing land his father and late brother had wangled from the Indians. Both Elijah Williams and Joseph Dwight could be fairly confident that the Stockbridges would satisfy their debts in some fashion—Williams was the county sheriff and Dwight was a justice. Within an eighteenth-century New England context, many creditors undoubtedly considered their actions to be charitable, since some of them probably made allowances for the Indians' situation. Indian debtors may have had more time to repay their debts than non-Indians did, and there was always the risk that a Mohican debtor might permanently relocate to another colony. But sympathy for Indians was not the dominant emotion among the growing population of western Massachusetts.

In the winter of 1763–64 Timothy Woodbridge petitioned the government seeking redress for the Indians, to no avail. The following November he wrote to Andrew Oliver describing their plight with regard to the law. Woodbridge expressed confidence that the government was honorable enough either to change the law restricting the Indians' sale of land, or to enact a new law preventing them from being abused as debtors. Hinting at the Stockbridges' then-contemplated trip to England, he concluded, "I am pleading for nothing but common justice that the Indians might have the same privileges with other subjects of the king. And I imagine such a procedure will make an ill appearance at the court of Great Britain if it should appear there."[40]

In January of 1765 Jacob Cheeksaunkun and other head men petitioned the government, echoing Woodbridge's remarks. Timothy Woodbridge was elected as the Stockbridge representative to the legislature that year, but various bureaucratic delays prevented any action until the fall. In October the General Court finally allowed the Stockbridges to sell some of their more remote holdings, which gave them the opportunity to redeem better land they had pawned and to settle their debts. The sales were to be scrutinized by Woodbridge and a county justice, who could also supervise maximum one-year leases for any Indians who left their improved lands temporarily to attend to other business. In addition, a committee headed by James Otis was designated to bring forth legislation to help the Indians keep the rest of their land.[41] Otis, however, was too busy organizing the Stamp Act Congress and protecting colonial American interests against British taxation to worry about protecting native Americans' interests. And Andrew Oliver, the sympathetic official to whom Timothy Woodbridge had appealed on the Indians' behalf, had the misfortune to be appointed an agent for the Stamp Act. After his home was sacked by a mob in protest of his appointment, Oliver had more immediate concerns besides the Indians.[42] No further measures to protect the Stockbridge Indians were taken.

The Indians did not expect others to solve all their problems, however. Combining native communal tradition with the lessons of New England organization and enterprise, in the 1760s they established committees of prominent tribesmen to deal with critical issues. In 1768, for example, the Indian proprietors appointed King Ben, David Naunauneekanuk, Johannis Mtohksin, John Naunauphtaunk, and Jacob Cheeksaunkun to apportion money received from land sales to resolve debts. Smaller committees also were formed whose function was to grant individual Indians permission to purchase goods on credit, using tribally held land as security. The committees provided notes to a merchant, stipulating articles of clothing or amounts of credit to be dispensed to an individual and charged to the Indian landowners as a group. The responsible tribesmen thus could control any potential abuses by individuals signing notes or deeds for communal land, and they could keep track of their land bank. In another example of tribal control, the Stockbridges assigned the land of an Indian who apparently had died without heirs to another Indian family.[43]

By 1767 more than a third of the Indians' township was nevertheless in colonial hands.[44] The need to sell tribal land to pay the debts of Indians who were land-poor or profligate undoubtedly created tension within the tribe. Their shrinking land base explains why they were anxious to sign an agreement with the Mohawks concerning the land north of Albany. Speculators and settlers were interested in that land, too, and soon after the agreement they sought to buy it from the Indians. Since the land was within New York, Timothy Woodbridge asked William Johnson to ensure that the Indians received fair treatment. Judging by later complaints from the Stockbridges, they did not get fair treatment.[45]

The Indians' low spirits may have been revived by the passage of a Massachusetts law declaring that after March 31, 1773, no one in the province could sue the Stockbridges for debts exceeding thirty-five shillings. If anyone did, the Indians could invoke the act and recover their costs in the suit. In passing this legislation the province finally acknowledged that persons in Massachusetts and New York had been advancing credit to the Indians "for the sake of gain," and that the Indians would soon "be reduced to a state of utter ruin."[46] The Indians could probably thank Timothy Woodbridge for that law. Passing the law in Boston and enforcing it in Berkshire County or Albany, however, were often different matters.

15

SEPARATION OF CHURCH, STATE, AND INDIANS

Some emigrants to western Massachusetts probably believed that despite thirty years of exposure to Christian civilization, the Indians seemed incapable of becoming responsible, progressive New England citizens. Colonial America was not the place to entertain a different cultural approach to life. Many New Englanders could not understand the Stockbridges' reluctance to accept English culture lock, stock, and barrel, since that had been the stated purpose of the mission in the first place. What the colonials also failed to understand, however, was how hypocritical that culture appeared to Indian eyes when it preached Christian love but too often practiced godless greed.

Many newcomers to Stockbridge, as well as the second generation of the original English families, did not view Stockbridge as an Indian town or mission, nor did they consider themselves to be role models. The fight against the French was hardly over and the graves of slain Stockbridges barely cold when a group of colonials complained to the province that they were under "diverse inconveniences by means of the Indian inhabitants." They wanted a separate school for their own children and roads to accommodate their carriages. Since the Indians did not pay provincial taxes, the English inhabitants petitioned to "be allowed to transact all matters relative to the premises by themselves, exclusive of the Indians." The Indians, still clinging to the notion that the town was theirs, naturally saw no reason to vote money or labor for another school, and since they probably did not own any carriages they felt no great need for a network of roads. The petition received sufficient backing, however, to introduce a bill "to enable the English inhabitants . . . to call town meetings and transact certain matters separately from the Indian inhabitants." Passage of the bill seemed certain until the Governor's Council voted that the petition be read to the Stockbridge Indians by Timothy Woodbridge.[1] That effectively killed the measure for the time being. But undaunted as usual by official stumbling blocks, the colonials appropriated money on their own over the next three years to build two schoolhouses and to obtain an English schoolmaster for their children.[2]

Factionalism once again divided the Christian Indian town. Those who favored separation sought to gain control of the town council and to elect Elijah Williams as representative to the legislature at Boston. While Woodbridge was away, Williams engineered a town meeting in March of 1763. Woodbridge was aware of the upcoming meeting but presumably was confident that the Indians and his friends and relatives would reelect him. Williams and his supporters, however, brought in their adherents, and the normal voting population of about forty suddenly jumped to sixty-one. Several eligible Indian voters, meanwhile, were away making maple sugar. Those Indians who attended the meeting found that a written ballot had replaced the normal procedure, whereby every nomination and measure was repeated in Mohican, giving the Indians time to digest and discuss each proposal and to register their votes by a show of hands. The outcome was the passage of a road measure that, according to opponents, benefited mainly Samuel Brown and Elijah Williams. Williams was chosen representative by a three-vote majority over Timothy Woodbridge.

The Indians and the Woodbridge allies were understandably upset. They protested to the government that several of the men who had voted were hired laborers and not Stockbridge residents, that no official announcement of the meeting had been made, and that therefore Williams had been illegally elected. They charged that some of the English were trying to "worm the Indians out of their privileges." Furthermore, it appeared "very injurious . . . for people by all ways and means to croud into the town to get estates and then cry out that they cannot bear to be a society with Indians nor to be controld by their votes." The Indians were beginning to wonder if the promise to introduce civilization to them had been a cruel joke.

It was early October before government investigators arrived in Stockbridge. They confirmed most of the allegations, including the assertion that not all of the voters were town residents, though most of them owned property in Stockbridge. Nevertheless, the investigators judged the election and the town meeting legal and laid part of the blame on John Naunauphtaunk, who had refused to serve as constable, the officer responsible for announcing town meetings. John's refusal was not unusual, however. Many New Englanders considered that office the most odious, and some refused to serve despite potential fines. The committee also concluded that the town's changing racial ratio and its cultural differences necessitated separate political entities.[3] The General Court subsequently ordered that the contested town meeting should stand, but that another meeting should be called to select a new constable.[4] A bill to divide the Indians and colonials into distinct and separate societies was introduced but went no further.

By 1764 nearly everyone in Stockbridge, including many of the Indians, favored a separation in town affairs, but for different reasons. Timothy Woodbridge claimed that some of the English had such violent and inconsiderate dispositions that he was unwilling to be governed by them. Woodbridge wanted to make sure that if a separate township were created, only those who favored separation would be in it. His own plan was to join with his family, his friends, and the Indians to create a new township for the separatists in the northern portion of Stockbridge, which was less agriculturally productive.[5]

The idea of separation met with sympathy not only in government, but also among the commissioners for the New England Company. At least one of them paid a visit to Stockbridge and saw the need for it. But the commissioners' version of separation alarmed the settlers. If the English became a separate religious congregation as well as a political entity, they would have to support a minister and a school. When the town voted on this proposal, nearly everyone opposed it.

Nevertheless, by 1767 the discontented were quietly and quickly negotiating for a viable separation, through Stephen West and young Samuel Hopkins, without the knowledge of Woodbridge and his faction. Twenty-four men, including John Sergeant's two sons, signed a confidential letter, in which they said that having initially opposed full separation, nearly everyone was now for it, except some (the Woodbridge faction), "that wanted . . . to make fools of the Indians in voting for them in town affairs. And we have reason to believe the Indians would all have been willing and chose to been separated if they had not been tampered with by such persons for sinister ends and views, which conduct is of very ill tendency and if not soon stopped may breed great disaffection between them and us."[6]

The proponents of separation suggested that Jonathan Edwards, Jr., who was tutoring at Princeton University, be invited to head the mission. Edwards, having grown up among the Indians while his father was missionary, had mastered Mohican and was interested in the Indians.[7] The petitioners "understood that the Indians not long since have mentioned they had a great desire for him and asked why they might not have him for their minister."[8] Edwards would also satisfy most of the English townsmen. Those who were content with Stephen West (the Williams faction, which now included the Sergeants), however, hoped that if there were a separation, West might be maintained at company expense until the English congregation could afford to support him by themselves. They were even willing, if the commissioners allowed, to hold their services at different hours from the Indian service, until they could afford to build their own meetinghouse.[9]

Stephen West more than once had expressed his willingness to step aside and let a better qualified man assume the Indian mission, even if it threatened his own livelihood as minister. He once admitted that the trust in him for the mission's success was a continual burden.[10] Both he and Samuel Hopkins let the authorities know that they favored a separation. At the end of March 1767, Hopkins wrote, "The Indians are truly in a deplorable state. And unless their present connexions with the English can be broken, and some laws can be made to prevent their getting into debt and alienating their lands, and a good schoolmaster introduced . . . there is little hope that any good will be done among them by all the money that is laid out upon them; but there is the greatest prospect that they will soon come to nothing, or that which is worse."[11]

By July an anxious Stephen West learned that the commissioners apparently favored separation and the attempt to secure Jonathan Edwards, Jr., as minister for the Indians. Edwards should not have been disagreeable to the Woodbridge faction since one of Joseph Woodbridge's sons had married Edwards's sister Lucy and settled in Stockbridge.[12] Her brother Timothy Edwards was soon to join them.

But according to Stephen West, Timothy Woodbridge and his allies opposed the idea and would either discourage Edwards from taking the mission or prevail upon the commissioners to put him in charge of both the English and the Indians.[13] Whether Woodbridge was successful or whether Edwards simply followed his own inclinations is not known, but young Jonathan chose not to become a missionary. Now, West said, the English at Stockbridge would be "universally opposed to separation, all dreading the cost and charge which will be incurred."[14] So for better or for worse the Indians remained connected with their English neighbors. If the company commissioners restricted his ministry to the Indians, West said, he would be willing to spend a great deal of time learning their language.[15] They did not restrict him, though, and he continued to shepherd both flocks for several years.

The contention over separation in part seems to have revolved around the minister's available time. Each Sunday John Sergeant had preached two sermons to the Indians and two to the English, except during the short daylight of winter, when he preached only one English sermon. The Sunday service did not end entirely until afternoon, after which he spent about an hour counseling the Indians. Since his death, the Indians had not had a missionary who could speak Mohican. Between the need for an interpreter and the attendant religious duties of a New England minister, the church service must have increasingly concentrated on the Indians. This had probably not been a problem a few years earlier, when the non-Indian Stockbridge population was smaller and fearful of rankling the Indians during the war. But with the war over, the growing colonial population was obviously impatient about the amount of time the minister spent on the Indians, not to mention the time and difficulty involved in getting the Indians to participate in town civil affairs. Just congregating the Mohicans together was a problem when many were frequently away hunting, trapping, fishing, trading, or consulting with other tribes. After several attempts, the Stockbridge families who sought to be separated from the Indians won a partial victory on March 9, 1774, when Massachusetts passed a law enabling them to incorporate into a distinct district. As for taxation and representation at Boston, however, those in the new district were still considered part of Stockbridge.[16] The Stockbridge Indians now had a token voice in a town that had been reduced by almost half. But the Indians who owned homes or property in what was now called West Stockbridge had no voice in their jurisdiction.

Religious observance among the Stockbridges, not surprisingly, was erratic during this tumultuous postwar period. In early 1763 Reverend West counted fifteen Indians in full communion with the church, and he estimated that between fifty and seventy attended services on Sundays, the lower number applying during the hunting and maple sugar seasons. Although he acknowledged that many of the Indians were sober and upright, he thought that the numbers attending Sunday services did

Stephen West, Stockbridge minister and missionary to the Stockbridge Indians, 1759–73. Source: David Dudley Field, History of the County of Berkshire *(Pittsfield, 1829).*

not accurately reflect the general tenor of their lives. They seemed, according to the minister, addicted to idleness and drinking, which made them "extremely barbarous and dissolute in their manners." Four years later, as the colonial families multiplied, West admitted that the Indians were being crowded out of their seats in the church "and actually make that an excuse (whether justly or not) for their neglect of the publick worship."[17]

The Indians' behavior did not mesh with West's Calvinism. In more than fifteen years as minister among the Indians of Stockbridge, he baptized forty-nine children but admitted only twenty-two Indians to full communion with the church, all but one of them women. By the early 1770s West was enforcing stricter church discipline. After public and private admonishment of professed sinners proved ineffective, he apparently decided to make examples of some of them. Over the next several years he excommunicated several prominent Indian men and women for drunkenness, adultery, and other infractions. Only one excommunicant was ever readmitted to the church, after a public confession of her sins more than nine years later.[18] But when Johannis Mtohksin was banned for what Reverend West called "extreme sottishness . . . and his unbridled appetite for strong drink," as well as his impertinent lack of remorse, Mtohksin fought back.[19] John Sergeant, Jr., said that Mtohksin also was charged with heresy, but that "discipline went down so hard with the old sachem that he mustered all his powers, got a number of the church which came into a confederacy to take all likely means to get Mr. West removed." At a later meeting Mtohksin read aloud a statement charging the reverend with a lack of charity and of proper religious sentiments. According to Sergeant, the majority of the town and the church backed West.[20] But of course the majority were not Indians.

Stephen West's church did not necessarily discriminate against Indians in its purges. A fifty-nine-year-old settler named David Pixley, who had lived in Stockbridge since 1742, took religion with a grain of salt. Besides confessing to fornication before marriage, he had been cited for drunkenness, as well as for being quarrelsome, profane, obstinate, and impertinent toward those who attempted to save his soul. He was publicly admonished once, but persisted until he, too, was excommunicated.[21] West's brother-in-law, Elijah Williams, did not set a good Christian example for the Indians either. A Berkshire County court on April 30, 1765, adjudged that he was the father of an illegitimate boy born of a young Stockbridge woman a year earlier. Williams was ordered to pay support, but there is no record that he was excommunicated or censured.[22]

Yet by the spring of 1773 Stockbridge was apparently experiencing another religious revival, or as West put it, "some fresh tokens of the divine presence with us in this poor, stupid town."[23] The awakening seemed most evident among those between thirty and forty years of age, he said; "most of the people, however, are still stupid and secure: Satan is not dispossessed of their hearts."[24]

Regardless of the revival, the company commissioners decided in November to dismiss Stephen West as missionary to the Indians. He continued to be a minister to the English, though some favored getting rid of him altogether.[25] West had already been searching his conscience about keeping the £80 sterling salary from the company, when he could do so little good. He was willing to give up half the money, if the more than fifty colonial families—who were not poor by any means—would at least pay the other half. After six months of reluctance, the families finally agreed. The reverend had been discouraged with, and tired of, the Indian service for some time and was seeking disengagement anyway. Of all the clergy with whom the Mohicans had been involved since Europeans first came to their land, West was probably the least suited to be a missionary. Yet his ministry among them lasted as long as John Sergeant's. In everyday application, he was a stricter Calvinist than even Jonathan Edwards. His comments regarding the town's moral stupor, therefore, especially with regard to the Indians, should be kept in perspective. In what became a regionally notorious case, for instance, he suspended a colonial woman from communion with the church " 'till she manifest a sense of her wickedness" for marrying, against the vote of the church, a man who publicly had confessed to using profane language.[26]

Two months before West's dismissal, Ezra Stiles noted that "Mr. West has excommunicated the last Indian out of his Church & turned over the mission to Mr. Sergeant."[27] John Sergeant, Jr., was the heir apparent to the Indian mission. In 1767 the New England Company authorized the commissioners to pay him to teach the mission school, and he probably assumed his duties the following year. John, who resembled his father, was then nineteen, and having grown up in Stockbridge he knew Mohican. Sergeant was considered to be of the yeoman class, however, and seemed to have no great ambitions. Stephen West surmised that he was "a man well disposed, and of peculiar steadiness and industry." Another contemporary described him as "not of college education but an ingenious, sensible and worthy man."[28]

Sergeant resembled his father in other ways. He was not ultraorthodox in his religious sentiments. He did not gain full membership in the Stockbridge church until 1771, and he later confided in his missionary friend Samuel Kirkland that he had heard from Boston that "my sentiments in religion will be a bar in the way of my ever taking the mission." At the time he thought it just as well, "for I am altogether unworthy; and an unlikely means of doing any good in the Lord's vinyard."[29]

Despite Sergeant's religious views the company commissioners supported him as West's replacement. Early in 1774 Sergeant reported that the Indians were attending two meetings each Sabbath, and were becoming friendlier toward him, partly because of his assurance that he would soon begin translating his sermons into Mohican. The religious stalwarts had admitted to Sergeant that the Indians' Christian moral status had fallen below that of his father's time, and that "therefore they should be dealt with more plainness and severity &c."[30] Nevertheless, young Sergeant was not an ordained minister, and since Stephen

West had excommunicated all the Indians, the Stockbridges now had no certified religious shepherd. Their wariness toward Sergeant, then, is understandable. If the Stockbridges knew that their first minister's son had favored separation in town affairs, they might have been suspicious of him on that account.

The progress of education in the postwar decade, like that of religion, was fitful. At the outset of the war Jonathan Edwards arranged to send a few Indian boys to his friend Joseph Bellamy in Bethlehem, Connecticut, for schooling. It took a while for the boys to become content there, partly because, according to Bellamy, "they love play too well." He also uncharitably described them as ignorant and stupid in religion (apparently not intended as a reflection on Edwards) and easily discouraged with arithmetic. "They will not indure hardship and bend their minds to business like English boys," Bellamy complained.[31] Stephen West also recommended sending some boys out of Stockbridge to be groomed to succeed Johannis Mtohksin as interpreter, though there is no evidence that this was done. West himself had tried to prepare one boy for the job, but felt that the other Indians' influence on the lad made success impossible.[32]

Timothy Woodbridge had stopped teaching school by May of 1762. He described himself at the time as old, infirm, and "with many avocations." At various times during this period, in fact, he was a county justice, a representative, an ex officio guardian for the Stockbridges, and an officer in the Susquehanna Company. Woodbridge therefore asked the New England Company commissioners—nine months *after* he had quit and in his place installed his twenty-two-year-old son—to relieve him of his teaching duties and to give his son the job. The son must have received the commissioners' support, since he taught until his death around 1767. It was said that Woodbridge then planned to recommend his son-in-law as teacher, and another son to succeed him.[33]

When Timothy stopped teaching, the number of children attending school fluctuated from sixteen to twenty-six. Many of them attended only in the summer, because in severe cold, when even the blankets they wrapped around themselves failed to keep them warm, the scarcity of firewood in the heart of town forced them to move a mile or two away for fuel.[34] Adding to the Indians' woes was illegal timber poaching by their provincial neighbors.[35]

After Eleazar Wheelock established his Indian academy (Dartmouth) in New Hampshire, eight to ten Indian boys attended it over a period of years starting in 1771.[36] In 1768 Timothy Woodbridge and others had tried unsuccessfully to persuade Wheelock to establish his academy in Stockbridge or in a developing township east of it. Woodbridge claimed that both the English and the Indians would welcome the school, and that the Indians were ready to grant 500 acres within Stockbridge to accommodate it. Wheelock, however, knew that influential men in Boston opposed his school for various reasons, and he opted for New Hampshire.[37] Dartmouth was shrouded in controversy and accusation in these early days of Wheelock's administration anyway, and the Stockbridge Indians did not need more of that. They themselves expressed concern one year when they asked that one of their young men at Dartmouth "not be disposed of in an unlawfull way, and in a clandestine manner."[38]

When John Sergeant kept school in Stockbridge, he received help from some of the Dartmouth graduates. And some Stockbridge Indians likely sent their youngsters to the Moravians for tutelage. Gradually more and more Stockbridges learned to read and write, as well as to speak and comprehend English, though perhaps just above a rudimentary level. About a dozen were at least capable of signing their names. Whatever education the Stockbridges were to receive would now be largely up to them, since the majority of their colonial neighbors were concerned only about their own children's education and future. Whether anyone else would be concerned with the interests of the Stockbridge Mohicans was a troubling question. William Johnson died in 1774. On May 11 of the same year their sixty-three-year-old teacher and mentor, Timothy Woodbridge, died after several weeks of illness. The future of the Stockbridge mission now rode squarely on the shoulders of the second and third generations.[39]

16

JOINING THE BROTHERS AGAINST THE FATHER

The Mohican struggle to stay alive as a nation coincided with the colonial struggle that resulted in the birth of a new nation. While the Stockbridges contended with poverty, debt, disposition of their land, and the condition of their souls, many other Americans contended with a stamp act, a tea tax, and the quartering of British soldiers. Rather than become the stepchildren of history, the Stockbridge Indians chose to join the Revolutionary family.

Berkshire County kept apace with, and sometimes anticipated, the rebellious steps being taken in Boston. On July 6, 1774, sixty delegates from several towns met in Stockbridge for two days. They passed resolutions that declared the tea tax illegal and the abolishment of trial by jury unconstitutional and oppressive. Timothy Edwards and Erastus Sergeant were members of a committee that forged an agreement to boycott British goods. The agreement also provided for a boycott of any trader or shopkeeper who refused to sign the agreement. Anyone who did not sign the agreement was to be treated with all due neglect. In the fall two militia regiments were raised.[1]

On November 2, Stephen West indicated that "we are making preparations for war. One man out of four is to be immediately inlisted. . . . The general officers are appointed, their names, however, at present kept secret." Commissaries were being established for "warlike stores," he said. "Everything forebodes the next to be a bloody summer. The

Canadians, it is expected, will fall upon us."[2] The two regiments were headed by John Patterson of Lenox and John Fellows of Sheffield. William Goodrich, a son-in-law of Timothy Woodbridge, was captain of one Stockbridge militia company, and David Pixley was first lieutenant.[3] Stockbridge Indians became minutemen in this company, with twenty-four-year-old Jehoiakim Mtohksin, son of Johannis, as second lieutenant.[4]

The Indians in general seemed perplexed by the militant quarrel between America and Great Britain. In their kinship frame of reference, this was like the child fighting against the father. Most of the charity the Stockbridges received came from England, and the king and his people had heard their pleas and entertained four of their chiefs just eight years earlier. How could their American brethren hope to win a fight against England? After all, Solomon Uhhaunauwaunmut, Daniel Nimham, and the others had observed the king's might in London.

It is not difficult to imagine the arguments and persuasions used to keep the Stockbridges on the American side. The theme of liberty struck a responsive chord among the Indians, and no doubt they were reminded that any taxes and acts forced on the colonies affected them as well. Then there was General Gage in Boston, imposed on the Massachusetts citizenry as their governor, ordering redcoats about the city and intimidating the people, the same Gage who had sent troops against the settlers and tenants in the disputes along the New York–Massachusetts border, and the same Gage who held the Indians in disdain.

Furthermore, despite the tumult of the past two decades, Stockbridge was the Indians' home. Most of the Indians in Stockbridge at this time had spent much if not all of their lives there, sharing the experiences of the community, bad and good. The core group of tribal councillors depended on the guidance of their colonial neighbors to successfully survive the changing order. When making decisions on issues of this magnitude, the Indians often had to consider the colonials' judgment. And their neighbors, including John Sergeant, Jr., espoused the rebel cause. In addition, the Six Nations' decision not to commit to either side left the Stockbridges free to make their own choice. This in turn afforded them an opportunity to finally throw off the Mohawks' political dominance.

Yet there were other, less idealistic reasons for leaning toward the Americans—the Stockbridges were surrounded by them. The same pressure exerted on colonials to conform to a boycott may have pressed the Stockbridges to the American side. The Stockbridges' constant indebtedness to their neighbors subjected them to subtle and not so subtle economic inducements. Forgiveness of their debts, however, was not one of them.[5]

Joseph Johnson, a Connecticut Mohegan preacher and a disciple of Eleazar Wheelock, related an example of such local pressure to Col. Guy Johnson. Accompanied by four Narragansetts, Joseph Johnson informed the colonel that sixty-four New England Indians intended to seek asylum with the Oneidas, who had offered them land on which to settle. Joseph Johnson said that the rest of the Indians, presumably meaning those in his home area, had been exhorted by Americans to fight with them and threatened if they refused. He further claimed that many who worked as laborers for Americans had been denied their wages unless they sided with the colonists. People in Farmington stopped Johnson and the others on their way to Oneida, insisting that they should stay to fight the British regulars. Johnson expressed surprise that "the people of New England [who] had got almost all our land from us, & thereby obliged us to go elsewhere should want to stop us now, when a year ago they seemed glad to get rid of us."[6]

One concern that was undoubtedly in the minds of the Stockbridges as they pondered joining sides was the question of the resolution of their claims on New York land. John Sergeant, Jr., at whose house they often conferred and whose advice they sought, and the Indians' other confidants probably assured them that if the Americans won the quarrel, they would ensure that the Indians received justice. And Sergeant could have reminded the Stockbridges that despite the sympathetic posturing by the king and his ministers, England had done nothing to restore their land rights. After all was said and done, however, a statement issued by some of the principal men a few years after the conflict probably reflected the Stockbridge Mohicans' general attitude toward the Revolution: "We had no immediate business with it."[7]

Having learned from John Patterson and William Goodrich that the Stockbridges had enlisted as minutemen, the Massachusetts Provincial Congress allocated £23 to purchase a blanket and a yard of ribbon apiece for those who had enlisted.[8] Wool blankets were always sought after, and the ribbon, probably made of silk, could be used as trim or decoration on Indian clothing or as a colored badge of distinction for those serving the patriot cause. The congress apparently also learned that the Stockbridges might need encouragement and an official explanation of what was happening. Since the rebellious leaders in Boston were eagerly looking for allies from all quarters in their growing confrontation with British authorities, they sent a message on April 1, 1775, to Jehoiakim Mtohksin "and the rest of our brethren, the Indians, natives of Stockbridge, Good Brothers!"

> It affords us great pleasure and satisfaction to hear . . . that our brothers the natives of Stockbridge are ready and willing to take up the hatchet in the cause of Liberty, and their country: we find you have not been inattentive to the unhappy controversy we are engaged in with our mother country. . . .

> This is a common cause, a cause you are equally engaged in with ourselves; we are all brothers, and if the Parliament of Great Britain takes from us our property and our lands without our consent, they will do the same by you; your property, your lands will be insecure; in short we shall not any of us have anything we can call our own. Your engaging in this cause discovers not only your attachment to your liberties; but furnishes us with an evidence of your gratitude to this province for their past favors. They have frequently, at your request, made laws and regulations for your protection and defence against the ravages and frauds of deceitful and designing men. They have constantly and chearfully afforded you aid and assistance because you have given them abundant proof of your fidelity; we have directed Col. Paterson and Capt. Goodrich to present each of you that have enlisted in the service with a blanket and a ribbon, as a testimony of our affection and shall depend upon your firm and steady attachment to the cause you have engaged in.[9]

After the Stockbridges received this address, they held council for nearly two days, discussing their response. Solomon Uhhaunauwaunmut, now head Mohican sachem, responded to John Hancock and the provincial congress on April 11. The tribe's answer revealed their self-image and portrayed the history of nations as a continuing saga of undying personal entities. The tribe's response also marked a significant change from previous decades, when the Stockbridges had been uncomfortable with the notion of fighting against their "fathers," the royal English governors. Now they were joining their brothers in fighting them.

> Brothers: You remember when you first came over the great waters, I was great and you was little—very small. I then took you in for a friend, and kept you under my arms, so that no one might injure you; since that time we have ever been true friends; there never has been any quarrel between us. But now our conditions are changed; you are become great and tall; you reach

up to the clouds; you are seen all round the world; and I am become small, very little; I am not so high as your heel. Now you take care of me, and I look to you for protection.

Brothers: I am sorry to hear of this great quarrel between you and Old England. It appears that blood must soon be shed to end this quarrel. We never till this day understood the foundation of this quarrel between you and the country you came from.

Brothers: Whenever I see your blood running, you will soon find me about you to revenge my brothers' blood. Although I am low and very small, I will grip hold of your enemy's heel, that he cannot run so fast and so light, as if he had nothing at his heels.

Brothers: You know I am not so wise as you are, therefore I ask your advice in what I am now agoing to say. I am thinking before you come to action, to take a run to the westward and feel the minds of my Indian brothers, the Six Nations, and know how they stand, whether they are on your side, or for your enemies. If I find they are against you, I will try to turn their minds. I think they will listen to me; for they have always looked this way for advice concerning important news that comes from the rising of the sun. If they hearken to me you will not be afraid of any danger from behind you. However their minds are affected, you shall soon know by me. Now I think I can do you more service in this way, than by marching off immediately to Boston, and stay there (it may be) a great while before blood runs. Now, as I said you are wiser than I, I leave this for your consideration, whether I come down immediately, or wait till I hear some blood is spilled.

By 1775, intentionally or not, the Stockbridges were in the process of breaking away from Mohawk political dominance. At this stage, however, they probably sought the Six Nations' opinion of the American conflict in order to crystallize their own attitude toward it. Yet Solomon was careful to reassure the Bostonians that the Stockbridges were not qualifying their endorsement of the patriot cause.

Brothers: I would not have you think by this that we are falling back from our engagements; we are ready to do any thing for your relief, and shall be guided by your counsel.

Brothers: One thing I ask of you if you send for me to fight, that you will let me fight in my own Indian way. I am not used to

fight English fashion, therefore you must not expect I can train
like your men. Only point out to me where your enemies keep,
and that is all I shall want to know.[10]

Previous wars apparently had reinforced the Indians' consciousness of
this aspect of their identity, which neither Christian influence nor Jeffrey
Amherst had changed. But even this cultural holdover was in its twilight.

Solomon was right in predicting that "blood must soon be shed," for
in less than two weeks word came that patriot blood was indeed running
at Lexington and Concord. An express courier arrived at Stockbridge
with the news at sundown on Friday, April 21, and by sunrise on Satur-
day two militia companies had set out to avenge their brothers' blood.[11]
William Goodrich's company included seventeen Stockbridges. Timothy
Yokun, son of Jehoiakim Yokun, was first sergeant, and three other
Indians filled the ranks of second sergeant, first corporal, and second
corporal.

The overland march east took nearly a week. By the end of April
Goodrich's company was at Cambridge, and the Stockbridge Indians,
painted for war, set up wigwams in the woods adjoining a farm owned
by a Tory, Ralph Inman, about a half-mile east of Harvard at the present
site of Inman Square.[12] A few days later six more Stockbridges joined
the company, and more joined as the siege of Boston began in earn-
est. Some veterans from the previous war were present, as were two
of Jacob Naunauphtaunk's sons, thirty-two-year-old Abraham and his
brother Jehoiakim, Jacob and Abraham Konkapot, and John Wauwaumpequunaunt's son, Daniel, and one of the Nimham clan. Chief Daniel
Nimham arrived with others in late June. A father and son, both named
William Notonksion, were part of the company, and some tribesmen had
brought their wives and children.[13] The Stockbridges would fight in their
own Indian way after all.

British redcoat sentries were excellent targets for guerrilla strikes
throughout the summer.[14] The Indians and the rough-cut Americans who
had adopted their tactics caused one British officer to lament: "Never
had the British army so ungenerous an enemy to oppose; they send their
riflemen (five or six at a time), who conceal themselves behind trees &c.
till an opportunity presents itself of taking a shot at our advanced sentries, which done they immediately retreat. What an infamous method
of carrying on a war!"[15]

When the Stockbridges were not shooting advance redcoats, they tried
to intimidate them by approaching the British lines, yelling insults, bran-

dishing their scalping knives, and—to the dismay of one New England Company official—turning their rumps in defiance to English vessels offshore.[16] That the Stockbridges might have been enjoying the rebellious spirit too much or been tempted by boredom during the long stretches of inaction during the siege was suggested in a petition to the provincial congress from Stockbridge in June. Most likely composed and sent to Cambridge by the tribal elders and John Sergeant, the petition was signed by eighteen of the Indians in camp, who agreed that: "We in our more serious hours reflect with shame upon our aptness to drink spiritous liquor to excess when we are under temptation; by which foolish conduct, when we are guilty of it, we render ourselves unfit for usefullness and service to our fellow men; and also disagreeable to those that have anything to do with us. We are senseable that we injure ourselves more than any one else; when we get a taste, we must some of us with shame say that sometimes no interest of our own will prevent us from procuring more, til we get too much. We therefore desire you would in your wisdom do something, (during our residence there) that we may get so much as will be good for us and no more."[17]

The signers further requested, to ward off temptation, that their army pay be given to Timothy Edwards and Joseph Woodbridge's son, Jahleel, who were then Stockbridge delegates to the provincial congress. The congress complied with both requests and issued a resolution calling on those who sold liquor not to let the Indians have too much, "as that wholly unfits them for any service."[18]

The Stockbridges' petition may have prompted a visit to their camp by a chaplain to the American troops, William Emerson, grandfather of Ralph Waldo Emerson. After being assured by Col. John Patterson that the Indians were fully under his control, Emerson enjoyed their company on July 7. "I had ye pleasure of sitting down with 'em at a fine mess of clams," he wrote to his wife, "cooked and eat in ye true genuine Indian taste. I wish you had been there to see how generously they put their fingers into ye dish, and picked out some of ye largest clams to give me, & with what a gust I eat them. Be sure it is the greatest diversion I have had since I have been in ye camp."[19]

The same day that Emerson visited the Stockbridge camp, George Washington arrived in Cambridge to take command of a motley army that was raw, ragged, at times unruly, and potentially dissolute. It is to the Stockbridges' credit as patriots that they took the side that had the least prospect of winning and few of the provisions and accouterments that made military service attractive to the Indians. Even at this late date the Stockbridges supplemented their firepower with bows and arrows and held target practice with them in camp.[20]

The Stockbridges learned firsthand the need for better discipline of the patriot militia. On the night of August 1, apparently during a sortie against redcoat sentries, Abraham Naunauphtaunk was shot through the knee and William Notonksion, Sr., was shot through the arm— by Americans.[21] Two days later Naunauphtaunk died.[22] Sometime afterwards Notonksion also died.[23] Naunauphtaunk and Notonksion thus were the first Indians to be killed on the patriot side in the Revolution, dying rather ignominiously at the hands of their fellow patriots.

What consequences, if any, followed is not known. John Sergeant, Jr., despite ill health, visited the army encampment in the middle of August, and he was aware of Naunauphtaunk's death and Notonksion's wound before he arrived.[24] Perhaps he came to smooth over any difficulties or simply to serve as a religious conscience for those tempted by unsavory influences around Boston. Despite the fatalities, some of the Indians remained at Cambridge and continued to terrorize British sentries for the next few weeks.[25]

Other Stockbridge Indians kept busy with different aspects of the patriot endeavor. The Reverend Stephen West expressed the fear of all New Englanders, that the Canadians would assault the frontier. If not the French Canadians and the Indians, then the British might come up the Lake Champlain–Lake George waterway to attack the rebellious colonies from the rear. Two expeditions departed in early May, therefore, to attempt to close the back door by taking the forts at Ticonderoga and Crown Point. Both expeditions were led by colorful, egotistical, and incompatible commanders, Ethan Allen and Benedict Arnold. Allen and his Green Mountain Boys were truculent, combative rebels before the Revolution made them legitimate. As squatters and speculators they had skirmished with New Yorkers over contested land between New York and New Hampshire. Governor William Tryon had put a price on Allen's head that escalated to £100 by 1774.[26] Allen, who had settled his family at Sheffield in 1767, became acquainted with the Stockbridges during his many wanderings between Massachusetts and what would become Vermont.

Ethan Allen and Benedict Arnold managed to surprise the British, taking Ticonderoga and Crown Point the second week in May. Less than a week after Ticonderoga fell, Abraham Nimham and two other Stockbridges arrived at the fort with a wampum belt, en route to Canada to learn the disposition of the tribes there toward the conflict.[27] Nimham had apparently enlisted with a militia outside Massachusetts and had the title of captain. Benedict Arnold handed Nimham a note addressed to a Montreal merchant friend and rebel collaborator, Thomas Walker, requesting any advice and assistance he could offer the Indian captain.[28] Abraham stopped at Crown Point for a couple of days before proceeding, and Ethan Allen also gave him a letter, long-winded and full of brotherly love, addressed with patriotic bravado to the Caughnawagas, the Saint Francis Indians, and two other tribes. He instructed Winthrop Hoit, who had once been captured by the Caughnawagas and adopted by the tribe, to accompany Nimham.

By advice of council I recommend our trusty and beloved friend and brother Capt. Abraham Nimham of Stockbridge as our Imbassador of peace to our good brother Indians of the four tribes.

. . . as King George's men first killed our men we hope as Indians are good and honest men you will not fight for King George against us as we have done you no wrong and would chuse to live with you as brothers. I always love Indians and have hunted a great deal with them. I know how to shute and ambush just like Indians and want your warriors to come and see me and help me fight Regulars. You know they stand all along close together rank and file and my men fight so as Indians do, and I want your warriors to join with me and my warriors like brothers and ambush the Regulars, if you will I will give you money, blankets, tomyhawks, knives and paint and the like as much as you say.

But if you our brother Indians do not fight on either side, still we will be friends and brothers and you may come and hunt in our woods and pass thro' our country in the Lake and come to our forest and have rum and be good friends.

We have sent our friend Winthrop Hoit to treat with you on our behalf in friendship. You know him for he has lived with you and is your adopted son and is a good man. Capt. Nimham and he will tell you about the whole matter more than I can write. I hope your warriors will come and see me. It may be at Crown Point or Saint John's and possibly at Montreal if I have good heart and fight well. So I bid all our brother Indians farewell.[29]

Nimham, the Stockbridges, and Hoit set out with their several messages on May 24, traveling down Lake Champlain on one of the captured vessels. As they approached Fort Saint John on the Richelieu, the Indians insisted on being put ashore for fear of being discovered on the water and taken prisoner. Hoit and one of the Indians apparently headed for Caughnawaga. Nimham and the other Stockbridge set out either for another Indian village or for Montreal, to contact Thomas Walker, but somewhere near Fort Saint John they were arrested.[30] They still had Allen's letter and Arnold's note, which ultimately found their way to Guy Carleton, the governor of Quebec. Carleton ordered a search for Hoit, who narrowly escaped capture.[31]

At Montreal the Stockbridges were court-martialed and condemned to be hanged for conspiring to incite the Canadian Indians against the British regulars. In the interim the Caughnawagas learned of the Stockbridges' fate and hotly protested to the governor. According to an anonymous letter to the Continental Congress from Stockbridge, angry exchanges took place between Carleton and the Canadian chiefs. They told him, "You have offered us money to fight for you, but we would not take it, as we would have nothing to do with your quarrel; but now we shall know who are our enemies. If you think it best for you to hang these our brothers, that came a great way to see us, do it; but remember, we shall not forget it."[32]

Some of the Canadian Indians reportedly offered to exchange their lives for those of the Stockbridge captives. Given these pleas and threats, Carleton thought it politic to release Nimham and his companion, but Nimham at least did not escape without a beating from the regulars at Fort Saint John and the loss of whatever material possessions he had with him.[33]

There was a practical reason why the Caughnawagas especially were so fervent in their defense of the Stockbridge emissaries. Ten of their boys were classmates of the Stockbridge boys at Dartmouth. Eight were descendants of colonial captives and one was the son of the head sachem at Saint Francis.[34] Eleazar Wheelock, among others, knew that in effect these boys were hostages, which gave him the sense that the school was secure against attack. It also gave him leverage to solicit money for the boys' support throughout the war. Persuasive Patrick Henry brought the situation to the attention of the Continental Congress, which appropriated $500 for the boys' support and renewed this grant in subsequent sessions.[35] Three ministers of rural churches also solicited support from their congregations for the Indian boys, specifically pointing out the youths' potential as a safeguard for the northern frontier.[36]

Despite their difficulties, the Stockbridges managed to convey messages to the Canadian Indians and to Arnold's friend, Thomas Walker, who apparently sent a return message with them back to Arnold. Five Canadian chiefs with their wives and children escorted the Stockbridges to Crown Point, arriving by June 10. Several officers under Ethan Allen contributed money from their own pockets to present to the chiefs as a gesture of friendship, and to compensate Abraham Nimham for his losses and for the marks of British abuse on his body.[37]

The Stockbridge Indian message to the Canadian Indians was that they should sit still, that is, stay out of the quarrel between the king and the Americans. Exchanging belts and strings of wampum with the Mohicans, the Caughnawagas replied, "I shall do as you tell me." But they also advised the Stockbridge tribe, "I would have you sit still too, and have nothing to do with this quarrel."[38] The Stockbridges, of course, were already in the thick of the quarrel. The Caughnawagas who accompanied Nimham to Crown Point assured the American officers that their tribe considered the fight a family feud and would not meddle. This sentiment was confirmed by an American missionary turned spy, connected with Dartmouth, who had been in Montreal throughout the spring. He reported that all the tribes around Montreal refused to join Carleton in an aggressive war, and that the Caughnawagas—for self-preservation mainly—had agreed to help the governor defend Montreal only if it were attacked. Eleazar Wheelock communicated this intelligence to the New Hampshire congress.[39]

Meanwhile, Solomon Uhhaunauwaunmut and his fellow Stockbridge chiefs were conducting diplomatic dialogues with other tribes and with American officials.[40] Before the year was out, the Stockbridges also sent a wampum message to their feisty younger brothers on the Ohio River, the Shawnees, inviting them to join the war on the American side.[41] In early May, according to an enthusiastic patriot minister at Pittsfield, Solomon had consulted with the Mohawks and reported that they "had not only gave liberty to the Stockbridge Indians to join us, but had sent them a belt denoting that they would hold in readiness 500 men to join us immediately on the first notice, and that the said Solomon holds an Indian post in actual readiness to run with the news as soon as they shall be wanted."[42]

This statement is interesting in its portrayal of the continuing diplomatic deference to the Mohawks by the Stockbridges, who probably did notify their uncles before committing themselves fully. But the rest of the statement seems to reflect wishful thinking. Though it was believed early on in some circles that the Mohawks might lean toward the patriot side, the Mohawks were largely neutral, as were most tribes at this stage of the conflict. The Mohawks did not have five hundred warriors, and even if they had, it is unlikely that they would have offered themselves as minutemen. The Six Nations were upset over failure to resolve the land contest in the Wyoming Valley, and over the failure of Americans to honor the Indian line established in 1768. There were, however, approximately five hundred Mohican men, women, and children scattered along the upper Hudson River who recognized Stockbridge as the central council fire. The fervent minister possibly mistook them for Mohawks.

The Stockbridge diplomats did not overlook the new Continental Congress. During part of June and July some of the tribe were in Philadelphia conferring with delegates on their present and future roll in the service.[43] The Stockbridges sought assurances that their land rights, particularly in New York, would be vindicated. The congress on at least one occasion promised "to protect you, to the utmost of our power, equally with ourselves, in the possession of all your rights and privileges."[44]

The Continental Congress formed commissions to treat with all the Indians in the hope of countering British influence and of persuading the Indians at least to remain neutral. Commissioners for the northern department met at German Flats and at Albany with the Six Nations during the last two weeks of August 1775, and Solomon Uhhaunauwaunmut represented the Stockbridges. Gatherings of this sort usually included entertainment. This time, besides the traditional Indian dances and rounds of rum, groups of Oneida and Stockbridge girls provided solemn evening entertainment by singing hymns. Tench Tilghman, a secretary-treasurer for the commissioners (and later aide-de-camp to George Washington), was a young man with an eye for the ladies. He believed that the Stockbridge girls far excelled the Oneidas in singing and were pretty, extremely clean, and spoke English tolerably well. With a few exceptions he found the Stockbridges superior to the Albany women. He also felt the urge to "make an acquaintance among them."[45]

While Tilghman was surveying the ladies, the Indians and the commissioners for the colonies were cautiously scrutinizing one another, but being careful not to commit themselves. On the last day of the conference Solomon spoke. A young New Jersey captain observed, "His behaviour is quite different from the rest of the savages, being polite & remarkeable free & easy in conversation."[46] Solomon's words contrasted sharply with the noncommittal tenor of the other tribes, and in effect asserted the Stockbridges' independence from them: "Brothers, appointed by the Twelve United Colonies: We thank you for taking care of us and supplying us with provisions since we have been at Albany. Depend upon it, we are true to you, and mean to join you. Wherever you go, we will be by your sides. Our bones shall lie with yours. We are determined never to be at peace with the red coats, while they are at variance with you. . . . If we are conquered, our lands go with yours; but if we are victorious, we hope you will help us to recover our just rights."[47]

This was bravery of a caliber that Americans would need for the coming Revolution. Here was a small, debilitated, nearly impoverished tribe clinging to a marginal existence astride two cultural worlds. Barely holding on to the little land they had left, the Indians were offering to risk it all for a patriot cause that surely seemed hopeless given England's far greater resources. In return, *if* the Americans were successful, the Indians asked only for help in recovering the land they believed was theirs by right. The public proclamation of the Stockbridges' allegiance with the Americans irrevocably severed the tribe's long-standing connection with the Mohawks. As a sign of how important the Christian ideal had become for the Stockbridge Indians, Solomon asked the commissioners to send a minister among them to instruct their women and children while the men were at war. Congenial as their relationship with John Sergeant, Jr., may have been, the Stockbridges knew that he was not an ordained minister and not as qualified to guide them in religion and education as their other missionaries had been. Lacking the authority to settle either the land issue or the question of a minister, however, the commissioners could only promise to represent the Indians' case to the Continental Congress, "and we dare say they will establish you in all your just rights."[48]

Within a year, the New England Company in London felt obliged to cut off funds for John Sergeant's salary, though it continued to honor the mission's other bills. The Stockbridges would be deprived of religious instruction unless someone was willing to donate his services. Sergeant petitioned the Continental Congress to maintain him as missionary, citing the Stockbridges' loyal service and his own role in advising them. Inexplicably, a congressional committee recommended supporting a missionary at Oquaga as well as Samuel Kirkland's mission to the Oneidas, even though Kirkland was living at Stockbridge. But the committee reasoned that the country "ought not to contribute to the support of a missionary to the Mohekon indians, of whom some resided at Stockbridge."[49] Perhaps the cost-conscious representatives chose to spend money on keeping potentially unfriendly Indians content rather than on placating those already loyal. Another possibility is that the congress expected the Stockbridges to take advantage of Kirkland while he was in their town. Kirkland's presence in Stockbridge probably served the American cause as much as or more than the Indians' spiritual needs, and the fervently patriotic reverend undoubtedly helped keep the Stockbridges in the Revolutionary family.

Indian involvement in the conflict between America and England was a thorny issue for both sides, but especially for frontier Americans, who had the most reason to be concerned. Now that the radical men of Boston had embraced Stockbridge participation in the fray, these Indians became propaganda symbols. The Massachusetts congress sent a letter to the Indians in Maine, encouraging them either to adhere to the Americans or stand neutral. As an enticement, the legislators noted that "our good brothers, the Indians at Stockbridge, all join with us, and some of their men have enlisted as soldiers, and we have given them that enlisted each one a blanket and a ribbon, and they will be paid when they are from home in the service, and if any of you are willing to enlist we will do the same for you."[50]

In April of 1775 the provincial congress wrote to the Mohawks, explaining the American version of the conflict and asking them to "whet your hatchet and be prepared with us to defend our liberties and lives."[51] The letter was sent via Samuel Kirkland, who was urged to use his influence to persuade the Mohawks to join the rebels or remain neutral.

The patriots felt justified in seeking Indian assistance because the British in Canada were rumored to be courting the Indians to their side. As early as June of 1774 Governor Tryon had supplied England with information about the numbers and the allegiance of the Indians in New York, in response to royal questions designed to determine the strategic disposition of the colonies.[52] Nevertheless, when Massachusetts drafted the Stockbridge Mohicans, the Americans became the first to employ Indians as soldiers in the conflict.

Thomas Gage's assessment of the importance of the Stockbridges depended on who was to receive his letters, what impression he wished to convey, and how exasperated he was. In May and June he wrote to the commander at Niagara and to Carleton, encouraging both men to woo the Indians to the British side. "The Rebels about this town have brought some Indians against us," he told Carleton, "and I would repay them in their own way. They are not distant Indians, but what the French would call domicilies, and not of great worth."[53]

After learning that Ticonderoga had been taken, Gage wrote to an official in London, "you may be tender of using Indians, but the rebels have shown us the example, and brought all they could down upon us here."[54] A creative exaggeration, but one that reflected Gage's frustration. The general was determined to overcome the home government's hesitation to use Indians against its own subjects and to justify his plan to raise Canadians and Indians to retake Ticonderoga. By July, George III agreed to employ the Six Nations and so instructed Guy Johnson.[55]

In September Gage was still using the Stockbridges for propaganda purposes. On the tenth he demeaned the patriot performance, telling William Tryon that "their Indians and rifle men have been firing above six weeks and have hit one poor marine, for which they [have] paid tenfold."[56] Ten days later he instructed the British superintendent of Indian affairs in the southern district to raise Indians to fight His Majesty's enemies, because "they have brought down all the savages they could against us here, who with their rifle men are continually firing on our advanced sentries."[57] In June the Stockbridges had been "domiciles," but by September they were savages.

Meanwhile, representatives from the Saint Francis, Saint John, and Penobscot tribes had visited Cambridge in August, and in the company of a Stockbridge Indian they met with George Washington to offer their services. Four Saint Francis Indians stayed on to join the Americans, and their chief returned with the Stockbridge to Ticonderoga.[58] Mohican influence with the northeastern tribes was now paying off for the Americans, since these tribes probably had lingering animosity toward the British. Washington and his advisers told the rest of the visiting Indians that they would be called if needed, and they were dismissed with suitable tokens of friendship. When Washington met with representatives from the Continental Congress and the New England governments to discuss war measures, they discussed whether it was proper to continue this posture of encouragement toward interested Indians. The delegates agreed to call on them if necessary, and that to encourage them with presents was appropriate. In early December the full Continental Congress agreed.[59]

As the Revolution entered 1776 and the prospect of taking Canada seemed real, the issue of actually employing the Indians remained unresolved. On February 22 Solomon Uhhaunauwaunmut arrived in Albany to offer the tribe's services in the fight that Benedict Arnold and Ethan Allen had carried to Canada. He delivered a note to Philip Schuyler from Timothy Edwards, who confided that "the refusing their proffered service is an affair of delicacy, to which you will readily attend."[60]

"Solomon urged me to let the Stockbridge Indians go to Canada,"

Schuyler reported to John Hancock. "I considered it as a matter too delicate for me to decide upon, and told him that I would lay his request
before Congress. He hinted he would expect pay."[61] Solomon's hint was
a response to the familiar specter haunting the Indians. The absence of
the men who participated in the siege of Boston, the commercial disruption of the war, ongoing problems with adjusting to a changing culture,
and the relentlessness of their creditors contributed to the Indians' financial woes. Uhhaunauwaunmut and the other principal men once again
were forced to petition the Massachusetts Provincial Congress to pass a
law that would give the Indians two years to pay their debts before they
could be sued. They wanted to pay all their debts by selling some of their
outlands, but had been thwarted by "the present troubles the country is
in. . . . We much fear and dread being sued." If it continued, "we fear
we shall be obliged to quit all and go off." The Stockbridges reminded
the congress of the expense and the imprisonment some of them had suffered in the past as a result of "being sued by almost every one to whom
we owed so much as a few shillings." They further asked the congress
to put "the tavernkeeper and retailer of spiritous liquors who live round
about us under some strict restraint in regard to the freedom they take
in selling us spiritous liquors, which ever has been ruinous to our souls
and bodyes, and always will be to those of us who are so foolish as to
give way to that most destructive practice of drinking to excess." The
committee that reviewed the petition recommended that it be granted
and that an appropriate bill be brought forward, but none appeared.[62]
The Stockbridges' debt problems, however, may have been temporarily
solved by Berkshire County radicals who were victims of similar lawsuits
and who ultimately shut down the courts.

American officials, meanwhile, had mixed feelings about using Indians
in the war. The Continental Congress, nevertheless, did order the raising
of Indians for an assault on Canada. Indian affairs commissioners Philip
Schuyler, Timothy Edwards, and Volkert P. Douw quickly tried to raise
two companies of eighty-four Indians each from among the Stockbridge
Indians and the Connecticut Mohegans.[63] The congress, to the confusion of George Washington and John Hancock, apparently had in mind
Canadian and Penobscot Indians, and it subsequently ordered a halt to
the enlistment of Stockbridges and Mohegans.[64] The effort was already
under way, however, and Schuyler feared that turning down the Stockbridges' services would give them "great umbrage." He advised Timothy
Edwards to inform them in a manner that would "give them the least
offence."[65]

The Stockbridges took offense anyway. At the end of July a contingent of them visited Washington's headquarters in New York and expressed their displeasure to Israel Putnam, who informed Washington. Since the Indians seemed so eager to join and had been led to believe they could by the commissioners at Albany, and since "we are under difficulties in getting men, and there may be danger of their or some of them taking an unfavourable part," Washington reasoned, "they had better be employed." [66]

Congress concurred and gave Washington authority to raise as many Stockbridges as he thought proper. The general in turn ordered them to reenlist quickly, and he later emphasized to Timothy Edwards the urgency of engaging as many of them as possible as soon as possible. To compensate for the inconvenience and affront they had experienced, Washington allowed them the option of joining him at New York or joining the northern army on Lake Champlain. [67]

It was mid-August before Schuyler and Edwards were able to reassemble the Indians. They increased the reparations to the young men by paying them for the month they had been discharged and inactive. [68] The Stockbridges contributed to the overall confusion when many of them at first decided to join Washington's army, but then changed their minds two days later and headed for Horatio Gates's forces on the lake. [69] This was strategically advantageous for the Americans, because with an invasion of Canada now impractical, there was a possibility that the British might move south from Canada. Gates placed the Indians under Capt. Ezra Whittlesey in Col. Samuel Brewer's command at Saw Mills, about a mile from Ticonderoga. To avoid another fatal mishap like the one outside Boston, the general ordered that each Stockbridge wear a blue and red cap, distinguishing them from the enemy's Indians: "Of this all officers and soldiers in this army are to take particular notice, to the end that we may not, by mistake, kill our friends instead of our enemies." [70]

The task of preventing the British from sweeping down from Canada on the Lake Champlain–Lake George waterway was assigned to energetic Benedict Arnold, who worked a minor miracle by assembling an impromptu navy from green timber and green troops by late summer. Thirteen vessels, plus three captured from the British the previous year, set out to challenge the king's men. Among the ships was the galley *Washington*, commanded by Gen. David Waterbury. Stockbridge Indians were serving with Waterbury, possibly as scouts sent out from the vessel to report on enemy movements. They may have been responsible for capturing the prisoners at the north end of Lake Champlain who informed Arnold that the British were assembling a sizable fleet as well as troops and Indians for an invasion. This armada ultimately overwhelmed Arnold's plucky backyard navy and gave it a bloody pounding on October 11 and 13. General Waterbury and 106 men surrendered the *Washington,* but were soon released under promise not to resume arms. Whether the Stockbridges were among the captives is unclear, but they returned to Ticonderoga in late October, a week after the release.[71]

The lateness of the season and the relentless approach of an overwhelming army may have made the Indians restless for home and family. And their old free habits, which in the past had aggravated militia officers, apparently were proving troublesome again. Whatever the reasons, the day after the Stockbridges returned from the naval fray, Captain Whittlesey pleaded with Colonel Brewer to dismiss them. "It is with the utmost difficulty," he said, "I have kept them in any order until now."[72] Brewer forwarded the request to Gates, who complied, and the Indians returned home that week.

The very day that Whittlesey requested the Stockbridges' dismissal, Philip Schuyler at Saratoga received a note from Washington's aide-de-camp. He asked that the Stockbridges be sent to Harlem Heights, New York, to serve as scouts against the British, who were pushing Washington's army around Manhattan. Schuyler simply replied that the Indians had left the army and returned home several days earlier.[73] This may have been technically true by the time Washington received Schuyler's reply, but the Indians were undoubtedly still available when Schuyler received the request. The general may have taken it upon himself not to recall the Stockbridges.

The Stockbridge Indians differed little in their lack of soldierliness from their rebel peers in the northern militia, judging by the officers' observations. Philip Schuyler wrote to Horatio Gates a few days after the Stockbridges departed: "The militia are deserting in great numbers. General Washington advises that if they are not absolutely wanted to dismiss them as he fears they will distress us as much as they have him, by eating our provisions and doing no service. Those at Fort George continue to refuse their aid in erecting the picket round the hospital and in mounting guard."[74]

Schuyler's orderly book for the preceding twelve months recorded numerous instances of drunkenness, insubordination, stealing, shooting guns around camp, sleeping on guard duty, and desertion.[75] In Stockbridge itself Timothy Edwards lamented the lack of patriotic fervor among his countrymen. Even though both Massachusetts and the town of Stockbridge had offered a bounty to men who volunteered for the Canadian expedition, "shameful to be told, the men are not all raised yet. Is this like a people struggling for their all? All that is valuable? . . . The truth is that we as individuals do not feel our lives liberties and properties to be in immediate danger."[76] There were some loyalists in Stockbridge; Elijah Williams was once jailed on suspicion of colluding with tories.[77]

Erastus Sergeant, at least, did join the northern army and served as a surgical officer at Ticonderoga. Though war disagreed with his delicate sensibilities, he admired the beauty of the well-disciplined army, particularly in contrast to the militia, "who at home are nearly on an equallity with their officers, and the time of their service is generally short, and I might mention the want of ability, honor and authority among many of the officers."[78] An officer at Ticonderoga, probably Arthur St. Clair, lamented in April of 1777, "It is with much pain I observe at least one-third of the troops now on the ground composed of negroes, Indians and children; . . . It is a melancholy reflection that we should be necessitated to retain Indians and negroes in our ranks. Have we not white men, have we not freemen sufficient without them? We certainly have."[79]

17

FIGHTING
AND
DYING
FOR
THE
UNAPPRECIATIVE

In 1777 the Stockbridges reenlisted for varying periods of duty as the northern colonies girded themselves for the enemy advance from the north. By mid-May at least fourteen Stockbridges had enrolled with Capt. Ephraim Cleaveland's company in Col. Michael Jackson's Eighth Massachusetts Regiment, now part of the Continental Army. Jehoiakim Mtohksin and two others served in a revived militia unit under David Pixley in Col. John Brown's regiment of the northern army from June 30 to July 26. Mtohksin was listed as a private in this outfit, but soon afterward acquired the title of captain, officially or unofficially. Abraham Nimham and several fellow tribesmen were identified with the regiments of Gen. John Nixon and Gen. John Fellows for about the same period.[1]

The Stockbridges joined in time to witness a large British army of regulars, Canadians, Hessians, and Indians under the command of John Burgoyne bearing down on Ticonderoga. Outmatched in quantity and quality of soldiers, Arthur St. Clair and his men retreated from the fort on the night of July 5, and the British reoccupied Ticonderoga nearly as easily as the Americans had taken it two years earlier. With Albany his goal, Burgoyne marched a little too leisurely south on the east side of Lake George, slowed down by his own equipment and by skirmishes with retreating Americans, who obstructed roads with felled trees.

Several weeks earlier Burgoyne had held a conference with his four hundred assorted Iroquois and Algonquin allies. Obviously alluding to the Stockbridge Indians, the British general claimed that "a few individuals alone, the refuse of a small tribe, at the first were led astray" by the rebels, but that "these pitiful examples probably have before this day hid their faces in shame."[2] The Stockbridge Indians were indeed hiding—behind rocks, bushes, and trees, as they monitored British movements and captured any overconfident enemy who strayed outside a camp perimeter.[3]

Burgoyne's army paused at Skenesborough (now Whitehall, New York), while the Americans continued to fall back toward dilapidated Fort Edward. Just north of the fort, the Berkshire County militia and the Stockbridge warriors under Nixon and Fellows were encamped near Wood Creek. On July 18 Fellows sent about six Stockbridge scouts under Abraham Nimham toward Skenesborough. Nimham's entertaining account of this sortie was published in a Boston newspaper:

We passed the Creek, and went within a mile or two of Skene's House, where we lay down in a thick spot of woods by the side of the road. It was not long before there came along two Regulars driving a number of horses; we jumped up and seized them; [The] Regulars were so very much frighted, that they made no resistance, neither could they speak plain. We found by the noise, there were a number more behind driving cattle. One of our prisoners called to the Serjeant for help; upon this, we thought it wise to make the best of our way into the woods. Our prisoners attempted to get away from us, we were therefore obliged to make them feel that our hatchets were heavy. I told them if you will behave like prisoners, we will use you well, but if you don't we must kill you; After this, they behaved well, and did every thing we bid them.

On our way to our encampment, we tho't we would take in with us as many Tories as we could find; and in order to find them out, we gave our prisoners their guns, taking out the flints. When we came near a house, we told our prisoners, you must keep before us, and if you see any man you must cock your guns and present them at them, and demand who they are for, the King, or Country? They did so, and the Tories answered, they were for the King or they should have moved off long ago. They seemed to be glad to see the Regulars, and told them, "you are our Brothers."

I knew one of the Tories as soon as I came in sight of him, I therefore put my hat over my face, for fear the fellow should know me, till the Red-Coats had done their duty. After he had in a most strong manner declared he was for the King, I asked him further will you be true to the King, and fight for him till you die? "O yes," said the Tory. Upon this he discovered his error, knew me, and immediately said, "What King do you mean? I mean King Hancock."

"Ah," said I, "we have found you out, we don't know Kings in America yet; you must go along with us."[4]

Nimham and his comrades collected two more tories on their way back, and as they approached camp produced a war cry that brought their Stockbridge brothers out to greet them. The scouts turned over the prisoners and collected their reward, while the American army collected some useful intelligence about British movements.[5] The information also assisted a council of officers at Fort Edward who were debating whether to let some of the militia return home to tend their farms. The council decided that half of them could go, and about half the Stockbridges returned with them. More than a dozen Indians, though, including David Naunauneekanuk the younger, Daniel Wauwaumpequunaunt, and John Nimham, signed up for a year as regular soldiers with the Continental Army under Colonel Jackson. Naunauneekanuk, however, still preferred the Indians' mode of warfare.[6]

Jackson's regiment was part of a relief contingent sent westward a month later to relieve Fort Stanwix, which was under siege by another arm of the British invasion. The men at Fort Stanwix successfully resisted the attack before the relief got there, and Jackson's regiment was able to return to help Horatio Gates resist Burgoyne's push southward. Those Stockbridges at home, meanwhile, joined Massachusetts militia to help American Brig. Gen. John Stark, one of their old officers from Rogers Rangers, defend against a force marching toward Bennington. By the time the Stockbridges organized themselves and set out, however, they were too late for the battle, and as Timothy Edwards put it, "too late to reape any of the glory of our late victory there."[7] The Indians returned to Stockbridge, but General Gates requested that they rejoin his army. Burgoyne was moving ominously toward Albany as the Americans continued to yield ground. Patriots in New York and western New England had good reason to defend themselves.

Timothy Edwards assembled the Stockbridge Indians, and after four days of preparation about fifteen warriors, some without guns, marched on August 26 with their captain, Jehoiakim Mtohksin. Edwards had supplied them with ammunition and enough provisions for the march to Albany. He also sent with them a note to Gates, saying that Mtohksin would probably "do well as long as he remains unconnected with Baccus." In other words, as long as he stayed sober. Abraham Nimham was to join them soon. "On him you may depend, for he forms no such connections," Edwards told the general.[8] Nimham had been in the service a little longer than the others and was esteemed enough to have received payment for "secret services."[9]

About this time John Sergeant, Jr., expressed concern about the Stockbridges' enlistment in the army, obviously fearing the Bacchus connection mentioned by Timothy Edwards. Sergeant was not only afraid that military service would "amazingly corrupt their morrals," he believed that the Indians would never last out the war and would therefore bring scandal on themselves and loss of respect.[10] Associating with the rabble in the militia certainly was not consistent with Calvinist discipline. But it is strange that Sergeant placed so little confidence in the Indians, given their enlistments throughout the French and Indian War. Furthermore, their service to the Revolutionary cause already exceeded that of many Americans, some of whom paid others to fight in their stead. The Stockbridge Mohicans on occasion headed for home when they felt it was necessary, rather than wait for official discharge, but so did other militiamen.

Mtohksin and his men joined Gates's growing army in time to help contain Burgoyne and served during the first conflict near Saratoga at Freeman's Farm on September 19. Those in Jackson's regiment likely saw action during the three-hour fight that afternoon. It is not known to whom Mtohksin and his men were assigned at this time, though they may have been with Col. John Brown's troops, as in July. Brown's men were part of a successful assault north against Ticonderoga's outer defenses. They captured the works and took three hundred enemy prisoners. Word of this feat reached the patriot army near Saratoga on the twenty-first. It cheered the Americans while dampening Burgoyne's hopes for a successful retreat should winter or Horatio Gates keep him from Albany.[11]

Mtohksin returned to Stockbridge with his men to help with the harvest, probably in late September.[12] Abraham Nimham also left, heading for Philadelphia to petition the Continental Congress for clothing. The scarcity of clothing and supplies was a continuing problem for the northern armies. In June, John Sergeant, Jr., had gone to Boston to buy blankets with the money the Indians had entrusted to him. The merchants who usually supplied the Indians had none, and Sergeant soon found that no private suppliers had any either. He then petitioned the provincial congress, which allowed him to purchase twenty from the government supply.[13]

Nimham pleaded the Stockbridges' case for clothing at Philadelphia on the first of October. Abraham acquainted the delegates with the warriors' service and added:

They always stand ready to the utmost of their power to oppose the enemies to this our country. But they are at present not fit to go into the service for want of comfortable cloathing. We Indians have no wool or flax, nor do we understand how to manufacture them to supply our own and the necessities of our families as you White people do. We cant buy any cloathing at all without giving a very great price for it, so that our money is good for but little. Neither can we find it any where about us for money.

I am now come this great distance in my own behalf, and in the behalf of my friends, to lay this matter before this Honourable Congress, beging of them to give such orders as they in their wisdom shall think fit, that we may be able to get necessary cloathing for ourselves and families at some reasonable price. That when ever we the warriors are called upon to join your armies we may all as one be ready to take up our guns and our tommyhawks and go immediately with this satisfactory consideration that we dont leave our wives and our children naked.[14]

Three weeks passed before the congress voted Nimham $200, which may have eased the Indians' plight for a while.[15] The difficulty of obtaining the necessary clothing delayed the Stockbridge Indian militiamen's return to General Gates's army until the last week in October. By then the general had engineered the significant defeat and capture of Burgoyne and his forces, minus the Canadian Indians, most of whom had deserted. Although those in Stockbridge knew of the victory by October 23, Mtohksin sent his lieutenant and the others to join Gates, and he wrote the general a polite, patriotic note: "Thank you sir in my own and the behalf of our people, for your kindness in leting these young men come home. They have been helpful to their families in gathering in their harvest. They have been delayed some in geting themselves shoes &c. We all rejoice with you Sir in the . . . suc[cess] you have had over your enemies since we left y[ou.] [M]ay the God of armies help you Sir to compleat [your] great and good work, and drive our enemies from their strong holds. This lets you know Sir that your brother warriors at

Stockbridge stand ready to go to your assistance, at any time you send for us."

Jehoiakim politely reminded Gates that the general had encouraged him and his lieutenant to expect that as Indian officers they would receive a little "something more than the common soldier." If Gates agreed, the lieutenant would kindly accept the bonus for both of them.[16] Mtohksin remained in Stockbridge, quite possibly because Solomon Uhhaunau-waunmut died around this time. As a principal tribal member, Mtohksin would have been needed to help with the tribe's civil affairs and the election of a new sachem. Joseph Shauquethqueat, apparently a son or grandson of King Ben, became sachem and also succeeded Solomon as a town selectman.[17] Descendants of the prominent early Stockbridge Indian families—the Naunauphtaunks, Konkapots, and Mtohksins—held office throughout this period, token as the positions may have been.

Up to this point, the Stockbridges were the Americans' only active Indian allies in the Revolution. The patriot commanders were satisfied with this arrangement, since their primary concern was that the Indians remain neutral in the conflict. Thus far Philip Schuyler, Timothy Edwards, and others had successfully maintained this neutrality in the northern department through negotiations with the Six Nations. Because of political, economic, and even religious pressures, however, combined with the prestige that warrior status brought to Indian males, their neutrality was short-lived. Missionary Samuel Kirkland's influence among the Oquaga Oneidas and Tuscaroras was strong enough to win most of them to his political views as well as his religious views. Tory officials such as Guy Johnson identified Kirkland as a potential subversive and discouraged his presence among the Iroquois.

Since 1770 Kirkland's fiscal support had come from the New England Company and from benefactors of Harvard College. As a consequence, his flock may have focused on Boston as the source of the charity, as the Stockbridges had, even though the funds ultimately came from England.[18] Kirkland's part-time residence at Stockbridge also may have helped cement Oneida and Tuscarora ties with their Mohican brethren. Even without Kirkland, however, relations between the Stockbridges, Oneidas, and Tuscaroras had strengthened since the early 1750s, when they hosted one another and became followers of Congregationalism.[19]

The British camp wielded greater influence with the Indians, between the prestige of the Johnson family and a powerful Mohawk named Joseph Brant, who, ironically, had been a pupil of Eleazar Wheelock. After visiting England with Guy Johnson in 1775, Brant was persuaded that the

Indians' true interests were guarded better by the British than by the Americans, too many of whom were displacing the Indians and ignoring the line between Indian and American territory. The Brant family was also strongly connected with the Johnson family. In addition, British agents vigorously pressured the Indians to join the king's fight, and they could draw upon the king's wealth for suitably persuasive gifts and necessities, items that were difficult to procure from the American side in wartime. And despite American appeals through patriots like Ethan Allen and Abraham Nimham, most of the Canadian Indians had sided with the British, however tentatively. Pressures increased in proportion to the tempo of the Revolution, and the Six Nations league was rent by disagreement. By the spring of 1776 several Oneida chiefs confided to Samuel Kirkland that their tribe, the Tuscaroras, and the Caughnawagas had agreed to a defensive alliance and would join the Americans if other tribes joined the British.[20]

In July of 1777, as Burgoyne was pushing south, the British military in western New York overwhelmed the rest of the Six Nations with gifts, rum, and patriotic persuasion. In the march against Fort Stanwix, the Mohawks and the western Iroquois carried the hatchet for the king. Among the American troops sent to relieve the besieged fort were sixty Indians, mostly Oneidas. At a fierce battle on August 6 between this American contingent and the enemy in ambush, many British Indian allies fell. In retaliation for the Oneidas' participation, the British Indian allies burned a nearby Oneida village, destroyed its crops, and killed or carried off its cattle. The Oneidas took similar revenge on the family of Joseph Brant and on a Mohawk town. The Iroquois in council then vowed to seek further revenge against the Oneida rebels.[21]

The Iroquois League now had serious internal rifts, and the Stockbridge Indians were no longer conspicuous as allies of the Americans. One hundred and fifty Oneida and Tuscarora warriors joined Horatio Gates's army on September 20. Wearing red woolen caps to distinguish them from enemy Indians, they wasted no time in capturing and scalping unwary enemy soldiers. Gates issued the authorized rewards for prisoners, but refused any for the scalps, apparently hoping to discourage the practice.[22] Timothy Edwards cautioned that the "affair of scalping as relating to Indians is delicate, but your knowledge of their disposition will conduct you into such measures as will not deprive them of trophies of war-like achievement."[23]

Although the Oneidas and other Indians were allies, Gates had to order his officers to prevent their men from crowding around the Indian camp, gawking and hurling insults. The Indians must have been thick-skinned and dedicated to withstand enemy fire and then take abuse from their own allies. Gates was pleased with their performance in the campaign and wrote John Hancock after Burgoyne's surrender that the "Six Nations having taken up the hatchet in our favor has been of great service."[24] The general was a little too optimistic, since a hundred or so Oneidas and Tuscaroras hardly constituted the Six Nations.

Most of the Indians who chose sides selected the British, as was all too evident by the summer of 1778. Having decided to fight, the British Indian allies vented their wrath on the Wyoming Valley, which had become the symbol of American intractability. The young settlements in frontier New York and Pennsylvania bore the brunt of Indian and tory raids. Hundreds of settlers lost homes, farms, crops, livestock, or their lives. In the meantime, the 1778 campaigns between the British and the Continental Army were concentrated in the settled eastern areas of New Jersey and New York. In terms of the outcome or resolution of the war they were not significant. But for the Stockbridge Indians they were highly significant.

By late summer the British were located in New York City and its environs, while the Continental Army formed a line of containment north at White Plains. Raiding parties from both sides skirmished on occasion in the neutral areas in between. This was appropriate duty for Indians, and Stockbridges and others offered their services. At least half the Stockbridge tribesmen who had been with Michael Jackson's regiment at Saratoga were serving under Gates at White Plains in late July. Four others were with Brig. Gen. Jedidiah Huntington.[25] Abraham Nimham commanded yet another group of Indians, and his father, Chief Daniel Nimham, joined him for this tour of duty. Besides Stockbridges, many of Nimham's men were probably members of scattered tribes, mostly from New York, who considered Stockbridge their capital.[26] Abraham also asked that regimental commanders under Gates allow Nimham's brothers to join him. "Now brothers," Nimham explained to the commanders, "I should be very glad if you will discharge them from their regiments. We always want to be in one body when we are in service. Do not think that I want [to] get these Indians away from their soldierings, but we want [to] be together always & we will be always ready to go any where you want us to go long as this war stands &c."[27] Nimham may have gotten not only his brothers but other Indians from Jackson's regiment as well, since by August he commanded nearly fifty.

The Mohicans wore deerskin mocassins, coarse linen trousers, and

A watercolor sketch of an Indian patriot in Abraham Nimham's 1778 Stockbridge militia company at White Plains and the Bronx, New York. From the manuscript diary of Hessian officer Johann von Ewald. Source: Bloomsburg University Archives, Bloomsburg, Pa.

long tunic-like linen shirts worn outside and reaching almost to the knees. A cinch around the waist held a tomahawk and one or more leather pouches containing probably powder, shot, or dried food. A broadbrimmed hat of woven basswood bark with a ribboned hatband covered a shaved head with only the silver-dollar-sized scalplock remaining. A bow and a quiver of about twenty arrows hung over one shoulder, and a musket was cradled in the other arm.[28]

The Stockbridge Indians, particularly the few who had fought in the French and Indian War, were in an ironic position. Based at Kingsbridge, within present-day New York City, was their old unit of rangers, still in the king's service. New faces appeared in its ranks, however. Robert Rogers's place had been taken by a British lieutenant colonel named John Simcoe, who also commanded a cavalry outfit and a corps composed primarily of loyalist volunteers. Simcoe's account paints a picture of events involving the Stockbridges in the waning days of August.

Nimham and his men were part of an American outpost located in the general area of present-day Tibbetts Brook Park in Yonkers.[29] By late August probing parties of rebels and Indians were sparring with Simcoe's men in the area now called Van Cortlandt Park in the Bronx. On one occasion Simcoe, Banastre Tarleton, the commander of the cavalry, and a few soldiers were patrolling a road near a farm. They intended to cross the farm, but the officers changed their minds and the party rode off in a different direction. Simcoe later learned that Nimham and his Stockbridges had been lying in wait around the farm, ready to ambush the British soldiers.[30]

On August 30 the corps of loyalist volunteers was patrolling ahead of Simcoe's force near the same area when they ran into a group of about a hundred patriots, half of them Stockbridges. Shooting began, and the loyalist corps retreated toward Simcoe, believing themselves heavily outnumbered. Simcoe learned through spies that the rebels and the Indians were elated at the loyalists' retreat and believed that they had forced Simcoe's entire command to fall back. Simcoe decided to encourage this belief. He ordered a day's provisions to be cooked and then marched his three units—about five hundred men—out of camp the next morning, moving forward to lay an ambush. As they moved north toward the farm where they themselves had almost been ambushed, Simcoe divided the units to the left and right of the road.

In the afternoon, the Stockbridge Indian company was moving south on the same road when it encountered the volunteer loyalist corps, which had wrongly positioned itself in the nearby woods. The Indians quickly

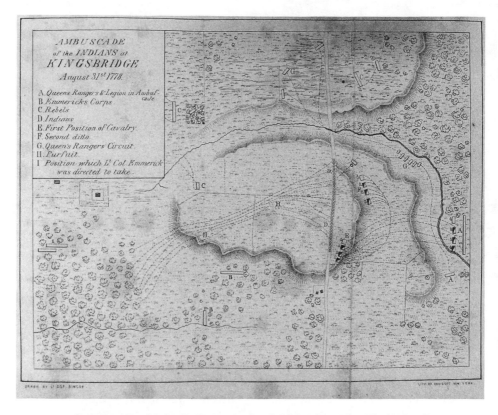

British colonel John G. Simcoe's sketch of the skirmish with the Stock-bridge Indians, August 31, 1778. Source: John G. Simcoe, Simcoe's Military Journal *(New York, 1844).*

spread out along a fence beside the road and peppered gunfire across a field into the woods. The British cavalry and Simcoe's rangers immediately moved up to the crests of ridges behind the Indians. Obstructed by fences on its side of the road, the cavalry had to drop back below the ridge, move north, and remount at another point. Simcoe then marched with grenadiers to the spot vacated by the cavalry, while rangers followed another ridge northwestward to encounter flanking rebels.

The Indians' attention was now divided between the loyalist corps at their front and the cavalry approaching from the rear toward the north end of their line. Simcoe and his men were thus able to approach undetected within ten yards of the southern end of the Indians' position. These Indians, Daniel Nimham among them, finally spotted Simcoe and his men, gave a yell, and turned their fire on the new attackers, wounding four grenadiers and Simcoe. The lieutenant colonel, who described the

Stockbridges as "excellent marksmen," credited Daniel Nimham with wounding him.

With overwhelming numbers pressing them from the north and the south, the chief called out to his people to flee, but said that he was old and would die there. He was right. Simcoe's orderly shot and mortally wounded the chief. Abraham had no time to mourn. He, too, was killed.

The rest did abandon the fence and headed west into the open field and toward the woods, still fighting as the cavalry rode them down and the foot soldiers closed in from the side. The Indians refused to give up and only a few received quarter from the enemy. The fighting was intense. Shots were fired at close range and swords, knives, and tomahawks flailed in a swirl of sweaty bodies slamming against frantic horses and one another, as the acrid smell of gunpowder, horses, leather, and blood filled the steamy air of the last day in August.

"The Indians fought gallantly," Simcoe acknowledged, "they pulled more than one of the cavalry from their horses." A German mercenary remarked that both the Indians and Americans "defended themselves like brave men." Banastre Tarleton lost his balance as he struck at an Indian and fell from his horse. He escaped death only because the Indian had already fired his gun, which had no bayonet attached. Another mounted soldier, a young bugler, struck at an Indian but missed. The Indian grabbed his hand and dragged him off his horse. As the Indian groped for his knife, he loosened his grip. The youth pulled a small pistol from his pocket and shot the patriot Indian through the head.[31]

Some of the rebel militia managed to join the Indians at the beginning of the skirmish, but Simcoe's men quickly captured about ten, one a captain. According to Simcoe, a larger body fled, leaving the Indians behind. Simcoe also reported that the British took two Indians captive, one of whom he described as the "Indian doctor." If he meant a shaman, this suggests that not all the Mohicans had abandoned Indian religion.

The skirmish was savage and lasted until about seven in the evening. Some Indians escaped into the woods, but many were wounded. And though the number of Indians reported killed varied, any number was a blow to the Mohicans. Simcoe claimed that nearly forty Indians were killed or desperately wounded. Another officer, who was likely not at the scene, repeated the same number.[32] An officer in the loyalist corps that first engaged the Indians put the figure at thirty-seven.[33] If these accounts are accurate, then most of the Indian victims could not have been Stockbridge Mohicans, since fewer than twenty Stockbridges were killed in action throughout the war. A loyalist newspaper said that "nineteen

Indians were killed on the field, refusing quarter, and many are supposed to have perished in the woods of their wounds." [34] An American report two days after the fight listed nineteen Indians as missing, six of whom were subsequently found dead on the field of battle. [35] This report is similar to intelligence received by Joseph Brant from the Oneida Indians, that the British "had killed some of the Stockbridge Indians [and] made 20 of them prisoners." [36]

According to an eyewitness to the battle's aftermath, "a great many dead Indians" lay on the field. Other bodies were found scattered around the farm and in the woods. The German soldier who had complimented their bravery examined the dead Indians mingled among their enemies and remarked that "one could see by their faces that they had perished with resolution." He was also astonished by the distinction between their well-built, sinewy bodies and those of the Europeans, though compared to his Teutonic ancestors the Stockbridges were as pygmies. One wounded Indian survivor was brought as a prisoner to a farmhouse to receive care, his face half cut away by a saber slash. After being nursed for several weeks, he managed to escape. He returned home with a terribly disfigured face.

This witness also said that shortly after the battle a local farmer suspected that his house dogs had been eating human flesh. Several farmers followed the dogs down a hill to a stream, where they reportedly found Chief Daniel Nimham's body, nearly devoured by the animals. It appeared that he had been severely wounded and had attempted to crawl to the stream, out of sight, or to the nearest farmhouse. The farmers soon found the mutilated bodies of two or three more Indians in the same area. They buried the bodies and piled stones on the graves to prevent further desecration. [37]

The chief who had gone to such lengths to reclaim his people's rights to New York land, who stood up to landed gentry and sided with the tenant class, and who traveled a vast ocean to present tribal claims to the king finally won a permanent claim to a small parcel of New York earth on the estate of a manor holder. Slain by the king's men and interred by members of the tenant class, his body was as inhumanely mutilated as was his people's inheritance.

It is possible to say only that as many as fourteen Stockbridge Mohicans died in this battle. After the war a total of seventeen were listed as killed in action, two of whom were killed during the siege of Boston and one of whom was still included on a military roster in 1779. [38] A few of these may have been killed in previous battles, such as Saratoga. Even though the Stockbridges continued to serve in the war, it is unlikely that any were killed in later actions.

Yet not only bullets and sabers took Stockbridge Indian lives. Others were struck down by the many camp diseases rampant at places like Ticonderoga. Many of those who died in the war had standing in the Mohican nation—Daniel and Abraham Nimham, Timothy Yokun, and Daniel Wauwaumpequunaunt—and the small Stockbridge tribe's vitality suffered from these losses.

The reports of the enemy's losses were as varied as those about the Indians. Simcoe reported only one of the cavalry killed, one wounded, and two hussars wounded, rather poor credit to the Stockbridges, whom he admitted fought gallantly and were excellent marksmen. The loyalist lieutenant said that four of his men had been killed and three rangers wounded. A German on the British side, however, tallied five dragoons killed, sixteen rangers killed or wounded, and nine horses killed, and another said that forty English were killed.[39]

By September 10 the remaining Stockbridges from Nimham's company were ready to go home. They would be greatly needed now that there were fewer men to help with the harvest and the hunt. Five of the slain had wives who must be told they were widows.[40] Those returning would have to help console the families of those slain and hold council on the tribe's future course in the war. A lieutenant from Nimham's company met with George Washington and received the company pay of $1,000.[41] The lieutenant also asked Washington to discharge the four tribesmen who were in Jedidiah Huntington's brigade, and the general so requested Huntington. "As they behaved well and were unfortunate in a late action," Washington's aide wrote, "His Excellency is inclined to indulge them."[42] Whether the Stockbridges assigned to the Eighth Massachusetts Regiment were included in Washington's permission to return home is unclear, but by November 1 most had been reported as deserters anyway.[43]

Later that month the Massachusetts General Court appropriated £100 for the relief of the families of Stockbridge officers and soldiers in the Continental Army. Spread among the entire town, £100 would have provided little relief. In the dead of winter clothing became scarce again for the Indians. The principal men petitioned Massachusetts for a supply, and the Board of War delivered twenty blankets to John Sergeant, Jr. Five were considered donations to the widows of the men killed with Nimham. But Sergeant had to pay $5 apiece for the others, which were to be distributed to the most needy.[44]

Who contributed the $75 for the blankets is not certain, though it was probably the Indians. Judging from an event in Stockbridge in 1778, there was no longer much sympathy for the Indian patriots. Massachusetts tried to establish constitutional government that year and submitted its proposed constitution to the various towns for a vote. Article five of this document extended the right to vote to "every male inhabitant of any town in this State, being free, and twenty-one years of age, excepting Negroes, Indians and molattoes." On April 21 seventy eligible Stockbridge folk assembled in a town meeting and voted thirty-nine to thirty-one to accept this constitution.[45]

If the Indians voted at all, their ballots probably made the vote as close as it was. Of the five selectmen who reported the vote, however, none were Stockbridge Indians. More than half the Stockbridge residents, whose lives, property, and revolutionary political values were being defended by their Mohican neighbors—and by blacks and mulattoes as well—clearly were willing to deny their patriot neighbors the opportunity to partake in the system for which they were risking and losing their lives. And this in a town that was established to teach Indians New England moral and political principles.

To the credit of most Massachusetts citizens, this constitution was rejected by a majority, and article five was one of the reasons. The citizens of Lenox, the new sister town bordering Stockbridge on the north, phrased their objections to the original version in eloquent Independence Hall language. Though they focused on article five's property requirement for each potential voter, their arguments were clearly applicable to citizens with differently colored skins: "We conceive this article declares honest poverty a crime for which a large number of the true & faithful subjects of the State, who perhaps have fought & bled in their countrys cause, are deprived of the above mentioned rights (which is tyranny) for how can a man be said to be free & independent, enjoying and defending life and liberty & protecting property, when he has not a voice allowed him in the choice of the most important officers in the legislature, which can make laws to bind him and appoint judges to try him in all cases as well of life & liberty as of property."[46] A subsequent draft dropped the racial exclusions.

18

THE
WAGES
OF
WAR
IS
DEATH

The next two years of the Revolution had the most impact on the Indi-ans. In 1779 the three-pronged attack called Sullivan's Campaign was launched against the Six Nations in New York and Pennsylvania. Samuel Kirkland joined Maj. Gen. John Sullivan's army at Easton as chaplain in mid-June, accompanied by Jehoiakim Mtohksin and three other Stock-bridges who served as guides directly under the general's commanding staff.[1] George Washington at West Point, meanwhile, on June 19 asked William Goodrich to enlist as many of the Stockbridge and Scaticook Indians as possible to join Sullivan's army, which had left Easton, Penn-sylvania, just the day before. Washington ordered that the Indians were to receive no more than private's pay, "unless you find it necessary to distinguish the chief of each tribe by some little pecuniary or other en-couragement." To Goodrich, who was now a major in the Massachusetts militia, he offered a captain's pay and rations.[2]

Apparently Goodrich did not like the terms offered by Washington and sent him a note to this effect via Lieut. Solomon Hendricks. Wash-ington stood firm, however, and hinted that because the matter had been delayed so long, the intended party might not be worth the original offer. Hendricks showed Washington a list of thirty-two Indians will-ing to accept his terms and to form a Stockbridge company for the expedition, with Solomon as their captain. Washington therefore gave Hendricks some sort of commission affirming the terms and stating "the good opinion I have of your bravery and attachment to the United States of America." He awarded Hendricks a captain's pay and promised that if he and his company distinguished themselves, after the expedition they would receive an additional "sum of money as a testimonial for your good conduct and services." Washington authorized $100 for Hendricks the same day and offered him the choice of joining Sullivan or George Clinton, whose brigade was to march southwest from Albany.[3] From this point forward Solomon's company disappears from the records.

The enthusiasm of the militia for harassing Indians bubbled over in Sullivan's army at Easton, where some soldiers ridiculed and cursed their own Indian allies. Informed of the men's conduct, Sullivan issued a reminder in his general orders that "nothing can be more ungenerous than to ridicule those who have come voluntarily to venture their lives in our aid; . . . All the warriors of the Oneidas, Tuscaroras and Stockbridge Indians are about to join us. . . . The person, therefore, who after this notice gives the least discouragement to these people, must in malice to his country far exceed the most inveterate Tory, and must expect to be treated accordingly." General Clinton had to issue a similar edict to protect the Indians with his army.[4]

Sullivan's army lumbered into Indian country throughout midsummer, skirmishing with retreating Indians and laying waste their empty villages. Mtohksin and his Stockbridges served as scouts, only occasionally spotting enemy Indians. Jehoiakim did return from one foray with two abandoned horses.[5]

By September 12 the army was approaching Conesus Lake, en route to a large Seneca town called Genesee Castle. Sullivan ordered a scouting party to cross a small river that flowed into the lake. A lieutenant gathered twenty-six men, including an Oneida and Jehoiakim Mtohksin, who cut cedars into poles, lashed them together for rafts, and crossed the river near midnight. The party failed to encounter any of the enemy that night. Returning the next morning single file through a fogbound swamp, the men suddenly received a withering volley of fire from tories and Indians hidden on both sides of their path. In a short time nearly all of the Americans had been killed and scalped. The lieutenant, another soldier, and the Oneida were taken captive.

Two young men managed to escape through the fog and gunsmoke, running north along the lake shore. They were pursued and attacked by three of the Indians' dogs. The men killed the dogs, but then spotted an Indian just ahead of them. Fortunately, the Indian was Jehoiakim Mtohksin. At the approach of enemy Indians, the two young men lost sight of Mtohksin as they again took flight for several miles until distance and nightfall provided a safe stop. During the night they spied Mtohksin passing nearby and called out to him. Jehoiakim joined them for the rest of the journey back to the main force. Around eight o'clock the next morning they arrived at the camp, but the army had crossed the river and was heading northwestward for Genesee Castle. The ambush and massacre that Mtohksin and the two soldiers had escaped at least disrupted an intended ambush of the main army, which proceeded unmolested. The three refugees then built another raft to cross the river and at last caught up with Sullivan as he reached the Seneca town, finding it abandoned except for the tortured and mutilated remains of the lieutenant and his fellow captives.[6] By the end of the campaign Sullivan's army had destroyed forty villages, up to 160,000 bushels of corn, and untold amounts of other crops. Only forty patriots were lost.[7]

Despite a brutal winter that added to their suffering, the British Indians victimized by Sullivan's scourge sharpened their hatchets and sought revenge on the frontiers in 1780. In addition, the Iroquois so intimidated the Oneidas for their part in the 1779 campaign that three hundred of them went over to the British side. Those who did not, including a group of Tuscaroras and a handful of Caughnawaga Mohawks, had their villages, possessions, and livestock destroyed. About four hundred of these destitute Indians were refugees at Fort Stanwix and later moved to the outskirts of Schenectady. Forty-four emigrant Connecticut Indians who had joined the pro-American Oneidas before the war fled to West Stockbridge, where they survived only through the charity of their new neighbors and occasional grants from Connecticut.[8] For most of 1780 the Stockbridges guarded the home front. If the Iroquois chose to carry vengeance to Stockbridge in pursuit of Jehoiakim Mtohksin and others who had participated in the Sullivan Campaign, the Stockbridge warriors would be there to protect their families.

Nevertheless, in the late summer about twenty Stockbridges under Captain Hendricks heeded General Washington's call for additions to his Continental Army, then in New Jersey. Washington put the Indians under the general command of the light infantry. The only significant battle in this part of the country had already been fought at Springfield, and the rest of the summer campaign consisted of occasional skirmishes, maneuverings, and stalemates between Washington's forces and the British. Whatever the Stockbridges' service, the commander in chief asserted that they "conducted themselves with great propriety and fidelity."[9]

By September 13 there appeared to be little prospect of operations suited to their talents, so the Stockbridges asked Washington to let them go and to pay them in clothing rather than money. They had evidently learned not to rely on the fickle currency. Washington complied with their request to leave but referred them to the Continental Congress for the clothing. He sent the Stockbridge captain to Philadelphia with an introductory letter, in which he praised the company and mentioned the losses they had suffered in the 1778 fight. The government subsequently provided the tribesmen with clothing, gunpowder, and money for their journey home.[10]

Between the war effort, the winter weather, the poor harvest the previous fall, and the cutoff of charity from England, times were harsh in Stockbridge. John Sergeant was also feeling the pinch, although the New England Company until this year had honored his bills for missionary expenses. Sergeant asked the state congress to exempt him from future taxes that might be imposed to support the war, since the war had already cost him nearly half his own support. Later that year he successfully petitioned to be exempted from all taxes and from military duty while he continued as missionary. He claimed that patriotism had moved him "to use great exertions" with the Stockbridges and that he had subjected "himself to considerable expenses in attending councils, consultations &c, in order to engage and secure their friendship and services in favor of the United States of America, in which he flatters himself he has not been unsuccessful." Further, Sergeant said, he had devoted nearly all his time to this matter, neglecting other business "that might be more lucrative."[11]

The Stockbridge warriors had hardly been home a month when they had to pack their fresh gunpowder and don their new clothing. Ethan Allen and the governor of Vermont had called for help with frontier defense. William Johnson's son, John, was leading a group of loyalists and Indians eastward through the Schoharie and Mohawk valleys of New York. William Goodrich assembled the Berkshire County militia, and eighteen Stockbridges joined in a sixty-mile march to Bennington on October 23. The scare in Vermont passed quickly, and the Stockbridges were home within sixteen days.[12]

The Stockbridges may have had a chance to display their new clothing in the spring of 1781. Daniel Brodhead at Fort Pitt informed the president of the Continental Congress that a few Delawares might remain on the American side if they were "well supplied." Brodhead further noted that "if a few of the Oneida or Stockbridge Indians could be sent to this place, their address would make a material change in the councils of the western tribes. But they ought to come in good clothing." [13]

The Stockbridges apparently were busy tending to affairs at home for most of 1781 and did not send a company to the Revolutionary army for the summer campaign. In any case, George Washington and the Continental Congress had concluded that periodically raising and disbanding militia units had created economic hardship, disrupted military order and discipline, and probably lengthened the war. The general and the congress both urged the states to require a certain quota of men to enlist for three years and so build a reliable Continental Army. Massachusetts passed a resolution requiring the raising of 4,240 men to fill its quota; Stockbridge was to contribute 12 men.[14] Long-term duty was not the forte of Indians or frontiersmen, but during the summer Abraham Konkapot, at least, enlisted as one of the twelve.[15]

The focus of the Revolution began to shift to Virginia. Leaving a token force outside New York, George Washington and French troops began the trip to Yorktown toward the end of August. William Goodrich and several old officers and gentlemen of Berkshire County volunteered to serve for a month. On behalf of the Stockbridge Indians, Abraham Konkapot, John Konkapot, Jr., and another tribesman made a similar offer to Washington at Philadelphia.[16] The Stockbridges also requested that a tribesman serving under Gen. William Heath in the Hudson Highlands be released from his enlistment. This may have been another Daniel Nimham, who was only fourteen at the time.[17] Following the devastation to the Nimham family in 1778, the tribe was probably determined not to lose any more members of that clan.

The commander in chief formally thanked both the Stockbridges and William Goodrich for their offers but politely declined them, suggesting that they offer their services to General Heath. It was this kind of short-term enlistment that Washington was trying to discourage. He also referred to General Heath the matter of releasing the other tribesman from duty. In a note to Heath, Washington told the general to employ the Indians if he thought they could be useful, "but it has ever been my opinion that their services never compensated the expense."[18] Not a very flattering remark considering Washington's compliments of a year before. Perhaps he was referring to the use of Indians in general, but his remark echoed those of other regular military officers. And what he said about the Indians was no worse than what he said about militias in general in a circular to all the states: "I solemnly declare I never was witness to a single instance that can countenance an opinion of militia or raw troops being fit for the real business of fighting."[19] The Stockbridges' expenses, then, probably did not contribute much to the patriots' woes. Ten years after Jehoiakim Mtohksin's service as scout in the Sullivan Campaign, in fact, the Indian captain had still not been paid.[20]

The sparse records for the period reveal little about the Stockbridges' military activity during the remainder of 1781. For a week in October one of them joined a militia company that marched to reinforce Gen. John Stark at Stillwater on the Hudson. Near the end of the year three more signed up for the Continental Army in the Fourth Massachusetts Regiment under the provisions of the state's resolution of the previous year.[21] The big incentive for Stockbridge enlistments came the following spring, when New York passed an act that offered a cash bounty and 600 acres to anyone who furnished an able-bodied man for a three-year enlistment or the war's duration; those who served two years would receive 350 acres. In this era a man could hire someone to take his place in the militia, so this legislation allowed the wealthy to send slaves or hire others to fight in their place and increase their landholdings at the same time. Presumably any free man who filled a slot in one of these units would receive the acreage, and thus this should have been an opportunity for the Mohicans to recover at least some New York land. As it turned out, however, twelve Indians, including four of the Nimhams, hired themselves out for enlistment instead of becoming eligible for land rights. They may have needed money more than land, or they may simply have been unaware of, or not allowed to take advantage of, the law.[22] The Indians were assigned to troops under Marinus Willett until just before the official peace of 1783, when they took their pay and headed home, not waiting for an official discharge.[23]

Cornwallis's surrender at Yorktown did not end the fighting on the frontier. Scattered hostilities continued for the next year, which explains New York's desire to continue encouraging enlistments. The Moravian Indians knew better than anyone that the frontier war had not ended. In the years between the French and Indian War and the Revolution an Ohio Delaware chief, who had been a friend to the Moravians, occasionally invited all Christian Indians to settle along the Muskingum River in Ohio. The Stockbridge Indians received an invitation in 1772, when there was a measure of shuttle diplomacy operating between eastern and western tribes.[24] The Stockbridges for the most part evidently were disinclined to move to Ohio, and one of them told John Sergeant, Jr., that the western Indians wanted to attract eastern Indians to their side and then go to war.[25] The Delaware chief, therefore, was likely acting under pressure from the Iroquois. It was a dispute over the merits of going to Ohio versus staying in Stockbridge that led to that fatal argument between the Saint Francis ex-slave and the old woman and her son, who both felt that Stockbridge was safer and more prosperous.

The Moravian Mohicans and Delawares at the Friedenshutten mission in Pennsylvania, however, did accept the Delaware chief's invitation. They soon established two mission towns on the Muskingum, one called Shoenbrun and the other given the popular name Gnadenhutten. Simply being on the frontier during the Revolution, however, caused problems for the peaceful flocks. Throughout the war they were suspected by the Americans of being pro-British and by the British of being pro-American. And they were suspected by frontiersmen just for being Indians.

On a day early in March of 1782 nearly two hundred frontiersmen, seeking revenge for a recent murderous raid by Wyandots, quickly formed a militia. They rode into peaceful Gnadenhutten, where they were welcomed by the Moravian Indians. The Americans gathered together more than ninety of them, including about twenty women and thirty children, under the pretense of placing them under American protection. When all of the Indians and their belongings were assembled in one place, the militia leaders condemned them to die, ignoring the Moravians' protests of innocence. Herded into two cabins, the Indians knelt, prayed, and sang hymns while the frontiersmen indulged in a bloody orgy of skull cracking and scalping. When it was over ninety Indians lay murdered on the cabin floors. The militia then made a funeral pyre of the cabins, seized the Indians' possessions as spoils of war, and returned home in triumph.[26] Something else died as a result of the Gnadenhutten massacre—the Moravian missionary effort in the United States and the progress of the conversion of Indians to Christianity in the Midwest for an entire generation.

19
==

RELOCATING
THE
COUNCIL
FIRE

A psychological blow hit the Stockbridge Indians about the time that the mortal blows smashed the heads of their brethren in Ohio. The Stockbridges thought that surely now, after demonstrating their loyalty to their neighbors and countrymen, they would receive justice regarding their land claims. On February 8, 1782, they addressed a letter to the New York General Assembly. Using the familiar tone of former addresses, it was at once a plea and a lament, but voiced by a new generation of tribal leaders, the sons of King Ben, Johannis Mtohksin, Jacob Naunauphtaunk, and Solomon Uhhaunauwaunmut. Yet the narrative assumed that the Stockbridges and the Americans were each a single undying entity, whose lives spanned the nearly two centuries of contact. With their oral tradition, the Stockbridge Indians had a better memory and feel for history than did many of their newly independent American brothers.

> Brothers, wise Men! attend. When you first came over the great water to this our Island, you was small, I was great. I then had a fullness of food and cloathing. I then was happy and contented. The sands and waters of this River, which you now possess were mine, that is those on the east side of it. Here I got my food and cloathing. You being then smaller I invited you to set down with me, and provide for yourself, your women and children. This you did. We were then happy in each other, your enemies were my enemies, your friends were my friends. Where

you bled by the hatchet of your enemies, there I bled also, for you and your friends. Where your fathers died in battle, my fathers died by their side. The waters of Lake George and Champlain, the hills about Boston and New York bear witness to this. The last time you took up the hatchet against the French King I went out with you with my hatchet, there I was with all my warriors many years.

The rewards for this service given to your warriors in land, were not given to mine. When I returned I found my hunting grounds ruined. You get food and cloathing by tilling the earth. I by killing wild beasts on my ancient hunting ground, they can now find no hiding places. You til it all. Some land my fathers told me they had given you, much they told me they had not given you. What they gave you not is still mine by the customs and laws of all nations. The great Spirit gave my fathers this what he has not taken away by conquest, and I or my fathers have not alienated, either by gift or sale, is certainly in the view of that Spirit, mine still.

This I related to my brothers the Bostonians who had also in their possession some of my land, they acknowledge my rights, and gave me full compensation. My claims are from Hudsons River, Wood Creek and Lake Champlain, to the mouth of Otter Creek on the north eastward.

Now Brethren; wise men; attend. You once was small, very small. I then was great at that time. I took you under my arm, and helped you. I am now become small, very small. You are become great, very great, you reach into the clouds. You are seen all over the world. I am not now as high as your ankles. I now look to you for help. I am weak through hunger and cold, through want of food and cloathing. My women groan and lament, and tears are in the eyes of all my children.

Brother! What I ask is that you resign to me that land, which is justly mine, which I have neither sold or given to you; or give me its value, that I may get food and cloathing for myself, my women and children and be happy with you as formerly; Remember too, that by this you will not leave room for lying birds to say, that you neglect to do me justice, because you are strong. Brothers should you give me anything, let it be given in such a manner, that men of evil minds may not deprive me, who am weak, of it unjustly.[1]

There is no record of the New York legislature or Governor Clinton ever receiving or acknowledging the Stockbridge petition. It is not mentioned in the state's legislative proceedings, and a gap exists in Clinton's papers for that period.

On February 25 the Indians had another tale to tell the Continental Congress, this time about their fellow patriots in Vermont, who had so loved the Indians when they needed their help during the war. The Indians told the congress that "your petitioners and their fathers before them have owned and occupied the country to the northward of their present place of abode as their hunting ground, comprehending part of a state now known by Vermont. . . . its now so overrun by the White People, that our hunting is at an end. Our tribe has therefore been disposed to sell their native right to the people, and to quit all claim to that country."

Some of those occupying the countryside as well as those contemplating the new townships, however, either ignored the Stockbridges' claims or agreed to pay them but never did. After three successive promises by Vermonters to set aside specific land for the Stockbridges, and three subsequent excuses for reneging on the promises, the Indians said, "this made us think hard. We thought we could not be used so by the White People of this country. That tho we are small and poor in comparison of the White People, who are great and rich, that we having taken an active part in the War, suffered very greatly by it in blood and interest, trusting in the good people of this island to do us justice with regard to our lands, we thought we deserved better treatment. We now send this our complaint to your Honourable Body, that as you have always kindly heard us, we now request you would look on your covenant with us and hold our rights in your power till such time as we have full satisfaction."[2]

Asa Douglas, a sympathetic Vermonter and one of Ethan Allen's former Green Mountain Boys, acted as the Stockbridges' agent in representing their claim. He sent the petition to the president of the congress, John Hanson, and requested him "to lay it before them as expressly as the business of Congress will admit, and before the dispute respecting Vermont be determined. I hope should it be made a state that the Indians property in, and right to that part of territory by them claimed be secured to them and their posterity."[3]

A congressional committee indifferently ordered that the petition be referred to the New York legislature, and merely added "that it be recommended to them to hear the said petitioners, and fully enquire into the matters . . . and that the . . . legislature do thereon what shall appear to them reasonable and just."[4] In other words, New York could do as it pleased about the Stockbridges' plea for Vermont land. Hanson forwarded the petition to Governor Clinton, stating noncommittally that "the reasonableness and propriety of the application will, no doubt, be investigated by the State in a fair & impartial manner and decided upon accordingly."[5]

Again, no official New York records indicate whether the state ever acknowledged the Stockbridge petition or the congressional prodding. Three years later the Oneida Indians interceded on behalf of the Mohicans' claim. The governor and the state's newly appointed Indian commissioners asserted that they had considered the Stockbridges' request just after the Revolution, but found that the Indians had been unable to prove their claim in 1766. The politicians noted that some New Yorkers had paid the Indians two or three times to avoid a dispute—a shallow point that ignored the nature of many of those purchases and glossed over the deep controversy. Obviously referring to the 1768 treaty between the Mohawks and the Stockbridges, the governor and the commissioners then said that the Mohicans, in the presence of the Mohawks, had relinquished their claim to land in New York on the east side of the Hudson. After reporting what was completely contrary to the facts, the government officials then had the audacity to comment on the faulty Stockbridge memory.[6]

In early July of 1783 sachem Joseph Shauquethqueat sent Captain Hendricks and four warriors to Washington's headquarters at Newburgh for one last conference with the general.[7] As in previous postwar situations the Stockbridges, though fortunate to be on the winning side, were likely to be harassed by Americans in outlying areas who felt that they had a score to settle with any Indian. In the past, the Stockbridge Mohican men had obtained statements testifying to their loyalty from locally known merchants or from their commanding officers so that they could trade and hunt without being taken for hostiles.[8] The Stockbridges needed such a statement now more than ever. This time all of them, including the women and children, were leaving Stockbridge for good.

In seeking justice from Vermont, the Stockbridges had been negotiating for a tract of land in their old hunting grounds, but became pawns once again in the territorial disputes between that state and New York. Vermont finally granted the Indians a tract of land, but it was not yet chartered.[9] The Indians decided to accept the invitation of their Revolutionary compatriots among the Oneidas to settle near them in the vicinity of Oneida Lake in New York. This was arranged through the auspices of the Connecticut refugee Indians who returned to Oneida country in 1783, accompanied by a few of the Stockbridges. The Connecticut Indians, remnants of Mohegans, Pequots, Narragansetts, and Montauks, had been adopted by the Oneidas as younger brothers in a ceremony at Sir William Johnson's in 1774. They were Christian Indians under the guidance of Mohegan preacher Samson Occom, who wanted to establish an all-Indian town modeled on those of New England, to be called Brotherton. When the Stockbridges met with the Oneidas after the war, the Oneidas adopted them, too, paving the way for the settlement.[10] According to Samuel Kirkland, who doubtless also played a part in the negotiations, some of his Oneida flock were among the Connecticut Indians when they sought refuge at Stockbridge, and it was they who made the offer to the Mohicans.[11] The Stockbridges were granted a tract of land six miles square on the site of an old Tuscarora village, and in the spring of 1784 most of the young men went there to plant corn and make provisions for the removal that began that year.[12] The Mohicans were finally awarded land in New York after all, but thanks to other Indians, not to the government.

The chiefs told the Massachusetts legislature that they were leaving Stockbridge and asked that a few trusted town friends and neighbors be authorized to sell or lease what little land was left.[13] The state appointed John Sergeant, Jr., one of Joseph Woodbridge's sons, and another resident as commissioners to review any deeds to ensure that the Indians had not been cheated.[14] The Stockbridges later sold their Vermont claim to one of their old militia captains, Isaac Marsh, a tavernkeeper in Stockbridge.[15]

New England civilization had come a little too quickly to the Stockbridge Mohicans. In the fifty years since John Sergeant had first set foot in a Housatonic village, the Indian population was never much more than two hundred. But as of September 1783, there were just under a thousand whites and forty blacks in Stockbridge alone. In all of Berkshire County, in fact, there were more than two hundred blacks. A few free blacks owned as much land as some of the Indians did. One of them married a Stockbridge Indian woman and therefore qualified for Indian land.[16] By the time the Indians were packing their belongings, the total non-Indian population of Berkshire County was almost twenty-five thousand.[17]

Had all of these Christians helped the Mohican nation accomplish the goals that John Konkapot and Aaron Umpachenee sought fifty years earlier? No and yes. Certainly the Mohicans' main hope, that the nation might increase in numbers by accepting Christianity, had been tragically disappointed. Accepting Christianity had only increased the number of non-Indians surrounding them. As a consequence the number of worldly temptations had increased and been placed near at hand, a problem the tribal leaders had wanted to solve, not reinforce.

The Stockbridges knew that the town had been set up for them, but they may have wondered if they had been set up for the town. They had defended Americans during the wars, making the frontier gradually safer and thereby encouraging more colonials to populate the area. By the time of the Revolution, the notion that Stockbridge was a town for the Indians had faded. Even missionary Samuel Kirkland bought Indian land in Stockbridge with money donated to him and then bragged about his bargain.[18]

Nearly half of the old township was now a separate entity completely governed by Massachusetts folk, and two years before the war those in the northern part of town had asked the government to annex them to Lenox. The token Indian participation in Stockbridge town affairs obviously did not persuade the majority of the town in 1778 that the Indians should have the right to vote.

Schools were separate, churches were separate, and the Indians were continually selling land to pay their debts in order to get out or stay out of smallpox-ridden jails. The contrast was sharp between the Indian have-nots and their neighbors, many of whom were relatively well-off farmers, businessmen, or professionals. Yet the rest of the citizens within and without Stockbridge were hardly handpicked Calvinist Christian examples for aspiring Indian youth to emulate. Counterfeiting was the latest illicit activity to scandalize the Stockbridge area.[19] On September 9, 1783, there was a jailbreak at Great Barrington, and among the escapees was one committed for forgery—an Indian.[20]

The area was not tailor-made, then, for impressing Christian morality on a people who had been taught that it was superior to their native ways. It is significant that the Stockbridge Indian leaders responsible for the decision to move did not include any non-Indians in their relocation plans. In this respect their thinking resembled that of Hopkins of Great Barrington, who as early as 1762 advised that even in a mission or boarding school project, "as few English should be among them as shall be consistent with the design, which would be instructors or overseers." As soon as the Indians learned these duties, Hopkins concluded, "the affair must be committed very much into their hands, which will tend to make them *the people,* and prevent them viewing themselves as *underlings,* despised by the English &c . . . which would frustrate the whole design."[21]

Why then did the Stockbridge Indians put up with the situation for fifty years, and on the whole accept Christianity and European-American civilization as a way of life? The first and probably the strongest explanation is that from the 1730s to the 1760s nearly all of western Massachusetts was in Mohican hands and served as a land bank upon which the Indians could draw when they needed money. Had they abandoned the area they would have destroyed the economic base that helped maintain tribal integrity. When that land base became depleted, they began the search for a new one farther removed from their Massachusetts brethren. To the credit of the Massachusetts government, it did generally recognize in principle the natives' right to the soil and paid them for it—however grudgingly—rather than just taking it. This was better treatment than the Mohicans received in Connecticut and New York.

Second, the impulse among tribal leaders to accept Christianity and obtain education for the tribe and its children was genuine. Religion was an integral part of Indian life before Europeans came among them, and it continued to be an important part afterward. When their old beliefs appeared to be failing them, the Indians reached out for new ones. Further, missions were usually accompanied by secular teaching, and after a hundred years of dealing with Americans the Indians had learned that they needed to know how to read and write to cope with the complex paper world around them. The Moravian Mohicans sought the same cultural amenities, and when they were forced out of New York and Connecticut they willingly established new religious communities in Pennsylvania. According to Mohican traditional history, as well as recorded historical accounts, several non-missionized western tribes invited the Mohicans to join them. After a generation of exposure to Christian culture, however, most preferred to keep company with tribes that had become similarly acculturated.

The Mohicans' endurance of the mission at Stockbridge, then, was pragmatic. The leaders realistically assessed the future and adapted to its approach accordingly. The mission provided a pause for the Indians—and more important, for their children and grandchildren—to adjust to the inevitable change in their way of living. By the third generation the Stockbridge Indians had absorbed enough European-American culture to try to manage on their own. Their parents and grandparents, however, like New World immigrants a century later, had to adjust to the problems of surviving in a dominant, alien culture that surrounded them faster than they would have chosen. Unlike those immigrants, however, they preferred to maintain some cultural separateness. And they chose not to relinquish their Indian identity or all of their Indian values. The Stockbridges, like most Indians, continued to seek the approval and to avoid the criticism of tribes that were not acculturated. In an ethnological study published in 1968, Marion Mochon found that despite the nearly complete outward assimilation of the Stockbridges into American culture, they maintained a definite sense of Indian separateness. What particularly distinguished them from the general culture was their environmental sense of harmony with nature, coupled with the value placed on sharing within the family and community, which contrasted with what they perceived to be the materialistic nature of the rest of society. For the Stockbridge Indians of the eighteenth century, this attempt to maintain dual personalities prolonged a painful involvement with the mission as the town rapidly evolved around them. In the end the adjustment process ultimately cost them their homeland and, ironically, their native culture, including their language. But despite their small numbers they thereby survived as a viable, distinct people with a rich cultural past and a more than respectable niche in American history.

The Stockbridge Indians of the 1780s were not forsaking Christianity and its moral discipline. The generation of Mohicans who made the decision to relocate grew up in a reasonable facsimile of a God-fearing community, where the religious rituals were as regularized as the native rituals of generations past had been. When the Indians proclaimed in 1734, "let us . . . leave our former courses and become Christians," when they said that Christianity was the religion "we intend to stand by and follow as long as we live" and "we wish and pray our whole nation may be brought into the same way," they meant it. They had turned corners in their tribal history that they would not go around again. Into the nineteenth century a few might cling to a wooden family idol or consult a powwow if superstition overrode their faith, but nearly all the Mohican religious and cultural practices of previous generations were disappearing.

When the Stockbridges relocated to New York, most of the church communicants were women, but baptism, church attendance, and religious conscience had become part of the Stockbridge Indian heritage. And though baptism was no guarnatee to the path of righteousness, a child reared in the religious New England environment of the eighteenth century could not deny its influence. In Oneida country, the Stockbridge men, women, and children alike traveled a good distance even in harsh weather to attend Samson Occom's or Samuel Kirkland's preaching. Both Kirkland and Occom were impressed by the piety, order, love, and kindness practiced by the majority of the Stockbridges at their new location.[22] Feeling the tug of religious conscience and the fear of abandonment by God, several principal tribesmen soon appealed to Occom to become the tribe's minister, whom they would support from their own earnings. Like Plymouth Colony pilgrims the Stockbridges declared: "We believe that there is but one the only true and living God. And that he is the Maker and preserver of our lives, and upholder of the same—that he has send his only begotten son into this world to be the Saviour of mankind, and we believe that this God has brought us up into this wilderness, where we might begin to serve him in sincerity and truth."[23] Probably the most important contribution that New England Christianity made to the Mohicans was inadvertent. In providing new beliefs to supplant old ones, it did so within a cohesive church body—an identity—that helped preserve tribal cohesion.

Nor did the Stockbridges abandon the important aspects of the new American culture they had learned in the mission town. Education continued to be essential in coping with society. When their own community was unable to provide schooling, Mohican boys received instruction elsewhere, and girls were occasionally placed in religious homes to learn the fruits of Christian "housewifery." The Indians were also pragmatic enough to seek and accept help from charitable religious groups like the Quakers and the Society for Propagating Christian Knowledge. Two members of the society visited the Mohicans at their new location in 1796 and reported that "two-thirds of the men, and nine-tenths of the women, are industrious. Agriculture, and the breeding of cattle and swine are their chief employments, by which they procure more than a sufficiency of food. They have but few sheep and a little flax; and they seem to be desirous of improving in both these articles." One admirable forty-year-old widow with several dependents was supporting her family by weaving woolen cloth. The sachem had an ox team, "a good field of wheat, Indian corn, potatoes and grass. . . . The fences in general are good, and the land under tolerable cultivation in New Stockbridge."[24] The Stockbridges even sold surplus meat and corn to their Oneida brethren. Perhaps the strict social and religious environment of Calvinist Stockbridge, even in the Stephen West years, had prepared the Mohicans to better cope with future American society.

Significantly, one cultural change that the Stockbridges adopted had been the source of contention and divisiveness in 1750: they allotted land parcels individually among themselves "so that each one holds his landed property as an estate in fee simple." The visiting society members viewed

this practice as "the *grand reason* of their superiority, in point of agricultural improvement, to their brethren the Oneidas, Tuscaroras, &c." The
tribe did retain one important restriction regarding their land, however:
"that it shall never be sold to white people." Even so, an internal tribal
division developed between those who wanted to lease land to their New
York neighbors for cultivation and those who preferred to cultivate it
themselves. At the time of the society members' visit those who preferred
self-determination were in control. The visitors also observed that the
"party who are in favour of leasing their lands are the most addicted to
intemperance."[25]

Not all of the Indians moved to New York right away. Jehoiakim
Mtohksin and some of the Konkapots were slower than the rest to leave
their ancestral home. The Konkapots and Mtohksins had been among
those most involved in adopting the New England social package, but
whether they preferred Stockbridge or merely stayed behind to settle the
Indians' affairs is uncertain. Also slow to join their brethren were several
widows, including the wives of Daniel Nimham and Solomon Uhhaunauwaunmut. Forty Stockbridges stayed behind until April of 1788.[26]

But these Stockbridges soon had an incentive to leave after they witnessed yet another upheaval. Outraged western Massachusetts farmers,
who were victims of the same social and economic forces that had
strangled the Mohicans, participated in the insurrection known as Shays'
Rebellion. Armed and angry, many of these men in Berkshire County
formed gangs that closed debtor's court and attacked the merchant and
professional class whom they viewed as their oppressors, ransacking
their homes and threatening their lives. In Stockbridge their victims included Elijah Williams (whom they physically attacked), Erastus Sergeant, Timothy Edwards, and Jahleel Woodbridge. Edwards and Woodbridge had been despised before and during the Revolution by many
Berkshire County radicals, both because of their wealth and because
they were judges in the hated courts, which seemed always to oppress
debtors. When the rebels were finished they had damaged and robbed
the homes of about thirty Stockbridge merchants and professionals and
captured more than twenty of the ruling gentry.[27] The rebels may have
drawn more attention to their problems than the Stockbridge Indians
ever did, but as always the gentry ultimately prevailed.

The remaining Stockbridges appear not to have participated in the
agrarian fray; if they had, it is hard to say which side they would have
taken, since they had friends on both. Most likely the upheaval was just
another impetus for the remaining Indians to leave the contentious, frac-

tious society of Stockbridge behind and head for more peaceful hills. And yet for years after the tribe relocated, thirty or forty Indians would come back to the Stockbridge area for the winter, build wigwams and make brooms and baskets to sell, rekindle fires on their old hearthstones, and visit the graves of their ancestors.[28]

It was 1794 before the nation's Founding Fathers formally expressed their gratitude to the Stockbridge Mohicans and fulfilled some of the promises made during the Revolution. As part of a treaty with the Oneidas and the Tuscaroras, the government publicly acknowledged them as faithful adherents of the United States. The government also agreed to establish a gristmill and a sawmill for the three tribes and to provide personnel and equipment for three years to train young Indian men in the work. "Some very few meritorious persons of the Stockbridge Indians" were to receive part of the $5,000 distributed mostly to the Oneidas and the Tuscaroras for their losses in the war.[29]

The certificate of allegiance that George Washington had issued in July of 1783 to safeguard the Stockbridge emigration asserted that "the Muhhekunnuk tribe of Indians have remained firmly attached to us and have fought and bled by our side; that we consider them as our friends and brothers, and as a peace is now established between all the powers who were at war, we do recommend it to all the different tribes of Indians as well as all other persons inhabiting the western country, not to molest them in any manner whatever, but to consider them as friends and subjects to the United States of America."[30]

About ninety years after the Mohicans had left Stockbridge, the town erected a monument in memory of the Housatonic band at what is reputed to be the tribe's ancestral burying ground. Echoing the sentiment in George Washington's certificate, the Indians were honored in stone as "friends of our fathers." The Stockbridge Indians were indeed the friends of our fathers; perhaps more so than our fathers were friends to the Stockbridge Indians. But alongside the intrigues, the cupidity, and the hypocrisy of some of those who managed Stockbridge Indian affairs— much of which may have been less apparent than historical scrutiny suggests—there were genuine demonstrations of charity and concern for the Indians. Somebody had to have taught them how to adapt to the religious, political, and material world of American culture, or the Stockbridges would not have elicited the favorable commentary of visitors to their new home in New York. Samuel Hopkins had maintained that "by the just treatment they for a course of years have met with from the government, from Mr. Sergeant, Mr. Woodbridge and others, they are become our hearty friends."[31] The Stockbridges took with them to New York a wealth of practical experiences with American culture that had been compacted in the fifty-year press of mission history—courts, lawyers, town government, farming, milling, lumbering, surveying, housebuilding, weaving, reading, writing, and revolution.

Unfortunately the Stockbridges' own contribution to their American friends and to American history was soon forgotten, as was their very identity. Generations of Americans preferred to believe in a novelist's invention—that the Mohicans were noble, mythic knights of the forest, as romanticized, elusive, and extinct as the men of King Arthur's Round Table. Yet it was an all-too-human struggle, sometimes painful, sometimes joyful, at times ignominious and at times noble, that kept a small group of native Americans from becoming the last of the Mohicans.

NOTES

INTRODUCTION

1. *Documentary History of the State of Maine*, ed. James Phinney Baxter, 9:253.

CHAPTER 1

1. "Extract from an Indian History," MHS, *Collections*, 1st ser. vol. 9 (1804): 100; "Documents Relating to the Stockbridge Mission, 1825–1848," Wisconsin Historical Society, *Collections*, vol. 15 (1900): 191; Timothy Pickering, "Captain Hendrick Aupaumut's Journal," Historical Society of Pennsylvania, *Memoirs*, vol. 2, pt. 1 (1827): 75.

2. "Extract from an Indian History," p. 100.

3. John Heckewelder, "An Account of the History, Manners and Customs of the Indian Nations . . . ," *Transactions of the Historical and Literary Committee of the American Philosophical Society*, vol. 1 (1819): 34–35, 69–70.

4. Speech of John W. Quinney, in "Celebration of the Fourth of July, 1854," Wisconsin Historical Society, *Collections*, vol. 4 (1857–58): 315–16; NYCD 7:118, 156; 9:1052; Electa Fidelia Jones, *Stockbridge, Past and Present*, pp. 16–17, appendix A; MA, 31:487, 647; Samuel Hopkins, *Historical Memoirs Relating to the Housatonic Indians*, p. 100; Charles James Taylor, *History of Great Barrington*, p. 108.

5. *Documentary History of the State of New York*, ed. E. B. O'Callaghan, 3:27; Stockbridge petition to Francis Bernard, May 27, 1762, Stockbridge Library Historical Room, item M.73-1.33 (1); NYCD 6:294; "Extract from an Indian History," p. 102; NYCD 2:133; 6:881; *Documentary History of the State of Maine* 12:288; NYCD 4:902–3.

6. Timothy Dwight, *Travels in New England and New York*, 4:177–78; NYCD 3:32.

7. Allen W. Trelease, *Indian Affairs in Colonial New York*, pp. 46–47; Ted Brasser, *Riding on the Frontier's Crest*, pp. 11–14; *Van Rensselaer Bowier Manuscripts*, ed. and trans. Arnold J. F. Van Laer, pp. 11–14; NYCD 2:769.

8. Robert Livingston, *The Livingston Indian Records, 1666–1723*, pp. 33–35.

9. NYCD 1:181–82; Neal Salisbury, *Manitou and Providence*, pp. 78–81.

10. Brasser, *Riding on the Frontier's Crest*, pp. 16–22; NYCD 1:181–82; John F. Jameson, ed., *Narratives of New Netherland, 1609–1664*, p. 172; *The Pynchon Papers*, ed. Carl Bridenbaugh, 1:64–65; 2:54–58; Livingston, *Indian Records*, p. 37; Deposition re Rensselaerwyck, Land Papers, Miscellaneous, New York, Columbia County, 1761–62, NYHS; Edward M. Ruttenber, *History of the Indian Tribes of Hudson's River*, p. 51; Petition by Muhheconnuk Nation, Nov. 20, 1820, Henry O'Reilly Papers, vol. 14, NYHS; Sherburne F. Cook, *The Indian Population of New England in the Seventeenth Century*, p. 70; Quinney speech, "Celebration of the Fourth of July, 1854," 316; Hampshire County Registry of Deeds, bk. 4, p. 833.

11. William C. Reichel, *Dedication of Monuments Erected by the Moravian Historical Society*, p. 168; William C. Reichel, *Memorials of the Moravian Church*, 1:144–54, nos. 8, 12, 13, 16, 33, 42, 50, 51; Augustus Schultze, "The Old Moravian Cemetery of Bethlehem, Pa. 1742–1897," Moravian Historical Society,

Transactions 5 (1899): 119 no. 30; 121 no. 9; 123 no. 25; 149 no. 16; 152 no. 9; *NYCD* 5:388. Several of the Indians at Shekomeko and virtually all of those at Kent, Connecticut, were called Wampanosch or Wampanoos by Moravian missionaries. Subsequent Moravians, including Carl J. Fliegel in his *Index to the Records of the Moravian Mission among the Indians of North America*, interpret these to mean Wampanoag, and barring any conclusive proof to the contrary, their interpretation may be legitimate.

12. *NYCD* 14:715–16.

13. *Pynchon Papers* 1:152, 171; Gordon M. Day, *The Identity of the Saint Francis Indians*, p. 19; *NYCD* 13:491–92; 14:715–16.

14. *NYCD* 13:501, 503, 495–97; 14:718; 3:255; *Public Records of the Colony of Connecticut*, ed. James Hammond Trumbull and Charles Jeremy Headly, 2:397–98, 436, 461, 462, 466, 467, 470, 472, 494, 404.

15. Livingston, *Indian Records*, pp. 39–40.

16. Ibid., p. 37.

17. *NYCD* 4:337; 3:800–805, 808; 4:195–96, 1067, 1077; 9:460–61, 490.

18. *NYCD* 5:661–64.

19. Hopkins, *Historical Memoirs*, p. 182.

20. Arnold J. F. Van Laer, ed. and trans., *Minutes of the Court of Fort Orange and Beverwyck, 1652–1656*, 1:165, 290–91; 2:135–36; Arnold J. F. Van Laer, ed. and trans., *Minutes of the Court of Rensselaerswyck, 1648–1652*, p. 97.

21. *NYCD* 13:332; *Pynchon Papers* 1:27; Robert Rogers, *Journals*, p. 207; Lois M. Feister, "Linguistic Communications between the Dutch and Indians in New Netherland, 1609–1664," *Ethnohistory* 20, no. 1 (1973): 32; Hendrick Aupaumut, "A Short Narration of My Last Journey to the Western Contry [sic]," Historical Society of Pennsylvania, *Memoirs*, vol. 2, pt. 1 (1827): 79; Thomas Allen to Seth Pomeroy, May 9, 1775, in David Dudley Field, *A History of the Town of Pittsfield*, p. 75; *Documentary History of the State of New York* 3:616; Jameson, *Narratives*, p. 172.

22. *Documentary History of the State of Maine* 9:50–53.

23. *Pynchon Papers* 1:102–7; *Correspondence of Jeremias van Rensselaer 1651–1674*, ed. and trans. Arnold J. F. Van Laer, p. 449.

24. *NYCD* 3:436, 444, 482, 808; 9:308, 569.

25. *Letters and Papers of Cadwallader Colden* 3:415–16; see also a speech by the Stockbridge Indians to the Mohawks circa 1747 in *JP* 1:125–26.

26. *Documentary History of the State of Maine* 9:50–53.

27. *NYCD* 13:17–18, 122–23, 126–27, 132, 136, 150–51, 162, 168–69, 170, 179–80, 264–65, 310; Van Laer, *Minutes of Fort Orange and Beverwyck* 2:284–86.

28. Livingston, *Indian Records*, pp. 64–69.

29. Hopkins, *Historical Memoirs*, p. 29; Stephen Williams to a gentleman in Boston, June 24, 1735, in Nathaniel Appleton, *Gospel Ministers Must Be Fit for the Master's Use*, p. iii.

30. Stockbridge Town Records, Book of Records, 1739–59; Hopkins, *Historical Memoirs*, p. 137.

31. Hopkins, *Historical Memoirs*, pp. 185, 196, 197.

32. *JP* 9:601.

33. MOA, Box 112, folder 8, item 2.

34. Arnold J. F. Van Laer, ed., and Jonathan Pearson, trans., *Early Records of the City and County of Albany*, 2:195–97.

35. *NYCD* 5:663.

36. Ibid.; David Brainerd's diary entry, May 18, 1743, in *Memoirs of the Rev. David Brainerd*, ed. Jonathan Edwards and Sereno E. Dwight, p. 101.

37. CA, "Indians," 1:244.

38. Stockbridge Indian petition to Sir Henry Moore, Apr. 1, 1766, British Museum, Additional MS. 22679 (LC copy misdated 1765); MA, 6:394.

39. John Sergeant, Jr., to Henry Storrs, Jan. 24, 1820, O'Reilly Papers, vol. 14.

40. MA, 46:378.

41. Daniel Gookin, *An Historical Account of the Doings and Sufferings of the Christian Indians*, p. 499.

42. Jonathan Edwards to Joshua Paine, Feb. 24, 1752, EP.

43. *NYCD* 5:562.

44. "Indian Treaties," Maine Historical Society, *Collections*, vol. 4 (1856): 129, 131, 141; *NYCD* 5:349, 351, 358; *JHRM* 11:48.

45. Hopkins, *Historical Memoirs*, p. 32; Jonathan Edwards to Isaac Hollis, July 17, 1752, EP.

46. John B. Dillon, *Oddities of Colonial Legislation in America*, pp. 74, 176.

47. Jones, *Stockbridge*, p. 16; Aupaumut, *Short Narration*, p. 87; Cadwallader Colden, *The History of the Five Indian Nations of Canada*, 1:20–21.

48. Sheldon Davis, *Shekomeko*, p. 17; petition, Nov. 20, 1820, O'Reilly Papers, vol. 14.

49. Hopkins, *Historical Memoirs*, pp. 24–25, 36–37; Land Papers, Miscellaneous, New York, Columbia County, 1761–62.

50. Stephen Williams in Appleton, *Gospel Ministers*, p. iii.

CHAPTER 2

1. William Kellaway, *The New England Company, 1649–1776*, p. 269; *JHRM* 12:94–95.

2. Hopkins, *Historical Memoirs*, p. 20.

3. Ibid.

4. Ibid., p. 22.

5. Jones, *Stockbridge*, p. 24; George H. Loskiel, *History of the Mission of the United Brethren among the Indians of New England*, pt. 2, pp. 65, 189; Dorothy Ripley, *The Bank of Faith and Works United*, p. 101; Ewald, Johann von, *Diary of the American War*, pp. 145, 148.

6. Hopkins, *Historical Memoirs*, p. 22.

7. Myron O. Stachiw, ed., *Massachusetts Officers and Soldiers, 1723–1743*, p. 199.

8. Hopkins, *Historical Memoirs*, p. 22.

9. Jones, *Stockbridge*, p. 18; Hopkins, *Historical Memoirs*, p. 25.

10. Hopkins, *Historical Memoirs*, p. 25.

11. Ibid., pp. 25–26.

12. Jameson, *Narratives*, pp. 86–87.

13. Hopkins, *Historical Memoirs*, pp. 28, 32.

14. Louis Mitchell, *The Woodbridge Record*, pp. 32, 59, 60.

15. Jonathan Law, *Law Papers*, ed. Albert Carlos Bates, 1:89–92.

16. Mason A. Green, *Springfield, 1636–1886*, p. 227.

17. Kellaway, *New England Company*, pp. 214–15; Letterbooks of the Company for the Propagation of the Gospel in New England, Mar. 11, 1741, Mather Collection, Tracy W. McGregor Library, University of Virginia, Charlottesville (LC MSS Div. microfilm 14, 705E).

18. Peter N. Carroll, *Puritanism and the Wilderness*, pp. 14–15.

19. *NYCD* 13:168.

20. Stephen Innes, *Labor in a New Land*, p. 43.

21. Robert Zemsky, *Merchants, Farmers and River Gods*, p. 107.

22. Jonathan Belcher Papers, vol. 5, p. 58, MHS.

23. Hopkins, *Historical Memoirs*, p. 177.

24. *NYCD* 4:652, 1067, 1074, 1077.

CHAPTER 3

1. Hopkins, *Historical Memoirs*, pp. 32, 33.

2. Appleton, *Gospel Ministers*, pp. iii, vi.

3. Hopkins, *Historical Memoirs*, pp. 34–35.

4. *NYCD* 7:969.

5. Housatonics to Nehemiah Bull, Feb. 5, 1734/35, Ayer Collection, Newberry Library, Chicago; Appleton, *Gospel Ministers*, p. vi; Hopkins, *Historical Memoirs*, p. 35; Stephen Williams diary, Jan. 30, 1735, Richard Storrs Library, Longmeadow Historical Society, Longmeadow, Mass.

6. Hopkins, *Historical Memoirs*, p. 35.

7. Housatonics to Bull, Feb. 5, 1734/35.

8. Hopkins, *Historical Memoirs*, pp. 35–36.

9. Appleton, *Gospel Ministers*, p. vii.

10. Hopkins, *Historical Memoirs*, pp. 40, 41.

11. *NYCD* 3:562–64; 4:498; 5:732; 9:669; 13:523, 527.

12. "Indian Treaties," pp. 127–35.

13. Ibid., pp. 133–35.

14. Ibid., p. 138.

15. Ibid., p. 140.

16. Ibid., pp. 142–43; Hopkins, *Historical Memoirs*, pp. 43–45; Williams diary, Aug. 28, 31, 1735.

17. Records of the Governor's Council (Mass.), Mar. 27, July 6, 1736, pp. 23, 38, ESR.

18. Belcher to John Sergeant, Dec. 11, 1747, Belcher Papers.

19. Hopkins, *Historical Memoirs*, p. 53.

20. Ibid., p. 47.

21. Appleton, *Gospel Ministers*, p. xi.

22. Hopkins, *Historical Memoirs*, p. 169.

23. John Sergeant letter, Mar. 1, 1736, in Hopkins, *Historical Memoirs*.

CHAPTER 4

1. Hopkins, *Historical Memoirs*, p. 55.

2. Ibid., p. 54.

3. MA, 29:309–16.

4. JHRM 15:85; RGCM, June 29, 1737, pp. 500–501 (the records incorrectly state one-sixteenth part for Sergeant and Woodbridge); Hampshire County Probate Records, bk. 7, p. 262.

5. Hopkins, *Historical Memoirs*, pp. 58–61.

6. Ibid., pp. 66–67.

7. *New England Weekly Journal*, Aug. 3, 1736.

8. MA, 29:324–32.

9. Hopkins, *Historical Memoirs*, p. 68; MA, 29:328.

10. *JHRM* 14:107.

11. Yasuhide Kawashima, *Puritan Justice and the Indian*, pp. 86–88, 91, 132.

12. Williams diary, Mar. 25, 1736/37.

13. Stockbridge Town Charter, Stockbridge Library Historical Room, M73-1.4 (This is a typewritten copy; the original was reported as stolen. The copy lists Sergeant's and Woodbridge's allotments as one-fortieth rather than one-sixtieth, which would have given each of them 576 acres, rather than 384. Since Sergeant's probate records report his holdings at 384 acres, the copy is probably in error.)

14. Hopkins, *Historical Memoirs*, pp. 74–75.

15. Hopkins, *Historical Memoirs*, p. 72.

16. Stockbridge Town Records, Births, Deaths, and Marriages, 1737–54.

17. Hampshire County Court Records, Inferior Court of Common Pleas and Court of General Sessions of the Peace, vol. B3, microfilm, Forbes Library no. 76, Northampton, Mass.

18. Charter of the Colony of Massachusetts Bay, in Edmund S. Morgan, *The Founding of Massachusetts*, p. 320.

19. *JHRM* 15:184, 191–92.

20. Henry Bond, *Genealogies of the Families and Descendants of the Early*

Settlers of Watertown, p. 314; "Ancestry of the Jones Family, Stockbridge, Mass.," *New England Genealogical and Historical Register* 6, no. 3 (1852):278; Daniel S. Lamson, *History of the Town of Weston*, pp. 39–40.

21. Called Wukhuautenauk by Sergeant. Seventeen Indians came to see him from this village, which as of Oct. 23, 1742, had thirteen men, fifteen women, and seventeen children. Hopkins, *Historical Memoirs*, p. 86; *Law Papers* 1:64.

22. Hopkins, *Historical Memoirs*, pp. 85–86.

23. *JHRM* 17:31.

24. John Sergeant journal, June 11, 1739.

25. *JHRM* 17:41–42; RGCM, June 20, 1739, pp. 46–47; Survey of Feb. 10, 1739, Dwight Collection, vol. 37, Chapin Library, Williams College, Williamstown, Mass.; David H. Wood, *Lenox*, pp. 8, 153; Hampshire Co. Registry of Deeds, Book L, pp. 98, 524, Book M, p. 475.

26. Hampshire Co. Court Records, vol. 76, pp. 299–300.

27. Hopkins, *Historical Memoirs*, p. 89.

28. "Letter from a Friend in the Country, Dated Aug. 2, 1739," *Boston Post Boy*, Sept. 3, 1739.

29. Hopkins, *Historical Memoirs*, p. 90.

30. Sergeant journal, Oct. 10, 1739.

31. Jones, *Stockbridge*, p. 19.

32. *The First Annual Report of the American Society for Promoting the Civilization and General Improvement of the Indian Tribes in the United States*, p. 45.

33. Sergeant journal, Oct. 21, 1739.

34. Ibid.; MA, 31:647–54.

35. MA, 3d Ser., 12:15, 221, Plan no. 557.

36. John Sergeant journal, in Philip S. Colee, "The Housatonic-Stockbridge Indians 1734–1739," pp. 193, 197–98.

37. Ibid., p. 183.

38. Hopkins, *Historical Memoirs*, p. 32.

39. Ibid.

40. Ibid., pp. 91–92.

41. Ibid., p. 153.

42. MA, 18:510–11.

43. Timothy Woodbridge letter, May 9, 1741, CHS.

44. Hampshire Co. Registry of Deeds, Book Q, p. 88, Aug. 7, 1744; Harry Andrew Wright, *Indian Deeds of Hampden County*.

45. Sergeant journal, Mar. 1740 (Stockbridge Library copy); Hopkins, *Historical Memoirs*, p. 137.

46. Hopkins, *Historical Memoirs*, p. 94.

47. Samuel Hopkins letter, July 3, 1735, in Appleton, *Gospel Ministers*, preface.

48. Hopkins, *Historical Memoirs*, p. 94.

49. Loskiel, *History of the Mission*, pt. 2, pp. 83–84.

50. Journals of Samuel Kirkland, 1796–97, p. 49, appended remarks Nov. 1799, Samuel Kirkland Correspondence, Burke Library, Hamilton College, Clinton, N.Y.

51. Hopkins, *Historical Memoirs*, p. 45.

52. Records of the Church in Stockbridge, Stockbridge Library Historical Room.

53. Hopkins, *Historical Memoirs*, pp. 63–64.

54. "Documents Relating to the Stockbridge Mission," 190–91.

55. Kellaway, *New England Company*, p. 272.

56. Sergeant to Williams, Feb. 14, 1742, Stockbridge Mission House Archives (Stockbridge Library copy).

57. Jones, *Stockbridge*, pp. 137–38.

58. Bond, *Genealogies*, pp. 120–22.

59. *JP* 9:581; Stockbridge Town Records, Book of Records, 1746, 1751.

60. Stockbridge Book of Records, 1746.

61. Jonathan Edwards to Jasper Mauduit, Nov. 24, 1752, EP; Loskiel, *History of the Mission*, pt. 2, p. 140.

62. Jones, *Stockbridge*, pp. 20–22.

63. MOA, Box 111, folder 1, item 1, Jan. 24, 1744; Box 112, folder 1, Feb. 4, 1744 (Price tr.); Box 112, folder 19, item 1, Feb. 4, 1744 (English). Moravian missionaries used the term *governor* to denote a local chieftain, and in their discussions of this and subsequent events involving this newly chosen chief they used this term. However, the term *captain* also referred to a chief or principal man of a village. In some cases the terms *governor* and *captain* seem distinct, and in others they seem interchangeable. Both terms were occasionally applied to Umpachenee, though he was most frequently called Captain Aron (Aaron). In his *Index*, Fliegel labels Captain Aron as "King of the Mahicans," implying that Umpachenee was sachem. The earliest evidence that Benjamin Kohkewenaunaunt was sachem is a letter from the Stockbridge Indians to William Johnson, Dec. 16, 1756, *JP* 9:581–82.

CHAPTER 5

1. Hopkins, *Historical Memoirs*, pp. 99–101.

2. Ibid.

3. Sergeant journal, May 19, 21, 27, June 10, 1739.

4. *Memoirs of the Rev. David Brainerd*, p. 36.

5. Ibid., p. 101.

6. Sergeant journal, Jan. 6, 1740; *Memoirs of the Rev. David Brainerd*, p. 101.

7. Ibid., p. 173.

8. MOA, Box 111, folder 2, item 8, Dec. 24, 25, 1743 (English); Box 112, folder 3, item 5, Aug. 2, 1744 (English); Loskiel, *History of the Mission*, pt. 2, pp. 54, 65.

9. *Law Papers* 1:64.

10. MOA, Box 114, folder 4, Aug. 8, 1751; Box 115, folder 14, items 1, 3 (Price tr.); Box 3191, folder 1, item 1; Loskiel, *History of the Mission*, pt. 2, p. 43; Reichel, *Memorials*, pp. 144–54, 210, 229–30; Fliegel, *Index*, p. 128 (see chap. 1, n. 16, above).

11. *Documentary History of the State of New York* 3:615.

12. Sergeant journal, in Colee, "Housatonic-Stockbridge Indians," pp. 180–81.

13. Loskiel, *History of the Mission*, pt. 2, p. 13.

14. The account thus far comes largely from Loskiel, *History of the Mission*, pt. 2, pp. 8–22.

15. Loskiel, *History of the Mission*, pt. 2, p. 88.

16. MOA, Box 111, folder 3, item 4, Feb. 22, 1743 (English).

17. Zinzendorf's journal in Reichel, *Memorials*, pp. 54–55.

18. MOA, Box 112, folder 7, drawing of Shekomeko, 1745 (reproduced in *A Memorial of the Dedication of Monuments Erected by the Moravian Historical Society*, p. 63).

19. Fliegel, *Index*, pp. 1342–47; Reichel, *Memorials*, p. 148; Schultze, "Old Moravian Cemetery," p. 149.

20. Formerly Shawas or Shabash, alias Maumauntissekun (various spellings). Fliegel, *Index*, pp. 9, 265; *NYCD* 7:246.

21. MOA, Box 111, folder 1, item 1, Oct. 5, 6, 1742; Box 111, folder 7, item 5, Oct. 5, 6, 11, 1742 (Price tr.).

22. MOA, Box 111, folder 1, item 1, Mar. 19, 1743; Box 111, folder 8, item 4, June 5, 1743 (Price tr.).

23. Timothy Woodbridge letter, May 9, 1741, CHS.

24. *Law Papers* 1:61–64, 89–92.

25. MOA, Box 111, folder 8, item 4, June 5, 1743 (Price tr.); Charles F. Sedgwick, *A History of the Town of Sharon*, pp. 38–44.

26. MOA, Box 112, folder 1, item 2, Mar. 2, 1743 (English); Box 111, folders 3, 4, 1743 (English); Loskiel, *History of the Mission*, pt. 2, pp. 50–51.

27. MOA, Box 221, folder 4, item 1, Jan. 1743 (English).

28. MOA, Box 111, folder 1, Apr. 16, 19, 1743 (Price tr.).

29. Timothy Woodbridge to Spencer Phips, Dec. 15, 1756, MA, 32:751; *NYCD* 7:206–7; Fliegel, *Index*, p. 200.

30. MOA, Box 111, folder 2, item 8, Aug. 21, 1743 (English); Box 111, folder 1, item 1, Aug. 21, 1743 (Price tr.).

31. Jonathan Edwards to Andrew Oliver, Feb. 18, 1752, EP.

32. Hopkins, *Historical Memoirs*, pp. 10, 174.

33. MOA, Box 111, folder 2, item 8, Nov. 6, 1743 (Price tr.); Box 111, folder 1, item 1, Feb. 5, 1744 (Price tr.); Box 112, folder 5, item 7, Dec. 19, 1744 (English).

34. MOA, Box 112, folder 19, item 6, Dec. 3, 6–9, 1743 (Price tr.); Box 112,

folder 6, item 11, Dec. 19, 1744 (Price tr.); Box 112, folder 5, item 7, Dec. 19, 1744 (English); Box 211, folder 5, item 5, Oct. 1742 (English). The last item is apparently a duplicate of the item in Box 112.

35. MOA, Box 112, folder 5, item 5, Oct. 1742 (English).

36. Hopkins, *Historical Memoirs*, pp. 169, 137; MOA, Box 112, folder 2, item 3, May 26, 1744 (English).

37. MOA, Box 111, folder 1, July 1, 1745 (Price tr.); Fliegel, *Index*, p. 324; MOA, Box 114, folder 3, May 27, 1751 (Price tr.); Box 112, folder 2, item 2, Apr. 25, 1744 (Price tr.); Box 112, folder 2, item 3, June 23, 1744 (English).

CHAPTER 6

1. Sergeant journal, Feb. 17, 1740.

2. *Boston Post Boy*, Sept. 3, 1739; Stockbridge Book of Records.

3. Sergeant journal, in Colee, "Housatonic-Stockbridge Indians," pp. 195–96; also in Hopkins, *Historical Memoirs*, pp. 87–88.

4. MA, 31:308.

5. *Correspondence of William Shirley*, ed. Charles H. Lincoln, 1:127–28; Hopkins, *Historical Memoirs*, p. 124; CA, "Indians," pp. 261, 262, 265L, 265x, 265y; ESR.

6. MOA, Box 112, folder 19, item 5, Aug. 26, 1744 (English); Box 112, folder 2, item 5, Aug. 25, 1744 (Price tr.); Box 111, folder 1, item 1, Aug. 26, 1744 (Price tr.).

7. MOA, Box 111, folder 1, item 1, May 21, 1744 (Price tr.).

8. Ruttenber, *History of the Indian Tribes*, pp. 204–5; MOA, Box 323, folder 8, item 1, June 5, 1744.

9. *Documentary History of the State of New York* 3:1013.

10. MOA, Box 112, folder 6, item 6, June 19, 1744 (English); *Documentary History of the State of New York* 3:616.

11. MOA, Box 112, folder 2, item 3, June 17, 19, 1744 (English).

12. Jacob J. Sessler, *Communal Pietism among Early American Moravians*, p. 64.

13. Loskiel, *History of the Mission*, pt. 2, pp. 63–64, 69.

14. *Documentary History of the State of New York* 3:616.

15. Loskiel, *History of the Mission*, pt. 2, pp. 68–69; MOA, Box 112, folder 6, item 11, Dec. 19, 1744 (English).

16. MOA, Box 113, folder 5, items 2, 4, 6, 8, 11 (English); Box 112, folder 6, item 5, folder 2, item 3, folder 11, item 2, May 1745 (English); Loskiel, *History of the Mission*, pt. 2, pp. 78–80.

17. MOA, Box 111, folder 1, item 2, Apr. 21, 26–29, 1745 (Price tr.); Box 112, folder 8, item 3, Apr. 29, 1745 (Price tr.).

18. MOA, Box 111, folder 1, June 16, 1745 (Price tr.).

19. MOA, Box 111, folder 1, May 22, 1745; Box 112, folder 11, item 2, May 1745 (Price tr.).

20. *JHRM* 22:51; RGCM, June 1745, pp. 426, 431–33, 451, 465.

21. James Logan to Richard Peters, Oct. 8, 1745, Conrad Weiser Papers, American Philosophical Society, Philadelphia; Weiser's account of Albany proceedings, Penn Manuscripts, vol. 1, Historical Society of Pennsylvania, Philadelphia (ESR); MOA, Box 111, folder 1, June 3, 1745.

22. *NYCD* 6:294.

23. *Law Papers* 2:118–20, 130–31, 148–49.

24. MOA, Box 111, folder 1, Dec. 21, 1745 (Price tr.).

25. *JHRM* 23:17–18, 23.

26. MA, 31:521–22; Samuel Hopkins, *The Works of Samuel Hopkins* 1:41.

27. MOA, Box 111, folder 1, Jan. 5, 6, 10, 15, 1746 (Price tr.).

28. Loskiel, *History of the Mission*, pt. 2, pp. 82–83, 85–86; MOA, Box 115, folder 11, Sept. 22, 1761 (Price tr.).

29. Fliegel, *Index*, p. 8; MOA, Box 111, folder 1, June 5, 1747 (Price tr.); Loskiel, *History of the Mission*, pt. 2, p. 113.

30. Hopkins, *Historical Memoirs*, p. 137; MOA, Box 131, folder 8, July 4, 1771 (Price tr.).

31. *NYCD* 6:320.

32. Ibid., pp. 322–23; Public Record Office (Kew), CO 5/1095, p. 17, in *Iroquois Indians: A Documentary History*, reel 13.

33. Samuel G. Drake, *Particular History of the Five Years French and Indian War*, pp. 133–34.

34. John Stoddard to Jacob Wendall et al., Apr. 29, 1747, *New England Historical and Genealogical Register* 20, no. 2 (1866): 134.

35. Drake, *Particular History*, p. 146; Benjamin Doolittle, "A Short Narration of Mischief Done by the French and Indian Enemy" (1750), reprinted in *Magazine of History*, extra no. 7 (1909): 16.

36. *Letters and Papers of Cadwallader Colden* 3:415.

37. *JP* 1:125–26.

38. Hopkins, *Historical Memoirs*, p. 127.

39. *Letters and Papers of Cadwallader Colden* 4:12.

40. John Sergeant's will, July 27, 1749 (typewritten copy, Stockbridge Library Historical Room).

CHAPTER 7

1. Hopkins, *Historical Memoirs*, p. 173.

2. Abigail Sergeant to her mother-in-law, Dwight Collection, vol. 8, p. 4 (misdated as 1739).

3. Loskiel, *History of the Mission*, pt. 2, pp. 115–16; Edward O. Dyer, *Gnadensee, the Lake of Grace*, pp. 74–76.

4. Stephen Williams diary (partial, LC MSS Div.), Aug. 25, 1749, Jan. 10, Mar. 14, 1750.

5. Stockbridge Book of Records, town meeting, Mar. 15, 1748.

6. MA, 115:430–31.

7. Stockbridge Book of Records, 1748; Stockbridge Proprietors Records, Berkshire County Proprietary Records, pp. 399, 406, 408, 410.

8. MA, 31:650–51, 653.

9. MA, 31:651, 654.

10. RGCM, Dec. 30, 1749, p. 107; MA, 31:647–54.

11. RGCM, Dec. 30, 1749, p. 107.

12. Hopkins, *Historical Memoirs*, p. 184.

13. Stockbridge Book of Records, Mar. 1750.

14. Stockbridge Proprietors Records, pp. 398–440.

15. MA, 32:62.

16. MA, 29:72, 77.

17. Stockbridge Proprietors Records, p. 406.

18. Letter of Mar. 11, 1755, Letterbooks of the Company for the Propagation of the Gospel in New England.

19. Hampshire Co. Court Records, vol. D5, Forbes no. 77, pp. 97, 147, 228, 229 (Forbes Library, Northampton).

20. MOA, Box 116, folder 6, Aug. 8, 9, 11–13, 20, 1749 (Price tr.).

21. MOA, Box 114, folder 2, Apr. 23, 24, 1750 (Price tr.).

22. MOA, Box 114, folder 3, Mar. 9, May 26, 1751 (Price tr.).

23. MOA, Box 114, folder 4, Aug. 24, 1751; Box 115, folder 15, Aug. 3, 1751 (misdated, should read September); Box 117, folder 2, Sept. 19, 1751 (Price tr.); Hopkins, *Historical Memoirs*. The Moravians apparently used the Gregorian calendar whereas the English used the Julian. Hopkins gives Umpachenee's death as Aug. 10, the Moravians as Aug. 22. On Aug. 19 the Moravians described Edwards's installation as imminent. The Aug. 8 date given in other sources reflects Julian usage.

24. MOA, Box 114, folder 3, May 26, 27, 1751 (Price tr.); Box 114, folder 4, Aug. 5, 8, 10–12, 1751 (Price tr.); Box 117, folder 2, Sept. 19, 1751.

25. Hopkins, *Historical Memoirs*, p. 171.

26. Abigail Sergeant to Ezra Stiles, Nov. 6, 1750, Ezra Stiles Papers, Beinecke Library, Yale University, New Haven, Conn.

27. Abigail Sergeant to Ezra Stiles, Oct. 6, Nov. 6, 1750; Stiles to Ephraim Williams, Apr. 25, 1750; Stiles to Abigail Sergeant, Sept. 14, 1750, Stiles Papers.

28. MOA, Box 114, folder 3, Feb. 17, 1751 (Price tr.); Jonathan Edwards to Joseph Bellamy, June 28, 1751, Joseph Bellamy Papers, Case Memorial Library, Hartford Seminary Foundation, Hartford, Conn., microfilm no. 81191; Edwards's petition, Oct. 1751, EP; Stockbridge Book of Records.

29. Berkshire County Registry of Deeds, bk. 2, pp. 234–43; Edwards's petition, Oct. 1751, EP; Jonathan Edwards to Timothy Dwight, June 30, 1752, EP; Josiah Willard letter, Oct. 19, 1751, Stockbridge Library Historical Room.

30. Ephraim Williams, Jr., to Jonathan Ashley, May 2, 1751, in Wyllis Eaton

Wright, ed., *Colonel Ephraim Williams: A Documentary Life*, p. 61.

31. Ibid., pp. 61–62.

32. Notes for children's sermon, Feb. 1750/51, EP.

33. Jonathan Edwards to Isaac Hollis, July 2, 1751, EP.

34. Jonathan Edwards to William Pepperell, Nov. 28, 1751, EP.

35. "A Letter from Rev. Gideon Hawley of Marshpee . . . ," July 31, 1794, MHS, *Collections*, 1st Ser., vol. 4 (1795):51.

36. In Ola E. Winslow, *Jonathan Edwards, 1703–1758*, pp. 284–85.

37. Jonathan Edwards to Andrew Oliver, Mar. 10, May 1752, EP.

38. MOA, Box 112, folder 2, item 2, May 1752 (Price tr.); Berkshire Co. Registry of Deeds, bk. 5, p. 437; note of Dec. 12, 1753, folder 71-230c.06, Stockbridge Library Historical Room.

39. MOA, Box 112, folder 2, item 2, Apr. 25, 1744 (Price tr.).

40. *NYCD* 7:970.

41. Edwards to Hollis, July 2, 1751; Samuel Hopkins, ed., *The Life and Character of the Late Jonathan Edwards*, p. 86; Edwards to Bellamy, June 28, 1751, Bellamy Papers; Jonathan Edwards to Timothy Edwards, Jan. 27, 1752, EP; Aaron Burr Letter Book, ca. 1752, Andover Newton Theological Seminary, Newton, Mass.

42. Abigail Sergeant to Ezra Stiles, Feb. 15, 1751, Stiles Papers.

43. Esther Edwards Burr diary, Jan. 21, Feb. 2, 1752, Beinecke Library, Yale University, New Haven, Conn. (photostat, Stockbridge Library Historical Room).

44. Jonathan Edwards, Jr., *Observations on the Language of the Muhhekaneew Indians*; reprinted in MHS, *Collections*, 2d Ser., vol. 10 (1823): 84–97.

45. Hampshire Co. Probate Records (Northampton), bk. 9, p. 165.

46. Wright, *Colonel Ephraim Williams*, p. 28.

47. Esther Burr diary, 1752; Jones, *Stockbridge*, p. 59; Stockbridge Book of Records, Mar. 28, 1757, and passim.

CHAPTER 8

1. Taylor, *History of Great Barrington*, pp. 91–94, 134, 153–54.

2. Hopkins, *Historical Memoirs*, pp. 137–38.

3. Ibid., p. 107.

4. MOA, Box 114, folder 1, item 2, Apr. 15, 17, 18, 1749 (Price tr.).

5. *JP* 1:233–34.

6. David Brainerd to John Sergeant, Mar. 25, 1745, in William B. O. Peabody, "Life of David Brainerd," frontispiece.

7. MA, 18:755; Sergeant's will, July 27, 1749 (typewritten copy, Stockbridge Library Historical Room); *JHRM* 26:96; 27:227.

8. Ephraim Williams to Elisha Williams, Oct. 11, 1750, Miscellaneous MSS, LC.

9. MA, 18:755; Ephraim Williams, Jr., to Elisha Williams, Dec. 21, 1750, in

Wright, *Colonel Ephraim Williams*, p. 59; Jonathan Edwards to Isaac Hollis, July 17, 1752, EP; Jonathan Edwards to Jasper Mauduit, Mar. 10, 1752, EP; Rhode Island Historical Society Manuscripts, vol. 6, pp. 1–12 (typewritten excerpt, Stockbridge Library Historical Room); Jonathan Edwards to Thomas Hubbard, Aug. 31, 1751, MHS, *Collections*, 1st Ser., vol. 10 (1809):148; *Documentary History of the State of New York* 3:627.

10. Hopkins, *Historical Memoirs*, pp. 143–49; Josiah Willard to Roger Wolcott, Oct. 11, 1751, CHS, *Collections*, vol. 16 (1916):104–5; CA, "Indians," Ser. I, vol. 2, item 63; Cadwallader Colden Report, Aug. 17, 1751, Penn Manuscripts, vol. 1; *JHRM* 29:33; 31:208.

11. Ephraim Williams to Elisha Williams, Oct. 11, 1750.

12. Jonathan Edwards to Andrew Oliver, Feb. 18, 1752, EP.

13. Edwards to Oliver, Feb. 18, 1752, Apr. 13, 1753; Edwards to Hubbard, Aug. 29, 1752, EP.

14. Edwards to Oliver, May, Aug. 27, 1752; Edwards to Hubbard, Aug. 29, 1752; Edwards to Josiah Willard, July 17, 1752, EP; *Sibley's Harvard Graduates* 7:56–66; CA, "Indians," Ser. I, vol. 2, p. 72a.

15. Note, Feb. 27, 1754; Edwards to Hollis, July 17, 1752; Edwards to Oliver, Oct. 1752, Apr. 13, 1753, EP; Ephraim Williams to Elijah Williams, Mar. 13, 1751, "Some Old Letters," *Scribner's Magazine* (Feb. 1895), p. 251.

16. MA, 32:304–5, 365–74; Edwards to Oliver, May 1752; *JHRM* 29:4.

17. Edwards to Oliver, Apr. 13, 1753, EP.

18. "Letter from Gideon Hawley," 54–56; Wright, *Colonel Ephraim Williams*, pp. 28, 66–69, 153.

19. MOA, Box 114, folder 7, Feb. 10, 1753; Box 117, folder 4, May 24, 1752, May 31, 1753; Box 118, folder 1, Jan. 15, 1754 (Price tr.); Fliegel, *Index*, p. 1349; Loskiel, *History of the Mission*, pt. 2, pp. 124, 147; *Documentary History of the State of New York* 3:633.

20. Edwards to Hollis, July 2, 1751, EP; MOA, Box 114, folder 3, May 27, 1751 (Price tr.).

21. Sereno E. Dwight, *The Life of President Edwards*, pp. 492–93.

22. Edwards to Josiah Willard, Mar. 8, 1754; Edwards to Hollis, July 17, 1752; Edwards, undated letter draft, folder 1, pp. 3–9, EP.

23. Edwards, postscript of letter to Hollis, Summer 1752; Edwards to Hollis, July 17, 1752.

24. Abigail Williams Sergeant to Ezra Stiles, Nov. 6, 1750, Stiles Papers.

25. "Letter from Gideon Hawley," p. 56n.

26. Timothy Woodbridge to Five Nations, AP, 39:262; Julian P. Boyd, ed., *The Susquehannah Company Papers*, 1:lxx–lxxxvii, 274, 303; 2:127–28; Penn MSS, Aug. 5, 1754, ESR.

27. Stockbridge Town Records, Births, Deaths, Marriages, 1737–54.

CHAPTER 9

1. Hopkins, *Historical Memoirs*, p. 183.

2. Sarah C. Sedgwick and Christina S. Marquand, *Stockbridge, 1739–1939*, pp. 72–73; MOA, Box 114, folder 8, Apr. 18, 1753.

3. MA, 32:542.

4. Ibid., pp. 542–45; Elisha Chapin to Israel Williams, Aug. 29, 1754, in *New Hampshire Provincial and State Papers*, ed. Nathaniel Bouton, 6:310.

5. Sedgwick and Marquand, *Stockbridge*, pp. 73–74.

6. Samuel Hopkins to Joseph Bellamy, Sept. 3, 1754, in Taylor, *History of Great Barrington*, p. 139.

7. Jonathan Edwards to John Erskine, Apr. 15, 1755, EP.

8. MA, 32:542–45.

9. Esther Burr diary; MA, 46:375, cited in H. F. Keith, "The Early Roads and Settlements of Berkshire," in *Four Papers of the Berkshire Historical and Scientific Society*, pp. 132–33.

10. MA, 32:542–45.

11. Edwards to Erskine, Apr. 15, 1755; Taylor, *History of Great Barrington*, pp. 154–55.

12. MA, vol. 32, Oct. 9, 1754, in *Iroquois Indians*, reel 16.

13. *NYCD* 6:909.

14. Beverly McAnear, ed., "Personal Accounts of the Albany Congress of 1754," *Mississippi Valley Historical Review* 39, no. 4 (1953): 738.

15. MOA, Box 115, folder 2, Oct. 10, 16, 1754; Box 115, folder 3, Feb. 6, 22, 1755; Loskiel, *History of the Mission*, pt. 2, p. 155; CA, "Indians," Ser. I, vol. 2, pp. 82–89; Sedgwick, *History of Sharon*, pp. 39–41; John W. DeForest, *History of the Indians of Connecticut*, pp. 403–5.

16. Hopkins to Bellamy, Sept. 3, 1754, in Taylor, *History of Great Barrington*, p. 139.

17. MA, 17:581–82.

18. Edwards to Erskine, Apr. 15, 1755.

19. MA, 32:542–45.

20. RGCM, Nov. 18, 19, 1754, p. 328.

21. In Joseph Edward Adams Smith, *The History of Pittsfield*, 1:99.

22. MA, 32:542–45.

23. Hopkins, *Historical Memoirs*, pp. 179–80, 184.

24. *NYCD* 6:881.

25. Ibid., pp. 857, 864, 865, 868.

26. *JHRM* 31:151, 161.

27. MA, 32:594–95.

28. William Williams account book, Dec. 4, 8, 1754, pp. 103–4, William Williams Collection, Berkshire Athenaeum, Pittsfield, Mass.

29. Stockbridge Book of Records, 1739–59; Church Records, Stockbridge

Library Historical Room; Stockbridge Proprietors Records, Berkshire Co. Proprietary Records.

30. CA, "Trade and Maritime Affairs," Ser. I, vol. 2, pt. 2, p. 287a.

31. Stockbridge Book of Records, 1739–59, pp. 7, 74, 87.

32. MOA, Box 117, folder 3, Aug. 26, Sept. 25, Oct. 30, 1752; Box 117, folder 4, Aug. 24, Sept. 4, 5, 21, 24, Oct. 9, Dec. 22, 23, 1753; Box 114, folder 7, Oct. 4, 5, 12, 1752; Box 119, folder 1, item 1019, Mar. 11, 1754 (Price tr.); Loskiel, *History of the Mission*, pt. 2, pp. 140, 149–51; Anthony F. C. Wallace, *King of the Delawares: Teedyuscung, 1700–1763*, pp. 47–55.

33. RGCM, May 6, July 8, 1755, pp. 402, 425; Nancy S. Voye, ed., *Massachusetts Officers in the French and Indian Wars, 1748–1763*, entry no. 1180.

34. *Correspondence of William Shirley* 2:355, 359–60.

35. *JP* 1:797; *NYCD* 7:25, 29–31; Milton W. Hamilton, *Sir William Johnson, Colonial American*, pp. 126–30.

36. Abigail Williams letter, July 29, 1755, Williams of Deerfield Collection, Massachusetts Papers, Box I, NYHS.

37. MOA, Box 115, folder 3, Feb. 14, Apr. 16, July 2–4, 6, 7, 14, 16, 1755 (Price tr.).

38. Fliegel, *Index*, "Christian (166)," p. 80, "Johannes (254)," p. 187.

39. Edmund De Schweinitz, *The Life and Times of David Zeisberger*, pp. 229–40; Reichel, *Memorials*, pp. 197–202, 234, 238; *NYCD* 7:50–51; *JP* 2:611, 613, 623, 624.

40. *NYCD* 7:152–53, 159–60, 253; MOA, Box 115, folder 6, Feb. 17, 1757.

41. MA, 32:718–19; *JHRM* 33 (pt. 1): 58, 66; RGCM, June 10, 1756, p. 216.

42. MOA, Box 115, folder 6, Dec. 11, 1756 (Price tr.).

43. Loudoun Papers, LO 1679, in Stanley M. Pargellis, *Lord Loudoun in North America*, p. 301n.

44. *Journals of the Hon. William Hervey*, ed. J. Clarence Webster and Sydenham H. Hervey, p. 23; *New York Mercury*, June 21, 1756.

45. *Journals of William Hervey*, pp. 24, 27.

46. MOA, Box 115, folder 6, July 1, 3, Aug. 14, 1756 (Price tr.); *JP* 9:590, 632; Rogers, *Journals*, pp. 19, 22, 26–28.

47. "A Journal of a Scout of Leiut Jacob of the Stockbridge Indaiens," Aug. 13, 1756, Loudoun Papers, LO 1480, Huntington Library, San Marino, Calif.

48. Rogers, *Journals*, pp. 26–28.

49. *Journals of William Hervey*, pp. 38–39; AP, 38:7; 46B:24; *Boston Weekly News-Letter*, Sept. 2, 1756.

50. Burt Loescher, *The History of Rogers Rangers*, 1:91–93.

51. MOA, Box 115, folder 6, Jan. 2, 5, 1757 (Price tr.).

52. Ibid., Jan. 23, 1757.

53. Loescher, *History of Rogers Rangers* 1:96, 415–16nn.

54. *JP* 9:590.

55. *JP* 2:678.

56. *JP* 9:632.

57. Esther Burr diary, Sept. 20, 1756; *The Journal of Esther Edwards Burr, 1754–1757*, ed. Carol F. Karlsen and Laurie Crumpacker, pp. 220–24; "The Journal of Esther Burr," *New England Quarterly* 3 (1930): 314.

58. Berkshire Co. Registry of Deeds, bk. 6, pp. 346–47.

59. Hopkins, *Life of Jonathan Edwards*, pp. 89–93.

60. Jonathan Edwards to Esther Burr, Nov. 20, 1757, Dwight Collection, vol. 5, p. 6; also in *Journal of Esther Edwards Burr*, p. 298. In the Dwight Collection letter, Woodbridge's name is condensed to "W–bge."

61. Hopkins, *Life of Jonathan Edwards*, p. 84.

62. Hopkins, *Works of Samuel Hopkins*, pp. 46–48.

63. Edwards to Gideon Hawley, Jan. 14, 1758, A. C. Thompson Papers, Case Memorial Library, Hartford Seminary Foundation; Timothy Woodbridge to Andrew Oliver, Oct. 9, 1758, Miscellaneous Bound MSS, MHS.

CHAPTER 10

1. AP, 38:23; 75:139. According to the *Oxford English Dictionary*, dollars at this period referred to the Spanish peso, or piece of eight, that was used as currency until the federal period.

2. CA, "Indians," Ser. I, vol. 2, p. 98; CHS, *Collections* 9:40, 112, 113, 182; 10:216, 242; 17:338–39; *Memoir and Official Correspondence of Gen. John Stark*, ed. Caleb Stark, pp. 439–40; *JP* 9:912–14.

3. AP, 76:138, 257, 258, 260; 81:92; John R. Cuneo, *Robert Rogers of the Rangers*, pp. 69, 82; Burt Loescher, *Genesis: Rogers Rangers* (vol. 2 of his *History*), pp. 1–2.

4. R. S. Embleton, "Rogers Rangers," *Tradition: Journal of the International Society of Military Collectors* 4, no. 23 (1967): 22–25; Loescher, *History*, pp. 435–36; AP, 76:96–97.

5. Rogers, *Journals*, pp. 105, 108; Loescher, *Genesis*, p. 2; *NYCD* 10:840. The French account said that forty Indians killed or captured all of the party.

6. AP, 75:179; Loescher, *Genesis*, pp. 2–3; *NYCD* 10:710.

7. *Boston News-Letter*, Mar. 15, 1759; *New York Mercury*, Mar. 19, 1759.

8. Loescher, *Genesis*, p. 15.

9. AP, 75:179; 76:260.

10. Rogers, *Journals*, pp. 122, 136; AP, 46A:11; 54:121–22.

11. AP, 46A:144a, 144b; *Correspondence of William Pitt*, ed. Gertrude S. Kimball, 2:44.

12. AP, 46A:21, 23, 150.

13. AP, 54:122–25; MOA, Box 115, folder 9, Apr. 2, 18, 1759 (Price tr.); James Gray letter, July 10, 1759, Sedgwick II Papers, MHS.

14. AP, 54:131–36.

15. AP, 30:52.

16. *The Journal of Jeffery Amherst*, ed. J. Clarence Webster, p. 112.

17. Ibid., p. 133.

18. Loescher, *Genesis*, p. 45; *Journal of William Amherst in America, 1758–1760*, pp. 42–43; *Journal of Jeffery Amherst*, pp. 133–34.

19. John Knox, *An Historical Journal of the Campaigns in North America*, ed. Arthur S. Doughty, 1:488, 492; James Gray letters, July 10, Aug. 2, 1759, Sedgwick II Papers; *Journal of Jeffery Amherst*, pp. 131–34; *Journal of William Amherst*, pp. 40, 44; *Boston News-Letter*, July 26, Aug. 2, 1759.

20. *Commissary Wilson's Orderly Book*, ed. E. B. O'Callaghan, p. 75; Howard H. Peckham, *The Colonial Wars, 1689–1762*, pp. 184–85.

21. AP, 8:10; 198:309. One of the men eventually taken captive with Cheeksaunkun was John Maunaumaug, the only John among them. When released in a prisoner exchange, this John was called John Jacobs. Capt. Jacobs was the name most colonials gave Jacob Naunauphtaunk, and John Jacobs apparently was the English name for Naunauphtaunk's son. Stockbridge town records indicate that Naunauphtaunk had four sons, one of whom was named John and was prominent in Stockbridge Indian affairs after the war. The gradual anglicization of Indian names continued throughout the tribe's history.

22. Extract of a letter from Crown Point, Aug. 23, 1759, in *New York Mercury*, Sept. 3, 1759; "Diaries Kept by Lemuel Wood," Essex Institute, *Historical Collections*, vols. 19–20 (1892): 188.

23. *Journal of Jeffery Amherst*, p. 160; Knox, *Historical Journal* 3:54.

24. *Journal of Jeffery Amherst*, pp. 153, 154–55; *Boston News-Letter*, Aug. 23, 30, Sept. 13, 1759; "Diaries Kept by Lemuel Wood," 19:184.

25. "Diaries Kept by Lemuel Wood," 20:156.

26. Gordon M. Day, "Oral Tradition as Complement," *Ethnohistory* 19, no. 2 (1972): 99–107.

27. Ibid. The spelling of this Indian's name hints that he may not have been a Mohican. In *Original Vermonters*, in a discussion of the Stockbridge Indian who forewarned the Saint Francis Indians, William A. Haviland and Marjory W. Power offer the plausible assertion that the Indian was an emigrant to Stockbridge from Schaghticoke when it was abandoned in 1754. Indians at Schaghticoke were closely associated with those at Saint Francis. It is possible, then, that either two or more non-Mohican Stockbridges were with Rogers, or that Samadagwis may have been the same Indian who had forewarned the Saint Francis people and then remained behind, only to be killed by mistake or in anger (pp. 217, 229, 238–39).

28. AP, 81:140; Knox, *Historical Journal*, 3:72.

29. Rogers, *Journals*, pp. 104–15; Loescher, *Genesis*, pp. 56–65; Cuneo, *Robert Rogers*, chap. 9; AP, 81:140, 199; 46A:194.

30. *Journal of Jeffery Amherst*, p. 173.

31. AP, 38:86.

32. MOA, Box 115, folder 9, Oct. 28, Nov. 10, 1759 (Price tr.).

33. AP, 54:151–53; 81:92.

34. *Journal of Jeffery Amherst*, p. 185.

35. AP, 46A:194; 81:199; 8:10; 198:309.

CHAPTER 11

1. Stephen West to Andrew Oliver, June 19, 1759, Misc. Bound MSS, MHS; MA, 33:154–55.

2. MOA, Box 115, folder 9, May 1, 1760 (Price tr.).

3. AP, 84:54; 51:12; 39:126.

4. AP, 48:237, 239; 52:38, 39.

5. AP, 52:43, 44.

6. *Journal of Jeffery Amherst*, p. 224.

7. AP, 51:22.

8. AP, 198:305; Rogers, *Journals*, p. 124.

9. AP, 51:55.

10. "Diaries Kept by Lemuel Wood," 20:204; AP, 51:63.

11. AP, 38:120; *Journal of Jeffery Amherst*, p. 212; "Samuel Jenks, His Journal of the Campaign in 1760," MHS, *Proceedings*, 2d Ser., vol. 5 (1890): 355, 357.

12. Hampshire Co. Probate Records (Woodbridge appointed executor of Naunauphtaunk's estate), bk. 9, p. 231, Feb. 5, 1761.

13. Rogers, *Journals*, pp. 136–38, 139–41; Loescher, *Genesis*, p. 110.

14. Thomas Mante, *The History of the Late War in North America*, pp. 305–6; AP, 38:141–42.

15. *Journal of Jeffery Amherst*, p. 241; AP, 52:87.

16. AP, 48:39, 55, 63, 69–71; 47:82; Loescher, *Genesis*, chap. 10.

17. MA, 32:545.

18. *JP* 3:402.

19. *JP* 3:281, 353, 402–3, 623, 660; 9:431–32; 10:409–15; *NYCD* 4:196, 216; AP, 39:241, 252.

20. AP, 39:386, 391; 38:248.

21. Canadian Archives, Ser. A, vol. 4, p. 232, Bouquet Papers, cited in Howard H. Peckham, *Pontiac and the Indian Uprising*, pp. 226–27.

22. *JP* 9:99–100; MA, 33:287.

23. "A List of the Different Nations of Indians That Met Sir William Johnson at Niagara, July 1764," MHS, *Collections*, 1st Ser., vol. 10 (1809): 121–22 (indicates that 120 Stockbridges attended).

CHAPTER 12

Except where specifically cited, background material for chapters 12–14 is drawn from the following sources: (1) "A Geographical, Historical Narrative or Summary of the present controversy between Daniel Nimham and . . . Frederick

Philipse . . . ," Lansdowne MSS, vol. 707, folios 24–51, British Museum (LC transcript); also published in Oscar Handlin and Irving Mark, eds., "Chief Daniel Nimham v. Roger Morris, Beverly Robinson and Philip Philipse—an Indian Land Case in Colonial New York 1765–1767," *Ethnohistory* 11, no. 3 (1964): 193–246; (2) Sung Bok Kim, *Landlord and Tenant in Colonial New York*; (3) Irving Mark, *Agrarian Conflicts in Colonial New York, 1711–1775*; (4) Franklin L. Pope, "The Western Boundary of Massachusetts," pp. 29–85; (5) Report of the Select Committee on the Stockbridge and Mohawk Petitions to the New York General Assembly, Mar. 26, 1853, Stockbridge Papers, no. 79, Miller Collection, Museum of the American Indian Library, Heye Foundation, New York.

1. NYCD 6:881–82; *Documentary History of the State of Maine* 12:289; NYCD 6:885.

2. MA, 56:327–28.

3. Township agreement, May 15, 1755; petition to the General Court, May 28, 1755, Stockbridge Indians, Miscellaneous MSS Collection, LC.

4. Stockbridge Indian petition to Volkert Douw, June 30, 1766, British Museum, Additional MS. 22679 (LC transcript).

5. *JHRM* 32 (pt. 1): 81.

6. *JP* 9:567–68, 581–82, 590–91.

7. *NYCD* 7:248–50.

8. *JP* 9:686, 766; Minutes of the New York Governor's Council, vol. 25, July 30, 1757, ESR.

9. MA, 32:751–59; Wright, *Indian Deeds*, Mar. 15, 29, 1757; Kim, *Landlord*, pp. 339–40.

10. *JP* 9:766.

11. *JP* 10:429, 431–32.

12. MA, 33:210–18.

13. *The Acts and Resolves, Public and Private, of the Province of the Massachusetts Bay* 4 (chap. 4): 369; MA, 33:210–18.

14. CA, "Trade and Maritime Affairs," Ser. I, pt. 2, vol. 2, pp. 305, 313b; Stockbridge Town Records, Indian Proprietors, 1749–90, pp. 70, 95.

15. *Public Records of the Colony of Connecticut* 12:310, 470; CA, "Trade and Maritime Affairs," Ser. I, pt. 2, vol. 2, pp. 275–306; Berkshire County Court Records, Inferior Court of Common Pleas, Apr. 1763 session, pp. 258–63; Sept. 1763 session, p. 272.

16. Petition, Feb. 8, 1782, M247, roll 73, item 59, vol. 3, p. 211, PCC.

17. *JHRM* 38 (pt. 2): 252–54.

18. MA, 33:10; *Acts and Resolves of Massachusetts Bay* 17 (chap. 258): 622–23.

19. *JP* 9:599–603, 620.

20. *NYCD* 7:891–92.

21. AP, 39:251.

22. *JP* 9:493–95.

23. "Statement of a Controversy between Daniel Nimham . . . and Philipse heirs . . . ," Philipse Gouveneur Land Titles, folio 13, no. 45, Columbia University Libraries, New York.

24. *JP* 11:735, 911–12.

25. Stockbridge Indian petition to Henry Moore, Apr. 1, 1766, British Museum, Additional MS. 22679; *NYCD* 7:849–50; James T. Flexner, *Lord of the Mohawks: A Biography of Sir William Johnson*, p. 296.

CHAPTER 13

1. *JP* 4:835–36.

2. Articles of agreement, Stockbridge Library Historical Room, M.73-1.33(3).

3. *JP* 12:97–98; *Daily Advertiser* (London), Aug. 7, 1766; *London Chronicle*, Aug. 7, 1766.

4. *Boston Evening Post*, June 30, 1766.

5. *NYCD* 7:886; Kim, *Landlord*, p. 386.

6. *London Chronicle*, Aug. 5–7, 1766; *Boston Evening Post*, Sept. 22, 1766.

7. *London Chronicle*, Aug. 5–7, 1766.

8. *Daily Advertiser*, Aug. 8, 13, 1766.

9. *London Chronicle*, Aug. 21, 1766.

10. *Daily Advertiser*, Aug. 19, 1766.

11. Edwin B. Chancellor, *The Eighteenth Century in London*, pp. 86–97.

12. *Daily Advertiser*, Aug. 20, 1766.

13. *London Chronicle*, Sept. 6, 1766.

14. *Citizen Soldier: The Revolutionary War Journal of Joseph Bloomfield*, ed. Mark E. Lender and James K. Martin, p. 79.

15. Earl of Shelburne to Lords of Trade, Aug. 16, 1766, *Calendar of Home Office Papers of the Reign of George III*, ed. Joseph Redington, 1766–69, no. 248, pp. 67–68.

16. *NYCD* 7:868–70.

17. *London Chronicle*, Sept. 2–4, 13–16, 1766.

18. *JP* 5:394–95.

19. *London Chronicle*, Sept. 30–Oct. 2, 1766; *Boston Evening Post*, Nov. 24, Dec. 1, 1766.

20. *NYCD* 7:886.

21. Kim, *Landlord*, p. 395.

22. MA, 118:202; 56:492.

23. MA, 6:331–32; Stockbridge Indians to Francis Bernard, July 1, 1766, British Museum, Additional MS. 22679.

24. Stockbridge Indians to mayor of Albany, June 30, 1766; same to Francis Bernard, July 1, 1766, British Museum, Additional MS. 22679.

25. *NYCD* 7:849–50.

26. *NYCD* 7:885–86; Kim, *Landlord*, p. 409.

27. *NYCD* 7:891–92, 913–14.

28. Samuel Monrow to John Kempe, May 5, 1767, John Tabor Kempe Papers, NYHS.

29. *JP* 12:282; New York, *Calendar of Council Minutes, 1668–1783*, ed. Berthold Fernow and Arnold J. F. Van Laer, p. 473.

30. *JP* 5:506.

31. *JP* 7:913–14.

32. *JP* 5:542–43.

33. *JP* 6:6–7.

34. *JP* 6:284.

35. Stockbridge Indian Proprietors, 1749–90, pp. 82, 90.

36. Timothy Woodbridge to William Tryon, Dec. 8, 1773, Ayer Collection, MS. 1015, Newberry Library; Stephen West, letter, Feb. 2, 1763, Misc. Bound MSS, MHS.

37. "A Chorographical Map of the Province of New York in North America," comp. Claude J. Sauthier (London: William Faden, 1779).

38. *JP* 12:600–604, 618, 973–74; CA, "Indians," Book II, p. 225, cited in Pope, "Western Boundary," appendix.

39. *The Writings of George Washington*, ed. W. C. Ford, 2:218–24.

40. New York Assembly Report, Mar. 26, 1853, Stockbridge Papers, no. 71, Miller Collection.

CHAPTER 14

1. Stockbridge Indian petition, May 27, 1762, M.73.1.33(1), Stockbridge Library Historical Room; MOA, Box 115, folder 11, Feb. 22, 1761 (Price tr.).

2. MA, 33:201; *The Colden Letter Books*, 1:157, 207; Loescher, *History of Rogers Rangers*, vol. 3 (Abraham Wnaumpos); Taylor, *History of Great Barrington*, pp. 280–81; Dwight Collection, vol. 7, pp. 9, 11. The murderer, Abraham Unkamug or Abraham Wanaumpos, had a brother named Jacob Unkamug, or Jacob Umpachenee. The victim, Chenegun or Chineagun, was probably James Chenegun, a brother of Jonas Etowaukaum, who shared home lots across from their father, Aaron Umpachenee.

3. Berkshire Co. Registry of Deeds, bk. 4, p. 417; Stockbridge Indian Proprietors, 1749–90, p. 58; Jonathan Edwards note, Feb. 27, 1754, EP.

4. John Sergeant, Jr., to Samuel Kirkland, Mar. 9, 1773, Kirkland Correspondence.

5. Stephen West letter, Feb. 2, 1763, Misc. Bound MSS, MHS.

6. Timothy Woodbridge to Andrew Oliver, Nov. 15, 1764, Misc. Bound MSS, MHS.

7. Samuel Hopkins to Andrew Eliot, Mar. 30, 1767, Misc. Bound MSS, MHS.

8. *JP* 12:481.

9. *JP* 12:498–99.

10. MOA, Box 131, folder 8, June 23, 1771 (Price tr.).

11. Ibid., Oct. 23, 27, 1771 (Price tr.).

12. John Sergeant, Jr., to Andrew Eliot, Jan. 11, 1774, Andrew Eliot Papers, 41.F.113, MHS.

13. MA, 33:286, 297–98.

14. Berkshire Co. Court Records, Inferior Court of Common Pleas, Sept. 1763 session, pp. 331–32; MA, 33:297–98.

15. *Acts and Resolves of Massachusetts Bay* 17 (chap. 291): 500.

16. MA, 33:297–98.

17. Loskiel, *History of the Mission*, pt. 2, p. 200.

18. CA, "Indians," Ser. I, 2:200.

19. Stockbridge Church Records.

20. MA, 33:287; Kellaway, *New England Company*, p. 275; Evarts B. Greene, *American Population before the Federal Census of 1790*, pp. 21, 30, 38.

21. Greene, *American Population*, pp. 21, 30, 38; Taylor, *History of Great Barrington*, p. 279.

22. MOA, Box 131, folder 2, May 30, June 12, 1765 (Price tr.).

23. MOA, Box 131, folder 8, June 17, 24, 1771 (Price tr.); John Sergeant, Jr., to H. Storrs, Jan. 31, 1820, O'Reilly Papers, vol. 14; MOA, Box 131, folder 7, Sept. 30, 1770; Box 131, folder 8, June 17, 23, 24, 26, July 28, 1771, Jan. 13, 1772; Box 131, folder 9, May 5, 1772 (Price tr.); Fliegel, *Index*, s.vv. "Jacob, s. of Marie" and "Stockbridge."

24. MOA, Box 131, folder 5, Apr. 4, 5, 8, July 17, Aug. 16, Sept. 23, 1768 (Price tr.); *JP* 12:644–45.

25. Hampshire Co. Colonial Proprietary Records (Stockbridge), p. 437; Stockbridge Church Records, p. 25.

26. Greene, *American Population*, pp. 198–99.

27. MA, 54:219–20; *JHRM* 35:29.

28. MA, 33:287–88.

29. *Acts and Resolves of Massachusetts Bay* 1 (chap. 2): 640–41; 4 (chap. 6): 163–64; Woodbridge to Oliver, Nov. 15, 1764, Misc. Bound MSS, MHS.

30. Woodbridge to Oliver, Nov. 15, 1764, Misc. Bound MSS, MHS.

31. MA, 32:765–66; *JHRM* 33 (pt. 2): 445; RGCM, Apr. 19, 1757, p. 475.

32. MA, 33:591–92.

33. MA, 33:311–16.

34. Woodbridge to Oliver, Nov. 15, 1764, Misc. Bound MSS, MHS.

35. MA, 33:286; Stockbridge Book of Records, Jan. 6, 1766.

36. MA, 33:322.

37. Stockbridge Indian Proprietors, 1749–90, pp. 68, 74, 77.

38. Berkshire Co. Proprietary Records, Stockbridge Proprietors Records, pp. 410, 413.

39. Dwight Collection, vol. 2, p. 34.

40. Woodbridge to Oliver, Nov. 15, 1764, Misc. Bound MSS, MHS.

41. MA, 33:311–16; *Acts and Resolves of Massachusetts Bay* 18 (chap. 135): 70–71; *JHRM* 41:270; 42:94, 144, 150–51, 158, 168, 181.

42. "The New England Company of 1649 and Its Missionary Enterprises," *Publications of the Colonial Society of Massachusetts*, vol. 38, *Transactions* (1947–51): 203.

43. Dwight Collection, vol. 7, p. 17; notes from Timothy Woodbridge to Elijah Williams, Mar. 30, Apr. 5, 8, 1773, MHS (photostats); Berkshire Co. Registry Deeds, bk. 5, p. 331.

44. Stephen West to Andrew Eliot, Jan. 20, 1767, Misc. Bound MSS, MHS.

45. *JP* 12:973–74; Stockbridge Indian petition to the Continental Congress, Mar. 25, 1782, M247, roll 50, item 41, vol. 4, p. 435, PCC.

46. *Acts and Resolves of Massachusetts Bay* 5 (chap. 38): 238.

CHAPTER 15

1. *JHRM* 38 (pt. 1): 47, 50, 52, 59, 65, 66.

2. Stockbridge Book of Records, town meetings, Jan. 12, Mar. 20, 1762, Jan. 4, Mar. 22, 1764, Mar. 1765.

3. MA, 33:249–52, 277–78; Robert E. Brown, *Middle-Class Democracy and the Revolution in Massachusetts*, pp. 40–44.

4. *Acts and Resolves of Massachusetts Bay* 17 (chap. 291): 500.

5. MA, 33:258–68.

6. John Sergeant, Jr., et al. to Samuel Hopkins, Mar. 27, 1767, Misc. Bound MSS, MHS.

7. Jonathan Edwards, Jr., *Observations on the Language of the Muhhekaneew Indians*, preface.

8. Sergeant et al. to Hopkins, Mar. 27, 1767, Misc. Bound MSS, MHS.

9. Samuel Hopkins to Andrew Eliot, Mar. 30, 1767, Misc. Bound MSS, MHS.

10. Stephen West letter, Feb. 2, 1763; Stephen West to Andrew Eliot, Jan. 20, 1767; anonymous, Jan. 30, 1767, Misc. Bound MSS, MHS.

11. Hopkins to Eliot, Mar. 30, 1767, Misc. Bound MSS, MHS.

12. Mitchell, *Woodbridge Record*, pp. 58, 94–96.

13. West to Eliot, July 2, 1767, Misc. Bound MSS, MHS.

14. West letter, Oct. 17, 1767, Misc. Bound MSS, MHS.

15. Hopkins to Eliot, Oct. 28, 1767, Misc. Bound MSS, MHS.

16. *Acts and Resolves of Massachusetts Bay* 5 (chap. 18): 325–26.

17. West letter, Oct. 17, 1767, Misc. Bound MSS, MHS.

18. Stockbridge Church Records, pp. 70, 72, 74; Catherine Pequunaunt, Sept. 1, 1782, Stockbridge Library Historical Room; MA, 33:545.

19. Stockbridge Church Records, p. 76; West letter, Feb. 2, 1763, Misc. Bound MSS, MHS.

20. John Sergeant, Jr., to Samuel Kirkland, Nov. 23, 1773, Jan. 11, 1774, Kirkland Correspondence.

21. Stockbridge Church Records, pp. 74–76.

22. Dwight Collection, vol. 7, p. 12.

23. Stephen West to Samuel Kirkland, Mar. 11, 1773, Kirkland Correspondence.

24. West to Kirkland, May 28, June 25, 1773, Kirkland Correspondence.

25. Sergeant to Kirkland, Nov. 23, 1773, Kirkland Correspondence.

26. Stockbridge Church Records, pp. 78–80.

27. *Literary Diary of Ezra Stiles*, ed. Franklin B. Dexter, 1:209–12, 413.

28. Kellaway, *New England Company*, p. 276; West to Eliot, May 9, 1767, Large MSS, MHS.

29. Sergeant to Kirkland, Feb. 22, 1773, Kirkland Correspondence.

30. Sergeant to Eliot, Jan. 11, 1774, Eliot Papers, 41.F.113.

31. Joseph Bellamy to Jonathan Edwards, May 31, 1756, EP.

32. West letter, Feb. 2, 1763, Misc. Bound MSS, MHS.

33. Woodbridge to Commissioners, Feb. 15, 1763; Woodbridge to Oliver, Nov. 15, 1764; Hopkins to Eliot, Mar. 30, 1767, Misc. Bound MSS, MHS.

34. Edwards letter, Apr. 13, 1753, EP; Woodbridge to Commissioners, Feb. 15, 1763, Misc. Bound MSS, MHS.

35. Stockbridge Indian Proprietors, 1749–90, p. 40, April 18, 1763.

36. James Haughton, "Additional Memoir of the Moheagans," MHS, *Collections*, 1st Ser., vol. 9 (1804): 97n; James D. McCallum, *The Letters of Eleazar Wheelock's Indians*, appendix A. Note: A boy named Aaron is described as son of "Harris," which should read "Honnis," a nickname used for Johannis Mtohksin, whose son Aaron was baptized by Stephen West on Mar. 6, 1774 (Stockbridge Church Records, p. 67).

37. Letters between Wheelock, Woodbridge, and Oliver Partridge, Sept. 24, 1768, MS. 768524.3; Nov. 12, 1768, MS. 76812.2; Dec. 12, 1768, MS. 768662; Dec. 26, 1768, MS. 768676; MS. 768680.2; MS. 769900.5, Dartmouth College Archives, Hanover, N.H.

38. Daniel Simon to Eleazar Wheelock, Dec. 7, 1778, MS. 778657, Dartmouth College Archives.

39. Sergeant to Eliot, Apr. 12, 1774, Eliot Papers, 41.F.114.

CHAPTER 16

1. Taylor, *History of Great Barrington*, pp. 229–32.

2. Stephen West to Samuel Kirkland, Nov. 2, 1774, Kirkland Correspondence.

3. Charles E. Hambrick-Stowe and Donna D. Smerlas, eds., *Massachusetts Militia Companies and Officers in the Lexington Alarm*.

4. L. Kinvin Wroth, ed., *Province in Rebellion: A Documentary History of the Founding of the Commonwealth of Massachusetts, 1774–1775*, p. 1498; William D. Love, *Samson Occom and the Christian Indians of New England*, p. 237.

5. MA, 180:156.

6. Minutes, Col. Guy Johnson, Mar. 24, 1775, RG 10, vol. 11, pp. 93–94, Public Archives of Canada (LC transcript).

7. Petition, Nov. 28–29, 1787, in Love, *Samson Occom*, p. 276.

8. Wroth, *Province in Rebellion*, p. 1497.

9. Ibid., pp. 1497–99.

10. Ibid., pp. 1557–58.

11. Hambrick-Stowe and Smerlas, *Massachusetts Militia Companies*, p. 53.

12. Frederick Mackenzie, *A British Fusilier in Revolutionary Boston*, diary entry, Apr. 30, 1775.

13. *Diaries and Letters of William Emerson*, ed. Amelia Emerson, pp. 79–80.

14. Richard Frothingham, *History of the Siege of Boston*, pp. 212–13.

15. Andrew F. Davis, "The Employment of Indian Auxiliaries in the American War," *English Historical Review* 8 (Oct. 1887): 715.

16. Israel Mauduit, "The Substance of a Speech Made at a General Court of the Company . . . ," 1785, in Kellaway, *New England Company*, p. 280; *Peter Oliver's Origin and Progress of the American Rebellion: A Tory View*, ed. Douglass Adair and John A. Schutz, p. 134.

17. Wroth, *Province in Rebellion*, p. 2480.

18. *American Archives*, ed. Peter Force, 4th Ser., 2:1483–84.

19. *Diaries and Letters of William Emerson*, pp. 79–80.

20. Frothingham, *Siege of Boston*, p. 212; "Diary of Jabez Fitch, Jr.," MHS, *Proceedings*, 2d Ser., vol. 9 (1894): 45; Ewald, *Diary of the American War*, p. 145.

21. *Caleb Haskell's Diary*, ed. Lothrop Withington, Aug. 1, 1775; Gamaliel Whiting diary entry, Aug. 2, 1775, in Taylor, *History of Great Barrington*, p. 206. Taylor supplied "enemies" after the words "our country's" in Whiting's entry, presuming that the diary inferred that the Indians had been shot by the British. Haskell's diary makes it clear, however, that they were shot by "our own men."

22. *Caleb Haskell's Diary*, Aug. 3, 1775; John Sergeant, Jr., to Eleazar Wheelock, Aug. 19, 1775, MS. 775469.1, Dartmouth College Archives.

23. Timothy Pickering Papers, 62:167, MHS.

24. Sergeant to Wheelock, Aug. 19, 1775, MS. 775469.1, Dartmouth College Archives.

25. *Caleb Haskell's Diary*, Aug. 27, 1775; MA, 180:190.

26. Charles A. Jellison, *Ethan Allen*.

27. "A Letter from Capt. Elisha Phelps, Commissary, to the General Assembly," CHS, *Collections*, vol. 1 (1860): 174–76.

28. Benedict Arnold to Thomas Walker, May 20, 1775, Public Archives of Canada, MG 11, C.O. 42, Q series, vol. 11, p. 192.

29. Ethan Allen to Caughnawagas, May 20, 1775, Public Archives of Canada, MG 11, C.O. 42, Q series, vol. 11, pp. 193–95.

30. Benedict Arnold, "Regimental Memoir Book," June 5, 1775, in *Pennsyl-*

vania Magazine of History and Biography 8 (1884); *American Archives*, 4th Ser., 2:1060.

31. Benedict Arnold, "Regimental Memoir Book," June 5, 1775, *Pennsylvania Magazine of History and Biography* 8 (1884).

32. *American Archives*, 4th Ser., 2:1060.

33. Crown Point Officers to Continental Congress, June 10, 1775, M247, roll 179, item 162, pp. 12, 16, PCC.

34. Eleazar Wheelock to Jonathan Trumbull, Mar. 16, 1775, MS. 775216.2, Dartmouth College Archives.

35. Nathaniel Whitaker to Wheelock, Aug. 15, 1775, MS. 775465.2, Dartmouth College Archives.

36. James Diman et al., open letter, Oct. 5, 1780, MS. 780555, Dartmouth College Archives.

37. Crown Point Officers to Continental Congress, June 10, 1775, M247, roll 179, item 162, pp. 12, 16, PCC.

38. *American Archives*, 4th Ser., 2:1002–3.

39. Wheelock to New Hampshire Provincial Congress, June 28, 1775, MS. 775378.1, Dartmouth College Archives.

40. *American Archives*, 4th Ser., 2:611; The Journals of Each Provincial Congress . . . , p. 312, ESR.

41. Case of the Stockbridge Indians as Related by Mr. Sergeant, Nov. 11, 1775, M247, roll 93, item 78, vol. 5, p. 57, PCC; Petition of John Sergeant, Jr., Nov. 27, 1776, M247, roll 52, item 41, vol. 9, p. 9, PCC.

42. Field, *History of Pittsfield*, p. 75; *New England Chronicle*, May 12–18, 1775.

43. *Journals of the Continental Congress*, ed. Worthington Chauncey Ford et al., 2:110–11, 185.

44. "Answer to Hendrick's speech," Dec. 6, 1794, Pickering Papers, 62:118.

45. *Memoir of Lieut. Col. Tench Tilghman*, ed. Samuel Alexander Harrison, Aug. 29 entry, p. 96.

46. *Revolutionary War Journal of Joseph Bloomfield*, p. 79.

47. *American Archives*, 4th Ser., 3:489.

48. Ibid.

49. *Journals of the Continental Congress* 6:983–84.

50. *American Archives*, 4th Ser., 2:611.

51. Wroth, *Province in Rebellion*, p. 1503.

52. *NYCD* 8:451–52.

53. Wroth, *Province in Rebellion*, pp. 2789–90.

54. *The Correspondence of General Thomas Gage*, ed. Clarence E. Carter, 2:684; see also 1:404.

55. *NYCD* 8:596.

56. Thomas Gage to William Tryon, Sept. 10, 1775, MS. 954, William L.

Clements Library, University of Michigan, Ann Arbor (LC transcripts, no longer held in LC).

57. Gage to John Stuart, Sept. 23, 1775, MS. 1020, William L. Clements Library.

58. Massachusetts Committee to Philip Schuyler, Aug. 19, 1775, Peter Force Papers, Series 7E, Box 28, pp. 328–29, LC.

59. PCC, M247, roll 40, item 33, p. 60, no. 17.

60. *American Archives*, 4th Ser., 4:1481–82; PCC, M247, roll 172, item 153, vol. 2, p. 9.

61. Philip Schuyler to John Hancock, PCC, M247, roll 172, item 153, vol. 2, p. 9.

62. MA, 180:156; *JHRM*, Jan. 29, 1776, p. 224 (ESR).

63. Schuyler to Hancock, PCC, M247, roll 172, item 153, vol. 2, p. 9; *The Jefferson Cyclopedia*, ed. John P. Foley, 1:420, entry no. 3898; *Journals of the Continental Congress* 4:394, 396, 412; *Writings of George Washington*, ed. John C. Fitzpatrick, 5:102; *American Archives*, 4th Ser., 6:914.

64. *Writings of George Washington*, ed. Fitzpatrick, 5:108, 163; Edmund C. Burnett, ed., *Letters of Members of the Continental Congress*, 1:481; *Journals of the Continental Congress* 5:473, 527; *American Archives*, 4th Ser., 6:1065.

65. Philip Schuyler to George Washington, July 1, 1776, George Washington Papers, Ser. 4, reel 36, LC.

66. *Writings of George Washington*, ed. Fitzpatrick, 5:356.

67. Ibid., pp. 386, 392, 409; warrant book, Aug. 10, 1776, Washington Papers, Ser. 5, reel 116.

68. Schuyler to Washington, Aug. 16, 1776, Washington Papers, ser. 4, reel 37; Schuyler Ledger Accounts, disbursements to Captain Solomon, Aug. 18, 1776, Philip Schuyler Papers, LC.

69. Schuyler to Horatio Gates, Aug. 29, 1776, reel 2, Horatio Gates Papers, NYHS; *American Archives*, 5th Ser., 1:1221, 1265.

70. *American Archives*, 5th Ser., 2:476.

71. Thomas J. Fleming, *1776: Year of Illusions*, pp. 387–96; *Revolutionary Journal of Col. Jeduthan Baldwin, 1775–1778*, ed. Thomas W. Baldwin, Oct. 21, 1776.

72. Ezra Whittlesey to Samuel Brewer, Oct. 22, 1776, Gates Papers, reel 2.

73. *American Archives*, 5th Ser., 2:1120; Schuyler to Washington, Oct. 23, 1776, Washington Papers, vol. 35.

74. Schuyler to Gates, Oct. 30, 1776, Gates Papers, reel 2.

75. Philip Schuyler orderly book, Oct. 1775–Oct. 1776, Schuyler Papers.

76. Timothy Edwards to Esther Burr, Feb. 22, 1776, Aaron Burr Papers, NYHS.

77. Edna Bailey Garnett, *West Stockbridge Massachusetts, 1774–1974*, pp. 25–26.

78. Erastus Sergeant to Theodore Sedgwick, Feb. 19, 1777, Sedgwick I Papers, MHS.

79. Correspondence of the New York Provincial Congress, Apr. 2, 1777, p. 430, ESR.

CHAPTER 17

1. MA, 22:72; Timothy Edwards to Horatio Gates, Aug. 26, 1777, Gates Papers, reel 4. *Continental Journal and Weekly Advertiser*, Aug. 21, 1777, p. 3.

2. John Burgoyne, *A State of the Expedition from Canada*, appendix 6, p. xii.

3. *Memoirs, Letters and Journals of Major General Riedesel*, ed. Max von Eelking, entry of Oct. 1, 1777.

4. *Continental Journal and Weekly Advertiser*, Aug. 21, 1777, p. 3.

5. Ledger Accounts, July 20, 1777, Schuyler Papers; Jared Sparks, ed., *Correspondence of the American Revolution* 2:515; Journal of the New York Council of Safety, July 20, 1777, pp. 1012, 1214, ESR. The two regulars were members of the Twenty-first Regiment of Foot under Brig. Gen. James Hamilton.

6. Journal of the New York Council of Safety, p. 1012; MA, 22:72; statement of John Hadocks, Mar. 10, 1852, in "Memorial of John W. Quinney," Wisconsin Historical Society, *Collections*, vol. 4 (1857–58): 325.

7. Edwards to Gates, Aug. 26, 1777, Gates Papers, reel 4.

8. Ibid.

9. Ledger Accounts, Aug. 5, 1777, Schuyler Papers.

10. John Sergeant, Jr., to Eleazar Wheelock, Aug. 6, 1777, MS, 777456, Dartmouth College Archives.

11. John F. Luzader, *Decision on the Hudson: The Saratoga Campaign of 1777*, pp. 411–46.

12. Jehoiakim Mtohksin to Horatio Gates, Oct. 22, 1777, reel 4, Gates Papers.

13. *JHRM*, June 16, 1777, pp. 26–27, ESR; *Acts and Resolves of Massachusetts Bay* 20 (chap. 72): 35.

14. Petition of Abraham Nimham, undated, M247, roll 55, item 42, vol. 5, p. 451, PCC.

15. *Journals of the Continental Congress* 9:770, 840.

16. Mtohksin to Gates, Oct. 22, 1777, Gates Papers, reel 4.

17. Stockbridge Town Records, Town Book, 1760–1835, for 1777; Stockbridge Indian Proprietors, 1749–90, p. 106; Berkshire Co. Registry of Deeds, bk. 26, o. 375, Feb. 21, 1785; MA, 33:545.

18. Barbara Graymont, *The Iroquois in the American Revolution*, pp. 39–46.

19. David Levinson, "An Explanation for the Oneida-Colonist Alliance in the American Revolution," *Ethnohistory* 23, no. 3 (1976): 281–82; *Documentary History of the State of New York* 3:627–33; Luna M. Hammond Whitney, *History of Madison County*, p. 751.

20. Graymont, *Iroquois*, p. 101.

21. *NYCD* 8:725.

22. *Revolutionary Journal of Col. Jeduthan Baldwin*, Sept. 22, 1777.

23. Edwards to Gates, Sept. 22, 1777, Gates Papers, reel 4.

24. William Torrey Orderly Book, Sept. 25, 1777, LC; Horatio Gates to John Hancock, Oct. 12, 1777, Gates Papers, reel 9.

25. Muster Roll, Greenwich, July 22, 1778, War Department, Revolutionary War Rolls, Mass. Jacket 11, M246, roll 37, National Archives; Richard Meade to Jedidiah Huntington, Sept. 11, 1778, Washington Papers, Ser. 3B, reel 51.

26. "Case of the Stockbridge Indians as related by Mr. Sergeant," T. Cushing to J. Hancock, Nov. 11, 1775, M247, roll 93, item 78, vol. 5, p. 57, PCC.

27. Abraham Nimham to Horatio Gates, in papers of 1778, Gates Papers, reel 6.

28. Ewald, Johann, *Diary of the American War*, pp. 145, 148.

29. Otto Hufeland, *Westchester County during the American Revolution*, p. 258.

30. John G. Simcoe, *Simcoe's Military Journal*, pp. 80–81.

31. Ibid., pp. 83–86; Ewald, *Diary of the American War*, p. 145.

32. Diary attributed to Brig. Gen. James Pattison or his aide, Aug. 31, 1778, in *Narratives of the Revolution in New York*, p. 254; Ewald, *Diary of the American War*, p. 145.

33. Thomas F. Devoe, "The Massacre of the Stockbridge Indians, 1778," *Magazine of American History* 5, no. 3 (1880): 193.

34. *Royal Gazette*, Sept. 5, 1778, p. 3.

35. *Public Papers of George Clinton*, ed. Hugh Hastings, 3:726–27.

36. Taylor & Duffin to Daniel Claus, Nov. 15, 1778, Claus Family Papers, Public Archives of Canada, MG 19, F1, vol. 2, pp. 67–68.

37. Devoe, "Massacre," p. 194; Ewald, *Diary of the American War*, p. 145.

38. Pickering Papers, 62:167.

39. Carl Baurmeister, *Revolution in America: Confidential Letters and Journals, 1776–1784, of Adjutant General Major Baurmeister of the Hessian Forces*, trans. and annotated by Bernard A. Uhlendorf; Ewald, *Diary of the American War*, p. 145.

40. Records of the Governor's Council, Jan. 11, 1779.

41. Warrant Book, Sept. 10, 1778, Washington Papers, ser. 5, reel 116.

42. Richard K. Meade to Jedidiah Huntington, Sept. 11, 1778, Washington Papers, ser. 3B, reel 51.

43. Military Service Records, Revolution, Eight Mass. Regiment, M246, rolls 437–39, National Archives.

44. *Acts and Resolves of Massachusetts Bay* 20 (chap. 336): 549; *JHRM*, Jan. 8, 1779, p. 90, ESR.

45. MA, 156:323, in Oscar Handlin and Mary Handlin, eds., *The Popular Sources of Political Authority: Documents on the Massachusetts Constitution of 1780*, pp. 209–10.

46. Robert J. Taylor, *Western Massachusetts in the Revolution*, p. 89.

CHAPTER 18

1. *Journals of the Military Expedition of Major John Sullivan*, pp. 246, 315.

2. *Writings of George Washington*, ed. Fitzpatrick, 15:286–87.

3. Ibid., pp. 367–68.

4. Louise Welles Murray, ed., *Notes from the Craft Collection in Tioga Point Museum on the Sullivan Expedition of 1779*, pp. 13–14; *The Order Book of Capt. Leonard Bleeker*, p. 66.

5. *Journals of John Sullivan*, pp. 108, 181, 249, 252, 260, 349.

6. Account of David Freemoyer, in John C. Dann, ed., *The Revolution Remembered: Eyewitness Accounts of the War for Independence*, pp. 288–89, 292–96; Albert Wright, *The Sullivan Expedition of 1779: The Losses*, p. 15; Albert Wright, *The Sullivan Expedition of 1779: The Regimental Rosters of Men*.

7. Graymont, *Iroquois*, pp. 217–19.

8. CA, "Indians," Ser. I, 2:226a–30.

9. *Writings of George Washington*, ed. Fitzpatrick, 20:44–45.

10. Ibid.; Pickering Papers, 62:167a; Record no. 20865, War Dept. Collection of Revolutionary War Records, MSS file, Misc. numbered records, M859, National Archives.

11. MA, 186:149, 275, 329; *Acts and Resolves of Massachusetts, 1780–81*, chap. 51, p. 160.

12. William Goodrich's Command, Military Service Records, Revolution, M881, roll 469, National Archives; Revolutionary War Rolls, Mass. Jacket 64, microfilm roll 41, National Archives (also in Vermont, *Rolls of the Soldiers . . .*, ed. John Ellsworth Goodrich and Chauncey L. Knapp, pp. 305–7); MA, 21:158.

13. Daniel Brodhead to S. Huntington, Mar. 10, 1781, M247, roll 92, item 78, p. 133, PCC.

14. *Acts and Resolves of Massachusetts, 1780–81*, chap. 104, pp. 190–201.

15. *Massachusetts Soldiers and Sailors of the Revolutionary War* 9:396.

16. Petition, Sept. 5, 1781, M247, roll 50, item 41, vol. 4, p. 422, PCC; *Journals of the Continental Congress* 21:935.

17. Military Service Records, Revolution, Ninth Mass. Regiment, M246, roll 441, National Archives.

18. *Writings of George Washington*, ed. Fitzpatrick, 23:75, 80–81.

19. Ibid., 20:209.

20. Kirkland's statement, Jan. 13, 1789, John Sullivan Papers, vol. 1 (1735–95), MHS.

21. Joseph Chenequin, Samuel Littleman, William Notonksion, and Isaac Wnaumpey enlisted in the Fourth Massachusetts Regiment. *Massachusetts Soldiers and Sailors*.

22. *New York in the Revolution as Colony and State*, pp. 12, 94–96.

23. Willett's New York Regiment, Capt. Simeon Newell's Co., Compiled Military Service Records, Revolution M246, rolls 773–74, National Archives.

24. Fliegel, *Index*, entries for Netawatwees; MOA, Box 141, folder 12, item 1, p. 5, June 5, 1772 (English).

25. John Sergeant, Jr., to Samuel Kirkland, Feb. 22, 1773, Kirkland Correspondence.

26. *Diary of David Zeisberger*, ed. and trans. Eugene F. Bliss, 1:81–85; Paul A. W. Wallace, *Thirty Thousand Miles with John Heckewelder*, chap. 22; John G. E. Heckewelder, *A Narrative of the Mission of the United Brethren*, ed. William E. Connelly, pp. 416–33; Henry S. Commager and Richard B. Morris, eds., *The Spirit of Seventy-Six: The Story of the American Revolution as Told by Participants*, pp. 1056–60.

CHAPTER 19

1. Petition, Feb. 8, 1782, M247, roll 73, item 59, vol. 3, p. 211, PCC.

2. Petition, March 25, 1782, M247, roll 50, item 41, vol. 4, p. 435, PCC (misdated, should read February).

3. Ibid.

4. *Journals of the Continental Congress* 22:127.

5. John Hanson to George Clinton, Mar. 11, 1782, M247, roll 24, item 16, p. 145; PCC.

6. *Proceedings of the Commissioners of Indian Affairs Appointed by Law for the Extinguishment of Indian Titles in the State of New York*, June 23, 25, 1785, pp. 93, 99.

7. Joseph Shauquethqueat to George Washington, July 2, 1783, Washington Papers, Ser. 4, reel 92.

8. Statement of Arent van Dyck et al., May 20, 1762, M73-1.33, Stockbridge Library Historical Room.

9. Records of the Governor and Council of the State of Vermont, Oct. 26, 1781, Mar. 15, 1788, Oct. 28, 1789, ESR.

10. Love, *Samson Occom*, pp. 208–28, 244–45.

11. Samuel Kirkland to James Bowdoin, Mar. 10, 1784, Kirkland Correspondence.

12. Ibid.; Kirkland journal, Mar. 27, 1789, Kirkland Correspondence; Samson Occom to Solomon Welles, Sept. 26, 1784, MS. 784526, Dartmouth College Archives.

13. Petition, Sept. 2, 1783, M73-1.30(1), Stockbridge Library Historical Room.

14. *Acts and Resolves of Massachusetts, 1782–83*, chap. 35, p. 578.

15. Stockbridge Indian deed to Isaac Marsh, July 20, 1789, town record, Marshfield, Vt.

16. Stockbridge Indian Proprietors, 1749–90, p. 79 and passim.

17. Massachusetts town populations, Sept. 1783, M247, roll 88, item 74, p. 370, PCC.

18. Samuel Kirkland to Eleazar Wheelock, Oct. 29, 1773; Kirkland to wife,

Nov. 1, 1773; Kirkland to John Thornton, Nov. 1, 1773, Kirkland Correspondence.

19. *JHRM* 49:162, 177, 221–23, 226, 228, 242–43.

20. *Massachusetts Gazette* (Springfield), Oct. 7, 1783.

21. Samuel Hopkins to Gideon Hawley, June 7, 1762, MS. 82685, A. C. Thompson Papers, Hartford Seminary Foundation.

22. Kirkland to wife, Sept. 10, 1785, Jan. 14, 1787, Kirkland Correspondence; Love, *Samson Occom*, pp. 250, 251, 252, and passim.

23. Hendrick Aupaumut et al. to Samson Occom, Aug. 29, 1787, MS. 787479, Dartmouth (copy in Stockbridge Library Historical Room, 71-230C.51).

24. "The Report of a Committee of the Board of Correspondents of the Scots Society for Propagating Christian Knowledge, Who Visited the Oneida and Mohekunuk Indians in 1796," MHS, *Collections*, 1st Ser. vol. 5 (1798): 22.

25. Ibid., pp. 26, 21.

26. John Sergeant, Jr., to Edward Wigglesworth, Mar. 24, 1788, MS. 788224, Dartmouth College Archives; Jones, *Stockbridge*, p. 85.

27. David P. Szatmary, *Shays Rebellion*, pp. 33–36, 108–14.

28. Timothy Woodbridge, *The Autobiography of a Blind Minister*, p. 37.

29. Charles J. Kappler, comp. and ed., *Indian Treaties, 1778–1883*.

30. *Writings of George Washington*, ed. Fitzpatrick, 27:53.

31. Hopkins, *Historical Memoirs*, p. 184.

BIBLIOGRAPHY

Primary Sources, Unpublished

Amherst, Jeffery. Papers. Great Britain, Public Record Office, War Office.

Ayer Collection. Newberry Library, Chicago.

Belcher, Jonathan. Papers. Massachusetts Historical Society, Boston.

Bellamy, Joseph. Papers. Case Memorial Library, Hartford Seminary Foundation, Hartford, Conn.

Berkshire County Court Records. Inferior Court of Common Pleas. Berkshire County Courthouse, Pittsfield, Mass.

Berkshire County Proprietary Records (Stockbridge). Berkshire County Courthouse, Pittsfield, Mass.

Berkshire County Registry of Deeds. Colonial Records, Stockbridge. Berkshire County Courthouse, Pittsfield, Mass.

British Museum Additional Manuscripts. (Library of Congress transcripts).

Burr, Aaron. Letterbook. Franklin Trask Library, Andover Newton Theological Seminary, Newton Centre, Mass.

——— . Papers. New-York Historical Society, New York.

Burr, Esther Edwards. Diary. Beinecke Library, Yale University, New Haven, Conn. Photostat, Stockbridge Library.

Canada. Public Archives. Record Group 10. Miscellaneous Collection on Indian Affairs (Library of Congress transcripts).

——— . Record Group MG 11.

"A Chorographical Map of the Province of New York in North America." 1779. Comp. Claude J. Sauthier. London: William Faden. Library of Congress.

Claus Family Papers. Record Group MG 19. Public Archives of Canada.

Company for the Propagation of the Gospel in New England. Letterbooks. Mather Collection, Tracy W. McGregor Library, University of Virginia, Charlottesville.

Connecticut Archives. Volumes for Indians, Trade and Maritime Affairs, and Towns and Lands. Hartford.

Connecticut Historical Society. Collections. Hartford.

Dartmouth College Archives. Hanover, N.H.

Dwight Collection. Chapin Library, Williams College, Williamstown, Mass. Microfilm. Originals in the Norman Rockwell Museum at Stockbridge.

Edwards, Jonathan. Papers. Franklin Trask Library, Andover Newton Theological Seminary, Newton Centre, Mass.

Eliot, Andrew. Papers. Massachusetts Historical Society, Boston.

Force, Peter. Papers. Library of Congress.

Gage, Thomas. Papers. William L. Clements Library, Ann Arbor, Mich. (Library of Congress transcripts).

Gates, Horatio. Papers. New-York Historical Society, New York.

"A Geographical, Historical Narrative or Summary of the Present Controversy between Daniel Nimham and . . . Frederick Philipse. . . ." Lansdowne MSS, vol. 707, folios 24–51, British Museum.

Hampshire County Colonial Proprietary Records (Berkshire County Records). Berkshire County Courthouse, Pittsfield, Mass.

Hampshire County Court Records. Inferior Court of Common Pleas and Court of General Sessions of the Peace. Forbes Library, Northampton, Mass.

Hampshire County Probate Records. Hampshire County Courthouse, Springfield, Mass.

Hampshire County Registry of Deeds. Hampshire County Courthouse, Springfield, Mass.

Journal of the Committee of Safety, New York (New York Council of Safety). Early State Records microfilm, Library of Congress.

Kempe, John Tabor. Papers. New-York Historical Society, New York.

Kirkland, Samuel. Correspondence. Burke Library, Hamilton College, Clinton, N.Y.

Land Papers, Miscellaneous, New York, Columbia County, 1761–62. New-York Historical Society, New York.

Loudoun Papers. Huntington Library, San Marino, Calif.

Massachusetts Archives. Boston.

Miscellaneous Bound MSS. Massachusetts Historical Society, Boston.

Moravian Archives. Bethlehem, Pa.

O'Reilly, Henry. Papers. New-York Historical Society, New York.

Papers of the Continental Congress. National Archives.

Paterson, Col. John. Orderly Book. Miscellaneous Manuscripts Collection, Library of Congress.

Penn Manuscripts. Historical Society of Pennsylvania, Philadelphia.

Philipse Gouveneur Land Titles, folio 13, no. 45. Columbia University Libraries, New York.

Pickering, Timothy. Papers. Massachusetts Historical Society, Boston.

Records of the Church in Stockbridge. Stockbridge Library Historical Room, Stockbridge, Mass.

Records of the Governor's Council of Massachusetts. Early State Records microfilm, Library of Congress.

Records of the Governor and Council of the State of Vermont. Early State Records microfilm, Library of Congress.

Reed, William. Orderly Book and Roll of Capt. William Reed's Co. Miscellaneous Manuscripts Collection, Library of Congress.

Schuyler, Philip. Papers. Library of Congress.

Sedgwick I Papers (Theodore). Massachusetts Historical Society, Boston.

Sedgwick II Papers. Massachusetts Historical Society, Boston.

Sergeant, John. Journal, April 1, 1739–March 30, 1740. Beinecke Library, Yale University, New Haven, Conn. Photostat, Stockbridge Library.

Stiles, Ezra. Papers. Beinecke Library, Yale University, New Haven, Conn.

Stockbridge Indians. Miscellaneous Manuscripts Collection, Library of Congress.

Stockbridge Library Historical Room Collections. Stockbridge, Mass. (A collection of original documents and copies from other collections pertaining to Stockbridge history).

Stockbridge Mission House Archives. The Trustees of Reservations, Stockbridge, Mass.

Stockbridge Town Records. Indian Proprietors, 1749–90. Town Hall, Stockbridge, Mass.

———. Births, Deaths, and Marriages, 1737–54. Town Hall, Stockbridge, Mass.

———. Book of Records, 1739–59. Town Hall, Stockbridge, Mass.

———. Town Book, 1760–1835. Town Hall, Stockbridge, Mass.

Stockbridge Papers, Miller Collection. Museum of the American Indian Library, Heye Foundation, New York.

Sullivan, John. Papers. Massachusetts Historical Society, Boston.

Thompson, A. C. Papers. Case Memorial Library, Hartford Seminary Foundation, Hartford, Conn.

Torrey, William. Orderly Book. Library of Congress.

War Department Collection of Revolutionary War Records (Record Group 93, microfilm groups M246, M859, M881), National Archives.

Washington, George. Papers. Library of Congress.

Weiser, Conrad. Papers. American Philosophical Society, Philadelphia.

Williams, Stephen. Diary. Richard Storrs Library, Longmeadow Historical Society, Longmeadow, Mass.

———. Diary, 1749–50. Miscellaneous Manuscripts Collection, Library of Congress.

Williams, William. Collection. Berkshire Athenaeum, Pittsfield, Mass.

Williams of Deerfield Collection. Massachusetts Papers. New-York Historical Society, New York.

PRIMARY SOURCES, PUBLISHED

The Acts and Resolves, Public and Private, of the Province of the Massachusetts Bay. 21 vols. Boston, 1869–1922.

Acts and Resolves of Massachusetts, 1780–81, 1782–83. 2 vols. Boston, 1880.

American Archives. Ed. Peter Force. Fourth and Fifth Series. New York and London: Johnson Reprint Corp., 1972.

American Board of Commissioners for Foreign Missions. *Report.* Boston, 1841.

Amherst, Jeffery. *The Journal of Jeffery Amherst.* Ed. J. Clarence Webster. Chicago: University of Chicago Press, 1931.

Amherst, William. *Journal of William Amherst in America, 1758–1760.* London: Butler and Tanner, 1927.

"Ancestry of the Jones Family, Stockbridge, Mass." *New England Genealogical and Historical Register* 6, no. 3 (1852): 278.

Appleton, Nathaniel. *Gospel Ministers Must Be Fit for the Master's Use.* Edinburgh, 1736.

Arnold, Benedict. "Regimental Memoir Book." *Pennsylvania Magazine of History and Biography* 8 (1884): 363–76.

Aupaumut, Hendrick. "A Short Narration of My Last Journey to the Western Contry [*sic*]." Historical Society of Pennsylvania, *Memoirs,* vol. 2, pt. 1 (1827): 61–131.

Baldwin, Jeduthan. *Revolutionary Journal of Col. Jeduthan Baldwin, 1775–1778.* Ed. Thomas W. Baldwin. Bangor: C. H. Glass, 1906.

Baurmeister, Carl. *Revolution in America: Confidential Letters and Journals, 1776–1784, of Adjutant General Major Baurmeister of the Hessian Forces.* Trans. and annotated by Bernhard A. Uhlendorf. New Brunswick: Rutgers University Press, 1957.

Benson, Adolph B., ed. *The America of 1750: Peter Kalm's Travels in North America.* Vol. 1. New York: Wilson-Erickson, 1937.

Bleeker, Leonard. *The Order Book of Capt. Leonard Bleeker.* New York, 1865.

Bloomfield, Joseph. *Citizen Soldier: The Revolutionary War Journal of Joseph Bloomfield.* Ed. Mark E. Lender and James K. Martin. Newark: New Jersey Historical Society, 1982.

Boston Post Boy. 1739.

Boston Weekly News-Letter. 1756–59.

Bougainville, Louis Antoine de. *Adventure in the Wilderness: The American Jour-*

nals of Louis Antoine de Bougainville, 1756–1760. Ed. and trans. Edward P. Hamilton. Norman: University of Oklahoma Press, 1964.

Boyce, Douglas, ed. "A Glimpse of Iroquois Culture History through the Eyes of Joseph Brant and John Norton." American Philosophical Society, *Proceedings* 117, no. 4 (1973): 286–94.

Boyd, Julian P., ed. *The Susquehannah Company Papers*. 11 vols. Ithaca: Cornell University Press, 1962.

Brainerd, David. *Memoirs of the Rev. David Brainerd*. Ed. Jonathan Edwards and Sereno E. Dwight. New Haven, 1822.

Burgoyne, John. *A State of the Expedition from Canada*. London, 1780.

Burnett, Edmund C., ed. *Letters of Members of the Continental Congress*. Gloucester: P. Smith, 1963–.

Burr, Esther. "The Journal of Esther Burr." *New England Quarterly* 3 (1930): 297–315.

————. *The Journal of Esther Edwards Burr, 1754–1757*. Ed. Carol F. Karlsen and Laurie Crumpacker. New Haven: Yale University Press, 1984.

Calendar of Home Office Papers of the Reign of George III. Ed. Joseph Redington. London: Her Majesty's Stationery Office, 1879.

"Celebration of the Fourth of July, 1854." Wisconsin Historical Society, *Collections*, vol. 4 (1857–58): 313–20.

Clinton, George. *Public Papers of George Clinton*. Ed. Hugh Hastings. 10 vols. 1899–1914. Reprint. New York: AMS Press, 1973.

Colden, Cadwallader. *The Colden Letter Books*. 2 vols. New-York Historical Society, *Collections*, vols. 9–10. New York: 1876–77.

————. *The History of the Five Indian Nations of Canada*. 2 vols. New York: Amsterdam Book Co., 1908.

————. *Letters and Papers of Cadwallader Colden*. 9 vols. New-York Historical Society, *Collections*, vols. 50–56. New York, 1918–37.

Commager, Henry S., and Richard B. Morris, eds. *The Spirit of Seventy-Six: The Story of the American Revolution as Told by Participants*. New York: Harper and Row, 1975.

Commissary Wilson's Orderly Book. Ed. E. B. O'Callaghan. Albany: 1857.

Connecticut Historical Society. *Collections*.

Continental Journal and Weekly Advertiser. 1777.

The Daily Advertiser (London). 1766.

Danckaerts, Jaspar, and Peter Luyter. *Journal of a Voyage to New York*. 1867. Reprint. Ann Arbor: University Microfilms, 1966.

Dann, John C., ed. *The Revolution Remembered: Eyewitness Accounts of the War for Independence*. Chicago: University of Chicago Press, 1980.

Dillon, John B. *Oddities of Colonial Legislation in America*. Indianapolis, 1879.

Documentary History of the State of Maine. Ed. James Phinney Baxter. Portland: Maine Historical Society, 1869–1916. (2nd series of Maine Historical Society's *Collections*)

Documentary History of the State of New York. Ed. E. B. O'Callaghan. 4 vols. Albany, 1850.

"Documents Relating to the Stockbridge Mission, 1825–1848." Wisconsin Historical Society, *Collections*, vol. 15 (1900): 39–204.

Documents Relative to the Colonial History of the State of New York. Ed. E. B. O'Callaghan. 15 vols. Albany, 1853–87.

Doolittle, Benjamin. "A Short Narration of Mischief Done by the French and Indian Enemy" (1750). Reprinted in *Magazine of History*, extra no. 7 (1909): 16.

Dwight, Timothy. *Travels in New England and New York.* 4 vols. London, 1823.

Edwards, Jonathan (Jr.). *Observations on the Language of the Muhhekaneew Indians.* New Haven, 1788.

Emerson, William. *Diaries and Letters of William Emerson, 1743–1776.* Ed. Amelia Emerson. N.p. 1972.

Ewald, Johann von. *Diary of the American War: A Hessian Journal.* Ed. and trans. Joseph P. Tustin. New Haven: Yale University Press, 1979.

"Extract from an Indian History." Massachusetts Historical Society, *Collections*, 1st Ser., vol. 9 (1804): 99–102.

Field, David Dudley. *An Historical Sketch, Congregational, of the Church in Stockbridge.* New York, 1853.

The First Annual Report of the American Society for Promoting the Civilization and General Improvement of the Indian Tribes in the United States. New Haven, 1824.

Fitch, Jabez. "Diary of Jabez Fitch, Jr." Massachusetts Historical Society, *Proceedings*, 2d Ser., vol. 9 (1894): 41–91.

Fliegel, Carl J. *Index to the Records of the Moravian Mission among the Indians of North America.* New Haven: Research Publications, 1970.

Franklin, Benjamin. *Papers of Benjamin Franklin.* Ed. Leonard Labaree. New Haven: Yale University Press, 1959–.

Gage, Thomas. *The Correspondence of General Thomas Gage.* Ed. Clarence E. Carter. 2 vols. New Haven: Yale University Press, 1938.

Gookin, Daniel. *An Historical Account of the Doings and Sufferings of the Christian Indians.* 1836. Reprint. New York: Arno Press, 1972.

Hambrick-Stowe, Charles E., and Donna D. Smerlas, eds. *Massachusetts Militia Companies and Officers in the Lexington Alarm.* Boston: Society of Colonial Wars in the Commonwealth of Massachusetts, 1976.

Handlin, Oscar, and Mary Handlin, eds. *The Popular Sources of Political Authority: Documents on the Massachusetts Constitution of 1780.* Cambridge: Harvard University Press, Belknap Press, 1966.

Haskell, Caleb. *Caleb Haskell's Diary.* Ed. Lothrop Withington. Newburyport, Mass.: 1881.

Haughton, James. "Additional Memoir of the Moheagans." Massachusetts Historical Society, *Collections*, 1st Ser., vol. 9 (1804): 77–99.

Heckewelder, John G. E. *A Narrative of the Mission of the United Brethren*. Ed. William E. Connelly. Cleveland: Burrows Brothers, 1907.

———. "An Account of the History, Manners and Customs of the Indian Nations. . . ." *Transactions of the Historical and Literary Committee of the American Philosophical Society*, vol. 1. (1819).

Hervey, William. *Journals of the Hon. William Hervey*. Ed. J. Clarence Webster and Sydenham H. Hervey. Bury St. Edmunds: Paul and Matthew, 1906.

Hopkins, Samuel (1693–1755). *An Address to the People of New England*. Philadelphia, 1757.

———. *Historical Memoirs Relating to the Housatonic Indians*. New York: Johnson Reprint Corp., 1972. Reprint of extra issue no. 17 of *The Magazine of History* (1911).

Hopkins, Samuel (1721–1803). *The Works of Samuel Hopkins*. 2 vols. Boston, 1852.

"Indian Treaties." Maine Historical Society, *Collections*, vol. 4 (1856): 123–44.

Iroquois Indians: A Documentary History Woodbridge, Conn.: Research Publications, 1985. Microfilm.

Jameson, John F., ed. *Narratives of New Netherland, 1609–1664*. New York: Scribner's Sons, 1909.

Jefferson, Thomas. *The Jefferson Cyclopedia*. Ed. John P. Foley. 1900. Reprint. New York: Russell and Russell, 1967.

Johnson, William. *Papers of Sir William Johnson*. Ed. Milton Wheaton Hamilton. 12 vols. Albany: University of the State of New York, 1921–57.

The Journals of Each Provincial Congress of Massachusetts in 1774 and 1775 and of the Committee of Safety. Boston, 1838.

Journals of the Continental Congress, 1774–1789. Ed. Worthington Chauncey Ford et al. New York: Johnson Reprint Corp., 1968.

Journals of the House of Representatives of Massachusetts. Boston: Massachusetts Historical Society, 1919–.

Journals of the Military Expedition of Major John Sullivan. Auburn, N.Y., 1887.

Kappler, Charles J., comp. and ed. *Indian Treaties, 1778–1883*. New York: Interland Publishing, 1972.

Knox, John. *An Historical Journal of the Campaigns in North America*. Ed. Arthur S. Doughty. 1914–16. Reprint. 3 vols. Freeport, N.Y.: Books for Libraries Press, 1970.

Law, Jonathan. *Law Papers*. Ed. Albert Carlos Bates. 3 vols. Connecticut Historical Society, *Collections*, vols. 11, 13, 15. Hartford, 1907–14.

"Letter from a Friend in the Country, Dated Aug. 2, 1739." *Boston Post Boy*, Sept. 3, 1739.

"Letter from Capt. Elisha Phelps, Commissary, to the General Assembly." Connecticut Historical Society, *Collections* 1 (1860): 174–77.

"A Letter from Rev. Gideon Hawley of Marshpee. . . ." Massachusetts Historical Society, *Collections*, 1st Ser., vol. 4 (1795): 50–67.

"A List of the Different Nations of Indians That Met Sir William Johnson at Niagara, July 1764." Massachusetts Historical Society, *Collections*, 1st Ser., vol. 10 (1809): 121–22.

Livingston, Robert. *The Livingston Indian Records, 1666–1723*. Ed. Lawrence H. Leder. Gettysburg: Pennsylvania Historical Association, 1956.

London and Its Environs Described. London, 1761.

London Chronicle. 1766.

McAnear, Beverly, ed. "Personal Accounts of the Albany Congress of 1754." *Mississippi Valley Historical Review* 39, no. 4 (1953): 727–46.

McCallum, James D., ed. *The Letters of Eleazar Wheelock's Indians*. Hanover, N.H.: Dartmouth College Publications, 1932.

Mackenzie, Frederick. *A British Fusilier in Revolutionary Boston*. Freeport, N.Y.: Books for Libraries Press, 1968.

Massachusetts Gazette (Springfield). 1783.

Massachusetts Soldiers and Sailors of the Revolutionary War. 17 vols. Boston, 1896–1908.

"Memorial of John W. Quinney." Wisconsin Historical Society, *Collections*, vol. 4 (1857–58): 321–33.

Morse, Jedidiah. *A Report to the Secretary of War of the United States on Indian Affairs*. . . . New Haven, 1822.

Murray, Louise Welles, ed. *Notes from the Craft Collection in Tioga Point Museum on the Sullivan Expedition of 1779*. Athens, Pa.: Tioga Point Museum, 1929.

Narratives of the Revolution in New York. New York: New-York Historical Society, 1975.

New England Chronicle. Boston. 1775.

New England Historical and Genealogical Register.

New England Weekly Journal. Boston. 1736.

New Hampshire Provincial and State Papers. Ed. Nathaniel Bouton. 7 vols. Concord, 1867–73.

New York. *Calendar of Council Minutes, 1668–1783*. Ed. Berthold Fernow and Arnold J. F. Van Laer. Albany: University of the State of New York, 1902.

New York Mercury. 1759.

Official Letters of the Governors of the State of Virginia. 3 vols. Richmond: Superintendant of Public Printing, 1926–29.

Oliver, Peter. *Peter Oliver's Origin and Progress of the American Rebellion: A Tory View* (1781). Ed. Douglass Adair and John A. Schutz. San Marino: Huntington Library, 1961.

Pickering, Timothy. "Captain Hendrick Aupaumut's Journal." Historical Society of Pennsylvania, *Memoirs*, vol. 2, pt. 1 (1827): 75.

Pitt, William. *Correspondence of William Pitt*. Ed. Gertrude S. Kimball. New York and London: Macmillan, 1906.

Proceedings of the Commissioners of Indian Affairs Appointed by Law for the Extinguishment of Indian Titles in the State of New York. Albany, 1861.

Public Records of the Colony of Connecticut. Ed. James Hammond Trumbull and Charles Jeremy Headly. 15 vols. Hartford, 1850–90.

Pynchon, John. The Pynchon Papers. Ed. Carl Bridenbaugh. 2 vols. Boston: Colonial Society of Massachusetts, 1982–85.

Rensselaer, Jeremias van. Correspondence of Jeremias van Rensselaer, 1651–1674. Ed. and trans. Arnold J. F. Van Laer. Albany: University of the State of New York, 1932.

"The Report of a Committee of the Board of Correspondents of the Scots Society for Propagating Christian Knowledge, Who Visited the Oneida and Mohekunuk Indians in 1796." Massachusetts Historical Society, Collections, 1st Ser., vol. 5 (1798): 12–32.

Riedesel, Friedrich A. Memoirs, Letters and Journals of Major General Riedesel. Ed. Max von Eelking, trans. William L. Stone. 1868. Reprint. New York: New York Times, 1969.

Ripley, Dorothy. The Bank of Faith and Works United. Philadelphia, 1819.

Roberts, Kenneth Lewis, ed. March to Quebec: Journals of the Members of Arnold's Expedition. New York: Doubleday, Doran, 1940.

Rogers, Robert. Journals (1765). Ed. Howard H. Peckham. New York: Corinth Books, 1961.

Royal Gazette. Tory newspaper. New York.

"Samuel Jenks, His Journal of the Campaign in 1760." Massachusetts Historical Society, Proceedings, 2d Ser., vol. 5 (1890): 353–91.

Sergeant, John. The Causes and Dangers of Delusions in the Affairs of Religion. Boston, 1743.

Shirley, William. Correspondence of William Shirley. Ed. Charles H. Lincoln. 2 vols. New York: Macmillan, 1912.

Simcoe, John G. Simcoe's Military Journal. New York, 1844.

"Some Old Letters" (letters from Ephraim Williams to his son, Elijah). Scribner's Magazine (Feb. 1895): 247–60.

Sparks, Jared, ed. Correspondence of the American Revolution. 4 vols. Freeport, N.Y.: Books for Libraries Press, 1970.

Stark, John. Memoir and Official Correspondence of Gen. John Stark. Ed. Caleb Stark. 1860. Reprint. Boston: Gregg Press, 1972.

Stachiw, Myron O., ed. Massachusetts Officers and Soldiers, 1723–1743. Boston: Society of Colonial Wars in the Commonwealth of Massachusetts, 1979.

Stiles, Ezra. Literary Diary of Ezra Stiles. Ed. Franklin B. Dexter. New York: Scribner's Sons, 1901.

Sullivan, John. Letters and Papers of Major General John Sullivan. Ed. Otis G. Hammond. New Hampshire Historical Society, Collections, vols. 13–15. Concord, 1930–39.

Tilghman, Tench. *Memoir of Lieut. Col. Tench Tilghman.* Ed. Samuel Alexander Harrison. New York: New York Times, 1971.

Van Laer, Arnold J. F., ed. and trans. *Minutes of the Court of Fort Orange and Beverwyck, 1652–1656.* 2 vols. Albany: University of the State of New York, 1920–23.

———. *Minutes of the Court of Rensselaerswyck, 1648–1652.* Albany: University of the State of New York, 1922.

Van Laer, Arnold J. F., ed., and Jonathan Pearson, trans. *Early Records of the City and County of Albany.* 3 vols. Albany: University of the State of New York, 1869–1919.

Van Rensselaer Bowier Manuscripts. Ed. and trans. Arnold J. F. Van Laer. Albany: University of the State of New York, 1908.

Vermont. *Rolls of the Soldiers. . . .* Ed. John Ellsworth Goodrich and Chauncey L. Knapp. Rutland: Tuttle Company, 1904.

Voye, Nancy S., ed. *Massachusetts Officers in the French and Indian Wars, 1748–1763.* Boston: Society of Colonial Wars in the Commonwealth of Massachusetts, 1975.

Washington, George. *The Writings of George Washington.* Ed. John C. Fitzpatrick. 39 vols. Washington, D.C.: GPO, 1931–44.

———. *The Writings of George Washington.* Ed. W. C. Ford. 14 vols. New York and London: G. P. Putnam's Sons, 1889.

Washington-Irvine Correspondence. Ed. Consul W. Butterfield. Madison, Wis., 1882.

Wolley, Charles. *A Two Years' Journal in New York.* 1902. Reprint. Harrison, N.Y.: Harbor Hill Books, 1973.

Wood, Lemuel. "Diaries Kept by Lemuel Wood." Essex Institute, *Historical Collections*, vols. 19–20 (1892).

Woodbridge, Timothy. *The Autobiography of a Blind Minister.* New York, 1856.

Wright, Harry Andrew. *Indian Deeds of Hampden County.* Springfield, 1905.

Wright, Wyllis Eaton, ed. *Colonel Ephraim Williams: A Documentary Life.* Pittsfield: Berkshire County Historical Society, 1970.

Wroth, L. Kinvin, ed. *Province in Rebellion: A Documentary History of the Founding of the Commonwealth of Massachusetts, 1774–1775.* 4 vols. Cambridge: Harvard University Press, 1975. Quoted segments are reprinted by permission of the publishers.

Zeisberger, David. *Diary of David Zeisberger.* Ed. and trans. Eugene F. Bliss. 2 vols. Cincinnati, 1885.

SECONDARY SOURCES

Anderson, Fred. *A People's Army: Massachusetts Soldiers and Society in the Seven Years' War*. Chapel Hill: For the Institute of Early American History and Culture by the University of North Carolina Press, 1984.

Axtell, James. *After Columbus: Essays in the Ethnohistory of Colonial North America*. New York: Oxford University Press, 1988.

Bond, Henry. *Genealogies of the Families and Descendants of the Early Settlers of Watertown*. Boston, 1855.

Bond, Richmond P. *Queen Anne's American Kings*. Oxford: Clarendon Press, 1952.

Brasser, Ted. *Riding on the Frontier's Crest: Mahican Indian Culture and Culture Change*. Ottawa: National Museums of Canada, 1974.

Brown, Robert E. *Middle-Class Democracy and the Revolution in Massachusetts*. New York: Russell and Russell, 1968.

Carroll, Peter N. *Puritanism and the Wilderness*. New York: Columbia University Press, 1969.

Chancellor, Edwin B. *The Eighteenth Century in London*. London: B. T. Batsford; New York: Scribner's Sons, 1921.

Colee, Philip S. "The Housatonic-Stockbridge Indians 1734–1739." Ph.D. diss., State University of New York, Albany, 1977.

Cook, Sherburne F. *The Indian Population of New England in the Seventeenth Century*. Berkeley: University of California Press, 1976.

Cuneo, John R. *Robert Rogers of the Rangers*. New York: Oxford University Press, 1959.

Davis, Andrew F. "The Employment of Indian Auxiliaries in the American War." *English Historical Review* 8 (Oct. 1887): 709–28.

Davis, Sheldon. *Shekomeko*. Poughkeepsie, 1858.

Day, Gordon M. *The Identity of the St. Francis Indians*. Ottawa: National Museums of Canada, 1981.

———. "Oral Tradition as Complement." *Ethnohistory* 19, no. 2 (1972): 99–107.

DeForest, John W. *History of the Indians of Connecticut*. 1851. Reprint. Hamden, Conn.: Archon Books, 1964.

De Schweinitz, Edmund. *The Life and Times of David Zeisberger*. 1870. Reprint. New York: Arno Press, 1971.

Devoe, Thomas F. "The Massacre of the Stockbridge Indians, 1778." *Magazine of American History* 5, no. 3 (1880): 187–94.

Drake, Samuel G. *Particular History of the Five Years French and Indian War*. 1870. Reprint. Freeport, N.Y.: Books for Libraries Press, 1970.

Dwight, Sereno E. *The Life of President Edwards*. New York, 1830.

Dyer, Edward O. *Gnadensee, the Lake of Grace*. Boston and Chicago: Pilgrim Press, 1903.

Earle, Alice M. *Customs and Fashions in Old New England.* New York, 1893.

Embleton, R. S. "Rogers Rangers." *Tradition: Journal of the International Society of Military Collectors* 4, no. 23 (1967): 22–25.

Feister, Lois M. "Linguistic Communications between the Dutch and Indians in New Netherland, 1609–1664." *Ethnohistory* 20, no. 1 (1973): 5–38.

Field, David Dudley. *A History of the Town of Pittsfield.* Hartford, 1844.

Fleming, Thomas J. *1776: Year of Illusions.* New York: Norton, 1975.

Flexner, James T. *Lord of the Mohawks: A Biography of Sir William Johnson.* Boston: Little, Brown, 1979.

Frothingham, Richard. *History of the Siege of Boston.* Boston, 1851.

Garnett, Edna Bailey. *West Stockbridge Massachusetts, 1774–1974.* West Stockbridge: Berkshire Courier, 1974.

Garratt, John G. *The Four Indian Kings.* Ottawa: Public Archives of Canada, 1985.

Graymont, Barbara. *The Iroquois in the American Revolution.* Syracuse: Syracuse University Press, 1972.

Green, Mason A. *Springfield, 1636–1886.* Springfield, Mass., 1888.

Greene, Evarts B. *American Population before the Federal Census of 1790.* Gloucester: P. Smith, 1966.

Hamilton, Milton W. *Sir William Johnson, Colonial American.* Port Washington, N.Y.: Kennikat, 1976.

Haviland, William A., and Marjory W. Power. *Original Vermonters.* Hanover, N.H.: For the University of Vermont by the University Press of New England, 1981.

Hopkins, Samuel, ed. *The Life and Character of the Late . . . Jonathan Edwards.* Edinburgh, 1799.

Hufeland, Otto. *Westchester County during the American Revolution.* Westchester County Historical Society, *Publications,* vol. 3. White Plains, 1926.

Innes, Stephen. *Labor in a New Land.* Princeton: Princeton University Press, 1983.

————, et al. *Early Settlement in the Connecticut Valley.* Westfield, Mass.: Historic Deerfield, Inc., 1984.

Jackson, Francis. *A History of the Early Settlement of Newton.* Boston, 1854.

Jellison, Charles A. *Ethan Allen.* Syracuse: Syracuse University Press, 1969.

Jennings, Francis. *The Invasion of America.* Chapel Hill: For the Institute of Early American History and Culture by the University of North Carolina Press, 1975.

Jones, Edward C., and Roscoe C. Scott, eds. *Westfield Massachusetts, 1669–1969.* Westfield: Westfield Tri-Centennial Ass'n, 1968.

Jones, Electa Fidelia. *Stockbridge, Past and Present.* Springfield, 1854.

Kawashima, Yasuhide. *Puritan Justice and the Indian.* Middletown: Wesleyan University Press, 1986.

Keith, H. F. "The Early Roads and Settlements of Berkshire. . . ." In *Four Papers of the Berkshire Historical and Scientific Society*. Pittsfield, 1886.

Kellaway, William. *The New England Company, 1649–1776*. Westport: Greenwood, 1975.

Kim, Sung Bok. *Landlord and Tenant in Colonial New York*. Chapel Hill: For the Institute of Early American History and Culture by the University of North Carolina Press, 1978.

Lamson, Daniel S. *History of the Town of Weston*. Boston: George H. Ellis, 1913.

Leger, Mary Celeste. *The Catholic Indian Missions in Maine*. Washington, D.C.: Catholic University of America, 1929.

Levinson, David. "An Explanation for the Oneida-Colonist Alliance in the American Revolution." *Ethnohistory* 23, no. 3 (1976): 265–89.

Loescher, Burt. *Genesis: Rogers Rangers*. San Mateo, 1969.

——. *The History of Rogers Rangers*. San Francisco, 1946.

Loskiel, George H. *History of the Mission of the United Brethren among the Indians of North America*. London, 1794.

Love, William D. *Samson Occom and the Christian Indians of New England*. Boston and Chicago, 1899.

Luzader, John F. *Decision on the Hudson: The Saratoga Campaign of 1777*. Washington, D.C.: National Park Service, 1975.

Macfarlane, Ronald O. "The Massachusetts Bay Truckhouses in Diplomacy with the Indians." *New England Quarterly* 11, no. 1 (1938): 48–65.

Mante, Thomas. *The History of the Late War in North America*. New York: Research Reprints, 1970.

Mark, Irving. *Agrarian Conflicts in Colonial New York, 1711–1775*. New York: Columbia University Press, 1940.

Melvoin, Richard I. *New England Outpost: War and Society in Colonial Deerfield*. New York: Norton, 1989.

A Memorial of the Dedication of Monuments Erected by the Moravian Historical Society. New York and Philadelphia, 1860.

Mitchell, Louis. *The Woodbridge Record*. New Haven, 1883.

Mochon, Marion J. "Stockbridge-Munsee Cultural Adaptations: 'Assimilated Indians.' " American Philosophical Society, *Proceedings* 112, no. 3 (1968): 182–219.

Morgan, Edmund S. *The Founding of Massachusetts*. Indianapolis: Bobbs-Merrill, 1964.

"The New England Company of 1649 and Its Missionary Enterprises." Publications of the Colonial Society of Massachusetts, vol. 38, *Transactions* (1947–51): 134–218.

New York in the Revolution as Colony and State. Albany, 1898.

Nobles, Gregory H. *Divisions throughout the Whole: Politics and Society in Hampshire County, Mass., 1740–1775*. New York: Cambridge University Press, 1983.

Pargellis, Stanley M. *Lord Loudoun in North America*. New Haven: Yale University Press; London: Oxford University Press, 1933.

Peabody, William B. O. "Life of David Brainerd." In *The Library of American Biography*, ed. Jared Sparks, vol. 8. New York, 1839.

Peckham, Howard H. *The Colonial Wars, 1689–1762*. Chicago: University of Chicago Press, 1964.

————. *Pontiac and the Indian Uprising*. 1961. Reprint. New York: Russell and Russell, 1970.

Pope, Franklin L. "The Western Boundary of Massachusetts." In *Berkshire Book*, vol. 1, pp. 29–85. Pittsfield, 1892.

Reichel, William C. *Memorials of the Moravian Church*, vol. 1. Philadelphia, 1870.

————. *Dedication of Monuments Erected by the Moravian Historical Society*. New York and Philadelphia, 1860.

Richter, Daniel K. "Cultural Brokers and Intercultural Politics: New York–Iroquois Relations, 1664–1701." *Journal of American History* 75 (1988): 40–67.

Richter, Daniel K., and James H. Merrell, eds. *Beyond the Covenant Chain: The Iroquois and Their Neighbors in Indian North America, 1600–1800*. Syracuse: Syracuse University Press, 1987.

Ritter, Priscilla R. *Newton, Massachusetts, 1679–1779*. Boston: New England Historic Genealogical Society, 1982.

Ruttenber, Edward M. *History of the Indian Tribes of Hudson's River*. Albany, 1872.

Salisbury, Neal. *Manitou and Providence*. New York: Oxford University Press, 1982.

Schultze, Augustus. "The Old Moravian Cemetery of Bethlehem, Pa. 1742–1897." Moravian Historical Society, *Transactions* 5 (1899): 99–267.

Schwarz, Philip J. *The Jarring Interests*. Albany: State University of New York Press, 1979.

Sedgwick, Charles F. *A History of the Town of Sharon*. Hartford, 1842.

Sedgwick, Sarah C., and Christina S. Marquand. *Stockbridge, 1739–1939*. Great Barrington: Berkshire Courier, 1939.

Sessler, Jacob J. *Communal Pietism among Early American Moravians*. 1933. Reprint. New York: AMS Press, 1971.

Sibley's Harvard Graduates. 16 vols. Boston: Massachusetts Historical Society, 1873–1919.

Smith, Joseph Edward Adams. *The History of Pittsfield*. 2 vols. Boston, 1869–76.

Smith, Wallace. *The History of the Province of New York*. 2 vols. Cambridge: Harvard University Press, Belknap Press, 1972.

Speck, Frank G. "The Delaware Indians as Women." *Pennsylvania Magazine of History and Biography* 70 (1946): 377–89.

Szatmary, David P. *Shays Rebellion*. Amherst: University of Massachusetts Press, 1980.

Taylor, Charles James. *History of Great Barrington*. Great Barrington, 1882.

Taylor, Robert J. *Western Massachusetts in the Revolution*. Providence: Brown University Press, 1954.

Thomas, Peter A. "Cultural Change on the Southern New England Frontier, 1630–1665." Pp. 131–61 in *Cultures in Contact*, ed. William W. Fitzhugh. Washington, D.C.: Smithsonian Institution Press, 1985.

Trelease, Allen W. *Indian Affairs in Colonial New York*. Ithaca: Cornell University Press, 1960.

Trigger, Bruce. "The Mohawk-Mohican War (1624–1628)." *Canadian Historical Review* 52, no. 3 (1971): 276–86.

Vaughan, Alden T. *New England Frontier*. Boston: Little, Brown, 1965.

Wallace, Anthony F. C. *King of the Delawares: Teedyuscung, 1700–1763*. Philadelphia: University of Pennsylvania Press, 1949.

Wallace, Paul A. W. *Thirty Thousand Miles with John Heckewelder*. Pittsburgh: University of Pittsburgh Press, 1958.

Weslager, C. A. "Further Light on the Delaware Indians as Women." *Journal of the Washington Academy of Sciences* 37, no. 9 (1947): 298–304.

Whitney, Luna M. Hammond. *History of Madison County*. Syracuse: 1872.

Winslow, Ola E. *Jonathan Edwards, 1703–1758*. 1940. Reprint. New York: Octagon Books, 1973.

Wood, David H. *Lenox*. Lenox, Mass.: Town of Lenox, 1969.

Wright, Albert. *The Sullivan Expedition of 1779: The Regimental Rosters of Men*. Ithaca, 1965.

———. *The Sullivan Expedition of 1779: The Losses*. Ithaca, 1965.

Wright, Harry Andrew. *The Story of Western Massachusetts*. 4 vols. New York: Lewis Historical Publishing, 1949.

Wynbeek, David. *David Brainerd, Beloved Yankee*. Grand Rapids: Eerdmans, 1961.

Zemsky, Robert. *Merchants, Farmers and River Gods*. Boston: Gambit, 1971.

INDEX

Abenaki Indians, 4, 8, 32, 108–9, 144.
  See also St. Francis Indians
Abercromby, James, 117, 124, 126–
  27, 127
Abraham (Moravian Mohican chief;
  alias Maumauntissekun, Shabash,
  Shawash): pre-Christian descrip-
  tion, 60–61; baptized, 63; land, 73,
  74, 129; move to Wyoming Valley,
  73, 74, 77, 113; and Stockbridges,
  73–74; King George's War, 77; son
  (*see* Jonathan)
Albany (Fort Orange), N.Y., 12;
  Indian trade, xii, 8, 13, 26, 32, 105;
  Indian conferences at, 6, 7, 8, 71,
  75, 77–78, 204–5; authorities in
  land dispute, 148–49, 151, 164–65.
  See also Albany Congress; Trade;
  Traders
Albany Congress, 109, 110–11, 146
Alcohol/alcoholism, 7, 9, 44–45, 49–
  52 *passim*, 60–61, 74, 88, 173–74,
  189, 199, 208; colonial, 42–43, 65,
  97, 189, 210

Allen, Ethan, 200–202, 203, 207,
  218, 230
Amherst, Jeffery: description and
  character of, 127–28, 144–45; opin-
  ion of Stockbridges, 129–31, 133,
  136–37, 138–40, 144; opinion of
  Rogers' Rangers, 131; assaults
  Ticonderoga, 132; defeats Canada,
  143; Pontiac's Conspiracy, 144–45
Andros, Edmund, 5–6
Arnold, Benedict, 200, 207, 209–10
Aron, Captain (Umpachenee),
  254n.63
Ashley, John, 29
Aupaumut, 7, 12, 20, 47; son, 32, 45
Austerlitz, N.Y., 165

Bear symbolism, 22
Bécancour, Canada, 108
Belcher, Jonathan, 18; attitude toward
  Indians, 26–27; proposes township,
  39–40, 45; meets with Housa-
  tonics, 31–36, 73–74
Bellamy, Joseph, 191

297

Gnadenhutten, Ohio (Muskingum River), massacre, 233

Gnadenhutten, Ohio (Tuscarawas River), 177

Gnadenhutten, Pa., 77, 89, 90, 102, 113; Indian attack on, 115

Goodrich, William, 194, 195–96, 198, 227, 230–31

Governor, as term for chief, 254n.63

Gravesend, England, 163

Great Awakening, xii, 15, 57, 62

Great Barrington, Mass., 20, 50, 97, 107, 239

Gregg, William, Jr., 160–61, 163

Hamilton, James, 275n.5

Hampshire County, Mass.: courts and justices in, 46, 47, 149, 179; militia, 110

Hancock, John, 196, 208

Hanson, John, 236–37

Hawley, Gideon, 101–2, 103, 104

Hendrick (Mohawk chief): visit to Queen Anne, 9, 27; at Albany conference, 75; and boarding school controversy, 99, 102; on T. Woodbridge, 104; death, 115

Hendricks, Solomon, 227–28, 229, 237

Henry, Patrick, 202

Hoit, Winthrop, 201–2

Hopkins, Samuel (of Great Barrington): and King George's War, 76; and Jonathan Edwards, 90, 93–94, 122–23; and tavern, 97; and French and Indian War, 107, 109; on Stockbridges, 173–74; town division, 185–86, 239

Hopkins, Samuel (of Springfield): and establishment of mission, 16, 19, 34, 48; on Indians, 27, 44, 105; opinion of John Sergeant, 38, 67–68; and

land, 48; opinion of Stockbridges, 87, 90, 110, 244–45

Housatonic Indians: and John Pynchon, 5; relocation of, 11; and Christianity, 13–17, 43–44; and Massachusetts land, 13, 44, 52; and mission, 19–21, 22–23, 28–30, 32–38; and establishment of Stockbridge, 40–43, 47–49, 50–51, 85–88. *See also* Mohican Indians; Stockbridge Indians

Housatonic River, 1, 11, 39, 94, 147

Howard, William, 24

Hudson, Henry, 3, 6

Hudson River and Valley: Mohicans along, xii, 11, 13, 98, 116, 174, 204; in Mohican tradition, 2–3; Mohican land in, 12; Stockbridge encampment on, 120

Huntington, Jedidiah, 219, 225

Ingersoll, David, 147, 148

Inman, Ralph, 198

Inman Square, 198

Jackson, Michael, 212, 214, 215, 219

Johannes (crippled Moravian convert; alias Tschoop, Wasamapah), 60–62, 63, 73–74

Johnson, Guy, 174, 195, 207, 217

Johnson, John, 230

Johnson, Joseph, 195

Johnson, William, 79, 103; on language translation, 94; and boarding school controversy, 98; and French and Indian War, 113–16, 117, 120, 124, 130, 139–40, 141, 143–44; and Pontiac's Conspiracy, 144–45; and Mohican land disputes, 149–53, 155–59, 161, 163, 168–69, 170, 182; and Mohican emigration, 176–77; death, 192

Jonathan (Moravian Mohican), 63, 151
Jones, Josiah, 46, 88, 90, 108, 180

Kaunaumeek Indians, 45–46, 58–59, 68–70, 98. *See also* Waunaupaugus, Solomon
Kellogg, Martin, 101, 102, 172
Kent, Conn., 60, 109, 114, 176, 249 n.11. *See also* Scaticook Indians
King Ben. *See* Kokhkewenaunaunt, Benjamin
King George's War, 70–71, 73–74, 76–81
King Philip's War, 5–6, 12, 44; refugees from, 15–16, 32, 109
Kingsbridge, N.Y., 221
Kingston, N.Y., 9
King William's War, 6, 9, 27
Kirkland, Samuel: and John Sergeant, 190; and American Revolution, 205–6, 217–18, 227; and Stockbridge emigration, 238, 241–42; and land, 239
Kokhkewenaunaunt, Benjamin: as sachem, 55, 56, 254n.11; and French and Indian War, 112, 127; and land disputes, 147, 150, 152, 154, 159, 165; and debt committee, 182
Konkapot, Abraham, 198, 231
Konkapot, John (alias Pohpnehounuwuh), 1; relocation of, 21; and land, 24, 46, 52, 85, 155, 174–75; and Mohican reaction to mission, 16–17, 28, 29–30; character of, 16, 23; and Christianity, 33, 36, 72; and Belcher, 33–35; establishment of Stockbridge, 47, 69; and French and Indian War, 112; son's debt, 174–75; death, 175. *See also*

Konkapot, Katherine; Konkapot, Mary; Konkapot, Robert
Konkapot, Katherine, 36, 80
Konkapot, Mary, 36, 53
Konkapot, Robert, 23, 31, 36, 79, 174–75; death, 175

Lake Champlain: Mohican boundary of, 2; King George's War, 70; French and Indian War, 109, 132, 136, 141; American Revolution, 200, 201, 209, 209–10. *See also* Crown Point; Ticonderoga
Lake George: King George's War, 112; French and Indian War, 115, 127, 131, 131–32; American Revolution, 212
Lenox, Mass., 48, 226, 239
Levis, Fort, 143
Liquor. *See* Alcohol/alcoholism
Livingston, Robert, Jr., 147, 150, 151, 152
London, England; Stockbridges' visit to, 162–64
The London Chronicle, 161, 163
Loudoun, Earl of. *See* Campbell, John
Louisbourg, Canada, 127

Malaria, 32
Marsh, Isaac, 238
Marylebone, England, 162
Massachusetts Bay Charter, 18, 42, 77
Mather, Increase, 24
Maunaumaug, John, 264n.21
Mayhew, Thomas, 18
Miami Indians, 8
Mochon, Marion, 241
Mohawk Indians: wars with Mohicans, 4–5, 9; Mohican relations after 1675, 5, 7–9, 72, 111, 144, 194, 197, 203–4, 205; King Philip's War, 5–6; and land, 12, 170, 182, 237;

and French and Indian War, 112; and land issues, 155, 165; and debt committee, 182

Naunauneekanuk, David (the younger), 214

Naunauphtaunk, Abraham, 198, 200, 272n.21

Naunauphtaunk, Jacob: background, 112; sons, 112, 132, 198, 234, 264n.21; and French and Indian War, 116, 117–19, 124–25, 129–32, 140; death, 141

Naunauphtaunk, Jehoiakim, 198

Naunauphtaunk, John: visit to England, 160–64; wife, 161; and debt committee, 182; as constable, 185; evidence as Jacob's son, 264n.21

Newburgh, N.Y., 237

New England Company: 18, 51; treasurer's embezzlement, 26; Sergeant's tombstone, 88; Edwards's salary, 92; and boarding school controversy, 98, 99, 101; town division, 185–90 *passim;* and American Revolution, 199, 205, 230; support for Kirkland, 217

New Lebanon, N.Y., 45

New Stockbridge, N.Y., 242

Nimham, Aaron, 112, 125–27

Nimham, Abraham: and American Revolution, 200–203, 212–16, 219–23; death, 223, 225

Nimham, Daniel (the elder), 112, 147; and New York land disputes, 156–60, 168–69; visit to England, 160–64; wife, 161, 243; and American Revolution, 198, 219–23; death, 223–25

Nimham, Daniel (the younger), 231

Nimham, John, 214

Nimham family, 89, 112, 155, 156, 198, 231

Nixon, John, 212–13

Noble, Robert, 165

Norridgewock Indians, 32, 70

Northampton, Mass., 24, 78, 90, 179

Notonksion, William, 198, 200, 272n.21

Notonksion, William, Jr., 198, 277n.21

Occom, Samson, 238, 241–42

Oliver, Andrew, 181

Oneida Indians: and boarding school controversy, 99, 101, 102; and French and Indian War, 114; at Ouaquaga, 177; and American Revolution, 195, 204, 205, 217–18, 224, 228–30 *passim,* 244; and Mohican land claims; and Stockbridge relocation, 237–38, 242–43

Otis, James, 181

Otsiningo, N.Y., 116, 150

Ottawa Indians, 2, 8, 16, 80

Otter Creek, 136, 235

Pachgatgoch. *See* Kent, Conn.; Scaticook Indians

Patterson, John, 194, 195, 196, 199

Penn, Thomas, 103–4

Penobscot Indians, 32, 70, 207, 208

Pequot Indians, xv, 238

Philipse, Phillip, 155

Pittsfield, Mass., 52, 112, 147, 203

Pixley, David, 189, 194, 212

Pontiac's Conspiracy, 144–45

Poohpoonuc, Ebenezer, 20, 30, 31, 36, 83, 89

Potawatomi Indians, 2

Powwow (shaman), 15, 16, 21–22, 30–31, 223, 241

Putnam, Israel, 209

Putnam County, N.Y., 147

Pynchon, John, 5, 6, 14

Queen Anne's War, 9, 24

Rauch, Christian, 60–62, 64, 65–66
Richelieu River, 134, 141
Robaud, Jean, 143, 144
Robinson, Beverley, 155, 157, 164
Rockwell, Norman, 95
Rogers, Robert: background, 117;
    creates uniforms, 125; Ticonderoga
    skirmish, 126; opinion of Stock-
    bridges, 129; Amherst's opinion of,
    131; and St. Francis raid, 133–36;
    assault on Canadian forts, 139–43.
    See also Rogers Rangers
Rogers Rangers: 1758 campaign,
    124–26; Stockbridges join, 117;
    Amherst's opinion of, 131. *See also*
    Rogers, Robert; St. Francis raid
Rum. *See* Alcohol/alcoholism

Sachem, in Mohican tradition, 22,
    55–56
St. Clair, Arthur, 211, 212
St. Francis Indians, 17, 32, 132–33;
    restitution to Stockbridges, 143–
    44; and American Revolution, 201,
    202, 207. *See also* St. Francis raid
St. Francis raid, 133–36, 264n.27
St. Frederic, Fort, 113
St. John, Fort, 141, 142, 202
St. John Indians, 207
St. Therese, Fort, 141
Salisbury, Conn., 12, 64–65, 71
Salisbury, England, 161
Samadagwis, 135, 264n.27
Saratoga, N.Y., 215
Scaticook Indians: location of, 60;
    and Moravians, 65, 130; and King
    George's War, 73, 75; visit to
    Umpachenee, 89–90; restricted,
    109; and French and Indian War,
    115–17, 120, 130, 137, 138; and

land, 175–76, 176–77; and Ameri-
    can Revolution, 227
Schaghticoke Indians: background,
    5–8 *passim;* and Christianity, 15,
    46; and Abenakis, 54; at Deerfield
    conference, 55; and King George's
    War, 70, 71; and Stockbridge at-
    tack, 108–9
Schoenbrun, 233
Schoharie Creek, 2, 230
Schuyler, Philip, 207–9, 210, 217
Seneca Indians, 57, 228
Sergeant, Abigail: marriage to John
    Sergeant, 13, 49; Sergeant's death,
    82–83; and Jonathan Edwards
    controversy, 90, 94; and board-
    ing school controversy, 99–101;
    marriage to Joseph Dwight, 100;
    Stockbridge's opinion of, 100;
    opinion of T. Woodbridge, 103;
    opinion of Stockbridges, 114
Sergeant, Erastus, 180, 185, 193,
    211, 243
Sergeant, John: background, 19–
    20; opinion of Indians, 19, 22, 47,
    50–51, 96–98; religious disposi-
    tion of, 19, 23–24, 93, 190; meets
    Housatonics, 20–23, 53; opinion
    of Konkapot, 42; ordination of,
    35; mission work of, 36–38, 51,
    187; opinion of Umpachenee, 37,
    43, 51; and establishment of Stock-
    bridge, 40–41, and land, 40–41,
    48, 252n.13; meets Belcher, 43–44;
    marriage, 45, 47, 49; proselytizing
    of, 45, 47, 57–58; and Moravians,
    64, 65–68, 77; opinion of Wanau-
    paugus, 69; and King George's War,
    70–71, 76, 80–81; and boarding
    school controversy, 96, 97–99, 101;
    death, 82–83, 99
Sergeant, John, Jr.: learns Mohi-
    can, 95; on Stockbridges, 174; on